Springer Series on **Behavior Therapy and Behavioral Medicine**

Series Editors: Cyril M. Franks, Ph.D., and Frederick J. Evans, Ph.D.

Advisory Board: John Paul Brady, M.D., Robert P. Liberman, M.D.,
Neal E. Miller, Ph.D., and Stanley Rachman, Ph.D.

Warren W. Tryon, Ph.D., is Professor of Psychology in both Fordham College and the Graduate School of Arts and Sciences at Fordham University where he teaches at the undergraduate and graduate levels respectively. Professor Tryon has published over 50 articles in scientific journals and presented nearly 40 papers at scholarly meetings. He is a diplomate in clinical psychology (American Board of Professional Psychology). In addition to supervising the clinical training of selected doctoral students, he maintains a private practice in the Scarborough-Briarcliff Manor area of Westchester County.

Behavioral Assessment in Behavioral Medicine

Warren W. Tryon, Ph.D.

Editor

Springer Publishing Company
New York

Springer Publishing Company, Inc.
200 Park Avenue South
New York, New York   10003

85 86 87 88 89 / 10 9 8 7 6 5 4 3 2 1

Library of Congress Cataloging in Publication Data

Main entry under title:
Behavioral assessment in behavioral medicine.
   (Springer series on behavior therapy and behavioral medicine ; v. 15)
   Includes bibliographies and index.   1. Medicine and psychology — Addresses, essays,
lectures.   2. Pain — Psychological aspects — Addresses, essays, lectures.   3. Obesity —
Psychological aspects — Addresses, essays, lectures.   4. Smoking — Psychological aspects —
Addresses, essays, lectures.   5. Alcohol — Toxicology — Addresses, essays, lectures.
6. Human physiology — Measurement — Addresses, essays, lectures.   I. Tryon, Warren
W.   II. Series.   [DNLM: 1. Behavior.   2. Behavioral Medicine — methods.
3. Diagnosis.   W1 SP685NB v.15 / WM 425 B4197]
R726.5.B4235   1985   616.08   84-14034
ISBN 0-8261-3910-8
ISSN 0278-6729

Printed in the United States of America

Contents

Preface

Measurement is fundamental to science and therefore to medical science, as the history of both reveals. Unfortunately, many investigators begin with theoretical hypotheses and end with measures of convenience. Measurements often lack fixed or standard units, making them partial or pseudo measurements. The present volume provides a different emphasis. Measurement is seen as an important first step since it provides the basis for noting similarities and differences among patient and control groups. Measurements having fixed or standard units are emphasized since they allow us to transcend concerns of reliability and validity, and address the matter of accuracy. (It is shown that measures can be both reliable and valid but inaccurate; see Chapter 1.) The basic thesis of this volume is that behavioral medicine is at a crossroad: It can make strides similar to those that have been documented regarding science in general and medical science in particular — if investigators will turn to the use of measures having fixed or standard units and then conceptualize the nature of disease and malfunction in terms of those measurements.

Contributors

LAURENCE A. BRADLEY, PH.D.
Bowman Gray School of Medicine of Wake Forest University

CAROL A. DENIER, M.A.
Jackson V.A. and University of Mississippi Medical Centers

WILLIAM FRANKENSTEIN, M.A.
Rutgers–The State University

MARK KANE GOLDSTEIN, PH.D.
V.A. Medical Center and University of Florida

WILLIAM M. HAY, PH.D.
Rutgers–The State University

CHARLES K. PROKOP, PH.D.
Texas Tech University School of Medicine

DONALD M. PRUE, PH.D.
Jackson V.A. and University of Mississippi Medical Centers

TODD ROGERS, PH.D.
Stanford Heart Disease Prevention Program

REDA R. SCOTT, PH.D.
Jackson V.A. and University of Mississippi Medical Centers

GERALD H. STEIN, M.D.
V.A. Medical Center and University of Florida

MARGRET K. STRAW, PH.D.
Bowman Gray School of Medicine

MARY C. WHITE, M.A.
University of North Carolina–Greensboro

1

Introduction and Overview

Warren W. Tryon

The quality of measurement establishes an upper bound upon the quantitative relationships that can be established between two or more variables. Mature sciences are never constructed on the basis of soft measurements. This is because clear replicable relationships can never be found between data sets that are unreliable and of questionable validity. It is all too common within the social sciences to hear investigators talking first about hypotheses, then about experimental design, and finally about measurement. The fewest concessions are made concerning hypotheses. Next come practical compromises in experimental design considerations. Only then is the topic of measurement raised. When the "best available" instrument is found to be of questionable worth, it is still used to test hypotheses under the rationale that it is the best instrument available. A preferable approach would be to abandon such hypothesis-testing efforts in favor of fundamental research concerning what is being measured and how it is being assessed. Concepts that are not reliably and validly translatable into solid measurements are almost always poorly framed concepts regardless of how psychologically relevant they may appear. Such vagueness will certainly cloud all relationships that one concept might have with another, particularly if the other concept is equally ill framed. In sum, measurement is the process by which concepts are given meaning; that is, are clarified to the point where they can be satisfactorily measured. Too often the pursuit of hypothesis testing is begun with poorly thought out concepts and therefore with inadequate measurements.

The major purpose of *Behavioral Assessment in Behavioral Medicine* is to advance the state of measurement in the multidisciplinary field of behavioral medicine. This objective is pursued by reviewing the measurement of several behaviors of medical interest. These include smoking, excessive drinking (alcoholism), overeating (obesity), and pain behaviors (behaviors associated with chronic pain). Behavioral measurements of interest to persons working in rehabilitative settings are also included. Activity is an important aspect of many behaviors that are relevant to medicine, such as obesity (and anorexia nervosa), chronic pain, and chronic diseases. The measurement of activity receives extended treatment in this volume because this topic has been underrepresented in the behavioral medicine literature.

Special emphasis is given to the highest-quality measurements that are currently available in the areas covered. This means that the measurements receiving special mention share certain attributes. First, such measurements often refer to overt rather than covert behaviors, primarily because overt behaviors are publicly observable. This allows several investigators to independently verify the nature and magnitude of the obtained measurements. Assessment of covert "behaviors" is limited by their privacy. Investigators are required to accept the subject's introspective report without any possibility of independent confirmation. Issues of reliability and validity can never be completely investigated when the object of study is out of public view.

A second characteristic of the highest-quality measurements is that they are often obtained objectively by instruments. Such devices are not influenced by factors such as fatigue, emotion, expectancies, and other human qualities that compromise the integrity of measurements. The physical consequences of behaviors can often be measured much better than the behaviors themselves. For example, smoking behaviors increase the thiocyanate levels in one's saliva. Hence, the biochemical consequences of smoking behavior can be monitored by measuring saliva thiocyanate even though no direct measurement is ever made of any specific smoking behavior. An added feature of measuring saliva thiocyanate is that such measurements are more directly related to health risks associated with smoking than are typical assessments of smoking behavior. This is because the saliva thiocyanate levels reflect ingested smoke, whereas "number of cigarettes smoked" and similar measures may or may not reflect ingestion.

A third characteristic of the highest-quality measurements concerns their units. Johnston and Pennypacker (1980) have discussed the historical development of two types of units of measurement within the behavioral sciences, and therefore only a brief overview of the main points is given here.[1] The preferred unit of measure has both a clear physical meaning and a standard size. Examples are the meter, kilogram, and second. Each unit has a specific meaning that is commonly shared and agreed upon within the scientific community due to the fact that standard quantities for these units have been adopted. What then are the units associated with most of behavioral science? What units do we employ to measure intelligence, anxiety, stress, and many other phenomena? The answer is arbitrary units! They either have no common definition or they have no fixed size, or both. These units are based upon estimates of within-group variability which are a function of the subjects tested. Different subjects or changes in the subject's performance cause changes in the size of the unit of measure. This is analogous to having elastic meter sticks, changeable scales, and variable clocks. Instruments that measure the physical consequences of behaviors do not share these limitations for they provide readings in terms of standard units of measure. Therefore, these measurements receive the greatest emphasis in this work.

Laboratory Analysis

Davidsohn and Henry (1974) wrote the following comments in the Preface to the 15th edition of Todd and Sanford's *Clinical Diagnosis by Laboratory Methods:*

> Our objectives or goals in this edition include the following:
> 1. Identify appropriate measurements and examinations for:
>   A. Diagnosis.
>   B. Confirmation of a clinical impression.
>   C. Screening or detection of disease.

[1]Johnston and Pennypacker (1980) used the term *indemniotic measurement* when discussing absolute units of measure and the term *vaganotic measurement* when discussing relative units of measure.

D. Prognosis.
E. Therapeutic or management guideline data.
2. Indicate the order in which such measurements and examinations should be requested.
3. Interpret and translate laboratory findings.
4. Recognize pitfalls, problems and limitations of laboratory data, including discussion of quality control and drug interaction as well as relative merits in terms of methodology, patient preparation and communication.
5. Understand pathophysiology or sequence of disease as reflected by laboratory measurements and examinations.

Most of these goals are applicable to behavioral medicine with little or no alteration. It seems reasonable that *Behavioral Assessment in Behavioral Medicine* should seek to "identify appropriate measurements and examinations for: A. diagnosis, B. confirmation of a clinical impression, C. screening or detection of disease, D. prognosis, and E. therapeutic or management guideline data." It also seems reasonable that *Behavioral Assessment in Behavioral Medicine* should seek to "indicate the order in which such measurements and examinations should be requested." These first two sets of goals are quite general and do not suggest one approach over others. However, the remaining three goals do reveal an orientation toward assessment about which we will say more shortly. This orientation is reflected by the title of Todd and Sanford's book: *Clinical Diagnosis by Laboratory Methods*. The first edition of this book was published in 1908. It was based upon lecture notes begun in 1905 by James C. Todd, who was offering one of the first courses in clinical diagnosis given in American medical schools. Todd states: "The subject matter was very limited, comprising little more than elementary microscopy, blood counts, and a few simple tests which any physician could readily carry out in his office" (Todd & Sanford, 1931, p. 9). Medical science was only just turning to physical measurements, long associated with laboratory sciences, to diagnose diseases, confirm clinical impressions, make prognostic statements, and provide therapeutic guidelines. The laboratory tests of blood, urine, etc., that we associate with the diagnostic and prescriptive aspects of modern medicine were not then a routine part of medical practice. Rather, research was being conducted to convince physicians of the utility of such laboratory measurements. *Behavioral Assessment in Behavioral Medicine* is in just this situation. Measurements of the physical consequences of behaviors such as smoking, drinking, overeating, chronic pain, and disease are just now being discussed in measurement chapters in works on behavioral medicine. Coverage of these measures occupies a small fraction of the pages on the subject, partly because the measures are new and not widely used. This is due to the small research base regarding laboratory analysis of the physical consequences of behavior. The benefits of such measurements are still being demonstrated. Practitioners feel particularly comfortable with existing non-laboratory-based measurements and are reluctant to de-emphasize their importance even while laboratory measures are gaining importance. This "multidimensional" assessment strategy is still the rule rather than the exception, as we see in the Overview section, which introduces the remaining chapters of this book.

The profound effect that instruments had on both the theory and practice of medicine is clearly illustrated by Reiser (1979) while discussing "The Medical Influence of the Stethoscope." Reiser observes that prior to the stethoscope, physicians arrived at a diagnosis by asking the patient questions and by observing the color of the patient's skin, tongue, etc. "The acceptance of the stethoscope led to the establishment of physical examination as the keystone of diagnosis. It worked a profound transformation in the practice of medicine, altering both the physician's perceptions of disease and his relation to the patient" (p. 148). The physician had to consider disease in anatomical terms in order to make sense of the sounds heard through the stethoscope. This caused a paradigm shift away from the accepted Greek view that disease was caused by an imbalance in body fluids called *humors* and toward the modern view that disease is associated with anatomical changes. Hence, the presence of a new measurement procedure, the stethoscope, occasioned a profound transformation in the theory of disease.

Realizing that the stethoscope would enable him to hear the sounds generated by the motion of all the organs in the chest, "Laënnec set to work to develop a systematic technique of diagnosis based on physical examination with the instrument" (Reiser, 1979, p. 148). Hence, diagnosis was now rendered in terms of measurements made possible by the new instrument. The results of clinical examinations via the stethoscope were correlated with clinical outcomes and the findings of autopsies confirming the new view that anatomical or structural changes were associated with disease. The physician had moved beyond exclusive reliance upon verbal report and visual inspection to base diagnosis primarily upon information obtained from a mechanical instrument.

By 1927 Todd and Sanford (1931) could say that "clinical pathology has undergone marvelous development, and the book has of necessity grown in size and scope with each new edition" (p. 9). In 1931 Sanford wrote: "The use of laboratory methods in clinical diagnosis has become recognized as a necessity in modern medical practice, so that clinical pathology is now considered an important speciality" (Todd & Sanford, 1931, p. 11). By 1974 Davidsohn and Henry could say that "it is virtually impossible to compress all of laboratory medicine into a single volume" (Preface). In short, a dramatic revolution took place within medicine as it began to embrace units of measurement common in the laboratories of natural scientists. The concept of disease was transformed from its prescientific state into an understanding based upon measurements obtained with instruments.

I sincerely believe that behavioral medicine stands upon the threshold of a similar "marvelous development" if only it will embrace units of measurement associated with the natural sciences. Significant advances in behavioral medicine are no more possible in the absence of standard natural science units than was the case with medicine per se. This is because the unit of measurement is a fundamental aspect of quantification. Nonstandard units result in noncomparable data in the strict sense of the word.

The Units Issue

All measurements contain two logical components. The first component is one or more digits indicating the number of units or quanta detected. The second component is the definition of the unit that was used. The unit of measurement is a statement regarding the quantity that is taken to be basic or fundamental to the phenomenon under study. For example, the centrigrade degree is taken to be 1 100th of the difference between the freezing point and boiling point of water. To say that it is $20°$ C outside has a particular meaning only because both the number 20 and the centigrade unit have clear definitions. Reporting either the number 20 or the unit C alone does not constitute a scientific measurement because neither component alone is sufficient to specify the magnitude of a measurement.

The value of a standard unit goes beyond mere standardization. It allows one to talk about the *accuracy* of one's measurements because the number of units times the size of a unit equals a particular magnitude. The absence of standard units of measure restricts discussions of accuracy and thereby diverts attention to the issues of reliability and validity, which do not together necessarily assure accurate results. However, accurate results must necessarily be both reliable and valid. The missing element represents a fundamental measurement flaw that is directly attributable to the absence of standard measurement units. Let us see how this can be. We provide evidence of our measurements' reliability by showing that two sets of numbers correlate with one another. The numbers 1, 2, 3, 4, and 5 correlate perfectly with the numbers 101, 102, 103, 104, and 105. However, the mean of the first series is 3, and the mean of the second series is 103. Such data would not be considered as evidence of reliability if they constituted five temperature measurements of five substances by the same instrument on two occasions, even if the two data sets were perfectly correlated. This thermometer clearly gave much higher readings during the second measurement session. The mean difference between the two series can be arbitrarily large and still preserve the correlation coefficient since a linear transformation does not affect the correlation coefficient. This fact is the major reason for not accepting the correlation coefficient as a sufficient index of reliability in behavioral assessment.

Validity is also a rank-order or correlational concept. All that is required to demonstrate the validity of an instrument is to show that higher readings go with more of the phenomenon. Consider the following hypothetical self- or peer ratings of intoxication: 1, 2, 3, 4, and 5. Let us suppose that these ratings were obtained on either the same person on five different occasions or on five different people on the same occasion. Let us further suppose that we obtained the corresponding blood alcohol measurements: 20, 40, 80, 160, and 320 mg/100 ml of blood. The ratings form a linear progression, while the alcohol readings form a geometric progression. The two series correlate much higher than most validity coefficients ($r[3] = 0.93$, $p < 0.05$) and therefore demonstrate that the ratings are valid measures of blood alcohol. Unfortunately, the linear progression of ratings is an inaccurate index of the geometric progression of blood alcohol levels. In short, correlations are insensitive to unequal consecutive differences. The absence of standard units can obscure fundamental aspects of the phenomenon under study.

Now let us consider the measurement of intoxication using an instrument providing readings in standard units, or milligrams of alcohol per 100 ml of blood. The accuracy of the instrument would be studied under laboratory conditions where exact concentrations of alcohol in specific blood or air samples would be prepared. The mixture would be separated into several specimens and each would be measured using the instrument in question. The accuracy of the instrument would be evaluated by comparing its readings with the standard quantities prepared under well-controlled conditions. The closer the correspondence of the readings to the prepared standard, the more accurate the instrument is said to be. Such an instrument will also be considered valid since it has been shown to measure what it purports to measure. The instrument will be considered reliable to the extent that the readings cluster about a single value, which will be the prepared standard value if the instrument is accurate and therefore valid. Consistent readings that are all over or under the prepared standard value can be adjusted in either of two ways. The most common method is to adjust the instrument so that it gives accurate readings. This process is referred to as *calibration*. The second method requires one to adjust the obtained readings by a *conversion* constant that is empirically derived by systematically studying the deviations from the prepared standard. Reliability places an upper bound on accuracy just as it does upon validity. The average accuracy of an instrument is limited by the extent to which repeated measurements of the same quantity cluster together. This is because systematic deviations from the standard can be corrected either by calibration or conversion. In sum, demonstrating that an instrument provides accurate readings shows that it provides reliable and valid data that can be directly compared from one study to another only because the data are expressed in standard units.

Contemporary psychology in general and behavioral assessment in particular are in the midst of a units crisis. Most of the measurements reported in the behavioral assessment literature do not contain any specification of the units of measure. Hence, these figures are not scientific measures in the strict sense. Controversy over the use of a particular set of units and the use of widely differing units is an index of the prescientific status of this area. Such a view is by no means original to the present writer since it has been widely recognized (Franks, 1980) that psychology is in a preparadigmatic phase, having yet to emerge into full scientific blossom.

Overview

The purpose of this section is to give an overview of the contents of the other chapters in this book in light of the previous comments. Particular emphasis is given to measurements having standard units.

Chapter 2: Obesity

Perhaps the area of behavioral medicine having the longest association with units of measure common to the natural sciences is the assessment of obesity. It is a common experience for people to stand on scales and read their weights in pounds or kilograms. Straw and Rogers discuss other measurements of obesity that have standard units. Densitometry is the measurement of body density, which is based upon weight per unit volume. Both weight and volume are measured in standard units. Skinfold measurements are obtained in millimeter units using calibrated calipers. Anthropometry involves measuring the girth and length of body parts as an index of obesity. Length is also measured in standard units. The next section of their chapter describes the health risks associated with obesity in terms of the standard units introduced previously. We find statements like the following: "For every 10% increase in relative body weight (using Framingham study norms), there is a 2 mg/dl increase in fasting blood sugar, a 6.5 mm Hg rise in systolic blood pressure, and a 12 mg/dl rise in total serum cholesterol" (p. 31). Such statements describe exact amounts of change and detail their interrelationships in a manner that allows other investigators to confirm or revise the exact relationships involved. This is possible only because the units of measurement are well defined and have standard meanings.

The next major section of the Straw and Rogers chapter concerns the measurement of activity of obese people and their energy expenditure. The most revealing feature of this chapter is that only a small fraction of investigators use mechanical devices to report activity in standard units (e.g., pedometers and actometers) or report energy expended. The use of methods that do not involve standard units prohibits quantitative statements such as those illustrated in the preceding paragraph. Surely it is time that we unburdened ourselves from the handicap of arbitrary units when measuring activity and expended energy.

A small part of the Straw and Rogers chapter concerns the assessment of eating behaviors and cognitive-emotional factors. It is noteworthy that this section is devoid of standard units of measure.

In sum, it appears that the study of obesity has endeavored to make use of standard units of measure. About half of the Straw and Rogers chapter involves a discussion of variables having standard units of measure. It is noteworthy that the more psychological aspects of obesity have not kept pace. The measurement of activity and energy expenditure under various conditions appears important to the scientific study and clinical management of obesity. Activity can be measured in standard units, but relatively few investigators do so. It is recommended that future investigators measure activity with instruments having fixed and preferably standard units of measure when studying obesity.

Physical measurements of activity can be used in two ways to conceptualize the nature of obesity. The first use is consistent with the general tenor of the Straw and Rogers chapter; that is, to describe a physical condition known as obesity. People who are said to be obese can be described as a certain number of standard units large on one or more measurement scales. One is reminded of clothing size in this connection. Clothes beyond a certain size are thought to be purchased by obese people. This is an end view of a process of overeating and/or underexercising.

The second understanding of obesity stemming from standard units concerns the consequences of overeating or underexercising that can be measured in terms of standard units. Too much eating behavior and/or not enough exercise behavior will alter the number of standard units large the person is. Change in the number of standard units is an index of change in a variety of behaviors influencing obesity. The more aspects of obesity that can be tracked in terms of standard units, the more precise the diagnosis can be as to what the person is or is not doing that is causing his obesity. It then becomes more likely that investigators will be able to track the developmental onset of behavioral patterns leading to obesity.

Chapter 3: Smoking

The first quarter of the Prue, Scott, and Denier chapter on smoking reviews methods used to obtain data regarding the rate of cigarette consumption. Their discussion begins with the lowest-quality measurements and proceeds to the highest-quality measurements currently available. Retrospective estimates of the number of cigarettes smoked are discussed first. Next they describe ways of monitoring cigarette consumption such as writing down the time of day each cigarette was smoked. The next higher level of measurement requires the subject to provide evidence of consumption. This can be done by having the subject send in all cigarette butts and/or empty cigarette packs. The next higher measurement level involves cigarette pack holders that count the number of cigarettes dispensed. A major problem with all of these methods is that the unit of measurement is the cigarette rather than any specific behavior with regard to the cigarette, such as puff rate, or with regard to any physical consequences of smoking, such as the volume of smoke inhaled. Perhaps the cigarette was lit, placed in an ash tray, and burned down while the subject was busy with some task. Clearly this is not the same as puffing at maximum frequency and at maximum volume. Cigarettes are not all made alike; they vary considerably in nicotine and tar levels. In sum, no standard unit of measure exists despite the illusion provided by single cigarettes.

The next section of the Prue, Scott, and Denier chapter on smoking concerns the topography of the smoking response. Such measures yield four parameters. The puff parameters include: number of puffs, puff length, total puff time, interpuff interval, and puff distribution. The cigarette parameters include: intercigarette interval and cigarette duration. The number of cigarettes per day can be deduced from these data. Therefore, this methodology is inclusive of the rate methodology. The volume and draw parameters are: volume of smoke inhaled, air flow through cigarette filter in terms of flow rate or velocity, and cigarette draw resistance. The respiration parameters include: depth of inhalation and exhalation, and pattern of inhalation and exhalation. These parameters are based upon standard units having clear physical significance. Many of the parameters are based on time, where the standard unit is the minute or second. Other parameters are based upon volume, which makes reference to standard units of length such as the meter, centimeter, or millimeter. It is not surprising that smokers cannot accurately report such data. Portable instruments have therefore been developed to obtain measurements of these parameters while the subjects behave in their natural environments. These data can be augmented by a physical analysis of the butts returned to the experimenter. It is possible to examine the cigarette filters for nicotine content and total particulate matter. Knowledge of the filter efficiency then allows one to estimate nicotine and total particulate matter exposure, provided one assumes that all butts returned were actually smoked by the subject in question rather than left to burn down. Perhaps it would be possible to identify which cigarettes have been truly smoked and which have been allowed to burn down by inspecting the physical contents of the cigarette filters. Deception remains a problem for topography measurements if the effort is to go beyond smoking style to measuring total exposure because it is possible that the subject · smoked cigarettes without using the topography measuring device.

The final portion of the Prue, Scott, and Denier chapter concerns biochemical measures of the physical consequences of smoking behavior; this section accounts for approximately half of the entire chapter. Such emphasis is appropriate for several reasons. First, the data have standard units of measure such as micromoles per liter. Second, the data are reliable within limits set by the laboratory equipment and skill of the technician, both of which are often considerable. Third, the matter of deception is largely put to rest. This is particularly true if repeated measurements are taken randomly. Fourth, biochemical data reflect injestion, meaning that they are sensitive to all of the topographical variables previously described. Hence, biochemical measures are inclusive of topographical measures with regard to total exposure. Fifth, saliva and breath samples can be more easily obtained than topography measures, which are the only other data based upon standard units. Taken together, these attributes make biochemical measures of smoking the highest-quality measures available. The authors discuss factors that must be considered when interpreting such data. One of them is activity. Greater activity produces faster excretion of carbon monoxide (CO_a) and quite probably faster excretion of other biochemical measures of smoking. Hence, the chapters concerning activity measurements take on additional significance for the field of behavioral medicine.

Chapter 4: Alcohol

The first third of the Hay and Frankenstein chapter discusses drinking behavior and how alcohol abuse is approached clinically. The next quarter of their chapter concerns data based upon the physical consequences of drinking alcohol that can be measured in terms of standard units; that is, the amount of alcohol present in the blood. Of particular importance is the report that heavy drinkers develop a tolerance for alcohol that makes them appear unintoxicated on behavioral sway tests and psychomotor tasks when they have high blood alcohol concentrations as measured by breath samples. The implications of this result are especially important for behavioral assessment. Breath samples are easily collected. Measurement of alcohol in breath samples can be accomplished by relatively inexpensive equipment that yields results in milligrams of alcohol per 100 ml of blood volume; that is, in standard units associated with natural science. Notice that these units of measurement control for the person's size since the number of milligrams of alcohol is divided by (is per) 100 ml of blood. Dubowski (1975) reported a correlation of $r = 0.95$ between breath and blood alcohol measurements. The result is a direct evaluation of the amount of alcohol injested by whatever means and therefore is immune to the vagaries of self-report. Gone are the problems of trying to find family members to spy on the client to determine drinking rate. The investigator is liberated from concerns about surreptitious drinking. The deception associated with "taste tests" is no longer necessary. Tolerance levels can be directly determined by comparing breath alcohol levels against behavioral tests rather than causing serious measurement errors, as would be the case if behavioral tests, self-reports, or behavioral observation data were used alone or together. These latter procedures are but indirect methods of estimating, via arbitrary units, what can be directly measured in standard units.

The next section of the Hay and Frankenstein chapter discusses the use of liver tests to evaluate the biological consequences of excessive alcohol consumption. The behavioral value of these tests is that the liver constitutes a cumulative record of the individual's lifetime drinking habits. The liver qualifies as a "nonreactive assessment" of drinking behavior in the full sense of the term, as discussed by Webb, Campbell, Schwartz, and Sechrest (1966). Moreover, such tests are direct indicators of the health consequences of alcohol consumption that control for individual differences regarding sensitivity to alcohol. Said otherwise, the same level of alcohol consumption may impair the health of one person substantially more than that of another person due to constitutional differences. It seems that investigators in the field of behavioral medicine should be particularly interested in nonreactive life history measures of alcohol consumption that are directly proportional to health risks. However, breath alcohol measures are probably the preferred measure of contemporary drinking behavior.

The final section of the Hay and Frankenstein chapter discusses special problems in evaluating female drinkers. It appears that the menstrual cycle and associated changes in sex steroids significantly influence the assessment of female drinking behavior. In sum, about half of the Hay and Frankenstein chapter is concerned with variables having standard units of measure.

Chapter 5: Chronic Disease

A major contribution of the Goldstein and Stein chapter is that it clarifies the central role that measurement of activity plays in the behavioral assessment of persons with chronic disease. Each major section of this chapter begins with a synopsis of the medical facts associated with each disease entity and how these aspects of the disease are reflected in the person's activity. For example, arthritis is a progressive crippling disorder that has the behavioral effect of making people less active. The degree of activity reduction is a measure of the person's functional status. Clinical improvement associated with various therapies can be evaluated via measurements of activity.

Cirrhosis of the liver is a consequence of excessive alcohol ingestion that attenuates ambulation in proportion to how far the disease has progressed. Hence, systematic activity measurements have a place in evaluating the behavior of alcoholics.

Chronic obstructive pulmonary disease is a consequence of excessive cigarette smoking, and it also reduces motor activity. Hence, systematic motor activity measurements have a place in evaluating the behavior of smokers.

Coronary heart disease impedes activity. Hence, activity measurements can be used to evaluate the extent to which the person's behavior has been affected by coronary heart disease. Moreover, exercise has been associated with lesser risks of contracting coronary heart disease. Measurements of activity can provide a comprehensive evaluation of a person's 24-hr activity cycle. Such measurements can determine if selected life-style changes are producing sufficient exercise to be considered prophylactic against coronary heart disease. Evaluations of this type are especially important given that many people are willing to make some life-style changes but may resist recommendations regarding jogging and sports that require special facilities or changing of clothes and showering during midday.

The importance of activity measurements to the evaluation and management of obesity are reiterated by Goldstein and Stein. In sum, the authors emphasize the relevance of measuring activity in standard units when researching and clinically treating people with various chronic diseases.

Chapter 6: Chronic Pain

Pain is a symptom common to many medical disorders. The first third of the White, Bradley, and Prokop chapter discusses the effects of chronic pain on activity. Some people respond to pain with hypoactivity while others respond with hyperactivity. Most of the research on activity in this area is based upon arbitrary units of measure because of the use of self-reports, ratings, and observational data. However, mercury switches are being used to measure "uptime," thereby evaluating how ambulatory chronic pain patients are.

The authors express concern that instrumental measurements of the magnitude of activity could be misleading in that the nature of the activity is not also recorded. It is possible for two people to expend the same amount of activity either by working or pacing. Clearly, the former alternative is preferable. Such concerns are based upon the fact that instruments do not duplicate the function of human observers; that is, they cannot infer the type of activity in addition to the magnitude of the activity. Such concerns are best addressed by letting instruments do what they do best and letting people do what they do best. Instruments can count the frequency of particular movements or measure the intensity of these movements far better than human observers can. Therefore, instruments should be used to measure the magnitude of activity. Such measurements can be conveniently taken over long time periods as the person continues to behave in his or her natural environment. It is also possible to have the patient or a relative record the general types of activity performed during the day. This could take the form of a checklist of positive and negative behaviors. The patient or a relative could indicate the types of behaviors engaged in during the day by checking the appropriate boxes on the sheet. Such a procedure would disclose whether or not particular activity measurements were obtained in questionable ways. It is quite likely that the rating forms could be discontinued once it was learned that a particular patient has consistently been engaging in desirable behaviors. This would ease the assessment burden on the patient and/or the relatives, thereby enhancing the possibility of obtaining extended follow-up measurements.

The last major section of the White, Bradley, and Prokop chapter concerns the assessment of pain via physiological measurements. Fraction I endorphins and L-tryptophan measurements taken on cerebrospinal fluid appear to be promising indices of chronic pain. Such variables clearly have standard units of measure.

Chapter 7: Activity—Measurement

It was mentioned earlier that the sounds made audible by the stethoscope occasioned a profound paradigm shift in our understanding and treatment of disease. A major thesis of this first of two chapters on measuring human activity by Tryon is that mechanical measurements of activity will require a similar fundamental shift in how we conceptualize behavior. Currently available instruments for measuring activity do not duplicate the behavior of human observers. Human observers respond to categories or classes of behaviors like hitting, throwing, sitting, and running. Instruments respond to selected physical forces occurring at the site of attachment consistent with the manner in which the device was constructed. Hence, two major conceptual shifts are required of investigators who use sensors to measure the observable movements of body parts such as arms, legs, head, and trunk that we will call *activity* for lack of a better term. The first required conceptual shift is from the general to the specific. It requires the investigator to take the perspective of the site of attachment rather than the entire person when interpreting data from an activity monitor. This requires one to think in terms of the movement of wrists, ankles, and waists rather than of persons. Often, one must think in terms of either left or right wrists or ankles. The second required conceptual shift is more difficult and has far greater ramifications for our theoretical understanding of behavior. Instruments respond to forces of acceleration (changes in velocity) and degrees of tilt relative to the vertical axis occurring at a particular site of attachment. Hence, we are obliged to talk in terms of physical forces and counts of displacement rather than the familiar behavioral terms of hitting, throwing, sitting, running, etc. This gives a completely new orientation to behavior that is based upon standard units of measure. It opens up a new conceptual frontier like the one explored by Laennec subsequent to inventing the stethoscope. Investigators can now begin to conceive of behavioral disorders in terms of the new measurements and systematically relate these new measurements to other aspects of the patient's medical records. Chapter 7 introduces the reader to the conceptual changes required by this paradigmatic shift.

Chapter 8: Motor Activity—Findings

The purpose of this second Tryon chapter is to review quantitative findings regarding activity. The reviewed articles appear in a wide variety of publications, many of which may be unfamiliar to psychologists. The quantitative findings are meant to provide a context for interpreting new data.

Conclusions

It appears that efforts are underway to measure medically relevant behaviors and the physical consequences of these behaviors using instruments yielding data that have fixed, if not standard, units of measure. Investigators are beginning to conceptualize behavior disorders in terms of these measurements, though much reliance yet remains upon data based upon arbitrary and variable units of measure. This situation is directly analogous to the circumstances surrounding laboratory medicine just prior to its explosive development into the foundation of modern medical science. Perhaps behavioral assessment is poised for just such a metamorphosis. I sincerely invite you to participate in this most exciting revolution.

References

Davidsohn, I., & Henry, J. B. *Todd–Sanford clinical diagnosis by laboratory methods* (15th ed.). Philadelphia: Saunders, 1974.
Dubowski, K. M. Studies in breath alcohol analysis: Biological factors. *Zeitschrift für Rechtsmedizin*, 1975, *76*, 93–117.

Franks, C. M. Conditioning and cognition in contemporary behavior modification. In W. W. Tryon, C. B. Ferster, C. M. Franks, A. E. Kazdin, D. J. Levis, & G. S. Tryon, (Eds.), On the role of behaviorism in clinical psychology. *Pavlovian Journal of Biological Sciences*, 1980, *15*, 12–20.

Johnston, J. M., & Pennypacker, H. S. *Strategies and tactics of human behavioral research*. Hillsdale, NJ: Lawrence Erlbaum, 1980.

Reiser, S. J. The medical influence of the stethoscope. *Scientific American*, 1979, *240*, 148–155.

Todd, J. C., & Sanford, A. H. *Clinical diagnosis by laboratory methods: A working manual of clinical pathology*. Philadelphia: Saunders, 1931.

Webb, E. J., Campbell, D. T., Schwartz, R. D., & Sechrest, L. *Unobtrusive measures: Nonreactive research in the social sciences*. Chicago: Rand McNally, 1966.

2

Obesity Assessment

Margret K. Straw and Todd Rogers

It is ironic that much of the early interest in obesity treatment among members of the behavioral community was prompted by the ease with which the effectiveness of treatment could be assessed. What seemed straightforward in the early 1970s has since been recognized as one of the most complex assessment problems in behavioral medicine. The issues and problems involved in obesity assessment take the behavior therapist outside of the familiar territory of behavioral assessment and into the realm of exercise physiology, nutrition, and medicine.

This chapter provides an overview of basic assessment techniques appropriate for obesity research and treatment. Additionally, we address some of the important issues in obesity assessment. Specifically, the chapter covers the assessment of body composition, health risk factors, food intake, activity, and behavioral concomitants of obesity. While this leaves a number of areas untouched, such as direct assessment of adipose cellularity, we have chosen to cover those topics most likely to be useful to researchers

During preparation of this manuscript, Dr. Straw was supported by Grant R01 AM 27333 from the National Institute of Arthritis, Diabetes, Digestive and Kidney Diseases.
During preparation of this manuscript, Dr. Rogers was supported by an NIH National Research Service Award (T32 HL 07034-07), Dr. John W. Farquhar, Director.

in behavioral medicine and to exclude techniques that are not yet widely available or systematized.

Measurement of Body Composition

Perhaps the most fundamental assessment problem in obesity research and treatment is the assessment of obesity itself. If we are to understand the relationship of obesity to various health risk factors, we must have a clear method of defining and assessing it. If we wish to evaluate treatment programs, we must be able to accurately assess changes in obesity status and to define a patient's success as it relates to some standard of normality. If we wish to explore personality or behavioral variables as possible correlates of obesity, we must feel confident in our definition and assessment tools. In short, we must be able to clearly define and measure obesity in order to study or treat it. In the extreme instance, we have no difficulty defining or identifying obesity. However, definitions and assessment techniques applicable to the borderline case and appropriate for evaluating change are needed. This section of the chapter is devoted to defining obesity, discussing several issues raised by our definition, and discussing specific assessment techniques.

Obesity is generally defined as a condition characterized by an excessive accumulation of adipose tissue or body fat (see Bray, 1980; Mahoney, Mahoney, Rogers, & Straw, 1979). This definition highlights several major issues in obesity assessment. First, note that obesity is defined in terms of body fat, not body weight. This approach to defining obesity is unfamiliar to many and remains somewhat controversial. Second, the definition leaves open the question of what constitutes excessive body fat. Third, it requires that we deal with the problems inherent in accurately measuring body fat.

We will not belabor the body weight–body fat controversy, but it would be remiss not to briefly discuss it. Because body weight is relatively easy to assess, because it is moderately correlated with body fat, and because body fat is difficult to assess, some experts recommend using body weight to determine obesity status (see Garrow, 1974/1978). Indeed, the Task Force on Definitions, Criteria, and Prevalence of Obesity of the 1977 Fogarty International Conference on Obesity concluded that, although *obesity* refers to an excess of body fat and *overweight* refers to an excess of body weight relative to height standards, in most instances the two terms are used synonymously (Bray, 1980). Nonetheless, the committee recognized that in certain borderline cases, obesity and overweight are not synonymous. For example, the professional athlete may be overweight because he is heavily muscled, not because he is overly fat. The sedentary office worker, on the other hand, may be overly fat but fall into a normal weight range because his muscles are not well developed. The use of weight would be misleading as a standard of obesity in these and similar situations. The use of body weight to evaluate treatment-related changes may also be misleading in certain circumstances. Because programs based on increasing physical activity may produce significant losses of fat, combined with increases in muscle weight, it is not unusual for body weight to remain stable or decrease only slightly. Without assessment of body fat, these programs would inappropriately be labeled failures. Thus, we prefer a definition of obesity based on body fat, even though there are problems inherent in its measurement.

A second issue in the definition of obesity is the development of a precise criterion of excessiveness. Before attempting this, it is important to know what constitutes normal body composition. For males, about 58% of the body mass is water, 20% is protein, 14% is fat, 5% is minerals, and 3% is glycogen; for females, 54% is water, 14% is protein, 24% is fat, 5% is minerals, and 3% is glycogen (for more detail, see Garrow, 1974/1978, or Mahoney et al., 1979). One standard deviation is 6% for both males and females. Thus, a reasonable normative definition of mild obesity would be 20% fat for males and 30% fat for females. Moderate obesity would be defined, using a criterion of body fat 2 or more standard deviations above the norm, as 26% and 36% fat, respectively.

Use of a normative definition does not, however, address the issue of excessiveness as it relates to health risk. Epidemiological data, most of which are based on body weight, suggests that mortality increases fairly dramatically for the individual who is 30% or more above weight standards for his or her height (Lew & Garfinkel, 1979; Society of Actuaries, 1959). Risk of death from diabetes, digestive diseases, and cerebrovascular disease all increase, with the average risk of early death being about 45% higher for those 30% or more overweight and 88% higher for those 40% or more overweight as compared to normal weight individuals (Lew & Garfinkel, 1979). Thus, excessiveness from the health risk point of view can be defined as 30% or more overweight, a criterion which is almost certainly synonymous with obesity.

Returning to the third issue in use of a definition of obesity based on body fat, we must find a way to overcome the difficulties in the measurement of body fat. The remainder of this section is devoted to briefly describing and evaluating various techniques for the assessment of body fat, including both precise laboratory-based techniques such as hydrostatic densitometry and inert gas uptake, and less precise but more widely available techniques such as skinfold calipering, anthropometric measures, and weight-based measures.

Densitometry

One approach to the measurement of body composition is based on calculation of body density. The densities of various components of the body relative to water are known. Given information on the relative densities of fat (about 0.9) and fat-free tissues (about 1.1), plus estimates of overall body density relative to water, researchers have developed several algebraic equations for estimating the percentage of body weight which is fat (e.g., the Grande equation proposed by Brozek, Grande, Anderson, & Keys, 1963; and the Siri equation, 1956; see Appendix A).

Since the development of standard equations, the major problem in determining percent fat has been the accurate measurement of total body density. One of the best approaches is based on hydrostatic densitometry, or underwater weighing (Garrow, Stalley, Diethelm, Pittet, Hesp, & Halliday, 1979). Body volume is calculated on the basis of the difference between the underwater weight and the dry weight of the subject, as corrected for the density of the water and the volume of the lung and intestinal gases. Density is then determined by dividing weight by volume.

Hydrostatic densitometry is considered to be very accurate and has often been used as a standard against which other assessment techniques are validated. However, the technique has a number of disadvantages for most clinical researchers. The procedure may be quite stressful for obese patients, since it requires complete submersion in a tank of water until an accurate underwater weight can be obtained. While this should take only about 30 sec, the obese patient, who floats easily, may have difficulty remaining underwater for the appropriate time period, making repeated measurements necessary. Furthermore, many obese patients find the procedure itself embarrassing. Even if these problems could be overcome, access to appropriate equipment and trained personnel may further limit the applicability of the technique for clinical research.

Inert Gas Uptake

Body composition can also be precisely assessed on the basis of inert gas uptake. When inhaled, a number of gases, including xenon, krypton, and cyclopropane, will dissolve in body fat but not in other body tissue. If one knows the exact amount of gas inhaled by an individual, the solubility of the particular gas in fat, and the concentration at which equilibrium is reached, then the individual's percent body fat can be calculated (Tiwary, 1977).

Although accurate, this technique also has drawbacks for the clinical researcher. The subject must breathe through air-tight equipment for up to 2 hr in order to reach equilibrium. Technically, obtaining a measurement without any air leakage may be difficult. Practically, both the inconvenience of the procedure for the subject and the lack of routine availablity of appropriate equipment are major limitations on the utility of the technique.

Total Body Water

A third approach to measuring body composition is through the assessment of total body water. Since body water is contained almost exclusively in lean body mass and since researchers make standard assumptions concerning the concentration of fluid in lean body mass, an assessment of the total volume of body water can be used as the basis for a calculation of lean body mass. To assess total body water the subject takes a dose of water labeled with either tritium oxide or deuterium oxide. Within about 4 hr the dosage is fully absorbed into the body waters, and a sample of body fluid (i.e., a plasma sample) is taken. The total volume of body fluid, and thus lean body mass, may be calculated on the basis of the dilution of the labeled liquid.

A number of potential problems exist with this technique. First, it is not clear that the assumptions about the percentage of water contained in fat-free weight, on which the technique is based, are accurate in obese adults (Tiwary, 1977). Furthermore, the technique offers ample room for error if the labeled liquid has not reached equilibrium when the fluid sample is obtained. To the behavioral researcher, a more pertinent concern is the relative difficulty of obtaining such a time-consuming measure, especially if multiple measurements are desired.

Total Body Potassium

Like water, potassium (K) is contained almost exclusively in lean body mass, and the amount of potassium per unit of lean body mass is known. Consequently, if we can measure total body K, lean body mass may be calculated. Since the natural isotope of potassium, 40 K, emits gamma rays, which may be measured using a gamma spectrometer, total body K can be measured indirectly. Using our assumption about the proportion of K in lean body mass, we can then calculate lean body mass.

This technique also has its drawbacks. On the theoretical level, it is not clear that the assumptions on the percentage of K in various body tissues are valid for obese adults (Garrow, 1974/1978). More practically, problems have been reported in excluding background radiation from measurements. It appears that this problem can be overcome, but only with extremely expensive measurement equipment.

More detailed discussion of these techniques may be found in Mahoney et al. (1979), Garrow (1974/1978), or Katch and McArdle (1977). To briefly summarize, each can provide accurate assessment of body composition in normal-weight adults. While the total body water and total body K techniques have been critiqued for use in obese adults, the others appear to be accurate across weight classifications, with underwater weighing considered the standard. The techniques share two fundamental problems: expense to the researcher and inconvenience for the patient. While their development and use is important for precise physiological research, for the purposes of behavioral medicine research, somewhat less precise measures that are more convenient, more acceptable to the patient, and less expensive are desirable. The following sections discuss several methods of assessment which are more practical for use in clinical and field research: skinfold, girth, and body weight measurements.

Skinfold Calipering

Assessment of body fat through skinfold calipering is based on the assumption that — across individuals of the same sex, race, and age — a fairly predictable proportion of body fat is stored subcutaneously. By measuring skin-fold thicknesses at representative sites, one can estimate the amount of subcutaneous fat, and thus total body fat. A number of equations have been developed to predict total body fat from skinfold measurements (see Appendix A). Perhaps the most widely used for clinical work are the Allen, Peng, Chen, Huang, Chang, and Fang (1956) and the Durnin (Durnin & Rahaman, 1967; Durnin & Womersley, 1974) equations, based on measurements at 10 sites and 4 sites, respectively. For epidemiological work, single skinfold measurements, usually at the triceps site, are often employed (Seltzer & Mayer, 1967).

For a number of reasons, we have found the Durnin equations to be especially appropriate for use in weight control research. First, they are highly correlated with body fat as estimated by densitometry (Womersley & Durnin, 1977; $r = 0.74$ to 0.92).[1] Second, these equations were developed using a population of both normal-weight and obese subjects; consequently, they remain accurate when used with an obese sample (see Rogers, Mahoney, Mahoney, Straw, & Kenigsberg, 1980). Finally, because measurements are obtained only at the tricep, bicep, supraileal, and subscapular sites, the process of calipering is relatively quick for the researcher and less embarrassing for the patient, who may object to completely disrobing for other measurement procedures.

The measurement technique used for skinfold calipering is described in detail by Franzini and Grimes (1976; Grimes and Franzini, 1977). To briefly summarize, one must first carefully identify and mark the site to be used for measurement. Accuracy in locating the site is important, since research has indicated that a variation of even 2.5 mm above, below, or to the side of a site can result in statistically significant differences in obtained readings (Ruiz, Colley, & Hamilton, 1971). Once sites have been identified, the assessor uses the thumb and forefinger to pull the fold of

---

[1]The correlations reported in this chapter all reached statistical significance and were based on adequate sample sizes. Precise information on degrees of freedom and significance level are not reported because of the tremendous variation in the availability of information across the literatures reviewed.

fat away from the underlying muscle. Often the obese patient must be instructed to move or flex his muscle to differentiate it from the fat. The calipers are then placed at the marked site and the reading is taken when the calipers stabilize (i.e., the indicator on the calipers is no longer moving). The precision of measurement can be enhanced if measurements are repeated until three identical readings have been obtained at each site.

Several excellent brands of calipers are available.[2] Generally researchers report very little difference in accuracy among them, and the decision to use a particular brand is based upon personal preference. It should be noted that for use with obese patients, the Lange calipers have the advantage of measuring somewhat larger skinfolds than can be measured with other calipers. They are also fairly compact and easy to handle.

Skinfold calipering has a number of distinct advantages for those involved in clinical research. Calipers are relatively inexpensive (under $200). They provide a quick method of measuring body fat and can be used easily within the clinic setting.

However, skinfold calipering has received a great deal of criticism as a method of assessing body fat. First, a number of researchers question the assumption that a predictable proportion of body fat is stored subcutaneously (see Garrow, 1974/1978). There are some indications that cross-cultural differences may exist. More important, there are strong indications that proportion of fat stored subcutaneously varies as a function of degree of obesity (Berry, 1974). However, those who have developed equations for predicting percent fat on the basis of calipering have attempted to address this issue, in part, by using data transformations to linearize the relationship between caliper readings and body density. For example, the Durnin equation requires a log transformation, which seems to handle the obese subjects' data much more effectively than would a simple linear regression equation.

Perhaps the most strenuous objection to the technique is that it takes highly trained personnel to caliper accurately, and even then the technique produces variable results. For example, Bray, Greenway, Molitch, Dahms, Atkinson, and Hamilton (1978) found significant variation in measurements of skinfolds by multiple rat-

---

[2]The most commonly used brands of caliper are the Lange and Harpenden calipers. The Lange caliper is available from Cambridge Scientific Instruments, Cambridge, MD. The Harpenden caliper can be obtained from British Indicators Ltd., St. Albans, Herts, United Kingdom.

ers. As noted earlier, Ruiz et al. (1971) found significant variability in measurement with an error of only 2.5 mm in marking the site. On the other hand, a number of researchers provide data suggesting that the error rate is not overly large. For example, Satwanti and Bharadwaj (1980) compared measurements of skinfold thickness obtained on two consecutive days from both obese and lean volunteers. These measurements correlated highly ($r = 0.84$ to 0.92). Furthermore, the magnitude of the correlations compared quite favorably to correlations obtained on consecutive days for body density as measured by water displacement ($r = 0.96$), for girths ($r = 0.84$ to 0.94), and even for body weight ($r = 0.96$). Burkinshaw, Jones, and Krupowicz (1973) had various raters measure skinfold thickness at both marked and unmarked sites. At marked sites, the agreement was considered very good; at unmarked sites, statistically significant differences in measurement were noted. However, when percent fat was calculated, using the Durnin and Rahaman equation (1967), those differences resulted in estimations of percent fat ranging from 15.5 to 16.1, a variation of less than 1 percentage point.

Some research also indicates that highly trained personnel are not a necessity. Straw and Straw (1980) trained undergraduate raters for a period of about a week and found that even with unmarked sites their agreement was acceptable. Coefficients of generalizability calculated for the sum of four sites (which is used to calculate actual percent fat) ranged from 0.81 to 0.93. Rogers et al. (1980), again using a rater with minimal training, obtained ratings which correlated highly with density measures obtained from underwater weighing ($r = -0.81$).

Although reliability is a serious threat to the utility of this technique, we feel that, in balance, the technique is a useful one. It is inexpensive and widely available. Data do exist suggesting that with careful training and repeated measures, calipering is fairly reliable. Therefore, for clinical research in which group data will be used, we recommend that skinfold calipering be seriously considered.

Anthropometry

A second approach to assessing body composition, also appropriate for clinical use, is based on physical anthropometry. Researchers have developed a number of equations using girth, length, and diameter measures to predict percent fat. The most frequently cited equations are those developed by Steinkamp and his colleagues (Steinkamp, Cohen, Gaffey, McKey, Bron, Siri, Sargent, & Isaacs, 1965a; see Appendix A).

As with calipering, a number of precautions must be taken to ensure reliable measurement. First, the sites must be carefully identified and marked. (For a listing of commonly used measurement sites, see Katch & McArdle, 1977; or Steinkamp, Cohen, Siri, Sargent, & Walsh, 1965b). Second, appropriate equipment must be used. Because standard cloth measuring tapes stretch with repeated use, steel spring-loaded tapes are recommended for girth measurements. Anthropometers are available for diameter measurements. Finally, a careful measurement technique is needed; the tape should be held snugly but should not compress the fat or skin.

Given these precautions, and adequate training, anthropometry can provide valid and reliable assessment of body fat. Steinkamp's equations correlate highly with body fat as assessed by hydrostatic densitometry (Steinkamp et al., 1965a). Furthermore, research on the test–retest reliability of the technique indicates that measures obtained on two consecutive days are highly correlated ($r = 0.84$ to 0.94; Satwanti & Bharadwaj, 1980).

Assessment techniques based on anthropometry are convenient and fairly inexpensive. As already noted, they have adequate reliability and validity. Their major drawback for use with an obese population is that the subject must disrobe for measurement. This may prove to be embarrassing to the obese client, making repeated measurements difficult to obtain.

Weight

Among the simpler techniques, body weight and weight-derived measures are the most widely used. As noted earlier, raw body weight measures do not correlate highly with body fat. Using a fairly heterogeneous sample of 49 obese men and women, Rogers et al. (1980) reported a correlation of only 0.44 between weight and percent fat as calculated through underwater weighing, although the correlations for women alone ($r = 0.72$) and for men alone ($r = 0.90$) were higher. In general, body weight has been found to predict body fat at approximately 0.6 ± 0.1 (Mahoney et al., 1979), with lower correlations found in heterogeneous samples.

Given the modest relationship between body weight and body

fat, one might question its use as an indicator of obesity. Garrow (1978) succinctly summarizes the rationale for its use as follows: "the simplicity and objectivity of body weight as a diagnostic criterion are advantages which, in practice, outweigh its theoretical shortcomings" (p. 230). In fact, body weight is easy to obtain, sensitive to small changes, and acceptable to the subject or client. Clinic balance beam scales that provide weights to 450 pounds are readily available, and use of a poise may allow accurate assessment of heavier individuals (King, 1977).

Given the practical advantages of using body weight as an indicator of obesity, researchers have attempted to develop weight-derived measures that correlate more highly with body fat. Common transformations include the ponderal index (W/H^3); the body mass, or quetelet, index (W/H^2); pirquet (H^3/W); and livi (W^3/H) where W equals weight and H equals height. Of these, the body mass index appears to consistently produce the strongest correlations with body fat, usually ranging from 0.7 to 0.8 (Bray, 1978). The ponderal index is generally viewed as fairly weak due to its high correlation with height and insensitivity to increasing weight (Keys, Fidanza, Karvonen, Kimura, & Taylor, 1972).

Several calculated indices of relative weight loss are also available for use as outcome measures in obesity treatment programs. These include Feinstein's reduction index (Wt. loss/excess wt.) × (initial wt./target wt.) × 100, the reduction quotient ([100 × wt. loss]/excess wt.), and percent body weight loss (wt. loss/initial wt.). Each of these indices has been criticized on several counts (see Stuart, Mitchell, & Jensen, 1981). First, they tend to represent lighter individuals as more successful than heavier individuals. Second, they may be insensitive to changes produced in brief programs. While these are valid criticisms, it is nonetheless important to assess whether subjects reached or approached their goal weights during treatment. Even with some misrepresentation or distortion due to differences in starting weights, there remains a need for a measure of progress that is clearly related to ideal weight.

Selection of weight-related measures for use in obesity research is necessary in order to maintain comparability with existing research. For any obesity research project, weight and body mass index (W/H^2) should be presented. These measures have become standards within the field. For the evaluation of treatment outcomes, presentation of three sets of data is recommended: absolute weight loss, change in body mass index, and relative weight change (e.g., Feinstein's reduction index or the reduction quotient).

In summary, there are a range of options available for assessment of body compositon. Where extremely precise measurements are needed and the resources are available, underwater weighing is the best choice with an obese population. When less precision is needed, a more economical option is the use of either skinfold or girth measurements, or an average of the two, in combination with weight and weight-derived measures.

Measurement of Health Risk

There are several major health risks associated with obesity, aside from the economic, social, and psychological problems that often accompany the condition. These health risks were summarized by the Task Force on the Risks, Hazards, and Disadvantages of Obesity, at the Forgarty International Center Conference on Obesity (Bray, 1980). The several possible hazards of obesity noted were:

- Increased risk of cardiovascular disease, particularly sudden death.
- Relation to the onset of hypertension. The prevalence of hypertension may be increased three to five times in individuals who are 50 percent or more above desirable weight.
- Increased risk of developing gallbladder disease.
- Increased risk of developing non-insulin-dependent (usually maturity-onset) diabetes mellitus.
- Aggravation of degenerative joint diseases.
- Economic and social handicap. (p. 8)

Cardiovascular disease (CVD; notably coronary heart disease and stroke) is the number one cause of death among American adults, and thus our discussion focuses on the relationship of obesity and CVD. Most equations of multiple logistic risk for CVD include an obesity indicator variable (e.g., relative weight or body mass index), implying that obesity is a direct risk factor for CVD. In fact, there is considerable controversy over the direct association of obesity and CVD (Lewin, 1981). Regardless of this controversy, the relationship of obesity and other atherogenic factors is well documented (Ashley & Kannel, 1974; Gorden & Kannel, 1973; Kannel, Gordon, & Castelli, 1979). Specifically, obesity has been related to blood pressure, plasma lipids, and lipoproteins, known atherogenic factors.

In their schematic representation of the comprehensive diet–lipid–heart disease hypothesis, Hulley, Sherwin, Nestle, and Lee (1981) clearly designate the position of obesity as an indirect risk factor in the chain of causality for coronary heart disease (CHD). In their model, based upon a detailed review of evidence from the entire spectrum of biomedical research, excessive dietary calories lead to obesity, which in turn is associated with high levels of low-density lipoprotein (LDL) cholesterol, low levels of high-density lipoprotein (HDL) cholesterol, and hypertension. Each of these risk factors is in turn associated with coronary artery disease, which leads to CHD. Obesity is not causally linked to CHD, except through its relationship with blood pressure, LDL, and HDL.

It should be noted that the inverse relationship between body weight and HDL found by many investigators in cross-sectional studies (e.g., Kannel et al., 1979; Rhoads, Gulbrandsen, & Kagan, 1976) has been inconsistently supported by prospective trials. For example, P. Thompson, Jeffery, Wing, and Wood (1979) found a decrease in HDL cholesterol among obese women who lost weight, while others have found an increase (e.g., Wilson & Lees, 1972) or no change (e.g., Hulley, Cohen, & Widdowson, 1977) in HDL cholesterol in obese individuals during weight loss. Brownell and Stunkard (1981) have even found differential changes in HDL levels in obese men and women who lost weight, with men showing an average 5% increase in HDL and women showing an average 3.3% decrease in HDL levels. Conceptually, since HDL cholesterol levels are inversely related to risk of CHD, one would expect that weight loss would increase HDL levels if obesity is indeed an indirect risk factor. Clarification of these inconsistencies, and a more complete understanding of lipid metabolism and its relationship to obesity, awaits further investigation.

Diabetes is another atherogenic factor, and obesity has been related to increases in blood glucose levels and glucose intolerance (Kannel et al., 1979). In fact, Kannel and Gordon (1980) have been able to quantify the relationship of obesity to fasting blood sugar, as well as to systolic blood pressure and total serum cholesterol. For every 10% increase in relative body weight (using Framingham study norms), there is a 2 mg/dl increase in fasting blood sugar, a 6.5 mm Hg rise in systolic blood pressure, and a 12 mg/dl rise in total serum cholesterol. In summarizing the obesity–CVD relationship, Kannel and Gordon conclude that, "because it reversibly promotes atherogenic traits like hypertension, diabetes, and hyperlipidemia, reduction of overweight is probably the most important hygenic measure (aside from the avoidance of cigarettes) available for the control of cardiovascular disease" (p. 140).

Given the excess health risks associated with obesity, it is clearly appropriate for all clinicians to expand their traditional obesity assessment packages to include measures of health risk. The following assessment battery, slightly different from the one offered by Rogers et al. (1980), is suggested:

• Blood pressure
• Plasma lipids and lipoproteins
• Fasting blood glucose
• Cardiovascular–respiratory fitness

The following sections present brief comments on each of these measurements.

Blood Pressure

Because blood pressure varies from moment to moment and is so sensitive to environmental, physical, and cognitive stimuli, it is essential that a standardized protocol be established and followed in all clinical research. Having one's blood pressure measured is somewhat of a stressful experience for some people, whether they realize it or not. Additionally, obese individuals who are being weighed as part of an intake or screening assessment session may also be anxious about getting on the scale. It is for these reasons that the measurement of blood pressure is best performed after weights have been taken.

The individual on whom blood pressure is to be measured should have been sitting quietly for at least 5 min prior to taking the measurements. The measurements should be made in a quiet, private room that is kept at a comfortable temperature. The individual should be sitting upright in a chair, with his feet flat on the floor and his right arm resting on a table.

Cuff selection is quite important. Inaccuracies in sphygmomanometric measurements of blood pressure due to improper cuff size have been documented; normal-size cuffs (26 cm long) have been shown to yield spuriously high blood pressure readings in obese individuals who have larger than normal arm girth (e.g., Karvonen, Telivuo, & Jarvinen, 1964). Large-size cuffs are available and should be used if the end of a standard cuff does not fall between the white lines marked on the cuff.

While most qualified medical personnel are adept at the measurement of blood pressure, a few specific techniques tend to yield more accurate measurements:

1. Inflate the cuff to about 20–30 mm Hg above the estimated systolic pressure (the level at which a palpated radial pulse disappears during cuff inflation).
2. Deflate the cuff slowly, at the rate of 2–3 mm Hg per second.
3. Note the systolic pressure, to the nearest even number, at the appearance of sound (Korotkoff's first phase).
4. Note the diastolic pressure, to the nearest even number, at the disappearance of sound (fifth phase).

After completely deflating the cuff and recording the blood pressure readings, repeat the measurement using the same procedure. Then average the readings from the two measurements.

Throughout the procedure, the individual should be encouraged to remain relaxed and should be kept informed of the procedure at each step. It has been noted that more than 50% of all individuals with elevated blood pressure at a first reading will have "normal" pressure when later rechecked (see Carey, Reid, Ayers et al., 1976). This high prevalence of labile hypertension may be due to any number of factors, such as the stress of the experience, regression to the mean, or adaptation to the procedure. It suggests that an uncontrolled, clinical outcome study that includes measurements of blood pressure in a single group of individuals will yield biased data. Whenever serial blood pressure measurements are being used as dependent variables in research, the inclusion of a reference group, to control for the effects of repeated testing, is advised.

Plasma Lipids and Lipoproteins

Plasma lipids include total cholesterol and triglyceride. As noted previously, obesity is positively related to total cholesterol, elevated levels of which lead to increased risk of CHD (Hulley et al., 1981). While obesity and triglyceride levels are positively related (Kannel et al., 1979), triglycerides do not seem to be related to CHD (Hulley, Rosenman, Bawol, & Brand, 1980). Lipoproteins, the fat–protein packets that "carry" cholesterol in the bloodstream, include HDL, LDL, and very-low-density (VLDL) cholesterol fractions. Obesity increases LDL and decreases HDL, both of which lead to CHD; the role of VLDL in the obesity–CHD relationship is not yet clear (Kannel et al., 1979).

Details on the measurement of lipids and lipoproteins are beyond the scope of this chapter. There are some general suggestions, however, that may be offered to increase the interpretative value of these measurements. First, blood samples should be made after individuals have been fasting at least 12 hr. Casual, or nonfasting, samples tend to elevate the values, especially those of triglycerides. Second, at least two samples, taken over 2 days in a week and averaged, will reduce the within-person variability that is also present in these measurements. Third, plasma lipid and lipoprotein measurements should be made using standardized analytic procedures, such as those of the Lipid Research Clinics (1974).

We should also mention that with new, more sophisticated analytic procedures, measurements of lipoprotein subfractions and apolipoproteins (all variously implicated in the development of CVD) are becoming increasingly more common (Anderson, Nichols, Pan, & Lindgren, 1978; Cheung & Albers, 1977). It is not recommended that the average clinical research study include these measurements. They are mentioned here only to point out the depth of our ignorance in this area and the degree to which new and more precise measurement techniques may in the future require us to reconceptualize the lipoprotein–CHD relationships.

Fasting Blood Glucose

Again, a detailed discussion of fasting blood glucose measurements is beyond the scope of this chapter. Most clinical laboratories can perform accurate determinations of fasting blood glucose using standard procedures. It should be noted that plasma or serum blood glucose levels are usually about 15% higher than "true" blood glucose (Boedeker & Dauber, 1974). Oral glucose tolerance tests are usually not necessary for initial diagnosis of diabetes mellitus and are inappropriate for inclusion in a screening battery of obese individuals.

Cardiovascular–Respiratory Fitness

The evidence has been mounting in support of the hypothesis that physical activity serves to prevent CHD (e.g., Froelicher, Battler, & McKirnan, 1980). As is the case with obesity, it is as yet unclear whether physical activity is a direct or indirect antiatherogenic factor. As a direct factor, echocardiographic techniques have revealed beneficial morphological and functional changes in the heart following exercise training (Froelicher et al., 1980). As an indirect factor, vigorous exercise appears to be associated with decreases in triglycerides and LDL and VLDL cholesterol, and increases in HDL cholesterol (Wood & Haskell, 1979).

The measurement of cardiovascular–respiratory fitness as part of an assessment package for obese individuals can serve two purposes. First, the measurements may be used as indicators of improvement in fitness as a function of a weight control program (which should include an emphasis on increasing physical activity, both for caloric expenditure and for increasing fitness). Second, fitness measurements are powerful motivators for participants, who can readily see their initial levels and improvements over time.

Clinicians have a wide range of fitness measures from which to choose, ranging from relatively simple, noninvasive procedures to elaborate, expensive, and invasive techniques. The spectrum includes the Master Two-Step Test, the Gradational Step Test, the Bicycle Ergometer Test, the Multi-Stage Treadmill Test of Submaximal and Maximal Exercise, and the Graded Exercise Test for Ischemic Heart Disease. Each of these procedures is described in detail in the American Heart Association publication *Exercise Testing and Training in Apparently Healthy Individuals* (American Heart Association, 1972).

For most clinicians, one of the step tests or the bicycle ergometer test will be a sufficient measure of fitness for use in obesity assessment packages. In most cases, however, these tests provide only electrocardiographic information, while the treadmill tests usually also provide information on functional aerobic power and maximal oxygen uptake (Vo_2 max) measures of respiratory function. Still, given the constraints on personnel and facilities, the step or bicycle tests should provide sufficient information on initial levels of fitness and changes over time.

Regardless of the test selected, a number of precautions should be taken in the measurement of fitness, especially with obese individuals. Only people with no history of CVD, who are not using any cardiovascular medications, and who are free of any known illness or disability at the time of the evaluation should be eligible for testing. Acute infectious disease, orthopedic disorders, or metabolic problems may also be exclusion criteria. Further, the American Heart Association (1972) recommends that multistage testing be supervised by a physician; and, while the step or bicycle tests are not multistage procedures, a nurse or other medically qualified individual should be present during these procedures as well.

In summary, the measurement of health risk among obese individuals can add important and interesting information to the typical behavioral assessment package. It can also provide an unanticipated, yet beneficial side effect since it requires that the behavioral scientist come in contact with medical concepts and personnel. This will surely expand the horizons of both disciplines and contribute to the development of the field of behavioral medicine.

Assessment of Nutritional Status

Because of the strong focus on behavior change and an "antidiet" stance taken in much of the behavioral obesity research, assessment of nutrient intake has frequently been neglected. (See Brightwell, Foster, Lee, & Naylor, 1979; and Ritt, Jordan, & Levitz, 1979, for two notable exceptions.) Nonetheless, nutritional assessment should play an important role in obesity assessment. First, given that reduced caloric intake is often the primary mediator of weight loss in behavioral treatment programs, it is important to assess that intake at various points during treatment to determine whether the behavioral interventions are having the desired impact on consumption. Second, quality of nutrient intake should be assessed as a desirable outcome of treatment. Given that the rationale for treatment is often a reduction in health risk from disorders such as hypertension and diabetes, both of which are directly impacted by diet, it also becomes important to determine whether appropriate changes in various nutrients are occurring. Finally, quality and quantity of food intake may be reasonable candidates in the search for predictors of long-term success. For all of these reasons, it is important that the behavioral researcher be familiar with the methods available to assess the nutritional status of an individual and the strengths and limitation of each.

Food Diary

For the behavioral researcher, the most familiar method for collecting food intake information is the food diary, or food intake record. The subject is asked to record everything that he/she consumes during a specified period of time. The record is presumed to provide an accurate assessment of current food intake.

Two primary decisions are required when using this method. First, one must determine how many days of recording are needed. Most nutritionists recommend a minimum record of 3 days including 1 weekend day to acquire a representative sample of intake (Young & Trulson, 1960). However, even this period may be too short. Trulson (1951, in Young & Trulson, 1960) reported a significant decrease in variability when using a 7-day record; others have argued that, if possible, several weeks of intake should be obtained (Yudkin, 1951). The most common compromise appears to be the 7-day record. Second, one must decide on the precision of recording which is to be required. Marr (1971) describes a range of recording procedures from precise weighing (which requires weighing and recording uncooked food, cooked food, and table scraps) to use of estimates of portion size and common household measures. Generally, the household measures approach will provide fairly accurate estimates with less work for the subject. For example, Bransby, Daubney, and King (1948) reported a correlation of 0.94 between calorie estimates based on recording weighed portions and recording portions using "homely measures."

As already noted, food intake records are assumed to provide an accurate estimate of what an individual is consuming during a given period of time. Unfortunately, the accuracy of this assumption is almost impossible to assess. However, the results obtained using the food diary have been demonstrated to be reproducible over time. For example, Marr, Heady, and Morris (1959) repeated individual weighed surveys for a group of subjects after 6 months. The mean daily consumption for the first survey was 2,769 calories per day while the mean daily consumption at Time 2 was 2,819 calories. The correlation between calorie intake at the two testings was 0.81. Considering that these surveys were conducted during different seasons of the year, a factor which must be assumed to have added some variability to the results, the weighed diet survey seems to be quite reliable. Other authors (Adelson, 1960; Huenemann and Turner, 1942; Thomson, 1958) obtained similar results retesting anywhere from consecutive weeks to 6 weeks later.

Use of the food intake record is not, unfortunately, without problems. First, there is ample evidence in the self-monitoring literature that the act of recording a behavior frequently changes it. Use of the food diary alone often produces a weight loss, suggesting that it does not provide an altogether valid measure of habitual intake (Romanczyk, 1974). Second, the subject whose intake is being examined must be both cooperative and accurate for the technique to be effective. Lansky and Brownell (1980) provide data suggesting that even among cooperative subjects, estimates of portion size are often very inaccurate. Third, the procedure may require a significant time commitment from the researcher. To overcome problems of inaccurate estimation and recording, it may be necessary to have a dietitian train subjects in recording procedures using food models to aid in estimation. Furthermore, repeated contacts and accuracy checks may be necessary.

24-Hour Recall

A second technique for assessing nutritional status, frequently used in dietary research but rarely used in behavioral research, is the 24-hour recall (Marr, 1971; Trulson, 1960). The subject is asked to report his most recent food intake and then to work backward in time, recalling earlier eating episodes. If he has difficulty reconstructing his intake, the interviewer may use a checklist of common foods to serve as a prompt or ask him to reconstruct the events of the day as an aid to recall. Food models illustrating common portion sizes are used as an aid to accuracy in the recall of quantity consumed.

This technique has a number of strengths. First, although it requires a reasonably good memory on the part of the subject, it does not require that the individual be extremely cooperative. Instead of having to record and weigh food as he would for a food intake record, the individual is generally asked only to respond to a half-hour interview. Second, the recall method is not as reactive as the intake record. Third, it is fairly reliable. Balogh, Kahn, and Medalie (1971) collected monthly 24-hour recalls over the period of 1 year. Although they did not succeed in getting 12 records per subject, about 75% of their subjects came in for eight interviews. The coefficient of variation within individuals after eight dietary recalls was 0.18 for total calories consumed. Thus, the standard deviation for the individual was, on the average, one-fifth as large as his mean caloric intake. The authors conclude that this level of reliability is acceptable, especially since the participants are reporting food intake over all seasons of the year and some variability is to be expected simply because of seasonal variations in the availability of food.

One of the major difficulties with a 24-hour recall of food intake is that the accuracy of the record is dependent on the memory of the subject. Campbell and Dodds (1967) compared the 24-hour recall of institutionalized subjects to a record of the foods actually eaten. They found that women were better at remembering their intake than were men, and that younger subjects were better than older subjects. When adequate prompting was not provided, the 24-hour recall missed as much as 35% of the calorie intake of older men. Thus, subjects must be screened for appropriateness before being included in a study depending on recall.

Another difficulty with the 24-hour recall method is that it cannot really be considered an adequate representation of habitual eating patterns unless the recall is repeated. Balogh et al. (1971) suggest that, to be accurate within ±20% of the individual mean of calorie intake for half of the population tested, at least 4 random recalls are required. To be that accurate for 90% of the population being studied, 9 reports are needed. Thus, between 2 hr and 5 hr of interview time alone is required to obtain relatively accurate estimates of mean calorie intake for most individuals. More interviews are necessary for similar accuracy in the estimations of carbohydrate, protein, or fat intake. A final problem with the 24-hour recall, if obtained only once or twice, is that it is not altogether clear what the recall is measuring. A 7-day food record is clearly measuring current intake. A dietary history is attempting to measure habits or usual food intake without much regard to current pattern. The 24-hour recall estimates calories for only 1 day, which cannot be assumed to represent either, although it is probably adequate when used to establish group means or when used as a rough screening device for the individual.

Dietary History

The dietary history, the final approach to assessing food intake, was developed by Burke (1947). Her rationale for using a history rather than food records is that "a detailed history of the dietary habits furnishes important information, since the nutritional status of an individual can be no better than his past and present food habits permit" (p. 1041). Thus, the dietary history approach is directed toward assessing long-term food habits. It is obtained during an hour interview. Subjects are first asked to provide information on their usual pattern of eating by answering questions such as "What do you usually eat for breakfast?" and "What did you eat for breakfast today?" After an estimate of the individual's habitual intake has been established, the interviewer cross-checks information by asking about the subject's preferences for and usual intake of a number of common foods. Finally, the subject is asked to keep a food diary for 3 consecutive days. This information is also used to round out the picture of the individual's eating habits. Representative foods and amounts are used to calculate nutrient intake. Although a very specific figure is obtained for each individual, a rating scale is generally used to present the data so that the exact figures will not give an unjustified impression of accuracy.

The dietary history is a useful tool for obtaining information on average consumption. It has demonstrated reliability over time. Reshef and Epstein (1972) conducted interviews on two separate occasions, 6.5 to 8.5 months apart. The mean calorie intake as estimated by the two interviews correlated at 0.81 for men and 0.79 for women. Furthermore, regardless of the number of different foods the individual reported eating, the relationship between calorie intake at Time 1 and Time 2 remained the same. A major problem with the dietary history is that it requires training and expertise on the part of the interviewer to obtain complete information and to integrate the information gathered in the three different phases of the interview.

How should a technique for the assessment of food intake be chosen? Studies comparing the 7-day food diary, 24-hour recall, and dietary history generally conclude that they do not give the same estimates of intake (e.g., Young, Hagan, Tucker, & Foster, 1952). In a review of various techniques, Young and Trulson (1960) concluded that the results obtained by one method cannot be predicted by another. Furthermore, "though comparisons of one method with another have been made, these comparisons are between methods whose accuracy and reliability are not known; therefore no conclusions may be reached regarding which method is the more accurate or reliable" (p. 808).

In the absence of empirical data on the validity of the tools at hand, the final decisions should be based on the appropriateness of the tool for the population of interest, on the ease with which the data can be collected, and on the questions of interest. We generally recommend the use of 7-day food records throughout treatment programs since they are an appropriate method for examining compliance with dietary guidelines. However, dietary histories might provide a very interesting starting point for modifications in diet and might be useful for follow-up assessments.

Tabulation Procedures

Once food intake information has been collected, a decision must also be made on how to convert that information into nutritional data. Although chemical analyses provide the most precise data on the nutritional value of foods, the technique is too expensive and time consuming for routine use. A number of food value tables are available, including the U.S. Department of Agriculture's *Nutritive Value of American Foods* (1971) and Pennington and Church's *Food Values of Portions Commonly Used* (1980). Studies have indicated that these tables provide reasonably accurate estimates of the values of foods. For example, Whiting and Leverton (1960) found that in 59% of the cases they examined, the total calorie intake agreed within 10% using the two procedures.

Finally, a procedure for tabulating the information must be established. Several very complete computer data bases are available for calculating nutrient intake (e.g., USDA Nutrient Data Bank in Hyattsville, Maryland). Additionally, smaller data bases have become available for microcomputers (e.g., Apple's *Diet Analysis*, Aslam & Tess Enterprises, 1980). The use of either of these computer resources will represent a dramatic savings in time over hand tabulation. For example, Young and Trulson (1960) estimated that hand tabulation, coding, and calculation may take as much as 27 hr per record. In contrast, we have found that a record can be processed using the Apple *Diet Analysis* program in under 2 hr.

A final decision to be made concerns the degree of detail desired in a nutritional analysis. At minimum, total calories and grams of protein, carbohydrate, and fat should be calculated. Recent behavioral work that assessed nutrient intake also examined dietary fiber, minerals, and vitamins (Brightwell et al., 1979; Ritt et al., 1979). To make the information more meaningful, the quantity of each nutrient obtained may be expressed as a percentage of recommended daily allowance.

In summary, nutrient intake information may be collected through a food intake record, 24-hour recall, or dietary history. Once information has been obtained, it must be processed in order to provide information on selected nutrients. Ideally, computer processing will be used to ensure consistency and to reduce the time required to obtain useful data.

Assessment of Activity

Physical activity, like nutritional information, has not been assessed routinely in behavioral weight control research. However, activity is increasingly recognized as an important factor in the development and maintenance of obesity (J. K. Thompson, Jarvie, Lahey, & Cureton, 1982). Moreover, it plays a number of important roles in weight loss. First, there is a convergence of evidence that exercise alone will promote weight loss (e.g., Epstein & Wing, 1980; J. K. Thompson et al., 1982). Second, the quality of weight loss obtained through a combination of diet and exercise is better than that produced with diet alone since a greater proportion of the loss is made up of body fat. Third, exercise can lead to increased physical fitness, which in turn may have health benefits. Fourth, activity may play an important role in increasing metabolic rate, partially compensating for decreases in basal metabolic rate (BMR) that are often noted in response to dietary restriction (Wooley, Wooley, & Dyrenforth, 1979). Additionally, its role as an alternative activity to eating; as a potential antidote to boredom, anxiety, and depression; and as an appetite suppressant (Oscai, 1973) make it an important obesity treatment component. Clinically, assessment is needed to determine a baseline level of activity on which to make treatment recommendations and, later, to determine whether the patient has complied with recommendations. From the standpoint of research, assessment of activity level is important as an intermediate-level outcome, given that it is a mediator of weight and fat loss. Accurate and practical assessment techniques are also important to the study of the role of activity in the etiology and maintenance of obesity.

Data on activity level may be collected in four ways. First, self-report techniques may be used to provide information on the routine pattern of an individual's activities and on the time spent in various activities. Second, mechanical devices are used to measure movement. Third, activities may be directly observed in a sample of settings. Fourth, fitness testing may be used to obtain an indirect indication of habitual activity level. The latter is not discussed in this section since it was briefly reviewed in our discussion of health risk assessment.

Self-Report

The primary tool for obtaining activity information in much of the activity research has been self-report, in one of three forms: activity records, interviews, or questionnaires. The activity record provides complete information on activity during a specified period of time. The subject is asked to note every activity in which he participates, its duration, and its intensity. This information is generally recorded in a formal diary that allows the subject to indicate the beginning and ending times of each activity (see Durnin & Passmore, 1967, for sample diaries).

With the cooperative subject, an activity diary can provide an excellent estimate of daily energy expenditure, as well as information concerning the pattern of his activity. However, it is usually regarded as a very cumbersome task (Durnin & Passmore, 1967) and is unlikely to be accurate for more than 3 to 4 days at a time (Garrow, 1974/1978). This limits its utility as an ongoing form of recordkeeping in clinical work with obese patients. Moreover, the act of recordkeeping is probably reactive, leading the subject to make changes in ongoing activity.

An abbreviated form of the activity diary may make the recording task simpler for the subject and still provide useful information for the researcher or clinician. A number of behavioral weight control programs that contain recommendations to increase planned exercise provide formats for recording exercise or extra activity. For example, Stuart and Davis (1972) provide a form that subjects use to check off every 5 min that they spend in light activity (4 kcal/min), moderate activity (7 kcal/min), or heavy exercise (10 kcal/min). Ferguson (1975) provides charts that allow patients to record the time spent per day in extra activities. This abbreviated format can minimize the time necessary to keep records and still provides helpful information. It may be a more appropriate clinical tool than the complete activity diary.

A second self-report procedure requires the subject to recall activities over a period of a few days or weeks. For example, Stefanik, Heald, and Mayer (1959) employed an interview technique to obtain 24-hr activity records by recall. Boys attending a summer camp were given a list of activities in which they might have participated. Based on this prompt, subjects indicated the activities in which they had taken part and the duration of each of those activities. McCarthy (1966), in a study of the dietary and activity patterns of obese women in Trinidad, obtained a 24-hr activity recall in which subjects estimated the amount of time they had spent lying down, sitting, standing, engaging in light work, or engaging in moderate to heavy work. Others have used similar interview techniques to establish long-term patterns of activity.

The use of an interview or recall procedure has a number of potential limitations. If the recall is to be accurate, the subject must identify all activities in which he has engaged within the time period in question, and estimate the duration and intensity of each. Given that activity is often a continuous, ever changing set of behaviors, it may be very difficult to remember and report, even for cooperative subjects. To partially overcome this difficulty, the subject may be informed that he will be questioned on activity so that he may more carefully observe his behavior. While this improves accuracy of recall, it may add to the reactivity of the measure.

A third self-report procedure is the use of a questionnaire or survey to assess habitual activity. For example, Lincoln (1972) asked respondents to rate their habitual activity on a four-point scale ranging from taking part in a great deal of activity to participating in hardly any activity. They were also asked to record the number of times per week that they exercised. While this particular survey did not obtain adequate information on types of exercise, duration of exercise, level of activity at work, and so on, the technique has potential if more systematically developed. Belding (1960) suggests a number of minimal criteria for a useful questionnaire on activity. For example, assessment of off-the-job activity should include routine activities, exercises, hobbies, and home maintenance chores. Assessment of on-the-job activity should provide information on the proportions of time spent sitting, standing, walking, climbing, lifting, etc. Given that these routine activities are measured and that the final survey provides the respondent with behavioral anchor points for various items, questionnaires could contribute greatly to our knowledge of average activity patterns. They should prove especially useful to epidemiological and basic research on obese–normal differences, but they could also be valuable for assessment of treatment-related changes in activity.

Mechanical Devices

The second major approach to the assessment of activity is the use of mechanical devices. In general, use of these devices minimizes the time and effort needed on the part of the subject to produce accurate assessment information since he only needs to remember to wear the device and to record at the end of the day.

The most commonly used mechanical instrument for recording activity is the pedometer. It has been used in a number of field studies of the activity level of obese and normal-weight individuals (e.g., Chirico & Stunkard, 1960; Maxfield & Konishi, 1966; Wilkinson, Parkin, Pearlson, Strong, & Sykes, 1977). Clinically, it is recommended for use in the assessment of routine activity in a number of behavioral obesity treatment programs (e.g., Ferguson, 1975; Mahoney & Mahoney, 1976). Additionally, it has been used as a portion of the routine assessment battery in obesity treatment outcome studies (Rogers et al., 1980).

The pedometer is a small, relatively unobtrusive device that records the number of miles walked by its wearer. Its major advantages are that it is inconspicuous, inexpensive (under $20), and easy for the client or subject to use. However, it has several disadvantages. Although it is often used as an indication of overall activity level, the pedometer records only miles walked. With a relatively inactive population for whom walking is the major form of activity, this problem is minimal; among active adults, the use of the pedometer alone to assess habitual activity may be misleading. Another significant limitation of the device is that the pedometer offers no information on the pattern of activities throughout the day, information which is desirable as a portion of any thorough assessment of physical activity. Technically, the pedometer also suffers from some shortcomings. To provide accurate measurements, it must be calibrated correctly and worn properly secured, yet be free to move slightly in response to each step taken. The artificiality of walking a short test course to determine stride length may produce atypical results, leading to an incorrect setting for the pedometer. The only way to overcome this is to have the subject walk several measured courses after the pedometer has been set, to ensure its accuracy. Even with these precautions, among extremely obese patients the devices may not function properly. Clinically, we have seen a number of patients whose fat folds prevented the device from moving freely, and thus from recording each step. Finally, pedometers have a high breakage rate. They not only fall apart (i.e., pins come loose, depositing the pedometer on the ground while the clasp stays firmly attached to the waist band), but they also simply cease to record. A quick survey of pedometers purchased for use by the first author in an obesity treatment clinic over an 18-month period indicated that over 25% had malfunctioned.

Several other, similar devices have been used to study activity levels. For example, an actometer, a small device designed to record movements of the limbs, has been used to study activity levels of infants (Rose & Mayer, 1968). Activity sensors have been built into seats to determine whether differences in amount of movement can be detected among obese and normal-weight individuals (Greenfield & Fellner, 1969). Thus far, these devices have enjoyed more limited use than pedometers, probably due to their lack of commercial availability.

One of the most promising developments in the area of mechanical assessment of activity is the advent of the large-scale integrated motor activity monitor (LSI monitor). This device, which is slightly larger than a wrist watch and may be worn at either the ankle or trunk, detects and records transverse and rotational movements (La Porte, Kuller, Kupfer, McPartland, Matthews, & Casperson, 1979). The number of movements detected are displayed on an LED screen. Preliminary testing of the device shows high interunit reliability. In a validity test, subjects wore the devices at both ankle and waist while walking on a treadmill. The number of units recorded by the device correlated with treadmill speed at 0.92 and 0.98 for the two sites, respectively. In a 2-day trial, trunk movements counted by the LSI correlated with calculated energy expenditure at about 0.69, again providing evidence that the device provides a reasonably valid measure of activity level. The device is currently being employed to measure activity in a variety of settings (e.g., with monkeys in research on heart disease). It shows promise for use in the study of obese–normal differences in activity level. However, at its present stage of development, it is not widely available, and it is too expensive for routine use in either treatment or treatment outcome studies.

Direct Observation

A final choice for collecting data on activity is to directly observe the subject in his natural environment. Several studies have been conducted in which activities of children were filmed (e.g., Bullen, Reed, & Mayer, 1964; Corbin & Pletcher, 1968) and later scored for type and intensity of activity. For example, Bullen and her colleagues, in their classic study, observed obese and normal-weight campers while they were swimming, playing volleyball, and playing tennis. A series of 3-sec film sequences were taken and later used to score campers as sitting, standing, walking, jumping, sliding, hopping, etc.

More recently, a number of observational studies have been conducted to examine obese–normal differences in the use of stairs (Brownell, Stunkard, & Albaum, 1980; Dean & Garabedian, 1979; Meyers, Stunkard, Coll, & Cooke, 1980). In these studies, unobtrusively posted observers rated potential subjects on obesity status and on use of stairs or escalators/elevators. No filming was used; rather, behavioral procedures for ensuring interrater reliability in recording the target information were employed.

Perhaps the most complex and complete study of activity that was based on direct observation is Waxman and Stunkard's (1980) study of several pairs of obese and normal-weight brothers. Over a period of months, each child was observed for a number of 15-min periods, at home and at school. Activity was rated every 15 sec as sitting, standing, fidgeting, walking, running, or fast running. This study stands out because it provides observations in a variety of settings over a period of time, thus giving a more realistic picture of habitual activity levels than have other studies based on direct observation.

The use of direct observation clearly has a long and important history in behavioral research. While it may be somewhat reactive initially, it is generally seen as decreasing in reactivity over time. With adequate training and repeated testing of observers, problems of unreliability and observer drift may be minimized. The major problem with its use in the assessment of physical activity is not a technical one but a practical one. It is difficult and time consuming to obtain a representative sample of an individual's activities on which to base the overall assessment of activity level. In single-subject research, it might be feasible. In group research and clinical practice, it is simply impractical on a routine basis. Thus, the primary use of direct observation continues to be in the naturalistic study of obese–normal differences.

In summary, self-report, mechanical recording, and direct observation are the three most common procedures for collecting data on activity habits. The choice of procedure clearly depends upon the questions being asked and the populations being studied. In the typical clinical outcome study, we recommend that a combination of self-report and of mechanical recording be used in which subjects record planned activities or exercise and rely on the pedometer to provide a rough assessment of routine activity. In basic research on obese–normal differences, more precise data should be obtained, including, if possible, self-report records, direct observation of a representative sample of activities, and precise mechanically recorded data such as that obtained through use of the LSI monitor.

   Once data on activities have been collected, they must be converted in some fashion to determine energy expenditure for the various activities. That is to say, we are concerned not only with what an individual routinely does but also with how many calories he burns while doing it. The following section discusses techniques available for determining the energy required for various activities.

Procedures for Conversion to Caloric Expenditure

Our ability to assess the caloric value of activities derives from the fact that all of the energy used by the body eventually becomes heat. Thus, if we can accurately measure the heat output of the body, we can also measure the energy expended by the body. The technique based on the measurement of heat output is referred to as *direct calorimetry*. It was first adapted to human research by Atwater at the turn of the century (Katch & McArdle, 1977). He constructed a completely insulated chamber in which a subject could live for several days. All of the heat given off by the subject was collected in water that circulated in pipes throughout the chamber. By measuring changes in water temperature, the investigators would arrive at a very exact estimate of energy expenditure. Clearly, this technique has limited utility because of its restrictiveness and expense. As a result, most experimental assessment of energy expenditure is currently done by indirect calorimetry.

   In order for the body to burn the energy stores it contains, it must make use of oxygen. Since the amount of oxygen needed to liberate specified amounts of energy is known, we can accurately estimate energy expenditure by determining how much oxygen is being consumed by the body. Measurements of energy expenditure based on calculating oxygen use or gas exchanges are referred to as *indirect calorimetry*. These measurements can be accomplished by collecting gases expelled by the individual in some tightly sealed apparatus.

   A number of systems of indirect calorimetry have been developed. In one of the oldest laboratory-based systems, the subject engages in activities of interest while wearing a vented hood. The composition of gases expelled from the hood is analyzed to determine energy expenditure. A second, less cumbersome laboratory system requires the subject to breathe into a mouthpiece. Tubing, attached to the mouthpiece, carries all expelled gases into a large bag (known as the Douglas Bag) for collection and analysis. Clearly, both of these techniques are severely limited by their bulkiness. For field use, systems have been developed in which a sample of expelled air is collected for analysis in a backpack. As with the Douglas Bag, subjects participate in activities while breathing into a mouthpiece that is connected by tubing to the collection vessels. The most commonly used pieces of field equipment are the Max-Planck respirometer and the Integrating Motor Pneumotachygraph, both of which have been in use for over a quarter of a century.

Another indirect method of assessing energy expenditure is to measure heart rate, which is closely associated with increased demand for oxygen, and thus with increased energy expenditure. During exercise, the heart rate is so closely associated with the consumption of oxygen that use of a heart rate monitoring system will result in no more than a 5% error in assessment. However, when an individual is not engaged in exercise, heart rate also increases in response to emotional pressures, and the measurement error will be greater. The most frequently used system for monitoring heart rate is the socially acceptable monitoring instrument (SAMI), which can record and store data on heart rate for a period of up to 24 hr. The major advantage of this system over the portable devices, which measure gas exchange, is that it may be worn for longer periods of time and is somewhat smaller and more comfortable than other systems.

Indirect calorimetry provides an accurate way of assessing the caloric cost of various activities for given individuals. For more detailed descriptions of the systems described here and discussion of their advantages and disadvantages, the interested reader should see Durnin and Passmore (1967), Garrow (1974/1978), or Katch and McArdle (1977).

Indirect calorimetry procedures have had important application in recent research on obese–normal differences. For example, Waxman and Stunkard (1980) converted the activity information collected on obese boys and their normal-weight brothers into caloric information through indirect calorimetry. Court (1972) was able to evaluate the activity of obese and normal-weight children in their natural environment by using the SAMI for periods of up to 24 hr.

Despite these exemplary cases, indirect calorimetry is too cumbersome and expensive for use in most clinical treatment, field research, or treatment outcome research. For these settings, a more common procedure for estimating the caloric costs of activities is to rely on normative data. For example, Durnin and Passmore (1967) provide normative data on the energy required for hundreds of activities ranging from walking, to house cleaning, to coal mining. Katch and McArdle (1977) also provide caloric estimates for an extensive list of activities.

In using activity tables to calculate energy expenditure, a number of cautions are required. Garrow (1974/1978) indicates that individual variability in the number of calories expended for an activity may make calculations based on normative information inaccurate by as much as 20 %. Practically, since the caloric cost of activity is partially based on body weight of the individual, normative data are often not available for extremely obese patients.

A second alternative for estimating the caloric cost of two common activities, bicycling and walking, is the use of regression equations. Drinkwater (1973) presents the following equation for estimating the energy expenditure required for bicycling:

$$\text{kcal/min} = 0.0467 \text{ WT (kg)} + 2.34$$

where WT is an individual's weight in kilograms. Durnin and Passmore (1967) present an equation for calculating the energy cost of walking:

$$E_w = 0.047 \text{ W} + 0.02$$

where E_w is the energy cost in kilocalories per minute of walking, and W is weight in kilograms. In cases in which an individual varies significantly from the weights given on standard charts of the caloric value of these activities, it is advisable to turn to these regression equations to obtain more accurate estimates of the energy costs for the individual.

Most field research on activity has relied on normative data to calculate the energy expenditure of subjects. For example, Bullen et al. (1964), in studying obese and normal-weight campers, estimated the calories used per minute for the various activities measured on the bases of norms. Normative data are also widely used in clinical practice to help patients determine how much of various activities is necessary to increase caloric expenditure by a set amount per day (see Ferguson, 1975; Stuart and Davis, 1972).

In summary, the assessment of activity requires two distinct phases. First, data must be collected to establish the routine level, types, and amounts of activity for an individual. Second, that information should be converted into an estimate of overall caloric expenditure. For most large-scale research projects and for clinical work, the use of pedometers plus logging procedures can provide a reasonable estimate of activity. The addition of normative data on caloric values for activities allows an adequate overall assessment of energy expenditure. However, there remains a very important role for specific, detailed logging procedures and direct observation, combined with indirect calorimetry, to provide the precise estimates of caloric expenditure needed to answer fundamental research questions on the role of activity in the development and maintenance of obesity.

Assessment of Behavioral, Cognitive, and Emotional Factors

Behavioral formulations of the problem of obesity diverge from other approaches to obesity in their emphasis on behavioral, cognitive, and emotional correlates of overeating. Indeed, behavioral theory suggests that most overeating occurs because of inappropriate responsiveness to cues (environmental, cognitive, or emotional) and because of inappropriate eating style. Consequently, behavioral treatment often focuses on changing the act of eating and the cues associated with eating. Unfortunately, this theoretical and treatment focus has not produced many systematically evaluated devices for assessing behavioral, cognitive, and emotional factors associated with obesity. Given that changes in these areas are presumed to mediate caloric reduction—which, in turn, produces weight loss—their assessment is as crucial as assessment of caloric intake or expenditure. Furthermore, with the recent interest in individualized behavioral treatments of obesity (see Straw & Terre, 1983), adequate behavioral assessment assumes an important role in providing the data base from which to develop and implement treatment plans. This section reviews the available techniques for evaluating psychological and behavioral factors relevant to obesity treatment and theory.

Assessment of Eating Behaviors

Assessment of eating behaviors and factors associated with over-eating has long been a key feature of behavioral obesity management. Probably the most commonly used procedure for assessing eating behaviors is the behavioral food diary. The patient logs not only food intake (on which dietary assessment is based) but also relevant behaviors and events such as time spent eating, feelings or emotions at the time of the eating episode, location of eating, and activities occurring during the eating episode. He may also be asked to provide information such as a rating of hunger prior to eating or thoughts associated with eating. This procedure, although used clinically by most behavior therapists, has not always been used for research purposes.

Straw, Henry, and Goldston (1981) tested a scoring system for use with food diaries. This procedure provides information on topics such as stimulus control of eating (percentage of eating episodes occurring with inappropriate activities or in inappropriate places), eating style (average time spent eating), emotional eating (percentage of eating episodes associated with emotional ups and downs), and food intake pattern (number of meals and snacks consumed per day). This system could be used reliably by trained raters, and it showed an interesting pattern of correlations with outcome measures in pilot testing. Posttest eating behaviors of subjects in a behavioral treatment program were correlated with indicators of success (including weight loss and relative weight loss) and with indicators of compliance. Low levels of snacking were associated with successful weight loss ($r = 0.48$). In turn, the average number of snacks consumed per day was correlated with percentage of eating episodes occurring with inappropriate activities and in inappropriate places ($r = 0.62$ and 0.69, respectively). Speed of eating was related to both weight change ($r = 0.36$) and to compliance ($r = 0.36$), such that those who ate more slowly showed a greater weight loss and better compliance with program recommendations. Although further testing of this coding system for food diaries is needed, it provides a useful model for the development of a systematic and reliable approach to extracting and summarizing the behavioral information available through self-monitoring.

Another tactic for assessing eating behaviors is through direct observation of the eating episode. Direct observation can provide very precise information on speed of eating, social influences on eating, food choices and preferences, and the influence of various cues on eating. Although primarily used in field and laboratory experimentation (e.g., Kissileff, Klingsberg, & Van Itallie, 1980; Stunkard & Kaplan, 1977), direct observation in the home has also been employed with patients undergoing obesity treatment (e.g., Coates, 1977). Direct observation in the field has provided a relatively nonreactive source of information on obese–normal differences (or lack thereof) in eating behaviors. In the laboratory, reactivity may limit the usefulness of direct observation. However, creative "cover stories" that distract the subject from the purpose of the research may be employed to minimize reactivity. More significant limitations on the use of direct observation exist when it is employed in the laboratory or at home as a portion of the assessment package used in treatment outcome research. When the subject is clearly aware of the changes expected, reactivity is a serious problem. However, even in that situation, direct observation can provide an interesting assessment of the extent to which the subject understands and is able to implement the changes suggested in treatment. On a more practical note, even if reactivity were not a problem, direct observation may be too time consuming for routine clinical use. In summary, direct observation of eating behaviors can provide an important source of information in the field and in the laboratory. For home use, it has more limited applicability. For a more complete discussion of direct observation, the interested reader should see Brownell (1981).

Finally, several paper-and-pencil devices that provide information on various eating behaviors have recently been developed and psychometrically assessed. For example, the Stimulus Control Scale of the Master Questionnaire (Straw & Straw, 1981; Straw, Straw, & Craighead, 1979) provides a brief, reliable assessment of the tendency to overeat in response to environmental cues. Scales are also available to assess whether binge eating is a component of the patient's eating behaviors (Gormally, Black, Daston, & Rardin, 1982; Hawkins & Clement, 1980).

In summary, systematic and replicable approaches to obtaining information on eating habits are important to refining and testing behavioral treatment procedures and behavioral theory. In treatment outcome research, food diaries with a clearly delineated coding system can provide fundamental information. Additional information can be obtained quickly and easily from paper-and-pencil measures. For field research, direct observation remains the assessment procedure of choice.

Assessment of Cognitive Factors

With the increasing emphasis in behavior therapy on the important role of cognitions, several devices have been developed to assess cognitions relevant to weight control. The focus of these devices is generally on goal setting and perfectionism, beliefs about ability to change, and knowledge concerning energy balance. Best known is Herman and Polivy's Restrained–Unrestrained Eating Scale (1975), which measures an individual's tendency toward constantly restricting food intake versus taking a more lenient, permissive approach to food intake and dieting. While not always classified as a cognitive scale, the device seems to tap perfectionism in dieting, which, according to cognitive theory (Mahoney & Mahoney, 1976), promotes overeating in response to relatively minor dietary infractions. Indeed, the research on restrained eaters has identified the expected pattern of overindulgence among restrained eaters but not among unrestrained eaters, following intake of high-calorie foods (Herman & Polivy, 1975; Spencer & Fremouw, 1979). Various other scales (e.g., Gormally's Cognitive Factors Scale, Gormally et al., 1982) attempt to assess the same problem of perfectionistic, rigid approaches to dieting. The Master Questionnaire provides Cognitive and Energy Balance Knowledge Scales (Straw et al., 1979). The cognitive subscales focus on feelings of helplessness regarding one's ability to lose weight; the knowledge subscale assesses the accuracy of the respondent's information on nutrition and exercise. Taken together, these scales have been good predictors of success in behavioral weight control programs (Straw & Straw, 1981). Recent data suggest that the cognitive factors scales have good reliability as well. Given the evidence suggesting that cognitions do play an important role in successful weight control and maintenance, and data suggesting that they may be predictive of success, some cognitive assessment strategy is advisable.

Assessment of Personality and Emotional Factors

Emotional and personality factors should also be routinely assessed in treatment outcome research for several reasons. First, since weight loss has sometimes been associated with emotional distress, especially depression, routine monitoring of mood is a therapeutic necessity. Second, in the search for predictors of success in various treatment programs, it is important to thoroughly assess emotional status and personality variables. Although there is little evidence for an obese personality, or for the use of a single scale as a predictor, it is very possible that several indicators in combination may be useful in determining whether a patient is a good candidate for treatment.

Two general strategies of assessment have been adopted in this area. In some research, general personality or symptom inventories have been used to provide information on current psychological functioning and emotional distress. Most commonly used are the MMPI (Minnesota Multiphasic Personality Inventory) and the SCL-90 (Symptom Checklist, Lipman, Covi, & Shapiro, 1979). The former is an extremely time-consuming procedure. Since it has not proved to be very useful in identifying an obese personality profile (Cooke & Meyers, 1980) and often provides more information than is needed for general assessment, a briefer inventory is recommended.

A second assessment strategy has been to use a variety of instruments to tap particular areas of interest to the researcher or clinician. For example, Rogers et al. (1980) assessed depression (Beck Depression Inventory, Beck, Ward, Mendelson, Mock, & Erbaugh, 1961), anxiety (Taylor Manifest Anxiety Scale, Taylor, 1953), and marital adjustment (Marital Adjustment Test, Locke & Williamson, 1958). Other appropriate additions might be an assertiveness inventory (e.g., Rathus Assertiveness Scale, Rathus, 1973), a life stress measure (e.g., Life Experience Survey, Sarason, Johnson, & Siegel, 1978), and a measure of locus of control (e.g., Internal–External Locus of Control Scale, Rotter, 1966; or Health Locus of Control Scale, Wallston, Wallston, Kaplan, & Maides, 1976).

In summary, a range of alternatives for the assessment of personality and emotional factors is available to the obesity researcher. Practically speaking, we find the use of a set of indicators (e.g., a depression measure, an anxiety measure) to be the preferred approach. Not only is it less time consuming for the subject than measures like the MMPI, but it allows the therapist or researcher to precisely target the information he finds most useful.

Conclusions

The behavioral medicine practitioner or researcher faces a fairly complex problem when dealing with obesity assessment. At minimum, the areas of body composition, health risk, nutrition, activity, behavior, cognition, and emotion must be considered as potential targets for assessment. The use of a thorough assessment package, especially in treatment outcome research, serves many purposes. It provides information on several levels of outcome, allowing an evaluation of both outcome and process. Thorough assessment is also important in the search for predictors of success, which in turn should eventually result in the empirical matching of patients and treatments. Finally, adoption of the suggested assessment package should foster interactions between behavioral psychologists and other health professionals, broadening the horizons of both and strengthening the field of behavioral medicine.

Appendix A
Common Formulas Used in the
Assessment of Obesity Status

I. Common transformations from body density to percent fat
    A. Grande equation (Brozek et al., 1963)

$$\text{Percent fat} = \left[\left(\frac{4.57}{\text{density}}\right) - 4.142\right] \times 100$$

    B. Siri equation (1956)

$$\text{Percent fat} = \left[\left(\frac{4.95}{\text{density}}\right) - 4.5\right] \times 100$$

II. Common transformations from skinfold thickness to percent fat
    A. Durnin and Womersley equations (1974)

Density (males) = 1.1765 − (0.0744 × log skinsum)

Density (females) = 1.1567 − (0.0717 × log skinsum)

where skinsum is the sum of the skinfold thickness at 4 sites (bicep, tricep, subscapula, suprailiac). Percent fat is calculated using either the Grande or Siri equation.
B. Allen equation (Allen et al., 1956)

$$kg\ adipose = Body\ weight\ (in\ kg)\ \sqrt{[(skinsum - 1)/1{,}000]}$$

where skinsum is the sum of the skinfold thickness at 10 sites (cheek, chest, upper arm, abdomen, back, waist, calf, side, knee, and chin).

$$Percent\ fat = \frac{kg\ adipose\ tissue}{kg\ body\ weight}$$

III. Common transformations from anthropometric measures to percent fat
A. Steinkamp equations (Steinkamp et al., 1965a)
  1. Males and females (ages 25–44)

$$kg\ fat = 0.592\ ICC + 0.360\ TC - 53.107$$

  2. White males (ages 25–44)

$$kg\ fat = 0.350\ WC + 0.444\ ICC + 50.560$$

  3. White females (ages 25–44)

$$kg\ fat = 0.337\ WT - 3.294\ WRC - 24.859$$

where ICC is iliac crest circumference, TC is thigh circumference, WC is waist circumference, and WRC is wrist circumference. All circumferences are measured in centimeters; weight (WT) is measured in pounds.

$$Percent\ fat = \frac{kg\ fat}{kg\ body\ weight}$$

References

Adelson, S. F. Some problems in collecting dietary data from individuals. *Journal of the American Dietetic Association*, 1960, 36, 453–461.

Allen, T. H., Peng, M. T., Chen, K. P., Huang, T. F., Chang, C., & Fang, H. S. Prediction of total adiposity from skinfolds and the curvilinear relationship between external and internal adiposity. *Metabolism*, 1956, 5, 346–352.

American Heart Association, Committee on Exercise. *Exercise testing and training of apparently healthy individuals: A handbook for physicians.* New York: Author, 1972.

Anderson, D., Nichols, A., Pan, S., & Lindgren, F. High density lipoprotein distribution: Resolution and determination of three major components in a normal population sample. *Atherosclerosis*, 1978, 29, 161–179.

Ashley, F., & Kannel, W. Relation of weight change to changes in atherogenic traits: The Framingham Study. *Journal of Chronic Diseases*, 1974, 27, 103–114.

Aslam, J., & Tess Enterprises, Inc. *Diet Analysis.* Cupertino, CA: Apple Computer, Inc., 1980.

Balogh, M., Kahn, H. A., & Medalie, J. H. Random repeat 24-hour dietary recalls. *American Journal of Clinical Nutrition*, 1971, 24, 304–310.

Beck, A. T., Ward, C. H., Mendelson, M., Mock, J., & Erbaugh, J. An inventory for measuring depression. *Archives of General Psychiatry*, 1961, 4, 561–571.

Belding, H. S. Subcommittee on methods for acquiring information on physical activity and body form. *American Journal of Public Health*, 1960, 50, 52–66.

Berry, J. N. Use of skinfold thickness for estimation of body fat. *Indian Journal of Medical Research*, 1974, 62, 233–239.

Boedeker, E., & Dauber, J. (Eds.). *Manual of medical therapeutics* (21st ed.). Boston: Little, Brown, 1974.

Bransby, E. R., Daubney, C. G., & King, J. Comparison of results obtained by different methods of individual dietary survey. *British Journal of Nutrition*, 1948, 2, 89–110.

Bray, G. A. Definition, measurement, and classification of the syndromes of obesity. *International Journal of Obesity*, 1978, 2, 1–14.

Bray, G. A. (Ed.). *Obesity in America* (NIH Publication No. 80-359). Washington, DC: U.S. Government Printing Office, 1980.

Bray, G. A., Greenway, F. L., Molitch, M. E., Dahms, W. J., Atkinson, R. L., & Hamilton, K. Use of anthropomorphic measures to assess weight loss. *American Journal of Clinical Nutrition*, 1978, 31, 769–773.

Brightwell, D. R., Foster, D., Lee, S., & Naylor, C. S. Effects of behavioral and pharmacological weight loss programs on nutrient intake. *American Journal of Clinical Nutrition*, 1979, *32*, 2005–2008.

Brownell, K. D. Assessment of the eating disorders. In D. H. Barlow (Ed.), *Behavioral assessment of adult disorders*. New York: Guilford Press, 1981.

Brownell, K., & Stunkard, A. Differential changes in plasma high-density lipoprotein-cholesterol levels in obese men and women during weight reduction. *Archives of Internal Medicine*, 1981, *141*, 1142–1146.

Brownell, K. D., Stunkard, A. J., & Albaum, J. M. Evaluation and modification of exercise patterns in the natural environment. *American Journal of Psychiatry*, 1980, *137*, 1540–1545.

Brozek, J., Grande, F., Anderson, J. T., & Keys, A. Densitometric analysis of body composition: Revision of quantitative assumptions. *Annals of the New York Academy of Sciences*, 1963, *110*, 113–140.

Bullen, B. A., Reed, R., & Mayer, J. Physical activity of obese and non-obese adolescent girls appraised by motion picture sampling. *American Journal of Clinical Nutrition*, 1964, *14*, 211–223.

Burke, B. S. The dietary history as a tool in research. *Journal of the American Dietetic Association*, 1947, *23*, 1041–1046.

Burkinshaw, L., Jones, P. R. M., & Krupowicz, D. W. Observer error in skinfold thickness measurements. *Human Biology*, 1973, *45*, 273–279.

Campbell, V. A., & Dodds, M. L. Collecting dietary information from groups of older people. *Journal of the American Dietetic Association*, 1967, *51*, 29–33.

Carey, R. M., Reid, R. A., Ayers, C. R., et al. The Charlottesville Blood-Pressure Survey: Value of repeated blood-pressure measurements. *Journal of the American Medical Association*, 1976, *236*, 279–298.

Cheung, M., & Albers, J. The measurement of apolipoprotein A-I and A-II levels in men and women in immunoassay. *Journal of Clinical Investigation*, 1977, *60*, 43–50.

Chirico, A., & Stunkard, A. J. Physical activity and human obesity. *New England Journal of Medicine*, 1960, *263*, 935–940.

Coates, T. J. *The efficacy of a multicomponent self-control program in modifying the eating habits and weight of three obese adolescents*. Unpublished doctoral dissertation, Stanford University, 1977.

Cooke, C. J., & Meyers, A. Assessment of subject characteristics in the behavioral treatment of obesity. *Behavioral Assessment*, 1980, *2*, 59–69.

Corbin, C. B., & Pletcher, P. Diet and physical activity patterns of obese and non-obese elementary school children. *Research Quarterly of the American Association for Health, Physical Education, and Recreation*, 1968, *39*(4), 922–928.

Court, J. M. Energy expenditure of obese children: Technique for measuring energy expenditure over periods up to 24 hours. *Archives of Disease in Childhood*, 1972, *47*, 153.

Dean, R. S., & Garabedian, A. A. Obesity and level of activity. *Perceptual and Motor Skills*, 1979, *49*, 690.

Drinkwater, B. L. Physiological responses of women to exercise. In J. H. Wilmore (Ed.), *Exercise and Sport Sciences Reviews*. New York: Academic Press, 1973, pp. 125–153.

Durnin, J. V. G. A., & Passmore, R. *Energy, work and leisure*. London: Heinenmann Educational Books, 1967.

Durnin, J. V. G. A., & Rahaman, M. M. The assessment of the amount of fat in the human body from measurements of skinfold thickness. *British Journal of Nutrition*, 1967, *21*, 681–689.

Durnin, J. V. G. A., & Womersley, J. Body fat assessment from total body density and its estimation from skinfold thickness: Measurements in 481 men and women aged 16 to 72 years. *British Journal of Nutrition*, 1974, *32*, 77–97.

Epstein, L. H., & Wing, R. R. Aerobic exercise and weight. *Addictive Behaviors*, 1980, *5*, 371–388.

Ferguson, J. M. *Learning to eat*. Palo Alto, CA: Bull Publishing Company, 1975.

Franzini, L. R., & Grimes, W. B. Skinfold measures as the criterion of change in weight control studies. *Behavior Therapy*, 1976, *7*, 256–260.

Froelicher, V., Battler, A., & McKirnan, M. D. Physical activity and coronary heart disease. *Cardiology*, 1980, *65*, 153–190.

Garrow, J. S. *Energy balance and obesity in man*. New York: American Elsevier Publishing Company, 1974; reprinted 1978.

Garrow, J. S., Stalley, S., Diethelm, R., Pittet, P., Hesp, R., & Halliday, D. A new method for measuring the body density of obese adults. *British Journal of Nutrition*, 1979, *42*, 173–183.

Gordon, T., & Kannel, W. The effects of overweight on cardiovascular diseases. *Geriatrics*, 1973, *28*, 80–88.

Gormally, J., Black, S., Daston, S., & Rardin, D. The assessment of binge eating severity among obese persons. *Addictive Behaviors*, 1982, *7*, 47–55.

Greenfield, N. S., & Fellner, C. H. Resting level of physical activity in obese females. *American Journal of Clinical Nutrition*, 1969, *22*(11), 1418–1419.

Grimes, W. B., & Franzini, L. R. Skinfold measurements techniques for estimating percentage body fat. *Journal of Behavior Therapy and Experimental Psychiatry*, 1977, *8*, 65–69.

Hawkins, R. C. II, & Clement, P. F. Development and construct validation of a self-report measure of binge eating tendencies. *Addictive Behaviors*, 1980, *5*, 219–226.

Herman, C. P., & Polivy, J. Anxiety, restraint and eating behavior. *Journal of Abnormal Psychology*, 1975, *84*, 666–672.

Huenemann, R. L., & Turner, D. Methods of dietary investigation. *Jour-*

nal of the American Dietetic Association, 1942, *18*, 562–568.

Hulley, S., Cohen, R., & Widdowson, G. Plasma high density lipoprotein cholesterol level: Influence of risk factor intervention. *Journal of the American Medical Association*, 1977, *238*, 2269–2271.

Hulley, S., Rosenman, R., Bawol, R., & Brand, R. J. Epidemiology as a guide to clinical decisions: The association between triglyceride and coronary heart disease. *New England Journal of Medicine*, 1980, *302*, 1383–1389.

Hulley, S., Sherwin, R., Nestle, M., & Lee, P. R. Epidemiology as a guide to clinical decisions. II. Diet and coronary heart disease. *Western Journal of Medicine*, 1981, *135*, 25–33.

Kannel, W. B., & Gordon, T. Physiological and medical concomitants of obesity: The Framingham Study. In G. A. Bray (Ed.), *Obesity in America*. (NIH Publication No. 80-359). Washington, DC: U.S. Government Printing Office, 1980.

Kannel, W., Gordon, T., & Castelli, W. Obesity, lipids, and glucose in tolerance: The Framingham Study. *American Journal of Clinical Nutrition*, 1979, *32*, 1238–1245.

Karvonen, M., Telivuo, L., & Jarvinen, E. Sphygmomanometer cuff size and the accuracy of indirect measurement of blood pressure. *American Journal of Cardiology*, 1964, *13*, 688–693.

Katch, F. I., & McArdle, W. D. *Nutrition, weight control, and exercise*. Boston: Houghton Mifflin, 1977.

Keys, A., Fidanza, F., Karvonen, M. J., Kimura, N., & Taylor, J. L. Indices of relative weight and obesity. *Journal of Chronic Diseases*, 1972, *25*, 329–343.

King, H. S. How to determine patient weights in excess of balance limits. *Journal of the American Medical Association*, 1977, *237*, 1198.

Kissileff, H., Klingsberg, H. R., & Van Itallie, T. B. A universal eating monitor for measuring solid–liquid consumption in man. *American Journal of Physiology*, 1980, *238*, 14–22.

Lansky, D., & Brownell, K. D. *Estimates of food quantity and calories: Errors in self-monitoring among obese patients*. Paper presented at the meeting of the Association for Advancement of Behavior Therapy, New York, 1980.

LaPorte, R. E., Kuller, L. H., Kupfer, D. J., McPartland, R. J., Matthews, G., & Casperson, C. An objective measure of physical activity for epidemiological research. *American Journal of Epidemiology*, 1979, *109*, 158–168.

Lew, E. A., & Garfinkel, L. Variations in mortality by weight among 750,000 men and women. *Journal of Chronic Diseases*, 1979, *32*, 563–576.

Lewin, R. Overblown reports distort obesity risks. *Science*, 1981, *211*, 258.

Lincoln, J. E. Calorie intake, obesity, and physical activity. *American*

Journal of Clinical Nutrition, 1972, *25*, 390–394.

Lipid Research Clinics. *Manual of laboratory operations, Vol. I: Lipid and lipoprotein analysis* (HEW Publication No. NIH 75-628). Washington, DC: U.S. Government Printing Office, 1974.

Lipman, R. S., Covi, L., & Shapiro, A. The Hopkins Symptom Checklist: Factors derived from the HSCL-90. *Journal of Affective Disorders*, 1979, *1*, 9–24.

Locke, H. J., & Williamson, R. C. Marital adjustment: A factor analysis study. *American Sociological Review*, 1958, *23*, 562–569.

Mahoney, M. J., & Mahoney, B. K. *Permanent weight control*. New York: Norton, 1976.

Mahoney, M. J., Mahoney, B. K., Rogers, T., & Straw, M. K. Assessment of human obesity: The measurement of body composition. *Journal of Behavioral Assessment*, 1979, *1*, 327–349.

Marr, J. W. Individual dietary surveys: Purposes and methods. *World Review of Nutrition and Dietetics*, 1971, *13*, 105–164.

Marr, J. W., Heady, J. A., & Morris, J. N. Repeat individual weighed dietary surveys. *Proceedings of the Nutrition Society*, 1959, *18*, xii.

Maxfield, E., & Konishi, F. Patterns of food intake and physical activity in obesity. *Journal of the American Dietetic Association*, 1966, *49*, 406–408.

McCarthy, M. D. Dietary and activity patterns of obese women in Trinidad. *Journal of the American Dietetic Association*, 1966, *48*, 33–37.

Meyers, A. W., Stunkard, A. J., Coll, M., & Cooke, C. J. Stairs, escalators and obesity. *Behavior Modification*, 1980, *4*, 355–359.

Oscai, L. B. The role of exercise in weight control. *Exercise and Sports Sciences Reviews*, 1973, *1*, 103–123.

Pennington, J. A. T., & Church, H. N. *Bowes and Church's food values of portions commonly used*. New York: Harper & Row, 1980.

Rathus, S. A. A 30-item schedule for assessing assertive behavior. *Behavior Therapy*, 1973, *4*, 398–406.

Reshef, A., & Epstein, L. M. Reliability of a dietary questionnaire. *American Journal of Clinical Nutrition*, 1972, *25*, 91–95.

Rhoads, G., Gulbrandsen, C., & Kagan, A. Serum lipoproteins and coronary heart disease in a population study of Hawaii-Japanese men. *New England Journal of Medicine*, 1976, *294*, 293–298.

Ritt, R. S., Jordan, H. A., & Levitz, L. S. Changes in nutrient intake during a behavioral weight control program. *Journal of the American Dietetic Association*, 1979, *74*, 325–330.

Rogers, T., Mahoney, M. J., Mahoney, B. K., Straw, M. K., & Kenigsberg, M. I. Clinical assessment of obesity: An empirical evaluation of diverse techniques. *Behavioral Assessment*, 1980, *2*, 161–181.

Romanczyk, R. G. Self-monitoring in the treatment of obesity: A comparative analysis. *Behavior Therapy*, 1974, *5*, 531–540.

Rose, H. E., & Mayer, J. Activity, caloric intake, fat storage, and energy balance of infants. *Pediatrics*, 1968, *41*, 18–28.

Rotter, J. B. Generalized expectancies for internal vs. external control of reinforcement. *Psychological Monographs*, 1966, *80* (Whole No. 1).

Ruiz, L., Colley, J. R. T., & Hamilton, P. J. S. Measurement of triceps skinfold thickness: An investigation of sources of variation. *British. Journal of Preventive and Social Medicine*, 1971, *25*, 165–167.

Sarason, I. G., Johnson, G. H., & Siegel, J. M. Assessing the impact of life changes: Development of the Life Experience Survey. *Journal of Consulting and Clinical Psychology*, 1978, *46*, 932–946.

Satwanti, I. P. S., & Bharadwaj, H. Fat distribution in lean and obese young Indian women: A densitometric and anthropometric evaluation. *American Journal of Physical Anthropology*, 1980, *53*, 611–616.

Seltzer, C. C., & Mayer, J. Greater reliability of the triceps skinfold over the subscapular skinfold as an index of obesity. *American Journal of Clinical Nutrition*, 1967, *20*, 950–953.

Siri, W. E. Gross composition of the body. In J. H. Lawrence and C. A. Tobia (Eds.), *Advances in biological and medical physics*. New York: Academic Press, 1956.

Society of Actuaries. *Build and blood pressure study, 1959* (Vols. 1 & 2). Chicago: Author, 1959.

Spencer, J. A., & Fremouw, W. J. Binge eating as a function of restraint and weight classification. *Journal of Abnormal Psychology*, 1979, *88*, 262–267.

Stefanik, P. A., Heald, F. P., & Mayer, J. Caloric intake in relation to energy output of obese and non-obese adolescent boys. *American Journal of Clinical Nutrition*, 1959, *7*, 55–62.

Steinkamp, R. C., Cohen, N. L., Gaffey, W. R., McKey, T., Bron, G., Siri, W. E., Sargent, T. W., & Isaacs, E. Measures of body fat and related factors in normal adults. II. A simple clinical method to estimate body fat and lean body mass. *Journal of Chronic Diseases*, 1965, *18*, 1291–1307. (a)

Steinkamp, R. C., Cohen, N. L., Siri, W. E., Sargent, T. W., & Walsh, H. D. Measures of body fat and related factors in normal adults. I. Introduction and methodology. *Journal of Chronic Diseases*, 1965, *18*, 1279–1289. (b)

Straw, M. K., Henry, W., & Goldston, D. *A behavioral coding system for food diaries: Reliability and a clinical demonstration.* Paper presented at the meeting of the Association for Advancement of Behavior Therapy, Toronto, 1981.

Straw, M. K., & Terre, L. An evaluation of individualized behavioral obesity treatment and maintenance strategies. *Behavior Therapy*, 1983, *14*, 255–266.

Straw, R. B., & Straw, M. K. *The generalizability of skinfold measures in obesity treatment outcome studies.* Paper presented at the meeting of the Association for Advancement of Behavior Therapy, New York, 1980.

Straw, R. B., & Straw, M. K. *Further evidence on the reliability and va-*

lidity of the Revised Master Questionnaire. Paper presented at the meeting of the Association for Advancement of Behavior Therapy, Toronto, 1981.

Straw, R. B., Straw, M. K., & Craighead, L. W. *Psychometric properties of the Master Questionnaire: Cluster analyses of an obesity assessment device.* Paper presented at the meeting of the Association for Advancement of Behavior Therapy, San Francisco, 1979.

Stuart, R. B., & Davis, B. *Slim chance in a fat world.* Champaign, IL: Research Press, 1972.

Stuart, R. B., Mitchell, C., & Jensen, J. A. Therapeutic options in the management of obesity. In C. K. Prokop & L. A. Bradley (Eds.), *Medical psychology: Contributions to behavioral medicine.* New York: Academic Press, 1981, pp. 321–353.

Stunkard, A., & Kaplan, D. Eating in public places: A review of reports of the direct observation of eating behavior. *International Journal of Obesity,* 1977, *1,* 89–101.

Taylor, J. A personality scale of manifest anxiety. *Journal of Abnormal and Social Psychology,* 1953, *48,* 285–290.

Thompson, J. K., Jarvie, G. J., Lahey, B. B., & Cureton, K. J. Exercise and obesity: Etiology, physiology, and intervention. *Psychological Bulletin,* 1982, *91,* 55–79.

Thompson, P., Jeffery, R., Wing, R., & Wood, P. Unexpected decreases in plasma high density lipoprotein cholesterol with weight loss. *American Journal of Clinical Nutrition,* 1979, *32,* 2016–2021.

Thomson, A. M. Diet in pregnancy. I. Dietary survey technique and the nutritive value of diets taken by primigravidae. *British Journal of Nutrition,* 1958, *12,* 446–461.

Tiwary, C. M. Obesity: Definition, measurement and some causes of treatment failure. *Nebraska Medical Journal,* 1977, *62,* 163–168.

Trulson, M. Subcommittee on methodology for diet appraisal. *American Journal of Public Health,* 1960, *50,* 39–52.

U.S. Department of Agriculture. *Nutritive value of American foods* (Agriculture Handbook No. 456). Washington, DC: U.S. Government Printing Office, 1971.

Wallston, B. S., Wallston, K. A., Kaplan, G. D., & Maides, S. A. Development and validation of the Health Locus of Control (HLC) Scale. *Journal of Consulting and Clinical Psychology,* 1976, *44,* 580–585.

Waxman, M., & Stunkard, A. J. Caloric intake and expenditure of obese boys. *Journal of Pediatrics,* 1980, *96,* 187–193.

Whiting, M. G., & Leverton, R. M. Reliability of dietary appraisal: Comparisons between laboratory analysis and calculation from tables of food values. *American Journal of Public Health,* 1960, *50,* 815–823.

Wilkinson, P. W., Parkin, J. M., Pearlson, G., Strong, H., & Sykes, P. Energy intake and physical activity in obese children. *British Medical Journal,* 1977, *1*(6063), 756.

Wilson, D., & Lees, R. Metabolic relationships among the plasma lipoproteins: Reciprocal changes in the concentrations of very low and
low density lipoproteins in man. *Journal of Clinical Investigation*,
1972, *51*, 1051-1057.

Womersley, J., & Durnin, J. V. G. A. A comparison of the skinfold method with extent of "overweight" and various weight-height relationships in the assessment of obesity. *British Journal of Nutrition*, 1977,
38, 271-284.

Wood, P., & Haskell, W. The effect of exercise on plasma high density
lipoproteins. *Lipids*, 1979, *14*, 417-427.

Wooley, S. C., Wooley, O. W., & Dyrenforth, S. R. Theoretical, practical, and social issues in behavior treatments of obesity. *Journal of
Applied Behavior Analysis*, 1979, *12*, 3-25.

Young, C. M., Hagan, G. C., Tucker, R. E., & Foster, W. D. A comparison of dietary study methods. *Journal of the American Dietetic Association*, 1952, *28*, 218-222.

Young, C. M., & Trulson, M. F. Methodology for dietary studies in epidemiological surveys. II. Strengths and weaknesses of existing methods. *American Journal of Public Health*, 1960, *50*(6), 803-814.

Yudkin, J. Dietary surveys: Variations in the weekly intake of nutrients.
British Journal of Nutrition, 1951, *5*, 177-194.

3

Behavioral Assessment of Smoking Behavior

Donald M. Prue, Reda R. Scott, and Carol A. Denier

Adequate assessment of tobacco consumption continues to be an important topic in behavioral medicine since smoking is a major risk factor in heart disease, cancer, and strokes—the three major causes of death in this country (U.S. Public Health Service, 1964, 1967, 1979). It has been estimated that more than 300,000 deaths per year are directly related to cigarette smoking, and that smokers' mortality rates are 72% higher than nonsmokers (Califano, 1980). In addition to mortality and morbidity estimates, businesses have projected that cigarette consumption costs them $43 billion a year (Luce & Schweitzer, 1977). This figure includes the costs of health care, absenteeism, lowered productivity, and accidents, and results in a substantial drain on this society's gross national product.

In recent years widespread publication of the enormous liabilities of cigarette smoking has resulted in positive changes in this country's smoking habits. For example, the percentage of smokers in the population has declined from 40.3 in 1964 to 32.5 in 1980. Over a 15-year period decreases have been reported for adult males (53% to 37.5%) and adult females (33% to 26.9%). Califano (1980) has reported similar decreases for teenagers. Yet 54 million

Americans still smoke despite increasingly obvious risks for disease and premature death (USPHS, 1981).

Although a large number of people continue to smoke, approximately 90% report that they would like to quit or have attempted to quit (USPHS, 1976). This substantial interest in quitting has encouraged psychologists to develop and evaluate smoking cessation programs. Behavioral psychologists, in particular, have been attracted to smoking research because cigarette consumption is a readily observable response that occurs in discrete units (Lichtenstein, 1971, 1982). In addition, smoking treatment has an easily defined goal, complete abstinence, which makes it particularly appropriate for outcome research. Finally, the significant social and personal implications of tobacco consumption make its modification one of the foremost challenges facing the behavioral medicine practitioner. These characteristics of smoking behavior have led to much research on its assessment and treatment.

The present chapter examines research on the measurement of smoking behavior. The intention of the chapter is to aid both the behavioral clinician and researcher in the selection of adequate assessment procedures for their work. Procedures that reliably measure the constituents of tobacco consumption most closely related to health risk are described and their advantages and disadvantages listed. Individual sections cover the assessment of rate of tobacco consumption, smoking topography, and biochemical measures of smoking. The biochemical measures highlighted include carbon monoxide, thiocyanate, and nicotine. A final summary section provides a prescription for the comprehensive assessment of tobacco consumption.

Behavioral Measures of Smoking

Rate of Consumption

Value of Rate

Daily rate of smoking is the most frequently reported measure of cigarette consumption. Its widespread use is based on three general considerations. First, rate of consumption is assumed to reflect amount of exposure to the toxic products contained in cigarette smoke and resulting health risk. Objective biochemical indices support this assumption. For example, body concentrations of two gas-phase constituents of tobacco smoke, carbon monoxide and hydrogen cyanide, show a positive correlation with reported rate of consumption. Also, epidemiological and clinical morbidity and mortality data support the use of rate as a valuable index of exposure. These data show a clear dose–response relationship between rate of smoking and numerous diseases.

Second, rate measures are widely employed for methodological reasons. For instance, information on rate can be obtained in a variety of ways, giving researchers and clinicians numerous options for data collection. Also, rate of cigarette consumption is a discrete, readily observable behavior that occurs at a fairly high frequency. These characteristics make rate measures attractive to behavioral psychologists who have traditionally focused on response rate as a primary dependent variable. Further, rate data are typically collected from smokers, the individuals in closest proximity to the target behaviors of interest. This proximity is assumed to ensure the reliability of rate data.

In addition to the impact as an index of exposure and the methodological advantages, a third consideration is that measures of rate have also been found beneficial to smokers in treatment. That is, studies (McFall, 1970; McFall & Hammen, 1971) have found that self-reports of rate lead to decreased consumption. This change in reported rate is presumably the result of response suppression and indicates the reactivity of self-recording. Thus, rate data obtained by the smoker can have a positive, therapeutic effect. A related advantage of rate measurement is that evaluations of treatments for obesity, and thus perhaps for smoking, indicate that subjects find self-recording to be an important component of comprehensive programs (Mahoney, 1977). A final reason for the popularity of rate is that numerical data enhance the psychometric qualities of smoking measurement and allow the use of more powerful parametric statistical procedures than simple measures of smoking status (Lichtenstein & Danaher, 1976).

Because smoking rate is related to health risk, readily available from smokers, potentially observable, possibly therapeutic, and rated as important by those in treatment, it has been widely used in smoking research studies. Frederiksen and Simon (1979) reported that 38 of 40 behavioral studies on smoking reduction have employed some measure of rate as their primary dependent variable. Similarly, a review of basic research on nicotine regulation found that 31 of 36 studies employed a rate measure (Moss & Prue,

1982). These data reflect an almost universal use of rate as the primary data for evaluation of human cigarette consumption.

Measurement of Rate

Methods for obtaining rate measures of cigarette consumption have varied along two major dimensions: the source of information and the method of assessment. Smoking researchers have generally relied upon either the smoker or some other person in the environment for provision of smoking rate data. Since smokers themselves are in the best position to continuously observe the target behaviors, they have been the preferred source of data. The use of smokers themselves is further supported by the possible therapeutic effect of this form of rate measurement. An alternative for collecting rate data has been the use of other persons in the smokers' environment including family, roommates, or trained observers (Best, 1975; Best & Steffy, 1975). Most studies employing significant-others' data have primarily used these data to corroborate the reports of smokers. The few studies that have relied on significant-others' reports as their primary dependent variable have been short term and laboratory based.

Rate data also vary in terms of method of assessment. Table 3.1 summarizes different methods used for obtaining rate. There are four general categories of measures that can be employed by either the smoker or significant other: rate estimates; monitoring measures, including self-monitoring; physical products; and automated data records.

Rate Estimates

Estimated rate typically involves simply asking either the smoker or significant other how many cigarettes have been smoked over a defined time period (e.g., cigarettes per day). The majority of epidemiological studies have relied on this method for evaluating the relationship between smoking rate and morbidity and mortality. Similarly, most smoking cessation studies have employed rate estimates during follow-up checks to evaluate program success. The benefits of this approach are ease of administration and low response cost to the smoker. Estimates require very little time for both the researcher and smoker or significant other. Estimates can also be obtained without requiring expensive in-clinic visits.

Although the advantages are considerable, rate estimates also

Table 3.1. Methods for Obtaining Smoking Rate Data

	Estimates	Monitoring	Physical products	Automated
		Smoker Self-Reports		
Advantages	1. Most convenient means for collecting rate data 2. Low response cost to smoker 3. Appropriate for determining status 4. Least intrusive	1. More accurate than estimates 2. Therapeutic 3. Temporal proximity to behavior 4. Easy to employ	1. Relatively convenient 2. Less response cost to smoker than monitoring 3. Less intrusive than monitoring	1. Low response cost to smoker 2. Independent of recall
Disadvantages	1. Inaccurate: digit bias, allows deception, unreliable 2. Susceptible to demand characteristics 3. Reactive	1. Reactive 2. Intrusive 3. Difficult to ascertain reliability 4. Deception 5. Increases subject attrition	1. Unknown reliability 2. Aesthetically unappealing 3. Allows deception 4. Expensive	1. High monetary cost 2. Reactive 3. Possible under-reporting 4. Has not received extensive investigation
		Observer Reports		
Advantages	1. Ease of data collection 2. Does not require face-to-face contact 3. Low cost to provider 4. Appropriate for determining status	1. Practical in basic research 2. Unobtrusive	1. May be useful for limited sampling 2. Unobtrusive	1. Not applicable

continued

Table 3.1. (continued)

	Estimates	Monitoring	Physical products	Automated
		Observer Reports		
Disadvantages	1. Pack bias 2. Restricted sampling 3. Inaccurate recall 4. Collusion	1. Not practical in applied settings 2. Restricted sampling 3. High response cost 4. Collusion	1. Has not receivsed extensive investigation	1. Not applicable

present a number of problems. Accuracy of rate estimates has been shown to be affected by several sources of bias. First, smokers' reports of their rates show a definite digit bias in multiples of 10 that may mask small, but significant, differences in rates of consumption (Vogt, 1977). Although the presence of digit bias in reports by significant others has not been conclusively demonstrated in research to date, the authors' experience suggests that significant others tend to respond in terms of packs of cigarettes unless requested to provide a number value for daily rates of consumption.

Despite the apparent unobtrusiveness of rate estimates, a second concern involves reactivity. A study by King, Scott, and Prue (1983) examined the reactivity of obtaining rate estimates in conjunction with a biochemical measure at two points during baseline. Both the rate estimates and the biochemical measure decreased significantly prior to the initiation of treatment. Although the combination of these two measures probably led to this decrease, the reactivity of obtaining rate estimates alone cannot be ruled out.

Rate estimates provided by significant others demonstrate a third problem. Others are seldom in a position to monitor the smoker for 24 hr a day. Thus, continuous, direct observations are impossible, and significant others must extrapolate rate from those time periods when in contact with the smoker. The latter strategy may be particularly unreliable if smoking is influenced by environmental constraints (e.g., no smoking in the office environment).

A fourth factor that may affect smokers' and significant-others' rate estimates is unintentionally inaccurate reporting. Most investigators have simply attempted to corroborate abstinence rather than actual rates (Frederiksen, Martin, & Webster, 1979); thus, little information exists on the reliability of rate estimates. One study (Vogt, 1977) has found that 20% of smokers demonstrated substantial discrepancies between two rate estimates obtained approximately 1 hr apart. Unfortunately, Vogt's (1977) subjects were participants in the Multiple Risk Factor Intervention Trial (MRFIT) program and thus may have been sensitized to the deleterious effects of high rates of consumption. Although information on self-reports of smokeless tobacco use also supports these concerns with estimates of tobacco consumption (Gritz, Baer-Weiss, Benowitz, Van Vunakis, & Jarvik, 1981), a more complete analysis of the reliability of rate estimates awaits further research.

A final problem with rate estimates, and probably the most critical, stems from smoker deception. A number of reports have provided convincing evidence that smokers will misrepresent their estimates, and thus smoking status, following completion of a treatment program. Research indicates that 20% to 48% of smokers are still smoking despite reporting abstinence posttreatment (Delarue, 1973; Ohlin, Lundh, & Westling, 1976; Sillett, Wilson, Malcolm, & Ball, 1978). It is generally assumed that these high rates of deception are due to the implicit demand for abstinence during follow-up evaluations. In addition, smokers' concerns with negative interpersonal evaluations by those conducting follow-up interviews certainly could affect reports of smoking status. Since data on deception indicate that smokers misrepresent their status, it should be expected that nonzero estimates of rate may be equally affected by variables that lead to unreliable reports of zero rate or abstinence.

Monitoring

Monitoring of rate refers to the use of more formal, ongoing records of cigarette consumption completed by the smoker or by significant others in the environment. This typically involves the observation and recording of discrete instances of cigarette consumption within specified time intervals. Monitoring methods have included tallying individual cigarettes, recording the time that each cigarette is lit, and counting the number of cigarette packs consumed.

Use of monitoring has several advantages over other data collection methods. Since it involves recording the behavior at the time of its occurrence, monitoring is potentially more reliable than estimations of rate that rely on retrospective accounts. As discussed earlier, self-monitoring may also have a therapeutic effect on subsequent rate of cigarette consumption and is considered by smokers to be a beneficial component in cessation programs. Because the reactivity of self-monitoring is not always desirable (as when data are collected for assessment purposes), it should be noted that recording methods can be varied systematically to enhance or minimize reactivity (Frederiksen & Simon, 1978). Overall, monitoring is an easily employed, efficient, and potentially therapeutic method of collecting rate data.

Although it has many advantages, monitoring is also affected by many of the same sources of error as rate estimates. For instance, the reliability of self-monitoring has not been high (McFall, 1970). One reason for this may be that reliability coefficients are likely to be extremely low when based on more discrete instances of cigarette consumption. A second reason may be difficulties associated with situating reliability observers in close enough proximity to monitor rate in the natural environment. For these two reasons smoking researchers have rarely reported reliability data on self-monitoring by smokers (Frederiksen et al., 1979).

Another reliability issue concerns the time at which data are recorded. Since smokers are instructed to record at the time of each cigarette, the temporal proximity of the observation of smoking and its subsequent recording is assumed to lead to more accurate data. When data are not recorded in a timely manner, the reliability of the rate data is lower than when recorded immediately after smoking (Frederiksen, Epstein, & Kosevsky, 1975). Yet, few studies have attempted to verify that smokers are recording as instructed. Typically, monitoring records are collected from smokers at weekly sessions without determining if the smokers are actually keeping records continuously. Again, difficulty in getting proximal reliability checkers is one likely reason for this.

Self-monitoring has been frequently employed in applied research, while the use of significant others has played a more important role in basic research. For example, nicotine regulation and smoking topography studies have employed trained observers to monitor rate. The restricted experimental situations and limited time intervals in basic research make the use of significant others quite practical for monitoring rate.

As with rate estimates (Delarue, 1973; Ohlin et al., 1976; Sillett et al., 1978), monitoring may also be influenced by smoker deception. It seems likely that self-monitoring is subject to the same demand characteristics that affect rate estimates, such that self-monitoring smokers may attempt to misrepresent rates. This point may be academic, however, since monitoring is rarely employed in posttreatment evaluations — the time period most likely to lead to deception. Typically, smokers monitor during baseline and treatment but provide only rate estimations for determining smoking status at follow-up.

A final problem with self-monitoring is reactivity. Studies have found that self-monitoring may affect a number of behaviors in addition to subsequent rate of consumption. Of particular interest to the behavioral medicine practitioner is a study by Frederiksen et al. (1975) conducted with college student volunteers participating for course credit. These authors found that a continuous monitoring procedure (smokers recording each cigarette) resulted in a greater reduction in smoking than two intermittent estimation procedures (smokers recording consumption on a daily or weekly basis). More important, however, was the finding that subject attrition was greater in the continuous monitoring group; smokers attributed this directly to the recording procedure. While the Frederiksen et al. (1975) study used college student volunteers participating for course credit, Moss, Prue, Lomax, and Martin (1982) examined the effects of self-monitoring on a veteran population in a V.A. hospital smoking cessation clinic. These treatment-seeking smokers showed even greater dropout rates when requested to self-monitor. Instructions to self-monitor for 7 days prior to returning to the clinic for the first treatment session resulted in a 53% attrition rate. Attrition was limited to 10% when smokers were asked to provide only estimates of rate. These differences in attrition point to the need for further evaluation of the effects of even relatively simple monitoring procedures.

Physical Products

Examining the physical products of cigarette consumption provides another means of rate assessment. One procedure is to require smokers to retain their empty cigarette packs (Prue, Krapfl, & Martin, 1981) or smoked butts (Schulz & Seehofer, 1978) for later collection and tabulation. Other methods include asking smokers to use only those cigarettes supplied to them (Creighton & Lewis, 1978) or allowing smokers to purchase cigarettes from the experimenters at a discount (Jaffe, Kanzler, & Friedman, 1980). Rate is then based on records of how many cigarettes have been provided to the smoker. Although physical product procedures have been useful in nicotine regulation research, they have been employed in few treatment evaluation studies. In addition, little has been done to assess the reliability of these measurement methods. While providing cigarettes or retrieving butts or packs may appear relatively straightforward and easy to employ, some potential problems merit consideration.

Several sources of error may affect the accuracy of rate data obtained by these methods. For example, collection of physical products may be incomplete. Smokers wishing to appear abstinent or compliant with treatment procedures may simply fail to turn in all empty packs or smoked butts. These same demand characteristics may also make smokers hesitant to request sufficient quantities of cigarettes when supplies are provided by the treatment staff. They may then purchase cigarettes on their own or borrow them from other smokers and not report these amounts, making reported rate lower than actual amount smoked. The use of these "extra" cigarettes has not appeared to be a problem in studies on nicotine regulation, but since the demand characteristics of treatment programs are quite different from those in more basic research, extra cigarettes represent a source of distortion that needs evaluation.

Another factor affecting physical product collection is the unpleasantness of handling smoked cigarette butts. The aversiveness of collecting these may decrease the likelihood of complete retrieval in the natural environment. For both the smoker and the research/ treatment staff, the difficulties in handling hundreds of cigarette butts each week may outweigh the advantages of this method of data collection. Employing empty cigarette packs instead of butts may be a more manageable procedure for all involved. Daily mailings of empty packs would be preferred in order to determine daily rate and maximize accuracy of rate data, yet the intrusiveness of this procedure may preclude smoker compliance.

Automated Data Records

This final category of rate assessment refers to the use of mechanical devices for automatic recording of cigarette consumption. To date, two types of devices have been employed to record smoking rate. Azrin and Powell (1968) provided smokers with a cigarette package that activated a counter each time it was opened. The counter thus recorded each cigarette consumed from the pack without any effort on the smoker's part. Despite its simplicity and apparent attractiveness, this type of mechanical recording device has not been employed in subsequent research evaluations. One likely reason for this lack of use is the substantial cost of supplying smokers with the device.

A second device for recording rate consists of a cigarette filter with a pressure-sensitive transducer and electromechanical relay that records each inhalation (Comer & Creighton, 1978). Smokers are instructed to use the filter for all cigarettes, and temporal patterns of pressure changes in the filter indicate each time a cigarette was lit. Rate data are obtained by tabulating these patterns. A number of laboratory studies of smoking topography and nicotine regulation have employed this type of filter system (Comer & Creighton, 1978; Creighton, Noble, & Whewell, 1978; Henningfield & Griffiths, 1979; Ossip-Klein, Martin, Lomax, Prue, & Davis, 1983). Although these studies focused on smoking topography and not specifically on rates of consumption, results indicate that filter devices can reliably measure rate of intake.

Laboratory and field work by Catchings (1982) also suggests the value of automated data recording for rate measurement. Catching's filter operates in much the same manner as the previously described laboratory devices but is portable, measuring just $5.5 \times 2.5 \times 1.5$ in. and weighing 14 oz. It can be easily used in the natural environment. Although the main value of a filter system has been its ability to provide topographical analysis, Catchings has shown the usefulness and reliability of this device in obtaining rate measures. Again, the portable filter recording device has the advantage of relying on mechanical input rather than the smoker's report for the collection of rate data.

Information on the strengths and limitations of mechanical devices for recording consumption is limited since their use has not been evaluated beyond early developmental work. Catchings (1982) found that use of the filter system had a slight but consistent suppression effect on rate of consumption; whether or not the suppression was just a short-term phenomenon was not investigated. In addition to reactivity concerns, further research on automated data recording is needed to examine the influence of factors that might distort records. Data collected by automated devices are subject to the same problems encountered when physical products are used to assess rate. Hence, smokers' reliance on other sources of cigarettes would lead to underestimates of rate. Although Azrin and Powell (1968) concluded this was not a problem in their study, treatment outcome evaluations may pose different demand characteristics that could influence results. Supplementary procedures to ensure the reliability of these devices for recording rate data should be considered.

Summary and Conclusions on Rate Measurement

Rate measurement is a valuable tool in the assessment of smoking behavior. A number of factors have contributed to its widespread use in basic and applied smoking research. Rate is directly related to toxic product exposure and subsequent health risk. Data on rate can be obtained through a wide variety of methods that are efficient and easy to employ. Despite these strengths, however, a number of problems have been noted. Traditional methods for assessing rate are limited by potential reactivity and the ease with which prescribed data collection can be circumvented. Since the advantages of rate assessment and its popularity in past research suggest that it will continue to serve as a primary measure of smoking behavior, a number of recommendations can be made to improve the usefulness of rate data for future research:

1. Multiple sources of rate (smokers and significant others) should be used for the evaluation of treatment programs. However, significant others may be reliable only in determining smoking status and of little help in validating actual daily rates of consumption. Whenever possible, using more than one significant other to provide information on smoking status would be advantageous.
2. Rate measures should be piloted to avoid unexpected and deleterious effects, such as the differential attrition rates reported by Moss et al. (1982). The therapeutic benefits of self-monitoring must be weighed against possible undesirable effects.
3. Since the reliability of rate data can be difficult to determine, the primary dependent variable in outcome research should be percentage of smokers attaining abstinence (Lichtenstein, 1971). The highest rate reported by the smoker or significant other should supplement abstinence data in outcome research for smokers not maintaining abstinence.
4. When assessment rather than treatment concerns are of primary interest, rate data should be obtained by the least reactive monitoring procedure. Frederiksen and Simon (1979) suggest postresponse, intermittent monitoring.
5. Rate data should be obtained for the same time period during baseline and posttreatment (Shipley, Rosen, & Williams, 1982) and with the same measurement procedures (McFall, 1978).
6. Steps should be taken to evaluate and improve the accuracy of self-report while decreasing the response cost for the smoker. For example, rate estimates combined with other minimally intrusive measures (e.g., biochemical indices) could be used to adequately assess exposure.

Topography Measures

Smoking topography is a summary term proposed by Frederiksen, Miller, and Peterson (1977) that refers to the measurement of how a person smokes. Frederiksen et al. noted the importance of topography when they stated that if two smokers are consuming equal numbers of the same cigarette, then any differences in exposure would be related to topography variables. Although this statement ignores differences in physiology, it does point out the importance of topography. Moreover, data indicating that rate measures account for only part of the variance in biochemical indices of smoke exposure also support the significance of topography measures. In fact, Vesey, Saloojee, Cole, and Russell (1982) argue that topography variables play a role at least as important as rate in overall exposure to harmful constituents in cigarette smoke.

Value of Topography Measures

Table 3.2 lists the variables subsumed by the term *smoking topography* (Adams, 1978; Creighton et al., 1978; Epstein, Dickson, Ossip, Stiller, Russell, & Winter, 1982; Frederiksen et al., 1977; Guillerm & Radziszewski, 1978; Rawbone, Murphy, Tate, & Kane, 1978). Topography variables generally are divided into five categories. Four concern exposure to smoke: puff, cigarette, respiration, and volume and draw parameters. An additional miscellaneous category considers properties of the amount and type

Table 3.2. Common Measures of Smoking Topography

1. Puff parameters
   a. Number of puffs
   b. Puff length
   c. Total puff time
   d. Interpuff interval
   e. Puff distribution
2. Cigarette parameters
   a. Intercigarette interval
   b. Cigarette duration
3. Volume and draw parameters
   a. Volume of smoke inhaled
   b. Air flow through cigarette filter, flow rate or velocity
   c. Cigarette draw resistance
4. Respiration parameters
   a. Depth of inhalation and exhalation
   b. Pattern of inhalation and exhalation
5. Miscellaneous
   a. Amount of cigarette consumed
   b. Substance smoked

of tobacco consumed. Variables listed in Table 3.2 are basically measures of how much smoke is presented to the smoker, yet each category attempts to account for exposure on a different dimension. The first two categories relate to overall exposure in a straightforward manner. For instance, within puff parameters, the greater the number of puffs a smoker takes, the greater the exposure to harmful constituents in cigarettes. Similarly, shorter intercigarette intervals lead to increased exposure by both increasing smoke intake and decreasing the time available for removal of toxic substances inhaled from prior cigarettes.

Volume and draw parameters, the third category in Table 3.2, are less overt measures of smoking than the previously mentioned variables, but they are more crucial to overall exposure. Volume and draw parameters are also more complicated because they interact to determine exposure. For instance, increases in the rate of flow of cigarette smoke through a filter decrease the filter's efficiency and therefore increase exposure. Thus, for a given volume of smoke, more rapid flow rates lead to greater exposure.

Respiration parameters also interact to determine exposure and may constitute the most important variables in determining exposure when combined with volume measures. Respiration parameters are important because they determine the amount and duration of smoke exposure to lung tissues. For example, the pattern of inhalation surrounding an inhaled puff of smoke will determine how long the smoke is exposed to lung tissues before it is washed out by inhaling clean air; the longer the time period, the greater the exposure.

The final category of topography variables in Table 3.2 considers the amount and type of substance consumed. The first measure, amount of cigarette consumed, is important because the per-puff delivery of harmful constituents in smoke increases as a cigarette is smoked down. Likewise, the type of substance also plays a role in exposure because there are wide variations in the tar, nicotine, and poisonous gas output of different cigarettes (Federal Trade Commission, 1981).

Evidence (Creighton et al., 1978; Rawbone et al., 1978) suggests that the volume and draw and respiration categories are the most critical for assessing exposure. Yet, each topography measure plays an important role in determining exposure. Unfortunately, as subsequent sections indicate, measurement of topography parameters is sometimes difficult and intrusive.

Measurement of Smoking Topography

Self-Report and Direct Observation

Topography variables have been measured in a variety of ways. The simplest procedure has involved using self-reports; smokers are asked to rate their smoking behavior along the dimensions outlined in Table 3.2. With this method of assessment, smokers might be asked to report on "how deeply they inhale cigarette smoke" or "how many puffs they take off a cigarette." Unfortunately, research has found that smokers cannot accurately evaluate their behavior on a number of topography variables (Henningfield & Griffiths, 1979; Vogt, 1977; Wald, Idle, & Bailey, 1978). The most extreme example of this problem stems from questionnaire evaluations of inhalation, an apparently simple behavior to report. Yet, Vogt (1977) found positive carbon monoxide levels in subjects who reported that they never inhale while smoking. Since carbon monoxide enters the body only through the lungs, positive carbon monoxide levels indicate that these smokers could not accurately report inhalation.

Direct observation of smoking is another method employed to assess topography (Schulz & Seehofer, 1978). Observations have been made *in vivo* and from videotapes of smokers (Frederiksen & Simon, 1979). Also, research employing direct observation has been conducted in both laboratory and applied settings (Comer & Creighton, 1978; Schulz & Seehofer, 1978). The laboratory setting is more convenient for research and facilitates more precise measurement. However, there is some question whether laboratory measures are representative of smoking in the natural environment (Comer & Creighton, 1978; Ossip-Klein et al., 1983; Schulz & Seehofer, 1978). In addition, direct observation of smoking topography is a labor-intensive and thus expensive assessment procedure. Thus, direct observation methodology seems most appropriate for basic research on topography where control of environmental conditions is more important than potential generalizability (Griffiths, Bigelow, & Liebson, 1976; Ray, Emurian, Brady, & Nellis, 1982). Additionally, direct observation procedures are limited to measuring the puff, cigarette, and miscellaneous parameters in Table 3.2; they cannot be used to assess either the volume and draw or respiration parameters.

Automated Data Records

A third way to assess topography is the use of automated measurement equipment. One type of apparatus employs a pressure-sensitive electrical switch (Henningfield, Yingling, Griffiths, & Pickens, 1980) to detect individual puffs on cigarettes. A second, more sophisticated procedure, which measures all the puff and cigarette parameters in Table 3.2, relies on pressure changes in a transducer to detect air movement in a cigarette holder. Pressure on the transducer is converted to proportional voltage and recorded on a polygraph or integrated into digital values (Epstein et al., 1982; Kumar, Cooke, Lader, & Russell, 1978). The use of a single pressure transducer in a cigarette holder detects pressure changes that measure all the puff and cigarette parameters in Table 3.2. The single transducer set-up provides reliable assessment of these parameters in both the laboratory (Comer & Creighton, 1978) and the natural environment (Catchings, 1982). In addition, the single-transducer apparatus yields an analogue measure of volume or, if calibrated with a series of known volumes, an estimated measure of volume (Epstein et al., 1982; Kumar et al., 1978). Volume measures from the single-transducer system, however, may not be valid because they assume that draw resistance remains constant across a cigarette as well as between different cigarettes. This latter assumption has not been supported by research on draw resistance (Creighton & Lewis, 1978; Creighton et al., 1978; Rawbone et al., 1978).

A more valid method of measuring volume and the other draw parameters, as well as puff and cigarette parameters, is the use of a more sophisticated cigarette holder. This second type relies on two transducers placed on either side of an orifice or filter within the holder. The first transducer measures pressure relative to atmospheric pressure on the distal side of the orifice (Creighton et al., 1978) or filter (Rawbone et al., 1978), while a second transducer measures pressure changes across the resistance (i.e., the orifice or filter). Comparisons of pressure across the resistance are necessary to provide draw resistance and flow rate measures. The two measures affect the volume of smoke inhaled (Rawbone et al., 1978; and Creighton et al., 1978) and thus are critical for its valid measurement. The two-transducer system uses a feedback loop to correct for changes in draw resistance and thus provides a measure of true volume. In addition to true volume, this system provides measures of the simpler puff and cigarette parameters in Table 3.2.

Measurement of respiratory parameters, the fourth category in Table 3.2, has been reported by Rawbone et al. (1978). These authors placed a mercury strain gauge across smokers' chests and related electrical resistance changes in the strain gauge to spirometer readings. An index of exposure to smoke is then obtained by summing the areas under the strain gauge tracings recorded on a polygraph over a range of known volumes. This allows measurement of the volume and duration of lung exposure to cigarette smoke and provides a valuable measure of dose of smoke and overall exposure.

Miscellaneous Measures of Topography

In Table 3.2 the final parameter of topography variables includes aspects of the amount and type of substance consumed by the smoker. The first variable, amount of cigarette smoked, has been measured because of its relationship to smoke exposure. Since the per-puff delivery of harmful constituents in smoke increases the longer a cigarette is smoked, each subsequent puff on a cigarette is more hazardous than preceding ones. Presumably, more puffs would lead to a smaller portion of a cigarette remaining unsmoked as well as a greater number of puffs on the proximal end of the cigarette. The amount of cigarette smoked is then calculated by either weighing the unsmoked butt or measuring its length. These measurements are then compared with values for whole, unsmoked cigarettes of the same brand (Schulz & Seehofer, 1978). The measure of exposure calculated by this procedure is expressed as percentage of cigarette smoked or tobacco consumed. The primary advantage of this method lies in its noninvasiveness. In addition, collecting butts also offers access to a more direct measure of exposure to smoke via examination of the contents retained in the filter. Filter analysis is conducted to measure the amount of nicotine and total particulate matter (TPM, or tar) trapped in the filter. The weights of nicotine and TPM in the filter, together with filter efficiency information, provide an estimate of mouth-level exposure to nicotine and TPM received during consumption of the cigarette.

Type of substance consumed by the smoker is the second variable in the fifth topography category. Cigarettes vary widely in their tar, nicotine, carbon monoxide, and hydrogen cyanide gas levels (FTC, 1981). Substance consumed can be measured by simply asking the smoker what brand is smoked or by direct observation of the cigarette pack. Assessment of substance is quite straight-forward and can be reliably reported by smokers (Prue et al., 1981). Yet, the importance of substance is a matter of some controversy in smoking research. Generally, the issue involves whether low tar and nicotine cigarettes are a "safer" alternative for those who continue to smoke. Recent studies by Rickert and Robinson (1981) and Feyerabend, Higenbottam, and Russell (1982) suggest that the importance of substance assessment may be exaggerated. Both these studies found that machine-determined data on the harmful constituents of different brands were not correlated with actual measures of the same constituents in smokers. Rickert and Robinson (1981) reported that since smokers today do not smoke in the same manner as the machines programmed to test and rate cigarettes, underestimations of smoke exposure are provided by machine testing.

Summary and Conclusions on Topography

Although research on topography variables is in its initial stages, several important issues have been highlighted in research to date. This information suggests a number of considerations to guide studies of topography variables:

1. Overall exposure appears to be a function of complex inter-relationships among many of the variables outlined in Table 3.2. Among the most important variables are measures of true volume, draw, flow, and respiration (Dunn & Freiesleben, 1978).
2. The technology of present topography assessment is intrusive as conducted in the laboratory. Future investigations should identify ways to minimize the reactivity of laboratory assessment (Schulz & Seehofer, 1978).
3. Work should continue on the development of devices to measure topography in the natural environment since even the newest available apparatus (Catchings, 1982) does not measure those variables most critical to accurate assessment.
4. The use of filter analysis procedures to determine mouth levels of exposure to smoke deserves greater attention because of their minimal intrusiveness (Schulz & Seehofer, 1978).
5. Problems noted in the earlier section on the electronic data

recording of rate are also likely to affect measures of smoking topography. For instance, smoking without the filter could seriously undermine assessments of overall exposure. Procedures should be developed to assess the validity of topography measures in the natural environment.

Biochemical Measures

Despite the utility of rate data, Densen, Davidow, Bass, and Jones (1967) contended that the relationship of health problems to smoking rate is a gross one at best. Thus, Densen et al. (1967) suggested that a more accurate and sensitive measure of exposure is needed for adequate study of smoking-related health disorders (e.g., respiratory disabilities). In a similar vein, Vesey et al. (1982) concluded that rate data can be used to estimate potential health risks on a group basis but that they fail to actually identify individuals at highest risk. The latter is largely because measures of rate ignore the importance of the manner in which each cigarette is smoked, individual biological differences in responsiveness to harmful smoke constituents, and differences in substances consumed by the smoker (Foy, Rychtarik, & Prue, 1981). All of these concerns have led a number of authors to suggest biochemical tests as a supplement to rate measures (Brockway, 1978; Densen et al., 1967; Vesey et al., 1982; Vogt, Hulley, Selvin, & Widdowson, 1977).

Biochemical tests of smoking exposure have a number of characteristics that make them extremely useful in assessing exposure to the harmful constituents in cigarette smoke. First, and foremost, biochemical measures can provide objective verification of smoking status (Prue, Martin, & Hume, 1980). Second, biochemical measures not only assess smoking per se but also are sensitive to variations in different patterns of consumption (Densen et al., 1967; Vesey et al., 1982). Third, biochemical measures are not affected by the same reliability problems that affect measures of rate (e.g., smoker deception, inaccuracy). Fourth, measures of biochemical exposure are relatively easy to obtain when compared to the steps necessary for improving rate measures (USPHS, 1979). Fifth, the use of biochemical measures can increase the accuracy of smokers' self-reports (Evans, Hansen, & Mittelmark, 1977). These characteristics suggest that direct measurement of the constituents of cigarette smoke can have important implications for the evaluation of smoking treatment programs. Three measures are addressed in subsequent sections: carbon monoxide, thiocyanate, and nicotine. Each measure's relationship to cigarette consumption and abstinence is discussed. Furthermore, the advantages and disadvantages of each are highlighted (see Table 3.3 for a summary).

Carbon Monoxide

One biochemical change produced by smoking is the elevation of carbon monoxide (CO) levels in the body. Carbon monoxide is a gas-phase constituent of smoke produced by the incomplete combustion of organic substances. As smoke is inhaled, CO is absorbed into the body through lung alveoli where it combines with circulating hemoglobin to form carboxyhemoglobin (COHb). Rates of CO absorption and elimination are influenced by a number of factors including smoking topography, lung diffusing capacity, alveolar ventilation, and circulation rate (Goldsmith, Terzaghi, & Hackney, 1963; Wald & Howard, 1975). Body levels of COHb increase within minutes of inhalation, and the half-life of CO is estimated at 2–4 hr, depending on activity level of the individual (Hawkins, 1976; Landaw, 1973).

Health Risks Associated with Carbon Monoxide

Carbon monoxide is thought to be one of the compounds most likely to contribute to the health hazards of smoking. Elevated levels have been implicated by numerous animal and human studies in the etiology of most cardiovascular diseases, including coronary heart disease (USPHS, 1979). Carbon monoxide is associated with peripheral vascular disease (Wald & Howard, 1975), reduced cardiac output and duration of exercise prior to angina (Aronow, 1976), and decreased oxygen content of fetal blood and subsequent complications in pregnancy (USPHS, 1980). Aronow (1981) has provided a review of the relationship between CO and morbidity and mortality. He concluded that both nicotine and CO contribute to the increased prevalence of fatal and nonfatal cardiovascular disease in cigarette smokers. Last, Wald and Howard (1975) suggested that CO may be the constituent of tobacco smoke most responsible for increased cardiovascular risk; they found that body levels of CO correlate more strongly than smoking history data with coronary disease.

The deleterious effects of CO are related to its impairment

Table 3.3. Biochemical Measures of Smoke Exposure

	Carbon monoxide	Thiocyanate	Nicotine
Advantages	1. Simple to assess 2. Immediate results 3. Reliable 4. Positive relation to rate 5. Index of exposure 6. Sensitive to short-term changes	1. Reliable 2. Sensitive to long-term changes because of half-life 3. Index of exposure 4. Positive relation to smoking patterns 5. Unaffected by recent physical activity	1. Tobacco only source 2. Cotinine's half-life, 30 hr 3. Reliable 4. Sensitive to recent smoking
Disadvantages	1. High individual variability 2. Relation to topography is unclear 3. Short half-life yields diurnal variability 4. Affected by alcohol	1. Flow rate effects 2. Deterioration of samples 3. Affected by time since last cigarette 4. High monetary cost 5. Influenced by diet 6. Concentrations fluctuate with levels of body fluids	1. Extremely short half-life of nicotine 2. Complex analysis 3. High monetary cost 4. Has received less investigation

of the oxygen-carrying capacity of hemoglobin (Wald & Howard, 1975). Since CO binds more readily than oxygen to hemoglobin, repeated exposure reduces the amount of hemoglobin available for oxygen transport. Carboxyhemoglobin also increases the affinity of hemoglobin for oxygen, which disrupts oxygen release at the tissue level. Anoxemia results, with heart and brain tissue affected first (USPHS, 1977). In addition, elevated CO levels may promote atherosclerosis by increasing the permeability of blood vessels to lipids (Astrup, 1980).

Sources of Carbon Monoxide

Cigarette smoking is by far the major source of exposure to CO and frequently leads to COHb levels above 8% (Ohlin et al., 1976; Wald & Howard, 1975). Thus, it is the major risk factor in the CO-associated diseases noted in the preceding section. However, other sources of CO exposure can also lead to elevated levels and increased risk. Occupational exposure is one such source. For instance, J. G. Jones and Walters (1962) compared blast furnace workers to unexposed controls and found CO levels of nonsmokers to be higher after exposure than the levels of unexposed control smokers. Automobile exhaust is another important environmental source of CO. Higher concentrations of CO have been found in workers who are exposed to dense automobile traffic — for example, traffic control officers, mechanics, and taxi, bus, and truck drivers (Goldsmith et al., 1963) — as well as in people living in urban areas (Stewart, Baretta, Platte, Stewart, Kalbfleisch, Van Yserloo, & Rimm, 1974). Exposure to smoke from other people's cigarettes can also lead to elevated CO levels (Aronow, 1981). Nonsmokers' exposure to high ambient CO levels can lead to COHb concentrations that approximate those of smokers (Russell, Cole, & Brown, 1973).

A final source of CO is endogenous production that does not involve environmental exposure. This occurs during the breakdown of hematic compounds (Cole, 1981) and results in a normal COHb level of approximately 0.5% (Goldsmith et al., 1963). This level can be substantially increased during certain pathological conditions (e.g., hemolytic anemia).

Measurement of Carbon Monoxide

Two methods have been used to measure CO levels: analysis of blood samples to determine the percentage of carboxyhemoglobin (% COHb) and analysis of expired air samples to determine parts per million of alveolar carbon monoxide (COa). These two measures have been found to be positively correlated ($r = 0.93$; Landaw, 1973). In addition, the relation between COHb and COa is expressed by the simple equation COHb = $0.5 + 0.2$ (COa) (Ringold, Goldsmith, Helwig, Finn, & Schuette, 1962). Because of the direct correlation between COHb and COa, selection of one procedure over the other is generally based on available personnel and laboratory equipment for collection and analysis. Carboxyhemoglobin assessment requires considerably more sophisticated analysis and collection procedures; therefore, COa has been the preferred measure in smoking cessation research because of its convenience and simplicity (Hughes, Frederiksen, & Frazier, 1978). However, both methods have been employed in studies examining the relationship between cigarette consumption and CO. In the remainder of this chapter, CO is used to refer to carbon monoxide levels in general, while COa and COHb are used when referring to CO as measured in the expired air or blood, respectively.

Carbon Monoxide and Smoking Status

The relationship between CO and smoking status (i.e., smoker or nonsmoker) has been investigated in a number of studies. Generally, research indicates that CO levels in smokers are consistently higher than those found in nonsmokers. For instance, Goldsmith and Aronow (1975) reported mean COa for smokers at 23 parts per million (ppm), which was significantly higher than the mean of 3.6 ppm reported for nonsmokers. Frederiksen and Martin (1979) also found significant differences in mean COa levels for smokers (34.38 ppm) and nonsmokers (4.93 ppm).

Comparison of smokers' and nonsmokers' CO levels allows the development of discrete CO ranges to distinguish between the groups. Frederiksen and Martin (1979) suggest a COa cutoff point of 8 ppm to discriminate smokers from nonsmokers. Although some false-negative classifications may occur with this cutoff point, Frederiksen and Martin found that less than 4 % of smokers would be misclassified. No false positives were found using the 8 ppm cutoff. Vogt (1977) employed the same cutoff point but found a higher incidence of false-negative classifications. He reported that 8 of 98 smokers (8 %) fell in the nonsmoker range with COa levels less than or equal to 8 ppm. Vogt attributed these data to the "marginal" smoking habits of misclassified subjects: All reported atypical patterns of smoking less than eight cigarettes per day, abstinence in the 24 hr prior to the test, or noninhalation of tobacco smoke.

When marginal smokers were removed from analysis, no false negatives were found. Three false positives still occurred in 42 nonsmokers; no information was provided on these subjects. For COHb measures, Sillett et al. (1978) suggest 1.7% COHb as a cutoff value based on data from 161 nonsmokers, while Turner (1976) suggests a COHb level of 2%. Although Russell (1976) has argued that firm cutoff points are not warranted by present research on COHb, the significant differences between smokers and nonsmokers reported here, as well as those found by other workers (e.g., Hawkins, 1976; Horan, Hackett, & Lindberg, 1978; Vesey et al., 1982), suggest the usefulness of at least tentative CO values as cutoff levels.

In summary, CO levels can discriminate between smokers and nonsmokers although care should be taken in the use of this measure given the data on false negatives and positives. The classification of smokers and nonsmokers on the basis of CO analysis has implications for the objective determination of abstinence following smoking cessation programs. Evaluations of treatment outcome have typically relied on subjects' reports of consumption, which suffer from the difficulties discussed earlier. For example, Ohlin et al. (1976) and Sillett et al. (1978) assessed COHb levels in subjects involved in smoking cessation treatment and found discrepancies between reported smoking status and COHb levels. When confronted with the discrepancy, a number of subjects reported that they had, in fact, been smoking. Thus, CO levels can be used not only to provide a more objective measure of consumption but also to increase the validity of self-reports of consumption.

Carbon Monoxide and Smoking Patterns

Objective determination of smoking status is important in cessation research, but the identification of different patterns of smoking may be even more valuable in studies of the etiology of disease. Since both elevated CO levels and rates of cigarette consumption have been implicated as health risk factors, comparisons of the two measures have been made to evaluate the effects of rate of smoking on CO level. A number of studies have reported positive correlations between estimates of rate of consumption and CO levels. Vogt (1977) evaluated patients in the MRFIT program and found a positive correlation of $r = 0.491$. Other studies have reported similar or higher correlations: Vesey et al. (1982) found a correlation of $r = 0.416$, Rickert and Robinson (1981) reported a correlation of $r = 0.63$, and Cole (1981) reported a correlation of $r = 0.82$ in a group of office workers. In general, the moderate correlation coefficients found indicate a general linear relationship between estimates of rate and CO but one which breaks down at both low and high rates. In addition, a great deal of individual subject variability in CO levels has been reported. Vesey et al. (1982) suggest that some heavy smokers (rate > 25 cigarettes per day) are likely to have the same risk — that is, CO levels — as nonsmokers, while some light smokers (≤ 5 cigarettes per day) may approach risk levels typically found in heavy smokers.

Factors Affecting Carbon Monoxide Levels

Rate of consumption accounts for only 17 % to 65 % of the variance in CO levels reported in these studies; this suggests that other factors play a crucial role in observed CO levels. In comprehensive reviews, Frederiksen and Martin (1979) and Cole (1981) consider the factors affecting CO levels. They report that tobacco product consumed, manner of smoking (smoking topography), temporal distribution of consumption, and smokers' activity levels greatly affect measured CO levels.

Tobacco products

There are wide variations in the CO yields of cigarettes, cigars, and pipes. Mainstream smoke of American cigarettes, analyzed in a standardized manner by smoking machines, contains between 0.5 and 26.0 mg CO (FTC, 1981). The differences in CO output stem largely from differences in tobacco and its packaging (Robinson & Forbes, 1975) and the type of cigarette filter and paper (Tiggelbeck, 1976). The major method of CO reduction is dilution of smoke via perforation of filters or cigarette papers. When dilution is limited by restricted ventilation, such as that found with nonporous cigar wrappers, CO output is increased. Cigarettes with air-stream filters have the lowest CO output.

In spite of these large variations in CO output, corresponding changes in measured CO levels as a result of smoking different products have not been clearly demonstrated. Prue, Krapfl, and Martin (1981) and Prue, Scott, Martin, and Lomax (1983) found CO level decreases following the introduction of low CO output cigarettes; however, the decreases appeared related more to rate changes than to substance consumed. Rickert and Robinson (1981) also reported that measures of CO output determined by smoking machine were not correlated with smokers' CO levels. These authors hypothesized that smoking machines are not programmed to smoke the same way smokers do. They suggest that there are large differences in average puff volume, puff duration, and interpuff interval between the two methods of smoking. Another factor that contributes to the lack of correlation is smokers' propensity to block the ventilation holes on air-stream filter cigarettes in order to increase the dose of smoke (Kozlowski, Frecker, Khouw, & Pope, 1980; Lombardo, Davis, & Prue, 1983).

Smoking topography

The way a cigarette is smoked also influences CO levels. A number of studies have found that differences in topography variables can have a significant impact on CO uptake (Frederiksen & Simon, 1978; Rawbone, Murphy, Tate, & Kane, 1978; Robinson & Forbes, 1975). Differences in CO levels have been related to holding smoke in the lungs, spacing of inhalation, and depth of inhalation (Rawbone, 1981), as well as amount of cigarette smoked (Cole, 1981). Vesey et al. (1982) have hypothesized that the way a person smokes accounts for 23% of the variation in COa levels, while rate of consumption accounts for just 21%. Thus, topography variables are critical to CO level differences found in smokers: Variables that increase amount of exposure to cigarette smoke result in higher levels of CO. (A more detailed description of topography assessment is considered in a subsequent section of this chapter.)

Temporal distribution

The spacing of cigarettes is closely related to rate of consumption and plays an important role in CO levels. The smaller the intervals between cigarettes, the higher the ultimate CO level. For instance, if environmental constraints restrict a pack-a-day smoker's consumption to a short time period (e.g., in the evening), that individual will have a higher CO level than a smoker who evenly spaces 20 cigarettes throughout the day. Short time intervals do not allow the body to eliminate any CO prior to consuming another cigarette; this results in higher overall CO levels (Frederiksen & Martin, 1979). Since peak CO levels may play an important role in morbidity, temporal spacing is a significant factor in overall health risk (USPHS, 1981).

Activity level

A final factor that affects CO levels is amount of activity. Hawkins, Cole, and Harris (1976) reported variations in the half-life of CO as a direct function of activity level. They compared sedentary workers with those engaged in heavy manual labor and found overall lower levels in the latter group. These differences existed despite the higher consumption rate in the more active group. The authors concluded that active individuals eliminate CO more rapidly so that CO peaks and basal levels are lower.

Summary and Conclusions on Carbon Monoxide

Carbon monoxide assessment has much to recommend its use as a supplement to rate data. Its sensitivity to variations in smoking behavior makes CO a valuable measure in both applied and basic research; it can provide objective verification of smoking status as well as detect changes in smoking patterns. In addition, its established association with cardiovascular disease makes CO an important variable for study in its own right. Carbon monoxide sampling is easily employed, reliable, and of little response cost to the smoker. However, some of the characteristics of CO, including its relatively short half-life and responsiveness to smoking patterns, suggest a number of factors that should be considered in the use of CO measurement:

1. The short half-life of CO in the body and resultant diurnal variability in levels should be considered in the assessment of smoking status. Thus, time of sampling should be equated across serial assessments. Since smokers may be able to reduce rates or abstain from smoking for short periods to circumvent discovery of their smoking status, afternoon samples may be more accurate indices of smoking status.
2. Subjects exposed to high levels of ambient CO either from occupational sources or in the sidestream smoke of others may be falsely labeled as smokers. Other environmental sources often encountered by smokers that may lead to elevated levels include defective automobile exhaust equipment and inadequately ventilated or defective space heaters. Thus, caution should be used in the designation of cutoff scores, and alternative explanations for elevated

levels should be entertained when CO levels fall near the cutoff.

3. Another factor that may confound valid assessments of COa is recent alcohol intake, which may increase levels obtained by Ecolyzer measurement (Horan et al., 1978). Similarly, certain medications, such as phenobarbital and diphenylhydantoin, result in the endogenous formation of CO and thus elevation of levels found (Stewart, 1975). The use of filters on COa-measuring equipment to remove alcohol fumes prior to sampling and an assessment of medication use are necessary for valid CO measurement.

4. Two additional factors should be considered when the purpose of CO assessment is to provide a measure of smoke exposure rather than simply smoking status. These are amount of time since last cigarette and time of day. Vogt (1977) found a correlation of $r = -0.405$ between elapsed time since last cigarette and CO levels. Since CO peaks immediately after smoking, assessment of time since last cigarette is necessary to fully evaluate amount of exposure. The time of day when CO level is sampled also merits consideration because of the diurnal variability in levels. Since levels increase throughout the day, samples obtained early are likely to be poor indices of CO exposure.

5. Careful attention should be paid to the procedures involved in sampling COa. In their work, the present authors have found a number of factors that potentially influence COa measurement. One problem is intake filter slippage on the Ecolyzer (Energetics Science, Inc., Elmsford, NY), which allows ambient air to dilute the COa sample. Another factor is the inability of some subjects to follow the standardized breath-holding procedure outlined by R. H. Jones, Ellicott, Cadigan, and Gaensler (1958) (i.e., [1] completely empty lungs of all air, [2] take a deep breath, [3] hold the inhaled air for 20 sec, [4] exhale approximately half the inhaled air, and [5] blow the remaining air into a polyvinyl bag). Patients with pulmonary disabilities, in particular, are often unable to inhale or exhale deeply. A number of subjects have also been found to take a second, almost imperceptible breath just prior to exhaling into the bag; this has the effect of diluting the sample. Finally, the size of the sample bag may affect volume of exhalation and subsequent CO concentrations in expired air.

6. For both COa and COHb measurement, more detailed descriptions of collection and analysis procedures should be provided to ensure standardization of samples. When measuring COHb levels, technicians' reliability should be assessed since the analysis of blood samples is a multistep process subject to human error.
7. A final factor to consider is the impact of CO measurement on smokers. Feedback can provide dramatic evidence of the immediate health consequences of smoking, thus making it more difficult for smokers to deny potential health hazards. Knowledge of CO levels is reactive and reinforcing, and may motivate smokers to initiate and maintain changes in their habits.

Thiocyanate

Thiocyanate is the primary metabolite of hydrogen cyanide (HCN), another gas-phase constituent of cigarette smoke. It has been estimated that a single cigarette may yield up to 0.4 mg of HCN, while the resulting smoke may contain up to 1,600 ppm (Vesey, 1981). Inhalation of HCN in cigarette smoke will yield subsequent elevations in thiocyanate (SCN) levels.

Health Risks Associated with SCN and HCN

Hydrogen cyanide gas has been established as the primary ciliatoxic agent in cigarette smoke (USPHS, 1979) and implicated in the development of chronic obstructive pulmonary disease, emphysema, and chronic bronchitis (Ross, 1976). Vesey (1981) has suggested that the combination of HCN with carbon monoxide may play a part in the development of atherosclerosis. Hence, measurement of HCN in smokers might serve as an excellent index of health risks associated with smoking.

Most of the cyanides entering the body are rapidly metabolized and converted to thiocyanate. The effects of SCN on bodily functions differ depending on the relative quantity. Moderate levels of SCN serve necessary biological functions (such as control of oral cavity disease), while elevated levels have been associated with the etiology of stomach cancer (Boyland & Walker, 1974; Langman, Doll, & Wilson, 1966). As with hydrogen cyanide, measurement of SCN may be useful in assessing exposure to the harmful effects of cigarette consumption.

Sources of Thiocyanate

Tobacco smoke has been confirmed as a major source of elevated SCN levels (Vesey, 1981). However, there are a number of naturally occurring sources of SCN and cyanogen compounds that may elevate SCN levels in nonsmoking subjects. For example, Vesey (1981) has reported that diet is a major source of SCN. Cyanogens are released from crushing almonds, apricot kernels, and apple and grape pips. In addition, cyanogens are present in large amounts in sugar cane and bamboo shoots, and are distributed in small amounts in legumes and foods from the cabbage family. Although diet has not seemed to play a major role in research to date, natural food sources could conceivably result in false-positive evaluations.

Vesey (1981) has suggested that smoking researchers may also need to consider a number of other possible contributors to SCN elevations that are unrelated to tobacco use. Cardiovascular patients and persons with peripheral vascular disease are sometimes treated with a cyanogenetic drug, sodium nitroprusside, which will increase SCN levels. Also, some bacterial infections will produce minor sources of cyanide and thereby increase SCN. In addition, changes in amount of body fluid can dramatically alter SCN. Recent vomiting, diuresis, pregnancy, menstrual cycle changes, and renal threshold differences can all affect SCN levels.

Finally, occupational exposure can alter SCN levels. Electroplating, precious metal cleansing, fumigation, and plastic manufacturing all produce cyanide, which may lead to increased SCN levels among nonsmokers (Vesey, 1981).

Measurement of Thiocyanate

Despite the health risks associated with hydrogen cyanide, this gas is metabolized so quickly that accurate measurement is precluded. However, thiocyanate has a half-life of 10 to 14 days; thus, elevations in SCN levels of smokers and nonsmokers may serve as excellent indices of smoking status.

Once metabolized, SCN accumulates in the body fluids, including blood plasma, saliva, gastric juices, urine, cerebrospinal fluid, and perspiration. Plasma, urine, and saliva have been used most frequently for assessing the relationship between smoking and SCN levels. Vesey (1981) has reported a strong correlation ($r = 0.89$) between saliva and plasma SCN levels. However, urine, blood, and saliva SCN have been generally found to be differentially sensitive to smoking exposure. For instance, a number of researchers have found that saliva sampling is more sensitive than blood or urine tests and that it provides the widest separation of groups with different smoking histories (Barylko-Pikielna & Pangborn, 1968; Densen et al., 1967). However, other comparisons of SCN levels in different fluids have produced inconsistent results. Maliszewski and Bass (1955) have reported that urine samples show the most change in SCN following smoking cessation, although saliva and plasma show similar decreases. The superiority of urine tests in this study may have been related to procedural differences. Maliszewski and Bass (1955) sampled all discharged urine over a 24-hr period while other, less successful researchers (Barylko-Pikielna & Pangborn, 1968) have sampled intermittently. Similarly, Vesey (1981) has reported that blood samples are more sensitive to smoking exposure than saliva. Despite the conclusions of Maliszewski and Bass (1955) and Vesey (1981), the bulk of data support the superior sensitivity of saliva SCN measures. In addition, Prue et al. (1980) suggest a number of other reasons for selecting saliva over other bodily fluids: (1) Saliva sampling is less intrusive relative to other procedures, (2) minimally trained personnel can obtain these samples, (3) smokers can perform their own sampling, (4) measures can be obtained openly in a wide variety of locations including the home or office, (5) the procedure is efficient in terms of time demands, and (6) saliva sampling and analysis are less expensive than the sampling and analysis of other fluids.

Thiocyanate and Smoking Status

Regardless of the body fluid used, research has demonstrated that measurement of SCN may be valuable in the discrimination of smokers and nonsmokers. For example, Butts, Kuehneman, and Widdowson (1974) reported only 3 false positives in 169 nonsmokers and 2 false negatives in 30 smokers when a cutoff value of 85 μmol SCN/liter of serum was employed. Vesey (1981) found a similar pattern in a sample of 234 smokers using a cutoff level of 80 μmol/ liter. Maliszewski and Bass (1955) found no overlap in SCN levels among smokers and nonsmokers. Vogt (1977) found both false negatives and false positives among his group of marginal smokers (i.e., those who denied inhaling, reported consumption of less than eight cigarettes per day, or reported abstinence 24 hr prior to sampling). These studies indicate that SCN levels of smokers and nonsmokers occasionally overlap, but levels have reliably distinguished smokers from nonsmokers with few exceptions (Prue et al., 1980).

The occasional overlap in single SCN samples has prompted the suggestion that serial samples may improve the discrimination of smoking status over single-sample evaluations (USPHS, 1979). For example, Maliszewski and Bass (1955) obtained daily samples in a smoker who abstained for 10 days and found 30% to 50% decreases in saliva, urine, and plasma SCN levels. Densen et al. (1967) reported similar changes in daily saliva and plasma samples following the initiation of abstinence, while Pettigrew and Fell (1972) reported decreases to nonsmoker levels after 2 weeks of abstinence. This latter study also found a return to baseline levels of SCN after resumption of smoking for 1 week. Thus, SCN levels can reliably discriminate smokers from nonsmokers with very little overlap. Comparisons of the same smokers during smoking and abstinence demonstrate the value of serial samples since large differences in levels make the discrimination of smoking status straightforward.

Thiocyanate and Smoking Patterns

The discrimination of smoking status, although necessary, is only one use of SCN levels. Another, perhaps more important characteristic is the relation of different patterns of smoking to elevated SCN levels. As with the CO measure, research has documented a relationship between SCN levels and rate of cigarette consumption. Butts et al. (1974) reported a positive correlation of $r = 0.46$ between estimated rate and SCN, Vogt (1977) reported a correlation of $r = 0.483$, Vesey et al. (1982) found a correlation of $r = 0.41$, and Vesey (1981) reported a correlation of $r = 0.50$ for plasma SCN and $r = 0.68$ for saliva SCN. Like CO, the correlations between rate and SCN are positive although rate accounts for little of the variance in SCN levels. One likely reason for the moderate correlations is that SCN levels demonstrate a sigmoid relation with rate as a function of floor and ceiling levels at extremely high (> 30 cigarettes per day) or low (< 10 cigarettes per day) rates (Barylko-Pikielna & Pangborn, 1968; Vesey, 1981; Vogt, 1977). In addition, empirical evidence suggests that consideration of other parameters of smoking—such as substance smoked (Djuric, Raicevic, & Konstantinovic, 1962), smoking topography (Barylko-Pikielna & Pangborn, 1968), and amount of cigarette smoked (Densen et al., 1967)—might improve the prediction of SCN levels in smokers.

Despite the limitation of a restricted focus on rate, most data indicate that SCN levels adequately discriminate smoking status. In addition, rate accounts for at least as much variance in SCN as it does in CO levels.

Factors to Consider When Using Thiocyanate Levels

Regardless of the body fluid used, past research has identified a number of factors that smoking researchers should consider when analyzing SCN levels:

1. When saliva levels are obtained, care must be taken to equalize saliva flow rates. Fischmann and Fischmann (1948) and Dogon, Amdur, and Bell (1971) have found that as saliva flow rates increase, mean SCN levels initially decrease and then asymptote in both smokers and nonsmokers. The distributions of SCN levels of smokers and nonsmokers tend to overlap at low flow rates but not at higher rates (>15 cc/hr). Therefore, most smoking researchers have stimulated flow rate prior to saliva sampling by having smokers chew on dental rolls (Densen et al., 1967) or paraffin (Maliszewski & Bass, 1955). Future research should continue this procedure prior to sampling. The authors have successfully used a small piece of tasteless parafilm, which is readily available in most laboratories.
2. When collecting urine specimens for SCN analysis, sole reliance on intermittent sampling is not recommended. Maliszewski and Bass (1955) have found that continuous, 24-hr sampling from subjects provides the most stable results. This has been confirmed by Densen et al. (1967), who report that random urine tests are poor indices of smoking because of large daily fluctuations.
3. When collecting fluid samples of any type, care should be taken to avoid deterioration and evaporation. Prue et al. (1980) have noted that deterioration of SCN leads to deflated SCN concentrations, while evaporation leads to inflated concentrations. Both deterioration and evaporation of SCN may stem from a number of factors related to sampling and storage. Thus, Prue et al. (1981) have suggested that SCN samples should be analyzed immediately after collection for best results.
4. Smoking patterns immediately prior to sampling should

be standardized or controlled for statistically, regardless of the type of procedures used. For example, saliva SCN has been shown to increase immediately after smoking a cigarette despite its 10- to 14-day half-life (Barylko-Pikielna & Pangborn, 1968). Although similar data have not been collected with plasma and urine samples, there is no a priori reason to assume that they would not be affected in a similar manner. Therefore, information regarding recent smoking should be systematically taken when obtaining fluid samples. Similarly, other factors that have been found to affect CO levels (e.g., time of day) should be considered when assessing SCN differences.

5. All laboratory procedures should be checked periodically to ensure that analyses are conducted in a standardized manner. The SCN analysis involves a large number of steps where technician error or bias could affect obtained values. Thus, technicians should be blind to the smoking status of individuals from whom samples are obtained. In addition, reliability checks with a second technician or a technician's analysis of the same sample twice should be routinely scheduled to ensure reliability.

6. A number of factors unrelated to tobacco use can produce marked changes in SCN levels. Thus, it is important for outcome researchers to routinely obtain information regarding diet, medications, hydration changes, and occupational exposure. This information should be systematically gathered during each assessment so that any discrepancies between self-report and SCN levels may be examined without reliance on post hoc information.

Despite the potential confounding variables, tobacco smoke remains a primary, indirect source of thiocyanate. In addition, SCN levels can successfully discriminate between the majority of smokers and nonsmokers, and are positively correlated with rate data. Analyzing SCN levels also directly measures health risks related to cyanide gas exposure, and the relatively long half-life of SCN (10–14 days) makes it less sensitive to variables affecting CO levels (e.g., time since last cigarette and time of sampling). Finally, SCN levels may be used to increase the accuracy of self-report (Brockway, Kleinmann, Edleson, & Gruenwald, 1977).

Nicotine

Each puff of inhaled cigarette smoke delivers a bolus of nicotine to the smoker; most believe this is the primary determinant of continued smoking (Russell, 1978). The amount of nicotine in one puff is equivalent to approximately 1 to 2 μg/kg given intravenously (Armitage, 1978). Approximately 14% to 22% of all nicotine in cigarette tobacco is available in the mainstream smoke (USPHS, 1979). Following its inhalation, nicotine subsequently enters the body, where it is absorbed in the lungs, the gastrointestinal tract, and the mucous membranes of the mouth and nose.

Health Risks Associated with Nicotine

Inhaled nicotine is absorbed from the lung so quickly that it can be found in the brain, the adrenal medulla, and the sympathetic ganglia within 5 min (Ashton, Marsh, Millman, Rawlins, Telford, & Thompson, 1978; Gilbert, 1979; USPHS, 1977). Despite its documented central nervous system effects and suspected cocarcinogenic effects (Bock, 1980), nicotine primarily acts upon the cardiovascular and respiratory systems. In fact, nicotine is known to cause three deleterious effects on the cardiovascular system including a hemodynamic response of the heart, increased circulation of fatty acids, and an increase in platelet adhesion and aggregation (USPHS, 1977). Finally, nicotine increases the amount of work of the heart while carbon monoxide reduces the amount of oxygen available to it; consequently, the combined action of carbon monoxide and nicotine has been linked to increased incidence of atherosclerosis and thrombosis (Cohen, Deane, & Goldsmith, 1969; USPHS, 1977).

Measurement of Nicotine

Despite its potential value as an index of health risk, accurate measurement of nicotine in bodily fluids is difficult since its half-life is only 30 min (Langone & Van Vunakis, 1975; Zeidenberg, Jaffe, Kanzler, Levitt, Langone, & Van Vunakis, 1977). Consequently, nicotine measurement is generally accompanied by or replaced with the assessment of cotinine, its primary metabolite (Langone, Gjika, & Van Vunakis, 1973). Cotinine has a number of advantages over nicotine: Its half-life is approximately 30 hr, it is found in larger amounts in bodily fluids, and the urinary excretion of cotinine has been found to be less affected by urine pH (Matsukura, Sakamoto, Seino, Tamada, Matsuyama, & Muranaka, 1979).

Both nicotine and cotinine concentrations have been measured by sampling the blood, urine, spinal fluid, and saliva of smokers. Various fluid samples have been analyzed using a number of different procedures (Beckett & Triggs, 1966; Feyerabend, Levitt, & Russell, 1975; Gritz et al., 1981; Haines, Mahajan, Miljkovic, Miljkovic, & Vessel, 1974; Zeidenberg et al., 1977). The authors have found only one report directly comparing the nicotine levels of different fluids. Feyerabend et al. (1982) found a strong correlation between urine and saliva nicotine concentrations ($r = 0.84$). Different analysis procedures have also been shown to be highly correlated (Langone et al., 1973; Langone & Van Vunakis, 1975); however, neither of these latter studies examined the relationship of urine to plasma nicotine. Thus, relatively little is known about the interrelationships among nicotine and cotinine levels in the different fluids.

Also, and perhaps more importantly, the effects of procedural and sampling variations within and across laboratories have not been investigated in research. The two primary methods of analyzing nicotine and cotinine are gas-liquid chromatography (GLC) and radioimmunoassay (RIA) procedures. Paxton and Bernacca (1979) have described the GLC procedure as simple, reliable, inexpensive, and brief; however, Langone et al. (1973) have argued that these procedures are too complex and demanding for large-scale studies. Langone et al. (1973) have suggested that the RIA procedure is preferable for large samples. A recent comparison of the two procedures by Gritz et al. (1981) has provided a formula for comparing nicotine and cotinine levels obtained via different procedures (Nicotine GLC = 2.35 + 0.76 RIA and Cotinine GLC = 31.34 + .71 RIA). Unfortunately, Gritz et al. (1981) did not discuss the advantages and disadvantages of each procedure. Thus, the rationale for using either GLC or RIA should be based on the availability of equipment or preferences of laboratory personnel until experimental data demonstrate the superiority of one of the procedures.

One final method of estimating exposure to nicotine has been through the analysis of nicotine retained in the cigarette filters. Schulz and Seehofer (1978) have noted that butt analysis is the only noninvasive method of estimating the amount of smoke inhaled. This indirect procedure relies on the standardized measure of the nicotine retention efficiency of a particular brand of cigarette's filter. Information on filter efficiency is combined with data on the amount of nicotine retained in the filter to calculate the proportion of available nicotine consumed by the smoker (Creighton & Lewis, 1978; Schulz & Seehofer, 1978). The rationale for this procedure is founded on the assumption that filter efficiency, calculated on the basis of constant flow rates, does not change during the consumption of a cigarette. Unfortunately, smoking in the natural environment does not support this assumption. Creighton and Lewis (1978) have found that filter efficiency changes while a cigarette is smoked; they also have noted numerous instances where flow rates have been affected by variations in puff volume, puff duration, inhalation patterns, and interpuff interval, with subsequent changes in filter efficiency. For instance, the "shape" of puffs, a function of duration and puff volume, affects cigarette filtering of nicotine, while the interpuff interval affects filter efficiency for the particulate matter. Variations in these parameters would lead to erroneous estimations of exposure based on filter analysis. Again, further research on butt analysis is necessary so that the advantage of noninvasiveness can be weighed against reliability problems associated with variations in smoking topography.

Nicotine and Smoking Status

Smoking researchers have investigated nicotine primarily because of its importance in the development and maintenance of smoking (Russell, 1978, 1979; Schachter, 1978). At this time it is generally agreed that individuals smoke to obtain pharmacologically satisfying doses of nicotine (Armitage, 1978; USPHS, 1979). Smokers become accustomed to certain levels of nicotine and subsequently maintain these levels by titrating nicotine intake by adjusting their smoking behavior (Hill & Marquardt, 1980; Russell, 1978). Therefore, nicotine should be an important measure of smoking status and is potentially valuable in differentiating degrees of exposure to smoke.

Although nicotine levels should be useful in discriminating smokers from nonsmokers, the one report of this use comes from Paxton and Bernacca (1979), who employed urine nicotine analysis. They reported extremely low probabilities of false-negative and false-positive classifications using urine nicotine cutoff of 0.4 μmol/liter. The study also found that as time since last cigarette increased beyond 15 hr, the probability of false negatives rapidly increased.

This report suggests the value of urine nicotine as a measure of recent smoking. Unfortunately, plasma and saliva measures of nicotine have not been studied, and thus little is known about their value in discriminating smokers and nonsmokers.

Nicotine levels have also been measured preceding and following cessation of smoking (Langone & Van Vunakis, 1975). This report found a characteristic pattern of rapidly declining nicotine levels in the plasma and urine of smokers following cessation. Levels dropped to minimal values within 1–3 days following initiation of abstinence. Unfortunately, no data were provided on nonsmokers, precluding comparison with levels obtained from smokers during the first 5 days and the eighth day following cessation. Yet, the rapid decline in nicotine levels suggests that serial measures may be a valuable index of changes in smoking status.

Nicotine and Smoking Pattern

The relationship between nicotine levels in the blood and urine and rate of cigarette consumption also has been investigated. For the most part, nicotine has not been significantly correlated with rate of cigarette consumption (Langone et al., 1973; Paxton & Bernacca, 1979). However, nicotine levels have been correlated with number of cigarettes smoked prior to sampling, time since last cigarette, and the number of cigarettes smoked in the hour preceding sampling (Feyerabend et al., 1982; Paxton & Bernacca, 1979; Russell, 1978). Again, the short half-life of nicotine likely leads to the observed effect on measured levels and resultant correlation coefficients.

Cotinine and Smoking

Since nicotine has limitations as a measure for assessing smoking status or rate, its primary metabolite, cotinine, has recently been investigated (Langone et al., 1973). Its longer half-life makes cotinine considerably more stable than nicotine (Zeidenberg et al., 1977) and provides a larger biochemical "window" through which to observe recent nicotine intake. Studies have reported that cotinine levels are related to number of cigarettes smoked on the day samples are taken (Rickert & Robinson, 1981), nicotine rating of brand smoked (Hill & Marquardt, 1980), average number of cigarettes smoked per day, and the total average nicotine intake (computed by multiplying estimated rate times cigarette nicotine content) (Zeidenberg et al., 1977). Zeidenberg et al. (1977) have also reported a strong correlation ($r = 0.73$) between estimated rate and cotinine levels, a particularly important finding given the weak correlations found between rate measures and nicotine. Although more research needs to be conducted, these results suggest that cotinine levels may play an important role in smoking assessment.

Factors to Consider When Measuring Nicotine and Cotinine

Despite its many shortcomings, nicotine analysis, and especially cotinine analysis, can be quite valuable in smoking research. For this reason, a number of factors need to be considered to maximize its value:

1. The short half-life of nicotine requires the assessment and experimental or statistical control of measures of recent smoking in order to ensure valid assessment. Similar concern is warranted in cotinine assessment although its greater stability should make recency of smoking variables less of a problem.
2. Cotinine's longer half-life, greater stability, and overall higher concentrations in the body make it more desirable than nicotine measures. In addition, saliva analysis, although largely uninvestigated, offers the least intrusive sampling procedure and thus should be evaluated in future research.
3. The importance of variability in smoking topography has to be considered in analyzing nicotine intake.
4. Differences in individual smokers' regulation of nicotine, such as Russell's (1979) distinction between "peak seekers" and "trough maintainers," should be considered in correlational studies of nicotine as well as in the design of treatment programs.
5. Individual differences in rates of nicotine metabolism (Zeidenberg et al., 1977) and excretion (Schachter, 1978) affect nicotine levels. Thus, these factors should be experimentally or statistically controlled for in nicotine assessment. Alternatively, serial measures may minimize the importance of individual differences.
6. Nicotine and cotinine measures may serve to enhance the accuracy of self-reports. Evans et al. (1977) found that giv-

ing information regarding saliva nicotine measurement as verification of self-report led to increased reports of smoking.

7. Finally, since GLC and RIA analyses are complex procedures requiring multiple steps, technicians should be blind to the smoking status of subjects, and their procedures should be routinely checked for reliability. Until more is known about effects of procedural variations, researchers should describe their methodology in precise detail.

General Summary

The preceding sections describe a variety of measures that have been used to assess smoking behavior. This review is limited to measures that have received attention in the smoking research literature. Recent studies on rate, topography, and biochemical assessment are reviewed. Alternative measures to rate of consumption have led smoking researchers away from a sole reliance on this dependent variable. This movement represents a more sophisticated approach to assessment. Until very recently, the assessment and treatment of smoking have been constrained by primitive, often unreliable (Ohlin et al., 1976) and limited measurement procedures (Densen et al., 1967). Unfortunately, the bulk of our knowledge of smoking behavior and its treatment stems from studies employing these procedures. Thus, smoking research, especially treatment outcome studies, must be considered in light of this chapter's discussion of smoking assessment. Research now provides a microanalysis of smoking behavior per se (i.e., topography measures) as well as a direct measure of health risk (i.e., biochemical measures). Hopefully, the development of these new approaches to assessment will result in new developments in smoking treatment.

References

Adams, P. I. The influence of cigarette smoke yields on smoking habits. In R. E. Thornton (Ed.), *Smoking behaviour: Physiological and psychological influences.* London: Churchill Livingstone, 1978.

Armitage, A. K. The role of nicotine in the tobacco smoking habit. In R. E. Thornton (Ed.), *Smoking behaviour: Physiological and psychological influences.* London: Churchill Livingstone, 1978.

Aronow, W. S. Carbon monoxide and cardiovascular disease. In E. L. Wynder, D. Hoffman, & G. B. Gori (Eds.), *Proceedings of the third world conference on smoking and health: Modifying the risk for the smoker* (DHEW Publication No. (NIH) 76-1221). Washington, DC: U.S. Department of Health, Education, and Welfare, 1976.

Aronow, W. S. Effects of cigarette smoking and of carbon monoxide on coronary heart disease. In R. M. Greenhalgh, (Ed.), *Smoking and arterial disease*. Bath, U.K.: Pitman Medical, 1981.

Ashton, H., Marsh, V. R., Millman, J. E., Rawlins, M. D., Telford, R., & Thompson, J. W. The use of event related slow potentials of the brain as a means to analyze the effects of cigarette smoking and nicotine in humans. In R. E. Thornton (Ed.), *Smoking behaviour: Physiological and psychological influences*. London: Churchill Livingstone, 1978.

Astrup, P. Carbon monoxide as a contributor to the health hazards of cigarette smoking. In G. B. Gori & F. G. Bock (Eds.), *Banbury Report 3: A safe cigarette?* Cold Springs Harbor, NY: Cold Springs Harbor Laboratory, 1980.

Azrin, N. H., & Powell, J. Behavioral engineering: The reduction of smoking with a conditioning apparatus and procedure. *Journal of Applied Behavior Analysis*, 1968, *1*, 193–200.

Barylko-Pikielna, N., & Pangborn, R. M. Effect of cigarette smoking on urinary and salivary thiocyanates. *Archives of Environmental Health*, 1968, *17*, 739–745.

Beckett, A. H., & Triggs, E. J. Determination of nicotine and its metabolite, cotinine, in urine by gas chromatography. *Nature*, 1966, *211*, 1415–1417.

Best, J. A. Tailoring smoking withdrawal procedures to personality and motivational differences. *Journal of Consulting and Clinical Psychology*, 1975, *43*, 1–8.

Best, J. A., & Steffy, R. A. Smoking modification procedures for internal and external locus of control clients. *Canadian Journal of Behavioral Science*, 1975, *7*, 155–165.

Bock, F. G. Cocarcinogenic properties of nicotine. In G. B. Gori & F. G. Bock (Eds.), *Banbury Report 3: A safe cigarette?* Cold Springs Harbor, NY: Cold Springs Harbor Laboratory, 1980.

Boyland, E., & Walker, S. A. Effect of thiocyanate on nitrosation of amines. *Nature*, 1974, *248*, 601–602.

Brockway, B. S. Chemical validation of self-reported smoking rates. *Behavior Therapy*, 1978, *9*, 685–686.

Brockway, B. S., Kleinmann, G., Edleson, J., & Gruenwald, K. Nonaversive procedures and their effect on cigarette smoking: A clinical study group. *Addictive Behaviors*, 1977, *2*, 121–128.

Butts, W. C., Kuehneman, M., & Widdowson, G. M. Automated method for determining serum thiocyanate to distinguish smokers from non-smokers. *Clinical Chemistry*, 1974, *20*, 1344–1348.

Califano, J. A. Remarks to the fourth world conference on smoking and health. In L. M. Ramstrom (Ed.), *The smoking epidemic: A matter of worldwide concern.* Stockholm: Almqvist & Wiksell International, 1980.

Catchings, P. M. *Effects of using a portable smoking recorder on normal smoking topography.* Unpublished doctoral dissertation, University of Minnesota, 1982.

Cohen, S. I., Deane, M., & Goldsmith, J. R. Carbon monoxide and survival from myocardial infarction. *Archives of Environmental Health,* 1969, *19,* 510–517.

Cole, P. Smoking habits and carbon monoxide. In R. M. Greenhalgh (Ed.), *Smoking and arterial disease.* Bath, U.K.: Pitman Medical, 1981.

Comer, A. K., & Creighton, D. E. The effect of experimental conditions on smoking behavior. In R. E. Thornton (Ed.), *Smoking behaviour: Physiological and psychological influences.* London: Churchill Livingstone, 1978.

Creighton, D. E., & Lewis, P. H. The effect of different cigarettes on human smoking patterns. In R. E. Thornton (Ed.), *Smoking behaviour: Physiological and psychological influences.* London: Churchill Livingstone, 1978.

Creighton, D. E., Noble, M. J., & Whewell, R. T. Instruments to measure, record and duplicate human smoking patterns. In R. E. Thornton (Ed.), *Smoking behaviour: Physiological and psychological influences.* London: Churchill Livingstone, 1978.

Delarue, N. C. A study in smoking withdrawal. *Canadian Journal of Public Health: Smoking and Health Supplement,* 1973, *64,* 5–19.

Densen, P. M., Davidow, B., Bass, H. E., & Jones, E. W. A chemical test for smoking exposure. *Archives of Environmental Health,* 1967, *14,* 865–874.

Djuric, D., Raicevic, P., & Konstantinovic, I. Excretion of thiocyanates in urine of smokers. *Archives of Environmental Health,* 1962, *5,* 18–21.

Dogon, I. L., Amdur, B. H., & Bell, K. Observations on the diurnal variation of some inorganic constituents of human parotid saliva in smokers and non-smokers. *Archives of Oral Biology,* 1971, *16,* 95–105.

Dunn, P. J., & Freiesleben, E. R. The effects of nicotine enhanced cigarettes on human smoking parameters and alveolar carbon monoxide levels. In R. E. Thornton (Ed)., *Smoking behaviour: Physiological and psychological influences.* London: Churchill Livingstone, 1978.

Epstein, L. H., Dickson, B. E., Ossip, D. J., Stiller, R., Russell, P. O., & Winter, K. Relationships among measures of smoking topography. *Addictive Behaviors,* 1982, *7,* 307–310.

Evans, R. I., Hansen, W. B., & Mittelmark, M. B. Increasing the validity of self-reports of smoking behavior in children. *Journal of Applied Psychology*, 1977, *62*, 521–523.

Federal Trade Commission (FTC), *Report of tar, nicotine and carbon monoxide of the smoke of 187 varieties of cigarettes*, Washington, DC: Author, 1981.

Feyerabend, C., Higenbottam, T., & Russell, M. A. H. Nicotine concentrations in urine and saliva of smokers and non-smokers. *British Medical Journal*, 1982, *284*, 1002–1004.

Feyerabend, C., Levitt, T., & Russell, M. A. H. A rapid gas-liquid chromatographic estimation of nicotine in biological fluids. *Journal of Pharmacy and Pharmacology*, 1975, *27*, 434–436.

Fischmann, E. J., & Fischmann, A. The thiocyanate content of saliva in normal and hypertensive subjects before and after ingestion of the drug. *Journal of Laboratory and Clinical Medicine*, 1948, *33*, 772–776.

Foy, D. W., Rychtarik, R. G., & Prue, D. M. Assessment of appetitive disorders. In M. Hersen & A. S. Bellack (Eds.), *Behavioral assessment: A practical handbook*. New York: Pergamon Press, 1981.

Frederiksen, L. W., Epstein, L. H., & Kosevsky, B. P. Reliability and controlling effects of three procedures for self-monitoring smoking. *Psychological Record*, 1975, *25*, 255–264.

Frederiksen, L. W., & Martin, J. E. Carbon monoxide and smoking behavior. *Addictive Behaviors*, 1979, *4*, 21–30.

Frederiksen, L. W., Martin, J. E., & Webster, J. S. Assessment of smoking behavior. *Journal of Applied Behavior Analysis*, 1979, *12*, 653–664.

Frederiksen, L. W., Miller, P. M., & Peterson, G. L. Topographical components of smoking behavior. *Addictive Behaviors*, 1977, *2*, 55–61.

Frederiksen, L. W., & Simon, S. J. Modification of smoking topography: A preliminary analysis. *Behavior Therapy*, 1978, *9*, 946–949.

Frederiksen, L. W., & Simon, S. J. Clinical modification of smoking behavior. In R. S. Davidson (Ed.), *Modification of pathological behavior*. New York: Gardner Press, 1979.

Gilbert, D. G. Paradoxical tranquilizing and emotion-reducing effects of nicotine. *Psychological Bulletin*, 1979, *86*, 643–661.

Goldsmith, J. R., & Aronow, W. S. Carbon monoxide and coronary heart disease: A review. *Environmental Research*, 1975, *10*, 236–248.

Goldsmith, J. R., Terzaghi, J., & Hackney, J. O. Evaluation of fluctuating carbon monoxide exposures. *Archives of Environmental Health*, 1963, *7*, 647–663.

Griffiths, R. R., Bigelow, G. E., & Liebson, I. Facilitation of human tobacco self-administration by ethanol: A behavioral analysis. *Journal of the Experimental Analysis of Behavior*, 1976, *25*, 279–292.

Gritz, E. R., Baer-Weiss, V., Benowitz, N. L., Van Vunakis, H., & Jarvik, M. E. Plasma nicotine and cotinine concentrations in habitual smokeless tobacco users. *Clinical Pharmacology and Therapeutics*, 1981, *30*, 201–209.

Guillerm, R., & Radziszewski, E. Analysis of smoking pattern including intake of carbon monoxide and influence of changes in cigarette design. In R. E. Thornton (Ed.), *Smoking behaviour: Physiological and psychological influences*. London: Churchill Livingstone, 1978.

Haines, C. F., Mahajan, D. K., Miljkovic, D., Miljkovic, M., & Vessel, E. S. Radioimmunoassay of plasma nicotine in habituated and naive smokers. *Clinical Pharmacology and Therapeutics*, 1974, *16*, 1083–1089.

Hawkins, L. H. Blood carbon monoxide levels as a function of daily cigarette consumption and physical activity. *British Journal of Industrial Medicine*, 1976, *33*, 123–129.

Hawkins, L. H., Cole, P. V., & Harris, J. R. W. Smoking habits and blood carbon monoxide levels. *Environmental Research*, 1976, *11*, 310–318.

Henningfield, J. E., & Griffiths, R. R. A preparation for the experimental analyses of human cigarette smoking behaviors. *Behavior Research Methods and Instrumentation*, 1979, *11*, 538–544.

Henningfield, J. E., Yingling, J., Griffiths, R. R., & Pickens, R. An inexpensive portable device for measuring puffing behavior by cigarette smokers. *Pharmacology, Biochemistry and Behavior*, 1980, *12*, 811–813.

Hill, P., & Marquardt, H. Plasma and urine changes after smoking different brands of cigarettes. *Clinical Pharmacology and Therapeutics*, 1980, *27*, 652–658.

Horan, J. J., Hackett, G., & Lindberg, S. E. Factors to consider when using expired air carbon monoxide in smoking assessment. *Addictive Behaviors*, 1978, *3*, 25–38.

Hughes, J. R., Frederiksen, L. W., & Frazier, M. A. A carbon monoxide analyzer for measurement of smoking behavior. *Behavior Therapy*, 1978, *9*, 293–296.

Jaffe, J. H., Kanzler, M., & Friedman, L. Studies of switching to low tar and nicotine cigarettes. In G. B. Gori & F. G. Bock (Eds.), *Banbury Report 3: A safe cigarette?* Cold Springs Harbor, NY: Cold Springs Harbor Laboratory, 1980.

Jones, J. G., & Walters, D. H. A study of carboxyhaemoglobin levels on employees at an integrated steel works. *Annals of Occupational Hygiene*, 1962, *5*, 221–230.

Jones, R. H., Ellicott, M. F., Cadigan, J. B., & Gaensler, E. A. The relationship between alveolar and blood carbon monoxide concentrations during breathholding. *Journal of Laboratory and Clinical Medicine*, 1958, *51*, 553–564.

King, A., Scott, R. R., & Prue, D. M. *The reactive effects of assessing reported rates and alveolar carbon monoxide levels on smoking behavior.* Manuscript submitted for publication, 1983.

Kozlowski, L. T., Frecker, R. C., Khouw, V., & Pope, M. A. The misuse of "less hazardous" cigarettes and its detection: Hole blocking of ventilated filters. *American Journal of Public Health*, 1980, 70, 1202–1203.

Kumar, R., Cooke, E. C., Lader, M. H., & Russell, M. A. H. Is tobacco smoking a form of nicotine dependence? In R. E. Thornton (Ed.), *Smoking behaviour: Physiological and psychological influences.* London: Churchill Livingstone, 1978.

Landaw, S. A. The effects of cigarette smoking on total body burden and excretion rates of carbon monoxide. *Journal of Occupational Medicine*, 1973, 15, 231–235.

Langman, M. J. S., Doll, R., & Wilson, J. Plasma and salivary thiocyanate in gastric cancer. *Gut*, 1966, 7, 549.

Langone, J. J., Gjika, H. B., & Van Vunakis, H. Nicotine and its metabolites: Radioimmunoassays for nicotine and cotinine. *Biochemistry*, 1973, 12, 5025–5030.

Langone, J. J., & Van Vunakis, H. Quantitation of cotinine in sera of smokers. *Research Communication in Chemical Pathology and Pharmacology*, 1975, 10, 21–28.

Lichtenstein, E. Modification of smoking behavior: Good designs – ineffective treatment. *Journal of Consulting and Clinical Psychology*, 1971, 28, 163–166.

Lichtenstein, E. The smoking problem: A behavioral perspective. *Journal of Consulting and Clinical Psychology*, 1982, 50, 804–819.

Lichtenstein, E., & Danaher, B. G. Modification of smoking behavior: A critical analysis of theory, research, and practice. In M. Hersen, R. M. Eisler, & P. M. Miller (Eds.), *Progress in behavior modification:* (Vol. 3). New York: Academic Press, 1976.

Lombardo, T., Davis, C. J., & Prue, D. M. When low tar cigarettes yield high tar: Cigarette filter ventilation hole blocking and its detection. *Addictive Behaviors*, 1983, 8, 67–69.

Luce, B. R., & Schweitzer, S. D. The economic cost of smoking-induced illness. In M. E. Jarvik, J. W. Cullen, E. R. Gritz, T. M. Vogt, & L. J. West (Eds.), *Research on smoking behavior* (NIDA Research Monograph 17, DHEW Publication No. (ADM) 78-581). Washington, DC: U.S. Department of Health, Education, and Welfare, 1977.

Mahoney, M. J. Some applied issues in self-monitoring. In J. D. Cone & R. P. Hawkins (Eds.), *Behavioral assessment: New directions in clinical psychology.* New York: Brunner/Mazel, 1977.

Maliszewski, T. F., & Bass, D. E. True and apparent thiocyanate in body fluids of smokers and non-smokers. *Journal of Applied Physiology*, 1955, 8, 289–291.

Matsukura, S., Sakamoto, N., Seino, Y., Tamada, T., Matsuyama, H., & Muranaka, H. Cotinine excretion and daily cigarette smoking in habituated smokers. *Clinical Pharmacology and Therapeutics*, 1979, *25*, 555-561.

McFall, R. M. Effects of self-monitoring on normal smoking behavior. *Journal of Consulting and Clinical Psychology*, 1970, *35*, 135-142.

McFall, R. M. Smoking-cessation research. *Journal of Consulting and Clinical Psychology*, 1978, *46*, 703-712.

McFall, R. M., & Hammen, C. L. Motivation, structure and self-monitoring: Role of non-specific factors in smoking reduction. *Journal of Consulting and Clinical Psychology*, 1971, *37*, 80-86.

Moss, R. A., & Prue, D. M. Research on nicotine regulation. *Behavior Therapy*, 1982, *13*, 31-46.

Moss, R. A., Prue, D. M., Lomax, B. D., & Martin, J. E. Implications of self-monitoring for smoking treatment: Effects on adherence and session attendance. *Addictive Behaviors*, 1982, *7*, 17-28.

Ohlin, P., Lundh, B., & Westling, H. Carbon monoxide levels and reported cessation of smoking. *Psychopharmacology*, 1976, *49*, 263-265.

Ossip-Klein, D. J., Martin, J. E., Lomax, B. D., Prue, D. M., & Davis, C. J. Assessment of smoking topography generalization across laboratory, clinical and naturalistic settings. *Addictive Behaviors*, 1983, *8*, 11-17.

Paxton, R., & Bernacca, G. Urinary nicotine concentration as a function of time since last cigarette: Implications for detecting faking in smoking clinics. *Behavior Therapy*, 1979, *10*, 523-528.

Pettigrew, A. R., & Fell, G. S. Simplified colorimetric determinations of thiocyanate in biological fluids, and its application to investigation of toxic amblyopias. *Clinical Chemistry*, 1972, *18*, 966-1000.

Prue, D. M., Krapfl, J. E., & Martin, J. E. Brand fading: The effects of gradual changes to low tar and nicotine cigarettes on smoking rate, carbon monoxide, and thiocyanate levels. *Behavior Therapy*, 1981, *12*, 400-416.

Prue, D. M., Martin, J. E., & Hume, A. S. A critical evaluation of thiocyanate as a biochemical index of smoking exposure. *Behavior Therapy*, 1980, *11*, 368-379.

Prue, D. M., Scott, R. R., Martin, J. E., & Lomax, B. D. Carbon monoxide levels and rates of consumption after changing to low tar and nicotine cigarettes. *Behaviour Research and Therapy*, 1983, *21*, 201-207.

Rawbone, R. G. The value of non-invasive methods for evaluating exposure to tobacco smoke. In R. M. Greenhalgh (Ed.), *Smoking and arterial disease*. Bath, U.K.: Pitman Medical, 1981.

Rawbone, R. G., Murphy, K., Tate, M. E., & Kane, S. J. The analysis of smoking parameters: Inhalation and absorption of tobacco smoke in studies of human smoking behavior. In R. E. Thornton (Ed.),

Smoking behaviour: Physiological and psychological influences. London: Churchill Livingstone, 1978.

Ray, R. L., Emurian, H. H., Brady, J. V., & Nellis, M. J. On the regularity of smoking. *Addictive Behaviors*, 1982, 7, 261–270.

Rickert, W. S., & Robinson, J. C. Estimating the hazards of less hazardous cigarettes. II. Study of cigarette yields of nicotine, carbon monoxide, and hydrogen cyanide in relation to levels of cotinine, carboxyhaemoglobin and thiocyanate in smokers. *Journal of Toxicology and Environmental Health*, 1981, 7, 391–403.

Ringold, A., Goldsmith, J. R., Helwig, H. C., Finn, R., & Schuette, F. Estimating recent carbon monoxide exposures: A rapid method. *Archives of Environmental Health*, 1962, 5, 308–318.

Robinson, J. C., & Forbes, W. F. The role of carbon monoxide in cigarette smoking. *Environmental Health*, 1975, 30, 425–433.

Ross, W. S. Poison gases in your cigarettes: Carbon monoxide. *Reader's Digest*, 1976, 109, 114–118.

Russell, M. A. H. Confirmation of abstinence from smoking. *British Medical Journal*, 1976, 1, 755–756.

Russell, M. A. H. Self-regulation of nicotine intake by smokers. In K. Batteg (Ed.), *Behavioral effect of nicotine*. Basel, Switzerland: Karger, 1978.

Russell, M. A. H. Tobacco dependence: Is nicotine rewarding or aversive? In N. A. Krasnegor (Ed.), *Cigarette smoking as a dependence process*. (DHEW Publication No. (ADM) 79-800). Washington, DC: U.S. Department of Health, Education, and Welfare, 1979.

Russell, M. A. H., Cole, P. V., & Brown, E. Absorption by non-smokers of carbon monoxide from room air polluted by tobacco smoke. *Lancet*, 1973, 7803, 576–579.

Schachter, S. Pharmacological and psychological determinants of smoking. *Annals of Internal Medicine*, 1978, 88, 104–114.

Schulz, W., & Seehofer, F. Smoking behaviour in Germany — The analysis of cigarette butts (KIPA). In R. E. Thornton (Ed.), *Smoking behaviour: Physiological and psychological influences*. London: Churchill Livingstone, 1978.

Shipley, R. H., Rosen, T. J., & Williams, C. Measurement of smoking: Survey and some recommendations. *Addictive Behaviors*, 1982, 7, 299–305.

Sillett, R. W., Wilson, M. B., Malcolm, R. E., & Ball, K. P. Deception among smokers. *British Medical Journal*, 1978, 1, 1185–1186.

Stewart, R. D. The effects of carbon monoxide on humans. *Annual Review of Pharmacology*, 1975, 15, 409–423.

Stewart, R. D., Baretta, E. D., Platte, L. R., Stewart, E. B., Kalbfleisch, J. H., Van Yserloo, B., & Rimm, A. A. Carboxyhemoglobin levels in American blood donors. *Journal of the American Medical Association*, 1974, 229, 1187–1195.

Tiggelbeck, D. Vapor phase modification: An underutilized technology.

In E. L. Wynder, D. Hoffman, & G. B. Gori (Eds.), *Proceedings of the third world conference on smoking and health.* (DHEW Publication No. (NIH) 76-1221). Washington, DC: U.S. Department of Health, Education, and Welfare, 1976.

Turner, J. A. M. Confirmation of abstinence from smoking. *British Medical Journal,* 1976, *2,* 755.

U.S. Public Health Service. *Smoking and health: Report of the advisory committee to the surgeon general of the Public Health Service* (PHS Publication No. 1103). Washington, DC: U.S. Department of Health, Education, and Welfare, 1964.

U.S. Public Health Service. *The health consequences of smoking: A Public Health Service review* (DHEW Publication No. 1696). Washington, DC: U.S. Department of Health, Education, and Welfare, 1967.

U.S. Public Health Service. *The health consequences of smoking. A reference edition* (HEW Publication No. (ADC) 78-8357). Washington, DC: U.S. Department of Health, Education, and Welfare, 1976.

U.S. Public Health Service. *The health consequences of smoking, 1975* (DHEW Publication No. (ADC) 77-8704). Washington, DC: U.S. Department of Health, Education, and Welfare, 1977.

U.S. Public Health Service. *Smoking and health: A report of the surgeon general* (DHEW Publication No. (PHS) 79-50066). Washington, DC: U.S. Department of Health, Education, and Welfare, 1979.

U.S. Public Health Service. *The health consequences of smoking for women: A report of the surgeon general* (DHHS Publication No. (PHS) 326-003). Washington, DC: U.S. Department of Health and Human Services, 1980.

U.S. Public Health Service. *The health consequences of smoking: The changing cigarette* (DHHS Publication No. (PHS) 81-50156). Washington, DC: U.S. Department of Health and Human Services, 1981.

Vesey, C. J. Thiocyanate and cigarette consumption. In R. M. Greenhalgh (Ed.), *Smoking and arterial disease.* Bath, U.K.: Pitman Medical, 1981.

Vesey, C. J., Saloojee, Y., Cole, P. V., & Russell, M. A. H. Blood carboxyhaemoglobin, plasma thiocyanate, and cigarette consumption: Implications for epidemiological studies in smokers. *British Medical Journal,* 1982, *284,* 1516–1519.

Vogt, T. M. Smoking behavioral factors as predictors of risk. In M. E. Jarvik, J. W. Cullen, E. R. Gritz, T. M. Vogt, & L. J. West (Eds.), *Research on smoking behavior* (NIDA Research Monograph No. 17, DHEW Publication No. (ADM) 78-581). Washington, DC: U.S. Department of Health, Education, and Welfare, 1977.

Vogt, T. M., Hulley, S. B., Selvin, S., & Widdowson, G. Expired air carbon monoxide and serum thiocyanate as objective measures of cigarette exposure. *American Journal of Public Health,* 1977, *67,* 545–549.

Wald, N., & Howard, S. Smoking, carbon monoxide and arterial disease. *Annals of Occupational Hygiene*, 1975, *18*, 1–14.

Wald, N., Idle, M., & Bailey, A. Carboxyhaemoglobin levels and inhaling habits in cigarette smokers. *Thorax*, 1978, *33*, 201–206.

Zeidenberg, P., Jaffe, J. H., Kanzler, M., Levitt, M. D., Langone, J. J., & Van Vunakis, H. Nicotine: Cotinine levels in blood during cessation of smoking. *Comprehensive Psychiatry*, 1977, *18*, 93–101.

4

Behavioral Assessment of Alcohol Abuse: Objective Measurement of the Drinking Response

William M. Hay and
William Frankenstein

Introduction

Alcohol abuse exacts a devastating toll from all aspects of our lives. Of the approximately 90 million Americans who consume alcohol, 9 million would be considered to be alcoholics (U.S. Department of Health, Education, and Welfare, 1978). Demographic studies of American drinking practices indicate that between 5% and 10% of adult males and 2% to 5% of adult females meet the criteria for alcoholism, with an additional 30% to 40% of young males evidencing problems related to their alcohol consumption (Cahalan, 1970). Even more dramatic is the fact that between 20% and 35% of medical and surgical inpatients meet fairly rigid diagnostic criteria for alcoholism (Moore, 1971; Schuckit, 1979). The higher incidence of alcoholism and alcohol-related sequelae in medical and surgical patients as compared to the general population documents the adverse impact of alcohol abuse on health (Korsten & Lieber, 1979). Liver cirrhosis, a traditional marker for alcoholism since more than 90% of cirrhosis cases are considered to be alcohol related, ranked as the seventh most common cause of death in the United States in 1978 (National Institute on Alcohol Abuse and Alcoholism, 1980). In addition to direct physical consequences, alcohol abuse has a negative impact on the abuser's level of functioning in other essential life areas including social relationships, marital and family stability, and work performance (McCance & McCance, 1969; P. M. Miller, 1981).

The emergence of the behavioral model for the assessment of alcohol abuse has produced important advances in the objective assessment of this clinically significant problem. This chapter provides the reader with an overview of the behavioral model for the assessment of alcohol abuse. Our major objective, however, is to review objective methods for measuring actual levels of alcohol intoxication in males and females.

Behavioral Assessment Model: The SORC Framework

The behavioral assessment model of alcohol abuse is initially "broad spectrum," encompassing a search for problems across a wide array of life areas (e.g., financial, sexual functioning, marital and family stability, employment, etc.). The pioneering work of the Sobells and their colleagues (e.g., M. B. Sobell & Sobell, 1978) and the recent Rand Report (Polich, Armor & Braiker, 1981) have underscored the importance of a "broad spectrum" approach to assessment. These investigators have demonstrated that drinking behavior should not be viewed in isolation, but rather in the context of its interaction with behavioral patterns in multiple life areas. The more traditional "narrow" focus on drinking behavior alone may not accurately reflect patient status following treatment (Nathan & Hay, 1980). Specifically, drinking disposition may change substantially (e.g., the client may be abstinent or maintaining a nonproblem drinking status) while serious problems in other life areas continue or perhaps intensify.

The results of a case study (Hay, 1982) illustrate the importance of a broad spectrum assessment strategy. In this case, both members of a married couple, Mr. and Mrs. L, were experiencing significant problems related to their heavy consumption of alcohol. The couple also had severe marital problems. In this instance, the results of a broad spectrum behavioral assessment indicated that each partner's excessive alcohol consumption intensified existing marital communication difficulties.

The specific assessment procedures employed in this case are presented in Table 4.1. The Michigan Alcoholism Screening Test (Selzer, 1971) was employed as a general diagnostic screening instrument for alcohol abuse. Questions drawn from the three semistructured interview formats helped to establish global alcohol use patterns, to identify problems in other life areas related to alcohol abuse (e.g., occupational, family, financial, legal, sexual, etc.), and to assess factors precipitating (antecedents) or maintaining (consequences) excessive alcohol consumption. Client self-reports provided more specific information on actual drinking behavior: Clients recorded the type of beverage consumed and the time span of consumption for each drink [1 drink = 1 standard ethanol con-

Table 4.1. Broad Spectrum Assessment Procedures

Alcohol assessment	Marital assessment procedures

1. Self-report instruments
  a. Michigan Alcohol Screening Test (Selzer, 1971)
	1. Self-report instruments
	  a. Locke-Wallace Marital Adjustment Scale (Locke & Wallace, 1959)

b. The Drinking Profile[a] (Marlatt, 1976)
  c. Pretreatment Data Sheet[a] (M. B. Sobell & Sobell, 1978)
  d. Behavioral and Alcohol Interview[a] (Hay, Hay, & Nelson, 1977)
	b. Intake Interview (Jacobson & Margolin, 1979)
	  c. Area of Change Questionnaire (Weiss & Margolin, 1977)
	  d. Marital Status Inventory (Weiss & Cerreto, 1975)

2. Client self-monitoring: daily drinking behavior	2. Client self-monitoring: marital happiness
3. Collateral reports of drinking	3. Videotape role play
4. Medical examination plus clearance	

5. Objective measures of drinking behavior
  a. Breath alcohol analysis
  b. Liver function screening	

[a]Items b, c, and d were administered in a semistructured interview

tent unit (SEC) = 0.5 oz or 15 ml of ethanol], the situation where consumption occurred, and concurrent thoughts/emotions. In addition, self-reports from collateral sources (e.g., spouse, relative, etc.) were used to validate client self-reports of drinking behavior. The two objective methods of measuring intoxication and alcohol abuse were employed at various points throughout assessment, treatment, and follow-up to provide concurrent validation of reported drinking status. Based on assessment data, treatment was conducted in two phases: Phase 1 focused on the modification of drinking behavior, while Phase 2 focused on marital issues with an emphasis on effective problem solving and communication. For this couple, drinking status and improvements in marital satisfaction were independent; dramatic reductions in individual alcohol consumption patterns did not result in substantial improvements in overall marital happiness. For the interested reader, P. M. Miller (1981), Marlatt (1979), and M. B. Sobell and Sobell (1978) provide excellent reviews of the self-report instruments presented in Table 4.1. Likewise, Stuart (1980) has provided a detailed and critical appraisal of the marital assessment procedures as well as a discussion of alternative assessment instruments.

Once the full range of problem areas related to alcohol abuse has been established, the focus of assessment shifts to a thorough SORC, or functional, analysis of the interaction of alcohol abuse and each identified problem area as well as a detailed assessment of the actual drinking response. The SORC assessment framework identifies three classes of variables critical in the determination of the factors precipitating or maintaining alcohol abuse: S, situational antecedents; O, organismic variables; C, consequences maintaining drinking (Goldfried & Sprafkin, 1976); and R, response. The fourth variable class, response, refers to the actual parameters of the drinking response (e.g., quantity of alcohol consumed, frequency of drinking, topography of the drinking response, intoxication level achieved, etc.).

Situational antecedents are cues or "triggers" that set the occasion for excessive alcohol consumption. Antecedents to alcohol abuse are typically assessed in five broad areas: situational, social/interpersonal, cognitive, emotional, and physiological/pain (P. M. Miller, 1976). Situational antecedents to excessive drinking must be determined for each individual. Situational antecedents include the time of day, location, and type of social gathering or meeting. In the case mentioned above, Mr. & Mrs. L (Hay, 1982), the situational antecedents identified included the train ride home, sales meetings, bridge with heavy-drinking friends, social gatherings, and being home alone at 5:00 P.M.

Excessive drinking also occurs in response to social/interpersonal antecedents. These antecedents may include an inability to say no to social pressure from friends to continue drinking, adverse reactions to personal criticism, or a reaction to an argument with a spouse, or the antecedent may arise as a way to cope with circumstances requiring an assertive response (Hamilton & Maisto, 1979; P. M. Miller & Eisler, 1977). Alcohol consumption is also affected by what has been termed the *social modeling effect*. Studies of alcohol consumption in naturalistic drinking environments have reported that drinkers in groups consume more alcohol than drinkers who are alone or with one other person (Cutler & Storm, 1975; Rosenbluth, Nathan, & Lawson, 1978). Sex differences in the impact of this social modeling effect have been noted. Males consume more alcohol at a faster rate when they are with other males rather than with females. Conversely, women consume more when they are with opposite-sex drinkers rather than other females (Rosenbluth et al., 1978). A study completed at the Alcohol Behavior Research Laboratory (ABRL) by Caudill and Lipscomb (1980) investigated the social modeling effect on the consumption patterns of three chronic alcoholics in two laboratory analogue drinking situations. The three alcoholics participated in a taste-rating task in which they were requested to rate the taste of three types of wine. The taste-rating task was followed by ad-lib drinking in a simulated bar situation. The alcoholics interacted with heavy- and light-drinking models (i.e., confederates) in both situations. The social modeling context exerted a significant influence on the drinking behavior of these alcohol abusers, with the alcoholics' consumption rates generally increasing or decreasing to follow the model's drinking pattern.

While situational and social influences on drinking behavior have been established empirically, the role of emotional factors as antecedents is unclear. The tension reduction hypothesis, which stresses the role of anxiety as a cue for excessive consumption, played a central role in early behavioral formulations of alcoholism. However, empirical substantiation of the tension reduction model has not been forthcoming (Higgins & Marlatt, 1975; Nathan & O'Brien, 1971). The causative status of other mood or emotional states such as depression and anger to excessive drinking also remains unclear (P. M. Miller, 1981). For the individual client, however, the careful assessment of emotion/mood factors that may precede or arise concomitantly with an abusive drinking episode is important. For example, a client's verbal report of "depression" may translate to a low frequency of reinforcing events, which may set the stage for excessive alcohol consumption at home. One component of the treatment intervention strategy, therefore, might be to increase the number of reinforcing activities that the drinker has access to outside of the home. A detailed assessment of emotional factors is also crucial for relapse prevention, since negative emotional states such as anger and frustration have been linked to alcoholic relapse (Marlatt & Gordon, 1980).

The causative influence of cognitive antecedents on excessive drinking also remains unclear. The impact of expectancy, however, has been well documented. The results of a series of well-controlled studies have indicated that the overall effects of alcohol are dependent on our individual expectancies concerning alcohol's purported effects on behavior as well as the actual pharmacological properties of the drug (e.g., Berg, Loberg, Skutle, & Ohman, 1981; Marlatt & Rohsenow, 1980). Typically these studies have utilized a balanced placebo methodology that includes four conditions: told alcohol/given alcohol, told alcohol/given placebo, told placebo/given alcohol, and told placebo/given placebo. Individuals told that they would be receiving alcohol, whether or not they actually consumed alcohol, showed less anxiety on both self-reports of anxiety and physiological measurements of heart rate (Wilson & Abrams, 1977), behaved in a more aggressive manner (Lang, Goeckner, Adesso, & Marlatt, 1975), and evidenced enhanced sexual arousal (Wilson & Lawson, 1976). In addition to the impact of expectancies, beliefs, or attitudes on drinking behavior, clinical assessment procedures usually reveal thought patterns that may precede or occur concomitantly with excessive drinking. For example, in the case mentioned earlier, Mrs. L's thoughts prior to and during drinking were usually self-depreciating or angry (e.g., "I work all day . . . make dinner, and he [spouse] doesn't care enough about me to call . . . ").

Physiological/pain antecedents are common "triggers" for excessive alcohol consumption. In many cases individuals with severe anxiety or pain symptoms "self-medicate" with alcohol. As we discuss later in this chapter, women frequently report the use of alcohol as a method of ameliorating menstrual symptoms (Belfer & Shader, 1976). In a recent case study (Hay, Frankenstein, & Nathan, 1981), a female alcoholic linked her resumption of heavy alcohol consumption after a prolonged period of abstinence to hormonal changes following a hysterectomy. Clinically, alcoholics frequently report that the onset of physiological discomfort related to withdrawal symptoms is a strong antecedent to renewed drinking.

Organismic variables are factors that function within the individual and are related to excessive alcohol consumption. These factors include, among others, purported genetic loadings and hereditary predispositions to develop alcoholic behavior (e.g., Goodwin, Schulsinger, & Hermansen, 1973), the interaction of initial tolerance to alcohol on subsequent drinking behavior (Lipscomb & Nathan, 1980), changes in cognitive ability during and following alcohol ingestion (Goldman, Williams, Dickey, & Weintraub, 1983), liver function status and general health, and hormonal factors related to phase in menstrual cycle (Jones & Jones, 1976a).

Within the behavioral model, excessive alcohol consumption and other problem behaviors are maintained by their consequences. Consequences are characterized as positive (maintains or increases the frequency of the response that immediately precedes it) or negative (suppresses or decreases in frequency the response that immediately precedes it), and as immediate or delayed. In the case of alcohol abuse, one typically finds that immediate positive consequences (e.g., positive feelings associated with being intoxicated, more assertive, decreased tension) function to maintain excessive consumption, while delayed negative consequences (e.g., deterioration in health, financial problems, spouse and family disruptions) exert little direct impact on the abusive response pattern. For Mr. L, in the case noted earlier (Hay, 1982), immediate consequences maintaining his drinking included avoiding offending his heavy-drinking boss by drinking with him, the expectancy that he was a more persuasive seller when intoxicated, a self-reported decrease in tension, and the enjoyment of drinking and socializing. Delayed negative consequences included a gradual decrease in productivity at work, an increased frequency of fights with his spouse, and health problems.

Measurement of the dimensions of the drinking response (e.g., frequency, magnitude, duration, pervasiveness, type of beverage, topography of the actual consummatory behavior) has received a significant amount of empirical investigation. Laboratory analogue measures including operant systems, taste-rating tasks, and simulated-drinking environments have been utilized to study drinking behaviors as well as the impact of various antecedent and consequent factors on consummatory behavior. Findings from initial laboratory-based studies using operant paradigms established the significant reinforcement value of alcohol for male alcoholics and revealed that many of these alcoholics followed a biphasic pattern of drinking (a weeklong spree followed by a much more lengthy period of maintenance-level consumption) (Nathan & Briddell, 1977). Female alcoholics studied in the same experimental context, however, showed a maintenance pattern of drinking that resembled the drinking profiles of heavy male drinkers who were not alcoholics (Tracey, Karlin, & Nathan, 1976). The taste test procedure requires subjects to sample a variety of beverages and to rate the beverages along taste dimensions. The objective of the procedure, however, is surreptitiously to measure actual alcohol consumption. The taste test methodology has been employed to study the effects of expectancy factors (Marlatt, Demming, & Reid, 1973), stress (Higgins & Marlatt, 1973), and modeling influences (Caudill & Lipscomb, 1980) on alcohol consumption.

Typical settings for simulated-drinking environments have included laboratory bars, living rooms, and party situations. This approach allows for the direct observation of drinking patterns, detailed analysis of the drinking response (e.g., number of drinks ordered, type of drinks ordered, number of sips, sip magnitude, intersip interval), and assessment of the amount of alcohol consumed as a function of various social contexts. Using this analogue assessment method, the Sobells and their colleagues were able to distinguish alcoholic and social drinking consumption patterns. The alcoholic's drinking profile, in contrast to the social drinker's profile, included a larger sip size (with slower sips but more consumed per sip), a much faster ingestion rate, and a preference for straight drinks versus the mixed drink preference of social drinking counterparts (Schaefer, Sobell, & Mills, 1971).

These analogue procedures, however, were developed to provide measurements of consummatory behavior in research contexts. Consequently, although analogue procedures may ultimately prove to be valuable adjuncts to clinical assessment, they have not been well integrated into clinical behavioral assessment process.

Self-report data including client self-monitoring of drinking behavior, responses to structured interview queries, and the validation of client reports of drinking by significant others (i.e., relatives, spouses, friends) remain the most commonly used assessment procedures to establish the dimensions of the drinking response. In general the literature supports the utility of self-report data in the assessment of drinking behavior (Marlatt, 1979). The test–retest reliability of self-report data generally has been high (L. C. Sobell & Sobell, 1975; L. C. Sobell, Maisto, Sobell, & Cooper, 1979). In addition, the level of agreement between alcoholics and collateral reports of drinking behavior has also been found to be accurate enough for most assessment purposes, especially when more global indices of consumption are employed (e.g., drinking disposition) (Maisto, Sobell, & Sobell, 1979). The weakest correlations, however, are found between measures of concurrent validity—for example, between self-reports of drinking and more objective measures of intoxication (e.g., breath alcohol analysis, liver function screening) (Marlatt, 1979). In addition, the discrepancies between self-reported drinking and the results of objective measures of alcohol abuse are most pronounced when the drinker is asked to provide self-report data after drinking (L. C. Sobell et al., 1979). The reliable and accurate measurement of intoxication, however, is the sine qua non of the broad spectrum behavioral assessment model. Based on these data, the use of objective measurement systems to ascertain actual levels of intoxication and extent of alcohol abuse is a critical component of a broad spectrum assessment approach. The remainder of this chapter, therefore, is divided into four sections that focus on physiologic measures of drinking behavior. The first section describes alcohol intoxication and related factors that affect the ultimate level of intoxication achieved and the resultant impairment—factors that are crucial to an accurate assessment of alcohol. The next section reviews the objective measurement of blood alcohol level (BAL). The third section examines the current status of liver function tests as objective screening tests for alcohol abuse. The fourth section considers the impact of variations in hormonal levels on the accurate assessment of intoxication in female drinkers.

Physiologic Measures of Drinking Behavior

Assessment of Alcohol Intoxication

Alcohol intoxication refers to the constellation of behavioral, neurological, and psychological sequelae of alcohol ingestion. For the individual who has not developed a high degree of tolerance to alcohol (i.e., the social drinker), the degree of intoxication and observed impairment correspond roughly to measured blood alcohol level (BAL: milligrams of alcohol per 100 ml of blood, or mg%).

The average-sized individual metabolizes between 7 and 10 g of alcohol per hour, which corresponds to approximately 1 oz of 90-proof spirits or 12 oz of beer (Becker, 1979). As the amount of alcohol ingested exceeds metabolic capacity, the level of alcohol in the blood increases. After one or two drinks, the nontolerant individual will note only minor changes in coordination, behavior, or mood.

As blood alcohol level increases above 100 mg%, (approximately five drinks in 1 hr for a 160-pound man), however, most social drinkers will begin to demonstrate significant signs of intoxication including dysarthria (slurring and thickening of speech), ataxia (unsteady gait), mood lability, impaired judgment, and memory and attention deficits. At dosage levels exceeding 200 mg%, these symptoms intensify. Marked dysarthria and ataxia are accompanied by extensive impairment of judgment, psychomotor skills, attention and memory, and mood control. At dosage levels exceeding 300 mg of alcohol per 100 ml of blood, the anesthetic action of alcohol predominates, with the possibility of coma, respiratory failure, and death increasing dramatically at blood alcohol levels between 400 and 700 mg of alcohol per 100 ml of blood.

In most states in the United States the legal limit of alcohol intoxication for the operation of an automobile ranges between 80 and 100 mg of alcohol per 100 ml of blood. These alcohol concentrations, however, do not necessarily correlate with actual level of impairment observed, especially for heavy alcohol consumers who have developed a high degree of acquired tolerance for alcohol. Acquired tolerance refers to the fact that after repeated consumption of alcohol (as well as a number of other drugs), a larger dose of alcohol must be consumed to experience the level of effects previously experienced with a smaller dose (Kalant, LeBlanc, & Gibbons, 1971; Lipscomb & Nathan, 1980). Laboratory studies of the metabolism of ^{14}C-labeled ethanol have indicated that, although chronic ingestion of alcohol results in an increased rate of metabolism in both alcoholic and nonalcoholic subjects, overall rate of metabolism does not differentiate the two groups (Mello, 1972; Mendelson, 1964; Mendelson, Stein, & Mello, 1965). The development of tolerance to alcohol, therefore, may be related to adaptive processes in the central nervous system rather than to alterations in the rate of metabolism of ethanol (Mendelson, 1968).

One important area of research related to the assessment of alcohol intoxication has been the examination of the differential abilities of alcoholics and nonalcoholics to estimate their own blood alcohol levels. Alcoholics have been found consistently to be less accurate than nonalcoholics in estimating their blood alcohol levels, both prior to and following training in internal cue discrimination (Huber, Karlin, & Nathan, 1976; Lansky, Nathan, & Lawson, 1978; Shapiro, Nathan, Hay, & Lipscomb, 1981). One hypothesis offered by Lipscomb and Nathan (1980) suggests that the development of tolerance by alcoholics may account for the observed differences between alcoholics and nonalcoholics in the ability to utilize internal cues of intoxication. To test this hypothesis Lipscomb and Nathan (1980) grouped nonalcoholic subjects according to differences in body sway when intoxicated and when sober. Recognized as an extremely sensitive measure of intoxication, body sway has also been put forward recently as a reliable measure of tolerance to ethanol (Moskowitz, Daily, & Henderson, 1974). In the research by Lipscomb and Nathan, low-tolerant subjects evidenced marked differences in body sway between sober and intoxicated states; high-tolerant individuals showed little difference in body sway between sober and intoxicated states. Following internal cue training, low-tolerant subjects were found to be significantly more accurate than high-tolerant subjects in their blood alcohol estimates, suggesting that increased tolerance may interfere with the utilization of internal intoxication cues.

The differential impact of tolerance on BAL discrimination accuracy has important implications for the behavioral assessment process. Since alcoholics and other individuals who exhibit significant tolerance to alcohol have difficulty associating internal cues of intoxication to BAL, they may lack stable internal reference points from which to make accurate BAL estimates. The resultant low or variable BAL estimation accuracy would call into question the reliability and validity of the self-reports of intoxication supplied by the alcohol abuser. We return to this issue in the next section when we discuss the use of automated breath alcohol analysis as an objective measure of alcohol consumption.

The final level of intoxication and resultant impairment is, therefore, a function not only of blood alcohol level but also of characteristics of the drinker, as well as pattern of consumption, general health and liver functioning, and the presence of other drugs in the blood. Among the characteristics of the drinker that can influence the observed level of impairment are the drinker's age, weight, prior experience with alcohol, learned expectations concerning the effects of alcohol (Wilson, Abrams, & Lipscomb, 1980), and degree of acquired tolerance for alcohol (Lipscomb &

Nathan, 1980). All of these factors, therefore, should be considered in the comprehensive behavioral assessment of alcohol abuse.

Measurement of Blood Alcohol Level (BAL)

As we have noted, the assessment of alcohol intoxication is complicated when tolerance for alcohol develops. Specifically, individuals who have developed a high degree of acquired tolerance may not evidence the impairments or exhibit the overt signs of intoxication observed in individuals who drink socially (Mello, 1972). Indeed, tolerant individuals have been found to perform quite well at blood alcohol levels between 200 and 300 mg% in tasks requiring psychomotor skills and good mentation (Mello & Mendelson, 1978; Talland, Mendelson, & Ryback, 1964). Anecdotally, there have been a number of occasions when we have interviewed "Bowery alcoholics" (residing at the Men's Shelter in New York City) who denied drinking and evidenced no overt signs of intoxication but who later registered "heroic" blood alcohol concentrations. Ironically, the impact of tolerance effects on the assessment process is, in all probability, greatest for individuals with extensive drinking histories, who may have developed physical dependence on alcohol (M. B. Sobell & Sobell, 1979). For these individuals, therefore, the accurate assessment of blood alcohol levels is all the more critical.

Given this potential lack of correspondence in the tolerant drinker between actual levels of intoxication and perceived impairment, estimates of intoxication based solely on observations of the drinker's behavior or appearance may not be valid. Research has demonstrated that even trained clinical observers (M. B. Sobell, Sobell, & Vander Speck, 1979) and law enforcement officers (Langenbucher, Nathan, Hay, & Wainer, 1981) are prone to frequent errors when estimating the actual levels of intoxication of alcohol abusers. In the M. B. Sobell et al. (1979) study, observers' ratings, alcoholics' self-reports of ingestion, and breath test assessments of alcohol intoxication were compared across three separate client populations. Trained clinical raters made more false-negative rating errors (i.e., failed to identify more individuals with positive blood alcohol levels) than false-positive rating errors (i.e., identified a sober individual as intoxicated). The rate of false-positive errors ranged between 0% and 16.7%, while the false-negative error rate ranged between 22.2% and 55%. The false-negative error rate increased dramatically, however, when intoxicated subjects provided invalid self-reports of drinking status (typically underreporting consumption), with only 50 % to 67 % of these subjects accurately identified by clinical raters. In a study conducted at the Alcohol Behavior Research Laboratory at Rutgers–The State University, the differential abilities of 31 police officers to estimate the blood alcohol levels of other persons were determined (Langenbucher et al., 1981). Estimation accuracy was found to be extremely variable, with most officers no more accurate than a similarly tested group of social drinkers (Nathan & Langenbucher, 1981). The problem of attaining an accurate assessment of alcohol intoxication is further complicated by the fact that the self-reports of drinking behavior by alcohol abusers have been found to be less valid on days when alcohol has been consumed (M. B. Sobell et al., 1979).

The assessment of blood alcohol level (BAL) circumvents measurement problems related to acquired tolerance level, observer error, and invalid self-report by providing a direct and objective measure of the level of alcohol intoxication. BAL is typically expressed in terms of milligrams (mg) of ethyl alcohol per 100 milliliters (ml) of blood volume, or as a percentage of blood volume. Estimates of the concentration of alcohol in the blood can be obtained directly from blood samples or by breath alcohol analyses. Alcohol partitions between the blood and the alveolar air in a ratio of approximately 2,000 : 1; therefore, breath alcohol content can be used to provide estimates of blood alcohol levels (Mason and Dubowski, 1976). Breath alcohol analysis correlates highly ($r = 0.95$) with direct blood alcohol screening (Dubowski, 1975).

At the Alcohol Behavior Research Laboratory breath alcohol analysis is accomplished by a Gas Chromatographic Intoximeter, Mark IV (manufactured by Intoximeters, Inc.). Intoximeters are extremely accurate and expensive pieces of equipment, typically ranging in price between $3,000 and $6,000, but are also essential clinical and research tools. The breath alcohol analysis process is initiated by having the subject blow into a breath inlet line. A carrier gas is used to transport the breath sample through a column where the alcohol is separated from other interfering substances. The alcohol then passes into a flame ionization detector, which burns the alcohol and thus creates an electrical signal. This signal is magnified via an amplifier and transduced to provide a digital readout of BAL. L. C. Sobell and Sobell (1975) have described the Mobat, an inexpensive, portable, and self-contained screening instrument for assessing blood alcohol concentration (Sober-Meter Kit SM-6, manufactured by Luckey Laboratories, Inc.). The Mobat has a maximum accuracy between 80 mg% and 150 mg% (BALs below 80 mg% will tend to be overestimated, while BALs over 150 mg% will tend to be underestimated) and is accurate enough for most clinical applications (M. B. Sobell & Sobell, 1979).

Breath alcohol analysis has been incorporated as an outcome measure into a number of studies to establish pretreatment baseline data on consumption, to monitor drinking during treatment and follow-up, and to provide a validity check of the alcohol abusers' reports of daily drinking behavior (P. M. Miller, 1975; P. M. Miller, Hersen, Eisler, & Watts, 1974; W. R. Miller, Taylor, & West, 1980; Pomerleau, Pertschuk, Adkins, & Brady, 1978). In a number of these studies, in-field breath tests were used on a "probe-day" basis to determine drinking status on a periodic basis during treatment and follow-up. Some investigators, however, have reported strategic difficulties in obtaining in-field assessments and have noted extensive client resistance to the *in vivo* breath alcohol analysis procedures (e.g., W. R. Miller et al., 1980). In spite of these difficulties, however, the results of studies such as that of M. B. Sobell et al. (1979) make it clear that breath alcohol analysis should be a mandatory assessment component of alcohol treatment programs as well as treatment evaluation studies.

As part of a broad spectrum assessment approach, breath alcohol analysis can serve a variety of functions. In our own clinical research work, clients undergo breath alcohol assessments prior to each treatment session. Treatment sessions are postponed for clients who register a positive BAL. In one study, Mobat assessments were administered to three female alcoholics on a random basis throughout an 18-month follow-up by their spouses (Hay, Frankenstein, & Nathan, 1981a). This assessment procedure provided a measure of treatment effectiveness (i.e., covert modeling) as well as a spot check on the validity of the daily self-reports of consumption. Mobat assessments can also be used to supply immediate feedback to clients regarding their level of intoxication. A survey conducted by Sobell, Vander Speck, and Saltman (1980) indicated that a number of participants in two countermeasures programs for drivers convicted for driving while intoxicated found the data supplied by self-administered Mobat assessments useful in making driving decisions.

Breath alcohol assessments have also been utilized to determine the differential abilities of alcoholics and nonalcoholics to estimate blood alcohol levels (Huber et al., 1976; Lipscomb & Nathan, 1980; Shapiro et al., 1980; Silverstein, Nathan, & Taylor, 1974). As standard procedure in all these studies, alcoholic and nonalcoholic clients consumed a fixed amount of alcohol and were asked to estimate their BALs at periodic intervals. Concurrent breath alcohol analysis provided objective measures of the accuracy of BAL estimates as well as a method for evaluating the effectiveness of training procedures. BAL discrimination procedures have already been incorporated into a number of treatment programs offering a controlled non-problem-drinking goal as an alternative to total abstinence (Lovibond & Caddy, 1970; Miller et al., 1980; M. B. Sobell & Sobell, 1973). Breath alcohol assessments, especially via portable systems, can be utilized as a training aid to supply clients with immediate feedback on the accuracy of BAL estimates and as an ongoing assessment device to help clients maintain BAL discrimination accuracy posttreatment.

Liver Function Tests

A number of biochemical indicators have been suggested as screening tests for alcoholism or excessive alcohol consumption. These tests include the measurement of serum γ-glutamyl transpeptidase and serum glutamic-oxalacetic transaminase (SGOT) levels, and determination of plasma α-amino-n-butyric acid to leucine acid ratios (the ratio of the plasma levels of these two amino acids has been found to increase in alcoholism but appears to remain normal in nonalcoholic liver disease) (Fink & Rosalki, 1978; Shaw, Stimmel, & Lieber, 1976; Shaw, Lue, & Lieber, 1978). Liver function tests have been incorporated into treatment studies to screen for excessive alcohol consumption and as outcome measures to assess progress during treatment and to monitor consumption/relapse patterns during follow-up (e.g., Miller et al., 1980; Pomerleau & Adkins, 1980). To date, the measurement of serum γ-glutamyl transpeptidase (GGTP) has received the most research attention. GGTP, a membrane-bound glycoprotein, is associated with the formation of the blood–brain barrier (Reyes, 1978). GGTP enzyme originates from the liver, where enzyme-inducing drugs including alcohol alter its activity level. The mechanism by which alcohol consumption produces an increase in GGTP activity, however, remains controversial (i.e., a direct alcohol induction or the result of poor nutritional status — reduced carbohydrate intake) (Shaw, 1979).

Higher than normal serum GGTP activity levels have been observed in alcoholics (both hospitalized inpatients and outpatients), problem drinkers, and heavy drinkers (Fink & Rosalki, 1978; Reyes, Miller, Taylor, & Spalding, 1978; Rosalki & Rau, 1972). Chronic alcohol abuse typically results in serum GGTP levels that average five times the upper limit of normal (Fink & Rosalki, 1978); although in some instances enzyme activity in chronic alcoholics has been observed as high as 20 times, and values up to 60 times the normal limit have been recorded (Fink & Rosalki, 1978; Reyes & Miller, 1980). When excessive consumption is discontinued, GGTP levels usually begin to return to the normal range within a few days, with the majority of patients evidencing a 50% reduction within 2 weeks and near-normal values within 5 weeks (Rosalki, 1977). The prolonged elevation of GGTP levels can result from underlying liver damage (e.g., cirrhosis); or in some cases, with the advanced hospitalized alcoholic, nutritional impairment (e.g., vitamin and mineral deficiency) may interfere with enzyme induction (Rosalki & Rau, 1972). Freer and Statland (1977) have reported significant elevations in serum GGTP activity in healthy individuals, who do not report excessive alcohol consumption, after the ingestion of approximately 2 oz of 100-proof alcohol. Generally, however, the "rule of thumb" appears to be that a minimum of 3 weeks of daily heavy alcohol consumption is prerequisite to the observation of pathological serum levels (Rosalki, 1977).

A positive correlation has been found between some GGTP activity and daily alcohol consumption, with a higher proportion of raised serum GGTP levels in individuals designated as heavy drinkers, as compared to individuals designated as moderate or social drinkers (Rollason, Pincherle, & Robinson, 1972). Pomerlean and Atkins (1979) reported a significant correlation between γ-glutamyl transpeptidase levels and the self-reported drinking levels of 20 of 32 outpatients participating in a treatment outcome study. Specifically, the greater the consumption reported, the higher the enzyme activity level observed. Further, six of seven subjects with abnormally elevated GGTP activity prior to treatment, but who reported substantial decreases in ethanol consumption between pretreatment and the end of treatment, also experienced decreases in enzyme activity at the end of treatment.

Shaw, Worner, Borysow, Schmitz, and Lieber (1979) compared the relative efficacy of mean red blood cell volume (MCV), GGTP, and α-amino-*n*-butyric acid (AANB) as outcome measures to determine the success of alcoholism treatment and to detect relapses. MCV, GGTP, and AANB values were measured in two alcoholic populations undergoing treatment at a Veterans Administration (VA) medical center and a private facility (Raleigh Hills Hospital). Assessments were made during withdrawal, subsequent abstinence, and follow-up as well as following any relapse. MCV values did not change significantly for either group of patients during the withdrawal period. GGTP and AANB values, however, evidenced steady and significant decreases throughout the withdrawal from alcohol, treatment, and follow-up (e.g., mean GGTP values for VA patients were: 124.1 IU at admission, 90.2 at discharge, and 71.1 during follow-up.) GGTP and AANB values, but not MCV assessments, were also sensitive to the resumption of heavy drinking: 26 of the 33 VA patients who resumed heavy drinking evidenced elevated GGTP and AANB levels. With this population of alcohol abusers the combination of GGTP and AANB measurements resulted in the detection of 80 % of the patients who relapsed, with a 10 % rate of false-positive identifications (Shaw, 1979; Shaw et al., 1979). The results of this study, therefore, support the efficacy of using GGTP and plasma AANB levels to assess withdrawal from alcohol, continued abstinence, and any resumption of heavy alcohol intake.

The availability of objective biochemical indicators that are readily accessible, inexpensive, and automated (see Rosalki & Tarlow, 1974) to validate self-reported alcohol consumption is an intriguing prospect. Recent research, however, has called into question the nature of the relationship of serum GGTP levels and alcohol intake (Reyes et al., 1978; Reyes & Miller, 1980; Robinson, Monk, & Bailey, 1979). Reyes and Miller (1980) assessed GGTP levels in a sample of male and female problem drinkers. Serum samples were taken at pretreatment assessment and at 3 and 12 months following treatment. Pretreatment GGTP activity readings were elevated into the alcoholic range (Rilder, Zurfluh, & Jegge, 1977). However, Reyes and Miller did not find a "robust" relationship between self-reported alcohol consumption and GGTP activity (the correlation between GGTP levels and weekly consumption was $r = 0.25$, significant at the $r = 0.05$ level). A higher correlation between GGTP levels and alcohol intake has been reported for females (Reyes et al., 1978). Research conducted by Robinson et al. (1979) produced minimal and nonsignificant correlations between serum

GGTP levels and reported alcohol consumption (correlation coefficients ranged from $r = 0.069$ to $r = 0.139$), suggesting that no particular level of alcohol consumption leads to liver impairment.

Reyes and Miller (1980) speculated that the absence of a strong correlation between GGTP activity and alcohol consumption in their own study may have been related to greater consumption by their subjects as compared to subjects in other studies (e.g., Rollason et al., 1972). Higher consumption coupled with the fact that GGTP levels can be elevated by the amount of recent alcohol consumption, by certain common medications (e.g., birth control pills, barbiturates), and by diseases (e.g., cancer, alcohol- or non-alcohol-related liver disease) may have also contributed to their discrepant findings. These authors also stress the importance of obtaining estimates of alcohol intake that are accurate enough to predict GGTP. The importance of obtaining collateral reports of drinking behavior is also clear, since Reyes and Miller found that GGTP was more highly correlated with alcohol consumption estimates supplied by significant others (correlation coefficient $r = 0.36$, significant at the 0.05 level) than with actual client self-reports.

A number of methodological problems make it difficult to interpret the results of studies comparing GGTP activity and drinking behavior. In a number of the studies reviewed here, diagnostic criteria (e.g., *Diagnostic and Statistical Manual*, 3rd ed., American Psychiatric Association, 1980) were absent. Further, in some cases, estimates of alcohol intake and subsequent assignment to consumption category (e.g., light, moderate, heavy, etc.) were made solely on the basis of clinical interviews (Rosalki, 1977), with minimal retrospective assessment "windows" (e.g., 1 week in Robinson et al. [1979]). The use of a variety of drinking cutoff levels to define consumption categories also makes it difficult to compare the populations included in various studies. Another important problem relevant to assessment is the fact that the absolute values of GGTP can vary significantly across client populations. Shaw et al. (1979) also compared changes in the absolute values of GGTP levels for the two populations of alcoholics studied, one group from a Veterans Administration hospital and the other group from a private treatment facility. At all assessment points — admission, discharge, and follow-up — the absolute GGTP levels of VA Hospital patients were two to three times higher than the levels observed for patients from the private facility. These differences may have reflected a higher incidence of liver damage in the VA population, resulting in persistently elevated levels of GGTP (Shaw et al., 1979). Since the frequency of false-positive tests (elevated levels interpreted as a relapse) among patients in remission was greatest for GGTP, clinicians should be cautious in this interpretation of absolute GGTP values. An alternative strategy that would seemingly diminish false positives would be within-subject comparisons of GGTP levels rather than comparisons of absolute values relative to the upper limit of normal.

In summary, the relationship between observed GGTP serum activity levels and particular levels of alcohol consumption remains equivocal. The value of GGTP assessment as a screening aid for the detection of established liver disease has been documented (Rosalki & Rau, 1972; Rutenburg, Goldbarg, & Pineda, 1963). However, the use of GGTP or related liver function indicators to assess precisely alcohol consumption or to verify client reports of daily drinking should be approached with caution. The nature of each drinking population must be considered in relation to the current status of alcohol- and non-alcohol-related physical disability; within-subject changes in GGTP levels rather than, or in addition to, absolute values should be assessed, and multiple GGTP assays should be performed during pretreatment assessment, treatment, and follow-up. One advantage of the broad spectrum approach to behavioral assessment described in this chapter is that it allows the clinician/researcher to interpret the results of each assessment instrument in relation to a variety of other assessment procedures. It is clear that changes in GGTP serum activity levels and other biochemical indices must be considered in the context of the entire assessment process. Further research should be directed at establishing the relationship between GGTP and consumption as well as the evaluation of other biochemical indicators (e.g., AANB), isoenzyme profiles (Reyes & Miller, 1980), and discriminant analysis of blood chemistry tests to aid in the identification of alcoholics (Ryback, Eckardt, & Pautter, 1980).

Assessment of Female Drinkers

Issues related to the assessment of female drinkers have become increasingly important given the recent emphasis on the identification and treatment of female drinkers. The results of a series of studies by Jones and Jones (1976a, 1976b) have identified a number of specialized areas that are relevant to the accurate assessment of alcohol use by the female drinker. Research has suggested a relationship between variations in women's responsiveness to alcohol as a function of hormonal level and stage in the menstrual cycle. It has been demonstrated consistently that women attain higher blood alcohol levels (Dubowski, 1976; Jones & Jones, 1976a, 1976b), absorb alcohol faster, and reach peak blood alcohol level sooner than men following an equivalent dose of alcohol (Jones & Jones, 1976b). In addition, women tested during the premenstrual phase (the day preceding the beginning of the next menstrual cycle, approximately Day 28) of the menstrual cycle have been found to attain significantly higher peak blood alcohol levels (BAL), with faster absorption rates, than women tested during either the menstrual phase (first day of menstrual flow) or intermenstrual phase (the middle of the menstrual cycle, approximately Day 14) (Jones & Jones, 1976a; Mello, 1980). Tests of three women on each day through a complete menstrual cycle indicated great variability in BAL following a constant alcohol dose; peak BALs occurred during premenstruum and about the time of ovulation (Jones & Jones, 1976a).

The finding that female drinkers may exhibit a higher level of responsiveness than male drinkers, to a particular dose of alcohol, carries a number of important implications for the assessment process. Objective assessment of intoxication by breath or blood analysis may register higher BALs than would be expected based on the drinker's self-reported alcohol consumption. This discrepancy between data sources may not indicate the lack of a valid self-report but rather reflect the female's enhanced responsiveness to a specific alcohol dose. In addition, the assessment of the absolute amount of alcohol consumed by the female drinker may not be an accurate index of drinking problem severity. To assess the degree of alcohol abuse the gender of the drinker should be considered as well as frequency and quantity measurements of alcohol consumption. Likewise, given the purported relationship between variations in women's responsiveness to alcohol as a function of hormonal level and stage in menstrual cycle, the assessment phase in the menstrual cycle is essential to allow for the accurate interpretation of self-monitored consumption data as well as the results of breath alcohol analysis.

In a subsequent study, Jones and Jones (1976b) also investigated the possible relationship of levels of the sex steroids, estrogen and progesterone, to variability and increased BAL in women.

Ethanol metabolism was examined in 11 women taking oral contraceptives and 11 female controls. The two groups of women achieved almost identical peak blood alcohol levels after a standard dose of alcohol (0.66 ml/kg). Women in the oral contraceptive group, however, metabolized ethanol significantly slower and as a consequence remained intoxicated longer than control women as assessed by three measures of ethanol metabolism: total time of intoxication, elimination rate of ethanol — mg/kg/hr, and disappearance rate of ethanol — %/hr. No significant differences were found between the two groups in the rate of ethanol metabolism as a function of the phase in the menstrual cycle (Jones & Jones, 1976b). Zeenir and Rugg (1980) also compared alcohol metabolism rates in 20 women, 10 taking oral contraceptives and 10 not taking oral contraceptives. Both groups were tested on Day 1 of the menstrual cycle, menstrual flow (low concentrations of estrogen and progesterone), and Day 24 of the cycle (high concentrations of estrogen and progesterone), prior to the onset of the next menstrual period. Ten of the subjects were taking oral contraceptives, which artificially elevated estrogen and progesterone concentrations on Day 24 with respect to levels on Day 1 and levels of the subjects not taking oral contraceptives. Peak blood alcohol concentration was found to be higher and alcohol clearance rates faster on Day 1 (hormonal levels were low) than on Day 24. In addition, subjects not taking oral contraceptives ("no pill") reached higher blood alcohol concentrations than subjects taking oral contraceptives on Day 24 but not on Day 1. These results suggest that high levels of female sex steroids appear to lower peak blood alcohol concentration and slow down ethanol metabolism.

A study conducted at the Alcohol Behavior Research Laboratory (ABRL) sought to replicate and expand the research of Jones and Jones by comparing 10 women using oral birth control methods to 10 women experiencing regular menstrual cycles (Hay, Nathan, & Heermans, 1981b). All subjects were social drinkers. Each woman was scheduled for a drinking session during each of the three phases of a full menstrual cycle: premenstrual phase, Days 23–30; menstrual flow, Days 1–5; and midcycle, Days 12–16. Alcohol was administered six times each session with subjects receiving approximately 7 oz of alcohol. Eight breath alcohol assessments were made; prior to each objective BAL assessment each subject was asked to estimate her level of intoxication so that the accuracy of BAL estimations could be assessed. Behavioral tolerance to alcohol was also measured throughout each session to assess the possible interrelationship of tolerance, stage in menstrual cycle, and BAL estimation ability.

Contrary to the earlier reports by Jones and Jones (1976a), no differences were found in the total time of intoxication (time to reach zero BAL) from onset of drinking between women on oral contraceptives and women not taking oral contraceptives. In addition, no differences were found between these two groups of women on the latency from onset of drinking to peak BAL or elapsed time from peak BAL to zero BAL. Preliminary analyses also indicated no differences between these groups on two other measures of ethanol metabolism reported as significant by Jones and Jones: elimination rate (milligrams of alcohol per kilogram of body weight per hour—mg/kg/hr) and disappearance rate of ethanol per hour (%/hr).

Again contrary to previous results (i.e., Jones & Jones, 1976a —females tested during the premenstrual phase developed significantly higher peak BAL and absorbed alcohol more rapidly than females tested during menstruum or intermenstrual phases), analysis of peak BAL attained and latency to peak BAL did not indicate a significant difference between premenstrual and other phases in the menstrual cycle. Consistent with earlier reports (Jones & Jones, 1976a), no differences in peak BAL were found between the two groups of women. Also consistent with earlier findings, no significant differences between these two groups were found in rate of alcohol metabolism as a function of phase in menstrual cycle.

Stage of menstrual cycle was not found to have a significant effect on the ability of women to make accurate blood alcohol level estimations. In addition, no significant differences in blood alcohol level discrimination ability was found for women using oral contraceptives compared to women with regular menstrual cycles not using oral contraceptive methods. A trend in the results that approached significance did suggest, however, that with increasing BAL, women with regular cycles who were not on oral birth control pills were prone to larger errors in their estimates of intoxication. In contrast to the results of earlier work at the ABRL with male social drinkers (Lipscomb & Nathan, 1980), initial tolerance levels did not appear to have a differential impact on BAL estimation accuracy in this sample of female drinkers. When phase in cycle was considered, however, initial tolerance levels did exert significant effects on BAL discrimination ability. High-tolerant female social drinkers exhibited a great deal of variability in BAL estimation ability compared to low-tolerant females. In addition, high-tolerant women were less accurate than women with low tolerance to the effects of alcohol at the premenstrual phase and especially at midcycle. This pattern reversed itself during the remainder of the cycle, with high-tolerant subjects more accurate than low-tolerant subjects.

These contradictory findings make it difficult to draw firm conclusions on the relationship between variations in a woman's responsiveness to alcohol that are related to hormonal level and menstrual phase and her ability to estimate BAL accurately. The results of one clinical survey of a sample of alcoholic women, however, indicated that 67 % of menstruating women and 46 % of nonmenstruating women related their drinking to their menstrual cycle, with drinking typically beginning or increasing in the premenstruum (Belfer & Shader, 1976). In addition, a number of investigators have speculated that differential sensitivity to alcohol across the menstrual cycle may increase the likelihood of an extended drinking episode among female problem drinkers (e.g., Mendelson & Mello, 1979). Whether variations in responsiveness to alcohol are ultimately linked to variations in hormone (i.e., estrogen) levels or to a psychological process such as expectancy (or an interaction of both processes), the assessment of female social drinkers and alcoholics should routinely consider all factors that might influence hormone level. These factors would include the type and dosage of oral contraceptive, hysterectomy, the prescription of estrogen supplements during menopause, and pregnancy (P. M. Miller, 1981). Given the accumulating evidence of alcohol's teratological impact on fetal development (e.g., Abel, 1981), we have incorporated pregnancy screening tests as a perfunctory part of our assessment procedures.

Conclusion

We wish to emphasize our endorsement of broad spectrum behavioral approaches to assessment that incorporate self-report; self-monitoring; direct or indirect observation of the drinking response; independent corroboration of drinking status and related effects from spouses, friends, and employment and police records; and the assessment of assertiveness and related marital, emotional, and cognitive skills as is indicated. However, each of these strategies, although integral to multidimensional assessment of alcohol abuse, has limitations to its utility.

The retrospective self-reports, obtained through structured and unstructured interviews and alcohol use instruments, are of use as they allow the assessor freedom to explore in great detail consumption patterns and provide information on the range of medical, social, legal, and employment-related consequences related to alcohol abuse. The disadvantages of retrospective self-reports, however, are in the reliance upon information that is subject to misrepresentation due to an alcoholic's inability or disinclination to recall information accurately. In addition, recall of behavior that occurred during periods of intoxication is even more subject to interpretive bias and reconstruction deficiencies on the part of the drinker.

Obviously, the utility of direct and indirect observational methods is for the most part confined to research applications. Although important normative information has been gained on the antecedents and consequences of drinking, these methods are of very limited clinical utility. These methods have led to a burgeoning research interest in expectancy effects and alcohol use; however, little has been done to date to integrate basic and applied research on expectancies. Consequently, at present no clear guidelines exist for the assessment of expectancies related to alcohol use (Wilson, 1981). One promising area for the development of clinical applications of expectancies concerns their relationship to the prediction of relapse after alcoholism treatment.

The self-monitoring of drinking behavior, which forms the cornerstone of the functional analysis, provides the greatest amount of detailed information on drinking patterns, consumption rates, and concomitant thoughts and emotions related to alcohol use. Self-monitoring yields the most representative sample of a client's drinking behavior. Clients have access to the entire universe of instances of their own drinking, much of which occurs in private or out of view of independent sources of verification. Self-monitored data, however, are subject to the same reliability and accuracy problems inherent in all self-reports. In addition, these methodological problems are, in all probability, intensified at higher blood alcohol concentrations.

Independent corroboration of drinking by spouses, friends, and/or official documents (e.g., police, employment, hospitalization, court records) is intended to supply the assessor with validity checks of patient reported data; however, even trained observers such as bartenders and policemen have trouble detecting intoxicated persons with accuracy. It may be unreasonable, therefore, to expect that untrained observers such as spouses will be accurate in their reports of how much alcohol their partners have consumed. Consequently, independent observers' reports may be as subjective in their appraisals of drinking behavior as client reports can be. Unfortunately, data can be reliable but not accurate in that spouses can corroborate misrepresentations. The spouse of a client we saw in our own research and treatment program confirmed fabricated drinking data that were based upon spouse-administered Mobats and spouse monitoring of drinking behavior (Hay, Frankenstein, & Nathan, 1981a). The Sobells have found that police and other official documentation can be woefully incomplete (L. C. Sobell & Sobell, 1980).

The difficulties that are encountered with traditional behavioral assessment methods underscore the advantages of incorporating objective physiologic assessment techniques into broad spectrum strategies. A caveat, however, is in order. Although physiologically based assessment procedures may not be subject to the vagaries of self-report data, we have considered a variety of other factors that can have a direct impact on the reliability, accuracy, and validity of physiologic measures of drinking behavior. It is anticipated that the reliability and validity of traditional behavioral assessment methods will be enhanced by the incorporation of physiologic assessment methods. These methods can be used to broaden the data base for evaluating patient status before, during, and after treatment; and with future development they will help provide critically important information for evaluating the degree and extent of patients' alcohol abuse and their resultant levels of impairment.

References

Abel, E. L. Behavioral teratology of alcohol. *Psychological Bulletin*, 1981, *90*, 564–581.

American Psychiatric Association. *Diagnostic and statistical manual of mental disorders* (3rd ed.). Washington, DC: Author, 1980.

Becker, C. E. Pharmacotherapy in the treatment of alcoholism. In J. H. Mendelson & N. K. Mello (Eds.), *The diagnosis and treatment of alcoholism*. New York: McGraw-Hill, 1979.

Belfer, M. L., & Shader, R. I. Premenstrual factors as determinants of alcoholism in women. In M. Greenblatt & M. A. Schuckit, (Eds.), *Alcoholism problems in women and children*. New York: Grune & Stratton, 1976.

Berg, G., Loberg, J. C., Skutle, A., & Ohman, A. Instructed versus pharmacological effects of alcohol in alcoholics and social drinkers. *Behavior Research and Therapy*, 1981, *19*, 55–66.

Cahalan, D. *Problem drinkers*. San Francisco: Jossey-Bass, 1970.

Caudill, B. D., & Lipscomb, T. R. Modeling influences on alcoholics' rates of alcohol consumption. *Journal of Applied Behavior Analysis*, 1980, *13*, 355–365.

Cutler, R. E., & Storm, T. Observational study of alcohol consumption in natural settings: The Vancouver beer parlour. *Journal of Studies on Alcohol*, 1975, *36*, 1173–1183.

Dubowski, K. M. Studies in breath alcohol analysis: Biological factors. *Zeitschrift für Rechtsmedizin*, 1975, *76*, 93–117.

Dubowski, K. M. Human pharmacokinetics of ethanol. I. Peak blood concentrations and elimination in male and female subjects. *Alcohol Technical Reports*, 1976, *5*, 55–72.

Fink, R., & Rosalki, S. B. Clinical biochemistry of alcoholism. *Clinics in Endocrinology and Metabolism*, 1978, *7*, 297–319.

Freer, E. D., & Statland, B. E. The effects of ethanol (0.75 g/kg body weight) in the activity of selected enzymes in sera of healthy young adults. 1. Intermediate-term effects. *Clinical Chemistry*, 1977, *23*, 830–834.

Goldfried, M. R., & Sprafkin, N. J. Behavioral personality assessment. In J. T. Spence, R. C. Carson, & J. W. Thibaut (Eds.), *Behavioral approaches to therapy*. Morristown, NJ: General Learning Press, 1976.

Goldman, M. S., Williams, D. L., Dickey, J. H., & Weintraub, A. L. Alcoholics' differential psychological recovery over three months as a function of age. *Journal of Consulting and Clinical Psychology*, 1983, *51*, 370–378.

Goodwin, D. W., Schulsinger, F., & Hermansen, L. Alcohol problems in adoptees raised apart from alcoholic biological parents. *Archives of General Psychiatry*, 1973, *28*, 238–243.

Hamilton, F., & Maisto, S. A. Assertive behavior and perceived discomfort of alcoholics in assertion-required situations. *Journal of Consulting and Clinical Psychology*, 1979, *47*, 196–197.

Hay, W. M. The behavioral assessment and treatment of an alcoholic marriage: The case of Mr. and Mrs. L. In W. M. Hay & P. E. Nathan (Eds.), *Clinical case studies in the behavioral treatment of alcoholism*. New York: Plenum Press, 1982.

Hay, W. M., Frankenstein, W., & Nathan, P. E. *The treatment of three problem drinkers using covert modeling procedures*. Paper presented at the Association for Advancement of Behavior Therapy, Toronto, Canada, 1981. (a)

Hay, W. M., Nathan, P. E., & Heermans, H. W. *Menstrual cycle, tolerance and blood alcohol level discrimination ability*. Unpublished manuscript, 1981. (b)

Hay, W. M., Hay, L. R., & Nelson, R. O. The adaptation of covert modeling procedures to the treatment of chronic alcoholism and obsessive compulsive behavior: Two case reports. *Behavior Therapy*, 1977, *8*, 70–76.

Higgins, R. L., & Marlatt, G. A. The effects of anxiety arousal upon the consumption of alcohol by alcoholics and social drinkers. *Journal of Consulting and Clinical Psychology*, 1973, *41*, 426–433.

Higgins, R. L., & Marlatt, G. A. Fear of interpersonal evaluation as a determinant of alcohol consumption in male social drinkers. *Journal of Abnormal Psychology*, 1975, *84*, 644–651.

Huber, H., Karlin, R., & Nathan, P. E. Blood alcohol level discrimination by nonalcoholics: The role of internal and external cues. *Journal of Studies on Alcohol*, 1976, *37*, 27–39.

Jacobson, N. S., & Margolin, G. *Marital therapy: Strategies based on social learning and behavior exchange principles*. New York: Brunner/Mazel, 1979.

Jones, B. M., & Jones, M. K. Alcohol effects in women during the menstrual cycle. *Annals of the New York Academy of Science*, 1976, *273*, 567–587. (a)

Jones, B. M., & Jones, M. K. Women and alcohol: Intoxication, metabolism and the menstrual cycle. In M. Greenblatt and M. A. Schuckit (Eds.), *Alcoholism problems in women and children*. New York: Grune & Stratton, 1976. (b)

Kalant, H., LeBlanc, A. E., & Gibbons, R. J. Tolerance to and dependence on some non-opiate psychotropic drugs. *Pharmacology Review*, 1971, *23*, 135.

Korsten, M. A., & Lieber, C. S. Hepatic and gastrointestinal complications of alcoholism. In J. H. Mendelson & N. K. Mello (Eds.), *The diagnosis and treatment of alcoholism*. New York: McGraw-Hill, 1979.

Lang, A. R., Goeckner, D. J., Adesso, V. J., & Marlatt, G. A. Effects of alcohol on aggression in male social drinkers. *Journal of Abnormal Psychology*, 1975, *84*, 508–518.

Langenbucher, J., Nathan, P. E., Hay, W. M., & Wainer, D. *Police officers' determination of inebriety*. Unpublished manuscript, 1981.

Lansky, D., Nathan, P. E., & Lawson, D. M. Blood alcohol level discrimination by alcoholics: The role of internal and external cues. *Journal of Consulting and Clinical Psychology*, 1978, *46*, 953–960.

Lipscomb, T. R., & Nathan, P. E. Effects of family history of alcoholism, drinking pattern and tolerance on blood ethanol level discrimination. *Archives of General Psychiatry*, 1980, *37*, 571–576.

Locke, H. J., & Wallace, K. M. Short marital adjustment and prediction tests: Their reliability and validity. *Marriage and Family Living*, 1959, *21*, 251–255.

Lovibond, S. H., & Caddy, G. Discriminated aversive control in the moderation of alcoholics' drinking behavior. *Behavior Therapy*, 1970, *1*, 437–444.

Maisto, S. A., Sobell, L. C., & Sobell, M. B. Comparison of alcoholics'

self-reports of drinking behavior with reports of collateral inform-
ants. *Journal of Consulting and Clinical Psychology*, 1979, 47, 106–
112.

Marlatt, G. A. The Drinking Profile: A questionnaire for the behavioral
assessment of alcoholism. In E. J. Mash & L. G. Terdal (Eds.), *Behavior therapy assessment: Diagnosis, design and evaluation*. New
York: Springer, 1976.

Marlatt, G. A. The Drinking History: Problems of validity and reliability.
In *Evaluation of the alcoholic: Implications for research, theory, and
treatment* (NIAAA Research Monograph No. 5). Washington, DC:
National Institute on Alcohol Abuse and Alcoholism, 1979.

Marlatt, G. A., Demming, B., & Reid, J. B. Loss of control drinking in
alcoholics: An experimental analogue. *Journal of Abnormal Psychology*, 1973, 81, 233–241.

Marlatt, G. A., & Gordon, J. R. Determinants of relapse: Implications
for the maintenance of behavior change. In P. O. Davidson & S. M.
Davidson (Eds.), *Behavioral medicine: Changing health lifestyles*.
New York: Brunner/Mazel, 1980.

Marlatt, G. A., & Rohsenow, D. J. Cognitive processes in alcohol use:
Expectancy and balanced placebo design. In N. K. Mello (Ed.), *Ad-
vances in substance abuse: Behavioral and biological research*.
Greenwich, CN: JAI Press, 1980.

Mason, M. F., & Dubowski, K. M. Breath alcohol analysis: Uses, methods
and some forensic problems — Review and opinion. *Journal of Forensic Science*, 1976, 21, 9–42.

McCance, C., & McCance, P. F. Alcoholism in northeast Scotland: Its
treatment and outcome. *British Journal of Psychiatry*, 1969, 115,
189–198.

Mello, N. K. Behavioral studies of alcoholism. In B. Kissin & H. Beg-
leiter (Eds.), *The biology of alcoholism* (Vol. 2: *Physiology and Behavior*). New York: Plenum Press, 1972.

Mello, N. K. Some behavioral and biological aspects of alcohol problems
in women. In O. J. Kalant (Ed.), *Alcohol and drug problems in
women*. New York: Plenum Press, 1980.

Mello, N. K., & Mendelson, J. H. Alcohol and human behavior. In L. L.
Iversen, S. D. Iversem, and S. H. Snyder (Eds.), *Handbook of psychopharmacology* (Vol. 12, Sec. 3: *Chemistry, pharmacology and
human use*). New York: Plenum Press, 1978.

Mendelson, J. H. Experimentally induced chronic intoxication and withdrawal in alcoholics. *Quarterly Journal of Studies on Alcohol*, 1964,
2, 1–126.

Mendelson, J. H. Ethanol 1 — C^{14} metabolism in alcoholics and nonalcoholics. *Science*, 1968, 159, 139.

Mendelson, J. H., & Mello, N. K. (Eds.). *The diagnosis and treatment
of alcoholism*. New York: McGraw-Hill, 1979.

Mendelson, J. H., Stein, S., & Mello, N. K. Effects of experimentally in-

duced intoxication on metabolism of ethanol 1-C¹⁴ in alcohol sub-
    jects. *Metabolism*, 1965, *14*, 1255.
Miller, P. M. A behavioral intervention program for chronic public drunk-
    enness offenders. *Archives of General Psychiatry*, 1975, *32*, 915–918.
Miller, P. M. *Behavioral treatment of alcoholism*. New York: Pergamon
    Press, 1976.
Miller, P. M. Assessment of alcohol abuse. In D. H. Barlow (Ed.), *Be-
    havioral assessment of adult disorders*. New York: Guilford Press,
    1981.
Miller, P. M., & Eisler, R. M. Assertive behavior of alcoholics: A descrip-
    tive analysis. *Behavior Therapy*, 1977, *8*, 146–149.
Miller, P. M., & Foy, D. W. Substance abuse. In S. M. Turner, K. S.
    Calhoun, & H. E. Adams (Eds.), *Handbook of clinical behavior
    therapy*. New York: Wiley, 1981.
Miller, P. M., Hersen, M., Eisler, R. M., & Watts, J. G. Contingent re-
    inforcement of lowered blood alcohol levels in an outpatient chronic
    alcoholic. *Behaviour Research and Therapy*, 1974, *12*, 67–72.
Miller, W. R., Taylor, C. A., & West, J. C. Focused versus broad-spec-
    trum behavior therapy for problem drinkers. *Journal of Consulting
    and Clinical Psychology*, 1980, *48*, 590–601.
Moore, R. A. The prevalence of alcoholism in a community general hos-
    pital. *American Journal of Psychiatry*, 1971, *128*, 130–131.
Moskowitz, H., Daily, H., & Henderson, R. Acute tolerance to behavioral
    impairment of alcohol in moderate and heavy drinkers. In *Report
    to the Highway Research Institute National Highway Traffic Safety
    Administration*. Washington, DC: Department of Transportation,
    1974.
Nathan, P. E., & Briddell, D. W. Behavioral assessment and treatment
    of alcoholism. In B. Kissin & H. Begleiter (Eds.), *Treatment and
    rehabilitation of the chronic alcoholic*. New York: Plenum Press,
    1977.
Nathan, P. E., & Hay, W. M. Invited comments on the Rand Report on
    patterns of alcoholism over four years – with apologies to Huxley and
    Shaw. *Journal of Studies on Alcohol*, 1980, *41*, 777–779.
Nathan, P. E., & Langenbucher, J. *Behavioral determination of inebri-
    ety*. Unpublished manuscript, 1981.
Nathan, P. E., & O'Brien, J. S. An experimental analysis of the behavior
    of alcoholics and nonalcoholics during prolonged experimental drink-
    ing. *Behavior Therapy*, 1971, *2*, 419–430.
National Institute on Alcohol Abuse and Alcoholism. *The public health
    approach to problems associated with alcohol consumption: A brief-
    ing*. Washington, DC: Author, 1980.
Polich, J. M., Armor, D. J., & Braiker, H. B. *The course of alcoholism:
    Four years after treatment*. New York: Wiley, 1981.
Pomerlean, O., & Atkins, D. Evaluating behavioral and traditional treat-
    ment for problem drinkers. In L. C. Sobell, M. B. Sobell, & E. Ward

(Eds.), *Evaluating alcohol and drug abuse treatment effectiveness: Recent advances.* New York: Pergamon Press, 1979.

Pomerleau, O., Pertschuk, M., Adkins, D., & Brady, J. P. A comparison of behavioral and traditional treatment for middle income problem drinkers. *Journal of Behavioral Medicine*, 1978, *1*, 187–200.

Reyes, E. Rat brain alpha-glutamyl transpeptidase: Effects of alcohol. *Research Communications Chemical Pathology and Pharmacology*, 1978, *21*, 145–148.

Reyes, E., & Miller, W. R. Serum gamma-glutamyl transpeptidase as a diagnostic aid in problem drinkers. *Addictive Behaviors*, 1980, *5*, 59–65.

Reyes, E., Miller, W. R., Taylor, C. A., & Spalding, C. T. The activity of gamma-glutamyl transpeptidase in the serum of problem drinkers. *Proceedings of the Western Pharmacological Society*, 1978, *21*, 289–297.

Rilder, H. P., Zurfluh, H., & Jegge, S. The activity of gamma-glutamyl transferase in serum of multiple sclerosis and other neurological diseases. *Clinica Chimica Acta*, 1977, *79*, 211–217.

Robinson, D., Monk, C., & Bailey, A. The relationship between serum gamma-glutamyl transpeptidase level and reported alcohol consumption in healthy men. *Journal of Studies on Alcohol*, 1979, *40*, 896–901.

Rollason, J. G., Pincherle, G., & Robinson, D. Serum gamma-glutamyl transpeptidase in relation to alcohol consumption. *Clinica Chimica Acta*, 1972, *39*, 75–80.

Rosalki, S. B. Enzyme tests for alcoholism. *Revue d'Epidemillogie et de Santé Publique*, 1977, *25*, 147–158.

Rosalki, S. B., & Rau, D. Serum gamma-glutamyl transpeptidase activity in alcoholism. *Clinica Chimica Acta*, 1972, *39*, 41–47.

Rosalki, S. B., & Tarlow, D. Optimized determination of alpha-glutamyl transferase by reaction rate analysis. *Clinical Chemistry*, 1974, *20*, 1121–1124.

Rosenbluth, J., Nathan, P. E., & Lawson, D. M. Environmental influences on drinking by college students in a college pub: Behavioral observations in the natural setting. *Addictive Behaviors*, 1978, *3(2)*, 117–122.

Rutenburg, A. M., Goldbarg, J. A., & Pineda, E. P. Serum gamma-glutamyl transpeptidase activity in hepatobiliary pancreatic disease. *Gastroenterology*, 1963, *45*, 43–48.

Ryback, R. S., Eckardt, M. J., & Pautter, C. P. Biochemical and hematological correlates of alcoholism. *Research Communications in Chemical Pathology and Pharmacology*, 1980, *27*, 533–550.

Schaefer, H. H., Sobell, M. B., & Mills, K. C. Some sobering data on the use of self-confrontation with alcoholics. *Behavior Therapy*, 1971, *2*, 28–39.

Schuckit, M. A. Treatment of alcoholism in office and outpatient settings.

In J. H. Mendelson & N. K. Mello (Eds.), *The diagnosis and treatment of alcoholism.* New York: McGraw-Hill, 1979.

Selzer, M. L. The Michigan Alcoholism Screening Test: The quest for a new diagnostic instrument. *American Journal of Psychiatry,* 1971, *127,* 1653-1658.

Shapiro, A. P., Nathan, P. E., Hay, W. M., & Lipscomb, T. R. Influence of dosage level on blood alcohol level discrimination by alcoholics. *Journal of Consulting and Clinical Psychology,* 1981, *48,* 655-656.

Shaw, S. Biochemical alternatives to the drinking history. In *Evaluation of the alcoholic: Implications for research, theory and treatment.* (NIAAA Research Monograph No. 5). Washington, DC: National Institute on Alcohol Abuse and Alcoholism, 1979.

Shaw, S., Lue, S. L., & Lieber, C. S. Biochemical tests for the detection of alcoholism: Comparison of plasma alpha-amino-*n*-butyric acid with other available tests. *Alcoholism: Clinical and Experimental Research,* 1978, *2,* 3-7.

Shaw, S., Stimmel, B., & Lieber, C. Plasma alpha-amino-*n*-butyric acid to leucine ratio: An empirical biochemical marker of alcoholism. *Science,* 1976, *194,* 1057-1058.

Shaw, S., Worner, T., Borysow, M., Schmitz, R., & Lieber, C. Detection of alcoholism relapse: Comparative diagnostic value of MCV, GGTP, and AANB. *Alcoholism: Clinical and Experimental Research,* 1979, *3,* 297-301.

Silverstein, S. J., Nathan, P. E., & Taylor, H. A. Blood alcohol level estimation and controlled drinking by chronic alcoholics. *Behavior Therapy,* 1974, *5,* 1-15.

Sobell, L. C., Maisto, S. A., Sobell, M. B., & Cooper, A. M. Reliability of alcohol abusers' self-reports of drinking behavior. *Behavior Research and Therapy,* 1979, *17,* 157-160.

Sobell, L. C., & Sobell, M. B. Outpatient alcoholics give valid self-reports. *Journal of Nervous and Mental Disease,* 1975, *161,* 32-42.

Sobell, L. C., & Sobell, M. B. Convergent validity: An approach to increasing confidence in treatment outcome conclusions with alcohol and drug abusers. In L. C. Sobell, M. B. Sobell, & E. Ward (Eds.), *Evaluating alcohol and drug abuse treatment effectiveness: Recent advances.* New York: Pergamon Press, 1980.

Sobell, L. C., Vander Speck, R., & Saltman, P. Utility of portable breath alcohol testers for drunken driving offenders. *Journal of Studies on Alcohol,* 1980, *41,* 930-934.

Sobell, M. B., & Sobell, L. C. Individualized behavior therapy for alcoholics. *Behavior Therapy,* 1973, *4,* 49-72.

Sobell, M. B., & Sobell, L. C. *Behavioral treatment of alcohol problems.* New York: Plenum Press, 1978.

Sobell, M. B., & Sobell, L. C. IBT: Interpretation of results. In *Behavioral treatment of alcohol problems.* New York: Plenum Press, 1979.

Sobell, M. B., Sobell, L. C., & Vander Speck, R. Relationships among clinical judgment, self-report, and breath-analysis measures of intoxication in alcoholics. *Journal of Consulting and Clinical Psychology*, 1979, *47*, 204–206.

Stuart, R. B. *Helping couples change: A social learning approach to marital therapy.* New York: Guilford Press, 1980.

Talland, G. A., Mendelson, J. H., & Ryback, P. Experimentally induced chronic intoxication and withdrawal in alcoholics. Part 5. Tests of attention. *Quarterly Journal of Studies on Alcohol*, 1964, *2*, 74–86.

Tracey, D., Karlin, R., & Nathan, P. E. Experimental analysis of chronic alcoholism in four women. *Journal of Consulting and Clinical Psychology*, 1976, *44*, 832–842.

U.S. Department of Health, Education, and Welfare. *Alcohol and health.* Washington, DC: U.S. Government Printing Office, 1978.

Weiss, R. L., & Cerreto, M. *Marital status inventory.* Unpublished manuscript, University of Oregon, 1975.

Weiss, R. L., & Margolin, G. Marital conflict and accord. In A. R. Ciminero, K. S. Calhoun, & A. E. Adams (Eds.), *Handbook for behavioral assessment.* New York: Wiley, 1977.

Wilson, G. T. Expectations and substance abuse: Does basic research benefit clinical assessment and therapy? *Addictive Behaviors*, 1981, *6*, 221–231.

Wilson, G. T., & Abrams, D. Effects of alcohol on social anxiety and physiological arousal: Cognitive versus pharmacological process. *Cognitive Therapy and Research*, 1977, *1*, 195–210.

Wilson, G. T., Abrams, D. B., & Lipscomb, T. R. Effects of intoxication levels and drinking pattern on social anxiety in men. *Journal of Studies on Alcohol*, 1980, *41*, 250–264.

Wilson, G. T., & Lawson, D. M. Expectancies, alcohol and sexual arousal in male social drinkers. *Journal of Abnormal Psychology*, 1976, *85*, 587–594.

Zeenir, A. R., & Rugg, P. Women and alcohol: Varying effects during the menstrual cycle. *Alcohol Technical Reports*, 1980, *8*, 18–20.

5

Ambulatory Activity
in Chronic Disease

Mark Kane Goldstein and
Gerald H. Stein

Each day thousands of observations of changes in human motion
are noted on hospital records and outpatient charts. These records
serve as important criteria for medical and surgical intervention
and rehabilitation efforts. An overwhelming majority of these observations are based on subjective estimates that may be misleading
or inaccurate; for example, an observation that "the patient is
walking more today" is frequently noted in hospital records as an
index of progress. In fact, without the aid of objective measurement, all that can be stated with certainty is that the patient appears to be walking more today, which may represent the biases
of the observer rather than a real change in the activity of the patient over some baseline condition. Conversely, the negative progress is observed in terms of attenuated patient activity.

  These observations often serve to initiate or change a therapeutic regimen, and they may even stimulate or forestall surgical
intervention. Decisions to replace a knee or hip joint, to increase
or decrease arthritic medicine or cortisone injections, to install or
remove prosthetic devices, to operate because of a patient's chronic
back pain, to intervene medically with a geriatric or a depressed
patient, to intervene in coronary artery disease, to prescribe port-

able oxygen for a patient with chronic obstructive lung disease — all are examples of decisions that depend, in part, on observations of ambulation and motion. Yet, these observations are made in acute hospital-based, time-limited circumstances and are almost always subjective.

In order to determine the relationship between clinical estimates of patient activity and actual walking, Saunders, Goldstein, and Stein (1978) asked the nursing staff of a psychiatric rehabilitation unit to make daily estimates of changes in physical activities of 36 patients between December 1974 and February 1975. The observations were based solely on the nurses' impressions of patients' daily activity and, as such, were similar to observations recorded in patient charts. During the same period, the investigators placed digital pedometers (Digi Manpo pedometer, Mitchell Mogul Co., New York) on all 36 patients. The pedometers were carefully calibrated in advance to minimize error (Figs. 5.1 and 5.2). Each day the pedometer readings were recorded but not seen by the nursing staff. The pedometer readings were sensitive to changes

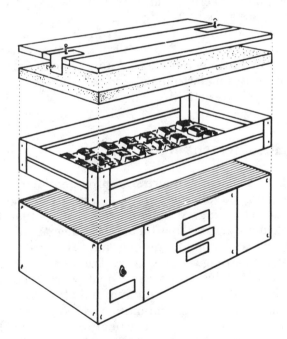

Figure 5.1. Eberbach single-speed reciprocating power unit used for calibration.

Figure 5.2. Digital pedometer.

in patients' status. Improvements in health and rehabilitation efforts were reflected in pedometer data, which showed increases in activity trends over time. The observations provided by the nurses did not reflect the systemic trends evidenced by the pedometer, and a statistical analysis comparing the slopes derived from the daily pedometer readings and daily activity ratings suggested that the two were not related to one another. Thus, there was little reason to assume that subjective analyses of patients' progress in terms of physical activity can reveal the trends and changes in activity that are actually taking place.

Accurate measurement of activity in chronic patients is both desirable and achievable. The intent of this chapter is to review those recent studies of chronic ambulatory patients that report using motion-measuring instruments and pedometers to analyze, diagnose, or prescribe activity changes.

Motion Measurement in Arthritis

Arthritis is a chronically progressive inflammation of the joints, producing pain and joint deformity, and in advanced situations, disability and crippling. Although there are more than 100 types of arthritis, most persons so afflicted have degenerative arthritis (osteoarthritis) and a smaller number have rheumatoid arthritis. The former is a cartilage degenerative disorder associated with aging and usually involves the larger weight-bearing joints, such as knees and hips, or the spine. An important alteration in the lifestyle of such patients is less ambulation as the process advances. In rheumatoid arthritis, the inflammation occurs in the lining (synovium) of multiple symmetrical joints of hands, wrists, feet, ankles, knees, hips, and shoulders. Characteristically most pain is present on arising in the morning and continues with rest as well as with use. The inflammatory swelling of the synovium of the joints accelerates the destructive processes. The causes of degenerative and of rheumatoid arthritis are unknown. The clinical course may produce markedly limited motion of all joints and significant loss of ambulation. Treatment consists of medications to suppress the inflammation or control the pain and reconstructive surgery to repair the individually damaged joints.

We (Goldstein, Stein, Shuster, & Harris, 1978) suggested that limitations of chronic motion can be more accurately assessed by patients than by clinically trained professional observers. Patients with chronic rheumatoid stable arthritis participated in a drug study that evaluated the effects of a new arthritis medication. Evaluations of joint involvement (tenderness and swelling) were made by rheumatologists at four 2-week intervals. Another rheumatologist transcribed their evaluations onto a skeletal form (Fig. 5.3). Using a scale from 0 to 8, where 0 indicated no joint involvement and 8 indicated severe swelling and tenderness, the

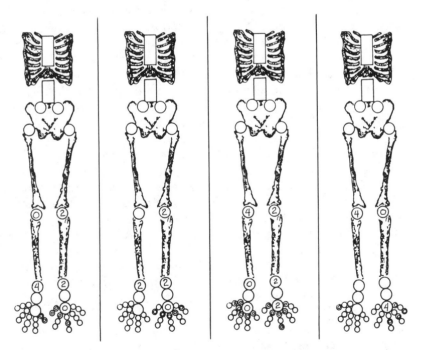

Figure 5.3. Skeletal form used to record evaluations of arthritis symptoms.

physicians (rheumatologists) rated joint involvement, pain, swelling, and tenderness in each patient.

The objective measure was the time to complete a 50-foot walk. We also requested patients to rate their own joint pain and swelling. The patients selected for the study had shown considerable variation in their time to complete a 50-foot walk, depending upon the degree of joint inflammation in the lower trunk. Thus, patients could complete a 50-foot walk in less time when their symptoms were ameliorated. Two physician–judges then reviewed the lower trunk joint ratings made by the patients and by the rheumatologists to determine which set of ratings better predicted 50-foot walk time. The judges were "blinded" by coding the data so that they were unable to determine the source of the ratings, and patients were unaware of the purpose of their self-ratings. The judges used the ratings of hip, knee, foot, and lumbar joints, to predict which "skeleton" would win a 50-foot walking race. The results indicated that patient self-ratings of lower trunk joint involvement were more useful than the ratings by the rheumatologists in predicting actual walk times. In fact, patient ratings were significantly associated with actual walk time, whereas physician ratings demonstrated no such association.

For 2 weeks Perlini and colleagues (Perlini, 1983) monitored the daily activity level of 20 patients with chronic stable rheumatoid arthritis. Then 10 of the patients were randomly selected to report daily to the investigators by telephone their pain-related symptoms, including pain and joint tenderness, and their pedometer readings. This group received attention for pain and suffering by appropriate sympathetic responses. The other 10 patients reported their activities but did not report painful symptoms. They were given attention and praise for appropriate activities. Over 4 months, the pedometer readings between the two groups revealed no differences. It was learned, however, that the pedometer readings were sensitive to change in arthritic inflammatory episodes; that is, the pedometer trends regularly predicted joint flare-ups and hospitalizations.

Algozzine, Stein, Doering, Araujo, and Akin (1982) studied the effects of a widely prescribed topical applied ointment (trolamine) for osteoarthritis of the knee. These investigators employed a pedometer (Digi Manpo, Mitchell Mogul Co., New York) as a dependent outcome measure of change in patient activity associated with the use of trolamine. Data collected from 20 patients over 3 weeks in a double-blinded cross-over design (AB vs BA) suggested no significant differences between pedometer readings of the two treatments in either phase (placebo or trolamine). The authors concluded, based in part on the continuously recorded pedometer data, that this commonly used topical remedy was ineffective.

The three studies suggest that it is possible to improve significantly the accuracy of our knowledge about the ambulatory capacity of chronically diseased arthritic patients and the effects of treatment. It is readily apparent that motion limitations may be more appropriately and effectively treated when they can be more accurately quantified and that the value of treatments can be assessed. The purpose of this chapter is to suggest how the treatment of chronic disease may be advanced through the use of simple, reliable mechanical monitoring systems and objective evaluation criteria. Whenever possible, patients themselves provide the crucial element in continuous monitoring of activity.

Motion Measurement in Cirrhosis

Cirrhosis is a common, chronic, slowly progressive disorder of the liver associated with scarring, destruction, and regeneration of liver cells. In its more advanced form, blood and lymph are unable to flow freely through the scarred, contracted liver; backup produces an internal hypertension, which in turn causes massive swelling of the abdomen (ascites) and legs (edema). Individuals may internally exsanguinate from rupture of the stretched vessels attempting to accommodate the inappropriately augmented blood flow; toxins normally eliminated by the liver accumulate, inducing a confusional syndrome (encephalopathy) and, ultimately, death. Chronic alcoholism is the leading etiologic factor in causing cirrhosis in the people of developed countries. It is sometimes referred to as Laënnec's cirrhosis, named after the famed French physician who described it about 100 years ago. Other causes include chronic hepatitis from viruses or drugs. Ambulation is attenuated in proportion to the advancement of the cirrhosis; weakness, edema, and confusion may all contribute to major motor limitations.

For 3 consecutive years, we (Goldstein, Stein, Smolen, & Perlini, 1976) daily monitored 13 ambulatory patients with Laënnec's cirrhosis. We reported data after the first 6 months of the study, analyzing patient self-measurements of daily liquid intake, alcohol consumption, abdominal girth, weight, and pedometer readings (Digi Manpo, Mitchell Mogul Co., New York). Patients transmitted all of their data to a monitoring facility daily, via a telephone call to an interactive answering service. We checked the reliability and validity of the self-reports during patients' visits to the hospital (tested blood for alcohol content, weighed the patient, confirmed the veracity of the patient's reports with a spouse, and analyzed the cumulative pedometer readings). The data suggested that trends and changes in daily activity were associated with other symptoms and functions. For example, computer analysis revealed a systematic positive relationship between hours worked and pedometer readings, and a negative relationship between hours worked and alcohol consumption. This report suggests that complex, multi-symptom, chronic disease states may be rapidly, accurately, and reliably monitored with the aid of simple motion-monitoring instruments to facilitate more precise and effective care, and measurement of clinical outcomes.

We (Smolen, Stein, Goldstein, & Rosenshein, 1978) also reported the development of an automated computer system for managing and analyzing the complex biobehavioral data generated by the previous study. This program, called NEW, produces computer "warnings" that rapidly scan daily data on behavioral and physiological changes in chronically diseased patients. The system prints an alert on those patients whose behavior or measures have exceeded preset limits, possibly requiring hospitalization if corrective intervention is not instituted. Pedometer readings are processed as one variable in the program yielding a general measure of patient change and status, which when combined with other procedures produces a profile for alerting the care team when needed.

Such a system allows acquisition and immediate comparison of daily readings on multiple variables such as abdominal girth, weight, pedometer readings, temperature, and blood pressure. For example, a change in ambulatory activity alone may not be regarded as significant, but when coupled with a change in blood pressure or rapidly increasing edema, it would provide a basis for further evaluation of the patient's condition. Computer-assisted analyses of the interaction among these variables can assist health professionals in more accurately managing a far greater number of ambulatory patients, and this is discussed further in a later section.

Motion Measurement in Coronary Heart Disease

Coronary heart disease represents a group of clinical disorders characterized by degenerative vascular damage to coronary arteries by a process of lipid deposition in the arteries (atherosclerosis) that nourish the heart muscle (myocardium). Obstruction of the blood flow by this atherosclerotic process is the major reason for insufficient coronary blood flow to the myocardium. Acute coronary thrombosis or arterial spasm can also impede the flow of blood.

Several clinical syndromes are associated with insufficient (ischemic) blood flow to the myocardium. Angina pectoris represents a relative deficiency of oxygen in the heart muscle. This ischemic situation is characterized clinically by chest pain or discomfort lasting 5–30 min, usually brought on by exertion or emotion and relieved by rest or nitroglycerin. A myocardial infarction, commonly called a heart attack, occurs when the myocardium literally dies (i.e., necrosis) from the oxygen deprivation produced from an obstructed coronary artery. Clinically, the patients have crushing chest pain lasting longer than 30 min. Most patients survive this attack; however, this is the leading cause of death in North America and Western Europe; it has an age-adjusted death rate of approximately 200 per 100,000 (1978 data), a mortality almost twice that of the second most frequent cause of death, cancer.

An additional clinical syndrome relating to coronary heart disease is congestive heart failure. In this condition, the cardiac limitations are due to insufficient pumping action, with its concomitant diminished blood flow to other vital organs, causing fluid retention and resulting in the complaints of shortness of breath (dyspnea) with exertion and swelling of the ankles (edema).

Motion limitation from coronary heart disease may be due to various mechanisms associated with the pathologic manifestations described. The anginal pains associated with coronary artery disease impose exertion-associated pains. The pain is usually so severe and frightening that patients discontinue their activity completely. Since angina may occur at variable intervals (e.g., as seldom as once a year to as often as 10 times a day), effects of limitation obviously depend on the frequency of the attacks. Hence, those patients with daily repetitive attacks are the most severely limited in their activities. Fortunately, medical and, more recently, surgical management may help many such patients lead active lives. Myocardial infarction also may cause activity to be considerably limited because of angina, congestive heart failure, and abnormal heart rhythms (arrhythmias). Congestive heart failure limits motion because of the shortness of breath. Symptoms of congestive heart failure are slowly progressive and may render patients totally unable to perform their jobs and, at the extreme, perform daily self-care activities. Arrhythmias may occur, producing either angina or congestive heart failure or both, which may severely curtail activities.

Most studies that report continuous monitoring of patients with heart disease use ambulatory electrocardiographic (ECG) monitoring to record the patient's electrocardiogram over extended periods of time in ambulatory settings. Electrical heart recordings are generated via a 10-lb portable recorder generally referred to as a "Holter monitor" after its developer, Herman J. Holter, who developed the instrument in 1952. Several papers have studied ambulatory monitoring in subjects without using pedometer measurements to determine the activity level during monitoring. Schang and Pepine (1977) studied 20 men with typical angina pectoris who had coronary artery narrowing documented by angiography. Continuous 10-hr Holter monitoring results, accompanied by detailed daily diaries of activities and symptoms, were obtained periodically over a 16-month interval. Data showed that 25% of the characteristic ECG changes of ischemia were associated with angina-type symptoms. The remaining 75% of ischemic ECG episodes were unrelated to symptoms or to posture. Most of these asymptomatic ischemic events occurred at rest or during very light activity such as slow walking or sitting. This suggested to the authors that events or factors that are unknown at this time frequently caused angina; that is, they do not appear related to physical activities.

This study is noteworthy because it attempted to collect physiological data from patients pursuing usual activities. As such, an unexpected finding came to light — that ischemic attacks occurred much more often than suspected and the cause was not evident in terms of relationship to physical activity. However, daily activity levels were not quantified; thus, it is difficult in this study to determine the precise physical activity on ischemic events.

Saris, Snell, and Binkhorst (1977) described a procedure including a heart rate recorder for monitoring subjects up to 3 weeks. Using microprocessor-based technology, they constructed a device weighing 220 g, which is considerably smaller and lighter than the Holter monitor. Its accuracy was calibrated against manual heart rate counts, and it was programmed to store heart rates in group-ings by 10s; that is, counting the number of times the heart rate is in the range 50–60, 60–70, 70–80, etc., during the interval of recording. The authors studied the effects of monitoring on the sub-jects' activity by obtaining premonitoring pedometer activity meas-ures for several days, thereafter initiating the monitoring process while maintaining the pedometer measurements. There was no dif-ference in pedometer results from the premonitoring to the moni-toring phase, which suggested that the heart rate monitor did not interfere or influence the subjects' daily activities. A disadvantage of this monitoring system is its inability to analyze the relationship of heart rate to time. The heart rates were presented in clusters over the total time. Moreover, the monitoring instrument could not store the obtained data.

These preliminary studies are encouraging in their attempts to obtain unincumbered home-based ambulatory data. The Holter monitor is limited to 24 hr of recording and lacks any means to correlate gross motor activity with electrocardiographic physio-logical events. The recording system that is used in conjunction with Holter monitoring depends on a handwritten daily diary for-mat, which is indeed cumbersome to use. The heart rate counter has some of the same difficulties of the Holter monitor but repre-sents state-of-the-art technology with its lightness and portabili-ty. This study demonstrates that the pedometer may be useful as a measure of overall activity in heart patients, but studies remain to be done on the relationship between ambulatory ECG moni-toring and daily pedometer readings.

A concern to clinicians is the need for accurate home-based data as more decisions regarding medication and surgery for man-agement of coronary artery disease place a greater burden eco-nomically on the patient and the community. A recent study by Leon, Rosing, Bonow, Lipson, and Epstein (1981) compared the effects of a standard medication for treating chronic angina (pro-panolol) with a new drug (verapamil). In this study, 11 men who had well-documented ischemic heart disease received either pro-panolol, verapamil, or placebo in a blinded controlled fashion. The dependent variable used to assess the efficacy of the drugs was data obtained by a calibrated bicycle ergometer. This device recorded total revolutions achieved until onset of symptoms. Their data in-dicated that verapamil was more effective in promoting exercise over a limited time interval. Obviously deficient in this study were the effects of these agents on the patients' symptoms at home or at work over a more realistic time base. The generalization of improvement from a short-time sample to the ambulatory environment is tenuous at best. The dissemination of incomplete information has led to acceptance of new interventions, but these may not truly benefit the functioning of a patient outside the hospital-based laboratory.

The issue of coronary heart disease prevention and its relation to ambulatory activity (exercise prevention of coronary heart disease) have not been adequately studied. Although there was a dramatic downtrend in the mortality rates of coronary heart disease during the 1970s, there has been supporting evidence that this was due to alterations of three major risk factors: (1) serum cholesterol, (2) blood pressure, and (3) smoking. The issue of exercise and the prevention of coronary heart disease remains confusing and inconclusive. Longitudinal motion measurement via pedometers could prove invaluable in determining the long-term effects of activity levels on heart disease. Further, the amount of exercise most individuals engage in appears to be less than that recommended for prevention of coronary heart disease. Hence, essential conclusions regarding the role of exercise must await more systematic and extensive ambulatory activity studies.

Motion Measurement in Chronic Obstructive Pulmonary Disease

The term *chronic obstructive pulmonary disease* (COPD) refers to a group of disorders in which the common physiologic abnormality is obstruction to air flow on expiration. The most prevalent diseases within this group are chronic bronchitis, chronic asthma, and pulmonary emphysema. Obstruction of air flow is most common; the prevalence is about 30% in men and women over 35 years of age and is even higher in smokers. It is a major cause of distress and disability in the elderly population. Numerous factors, both internal and environmental, may contribute to the development of COPD, including allergy, infection, atmospheric contaminants (such as dust and vapors), and, most importantly, cigarette smoke. The predominant symptoms are cough with production of sputum, wheezing, or shortness of breath, or a combination of the three. Documentation of the severity of the disease is based on physiological measures including pulmonary function tests that measure breathing capabilities under standard conditions in a hospital laboratory. The clinical manifestations vary, with some persons being mildly afflicted and others being severely limited. Severe COPD prevents patients from performing normal daily activities that involve exertion such as walking or mild exercise. At the extreme, patients do not have enough breath to walk to the bathroom and are bedridden by dyspnea. They cannot store adequate amounts of oxygen, and carbon dioxide is retained as a waste product. The altered physiologic changes produce a type of heart failure, and ultimately the patient succumbs from combined cardiopulmonary deterioration.

The clinical management of these disorders involves compliance with complex medical regimens as well as alterations of lifestyle, but most important is the cessation of smoking.

In a recent study, Moser, Bokinsky, Savage, Archibald, and Hansen (1980) attempted to evaluate the physical and physiologic effects of patients with COPD in a comprehensive rehabilitation program.

Forty-two patients with COPD participated in a regular treadmill exercise regimen for 6 weeks. Physiologic measures such as pulmonary function tests and arterial blood gases were obtained. In addition, functional activity self-reported questionnaires were completed at pre- and poststudy intervals. Most of the physiologic measurements showed improvement at the end of the 6-week study interval. However, some important observations, such as arterial blood oxygen pressure, declined (worsened) in the majority of patients. Most patients who improved physiologically also improved functionally as measured by the treadmill. There were some patients whose daily activity showed increases without concomitant improvement in the physiologic measures. This study is of great importance because it establishes that an in-hospital exercise training program can be safely conducted with favorable results for a majority of patients with COPD. However, the issues are far from settled; it may be that the rehabilitation program desensitized patients to their fear of dyspnea. A reduction in fear could have led to their functional improvement rather than physiologic improvement, which was minimal at best. Without ambulatory daily pedometer readings, it is difficult to assess the long-term effects on the patients' rehabilitation. Such hospital-based rehabilitation programs with COPD or with heart patients present no conclusive data about continuation of improvement outside the hospital environment.

In an attempt to overcome methodological problems, Lilker, Karnick, and Lerner (1975) conducted a study on patients with

COPD comparing the efficacy of a portable oxygen gas apparatus (Linde Walker) to a control situation using liquid air as the gas. Patients were evaluated by standard pulmonary function tests and arterial blood gases. Under various controlled conditions, they were requested to record the amount of walking by pedometer on a daily basis. Each of the nine patients received 5 weeks of liquid oxygen therapy and 5 weeks of liquid air treatment with the portable gas apparatus on a daily continuous blinded basis. Although patients stated they felt better with the gas apparatus, there was no improvement in any of the measures using the liquid air.

However, while receiving liquid oxygen there was significant improvement in the arterial blood oxygen pressure. Nonetheless, only three of the nine patients significantly improved their walking capacities as judged by pedometer readings. These three patients also experienced the greatest degree of subjective improvement.

This study explored the association between physiologic and functional measurements obtained from the home in a continuous fashion. Home oxygen treatment by the portable gas apparatus is an expensive therapeutic tool and is widely employed. Patients were noted to feel subjectively improved by having the apparatus whether they were receiving oxygen or air. Air was not associated with an improvement in either physiologic or functional measurement, and only three patients improved in functional capacity with oxygen. Hence, it appears that the data provided by the pedometer in this study suggest that the widespread use of this expensive therapy for COPD may be only marginally beneficial in increasing patient activity, though it is freely prescribed for such a purpose.

Motion Measurement in Psychiatric Disorders

Schizophrenia represents a group of chronic psychiatric disorders associated with severe disturbances of thinking and of appropriate behavior. Such individuals may be withdrawn, paranoid, and tangentially uninterested in their daily activities, and have impaired cognitive processes. Memory recall, however, is intact. The cause of the disorder is unknown, with the exception of certain well-established organic causes. Genetic factors are believed to be important in some cases.

Inactivity, inability to function in the home environment, and symptomatic treatment remain the hallmarks for this psychiatric disorder, as they do for the disorders affecting most chronically impaired individuals.

Contemporary reports of psychiatric management of schizophrenia show a striking paucity of objective data on the efficacy of treatment. Standard evaluation questionnaires administered by trained observers based on patients' comments about functioning in the home or on the job have not proved adequate as tools in defining objective change in the schizophrenic process.

Nonetheless, since these patients are in great part inactive, measurement of their activity level seems a more precise approach to evaluation of treatment effects. Interestingly, one such study was performed by Perris and Rapp (1974), evaluating a long-acting psychotropic agent (fluspirilene) in the management of 10 schizophrenic inpatients. The dependent variable was the change in pedometer recordings of ambulatory activity. The 10-week study was designed with three control intervals: During the first 3 weeks of the study (Phase 1) subjects received their usual maintenance dosage of their prescribed medications. During the fourth week (Phase 2), the Phase 1 psychotropic was withheld. During the final 3 weeks (Phase 3), the study drug was administered. The results suggest significant increases in activity during the fluspirilene phase compared with the other phases of the study. The authors concluded that the pedometer is an effective way to objectively assess ambulatory activity in chronic psychotic patients and that it showed the efficacy of their particular study drug.

Depression is another psychiatric disorder, characterized by a set of affective cognitive behavioral and somatic symptoms. Those symptoms include a sense of hopelessness, gloominess, and sadness; lack of interest in surroundings; an inability to concentrate; slowness of speech and thought; and a variety of sleeping, eating, and pain disorders that are poorly understood. Psychomotor retardation is frequently a dominant clinical problem. Thus, the measurement of activity levels would greatly enhance the objectivity of therapeutic interventions. In one such study, Matussek, Romisch, and Ackenheil (1977) used pedometers to assess gross ambulatory activity in a group of depressed patients who were undergoing biochemical studies. The authors theorized that sleep deprivation generated a biochemical change that was associated with activity changes. The results indicated that patient activity as measured by the pedometer was unaffected by sleep deprivation or physiologic changes measured in the study. In the report by Saunders and associates (1978), several patients had histories of depression, and their pedometer records reflected change in activity levels associated with important changes in treatment and rehabilitation. Thus, continuous monitoring of movement may be a sensitive tool for evaluating clinical change in depression and associated psychiatric disorders.

Motion Measurement in Obesity

Obesity is a chronic disorder currently considered to be an energy imbalance between caloric intake and expenditure of voluntary and involuntary muscular work. Overeating remains the primary cause, although some research has focused on the measurement of activity to determine the net contribution of activity levels to obesity.

Albert Stunkard was a pioneer in the direct measurement of unrestrained human activity in the United States. One of the earliest reports was by Dorris and Stunkard (1957), in which they observed that the instruments recorded a mean of less than 2 miles walked per day for obese women and a mean of 4.9 miles per day for nonobese women. Chirico and Stunkard (1960) expanded this investigation, finding that a group of nonobese men exhibited a mean of 6.0 miles per day, whereas the mean for obese men was 3.7 miles per day. Stunkard and Pestka (1962) used pedometers to study the activity of 15 matched pairs of obese and nonobese girls aged 10 to 13 years. It is not surprising that there was no difference between the activity levels of the two groups because at the time the subjects were in a Girl Scout camp, where differences in activity were likely to be minimal because of uniformity and regimentation in the program. Nevertheless, these observations represent an advance in the direct continuous measurement of human activity, without which these discoveries would not have been possible.

A study by Epstein, Wing, and Thompson (1978) also presented interesting objective data suggesting that much of the problem in obesity appears associated with a lower activity level rather than an increased intake. The former is felt to be the main reason for an energy imbalance leading to caloric excess, resulting in obesity. The authors point out that there are few studies concerning the relationship of obesity to activity because of difficulties in obtaining accurate measurement of activity levels in the natural environment. One phase of their study used the pedometer as a method to obtain continuous activity data over 1 week on patients' activity levels. In a pretest subjects ran as far as they could in 12 min on a 1/8-mile indoor track. Thereafter, each subject recorded daily food intake and activity for a full week after the 12-min pretest. Food intake was self-monitored and converted to calories by the experimenters. Daily activity was recorded using a digital pedometer and an activity log. The activity log provided for the recording of 29 common activities such as running, sleeping, and dancing. After 1 week of the self-monitoring, each subject was given another 12-min running test. The results showed that the pre and post 12-min running tests correlated highly with daily pedometer readings and logging of specific activities. The authors concluded that there are orderly and predictable relationships between caloric intake, weight, and activity level such that obesity is predictably associated with an imbalance between activity level and caloric intake.

Conclusion

Motion limitations are an important feature of chronic medical illness. However, few studies have measured motion changes associated with chronic disease or measured the improvement in home or work activity resulting from medical treatment. The reason for this lack of interest in measurement in chronic disease is speculative. Clinicians are not accustomed to using daily acquired data in their patient evaluation. It may appear time consuming, laborious, and unnecessary. Most clinicians have been trained to treat chronic illness only in the acute manifestations of the underlying chronic process by treating the patient with the latest available therapeutic agents.

The problem is compounded by the financial disincentive for the physician to spend more time with the patient to understand his limitations in the home. Physicians tend not to charge their patients on an hourly basis, and those few who do find that their services are restricted to the financially secure segment of the population. One possible method to overcome such powerful obstacles to the use of home-monitored data is computerization of the data. Such a technique (NEW) has been proposed (Smolen et al., 1976), and as mentioned earlier, automated computer analysis of patient data provides profiles of responses indicative of progress.

It is clear that patients may be trained to enter clinically relevant data into self-contained terminals capable of storing data for transmission to the clinical laboratory on a daily basis. At the laboratory, the data are retrieved and analyzed for clinical relevance. Data of possible clinical significance are extracted for presentation to the clinician for daily review. Any alterations in the regimen can be relayed by telephonic communications directly to the patient. Thus, an interactive loop of computer-assisted patient–clinician management may enable patients to assume a greater role in their own chronic disease management, leading to greater rehabilitative gains (Goldstein, Thomas, Moulder, & Stein, 1979).

References

Algozzine, G. J., Stein, G. H., Doering, P. L., Araujo, O. E., & Akin, K. C. Trolamine salicylate cream in osteoarthritis of the knee. *Journal of the American Medical Association*, 1982, *247*, 1311–1313.

Chirico, A. -M., & Stunkard, A. J. Physical activity and human obesity. *New England Journal of Medicine*, 1960, *263*, 935–940.

Dorris, R. J., & Stunkard, A. J. Physical activity: Performance and attitudes of a group of obese women. *American Journal of the Medical Sciences*, 1957, *233*, 623–628.

Epstein, L. H., Wing, R. R., & Thompson, J. K. The relationship between exercise intensity, caloric intake, and weight. *Addictive Behaviors*, 1978, *3*, 185–190.

Goldstein, M. K., Stein, G. H., Schuster, J., & Harris, G. *Progress in assessing rheumatoid joint involvement.* Paper presented at the annual scientific meeting of the Arthritis Foundation, New York, June 1978.

Goldstein, M. K., Stein, G. H., Smolen, D. M., & Perlini, W. S. Bio-behavioral monitoring: A method for remote health measurement. *Archives of Physical Medicine and Rehabilitation*, 1976, *57*, 253–258.

Goldstein, M. K., Thomas, R. G., Moulder, P. V., & Stein, G. H. Microprocessing. 2. The patient operated portable analyzer. In *Proceedings of the American Association for Medical Instrumentation.* Las Vegas: AAMI, 1979, p. 97.

Leon, M. B., Rosing, D. R., Bonow, R. O., Lipson, L. C., & Epstein, S. E. Clinical efficacy of verapamil alone and combined with propranolol in treating patients with chronic stable angina pectoris. *American Journal of Cardiology*, 1981, *48*, 131–139.

Lilker, E. S., Karnick, A., & Lerner, L. Portable oxygen in chronic obstructive lung disease with hypoxemia and cor pulmonale: A controlled double-blind crossover study. *Chest*, 1975, *68*, 236–241.

Matussek, N., Romisch, P., & Ackenheil, M. MHPG excretion during sleep deprivation in endogenous depression. *Neuropsychobiology*, 1977, *3*, 23–29.

Moser, K. M., Bokinsky, G. E., Savage, R. T., Archibald, C. J., & Hansen, P. R. Results of a comprehensive rehabilitation program: Physiologic and functional effects on patients with chronic obstructive pulmonary disease. *Archives of Internal Medicine*, 1980, *140*, 1596–1601.

Perlini, W. S. *The effects of differential attention on the self-monitoring responses and activity levels of a group of rheumatoid arthritic patients*. Unpublished doctoral dissertation, University of Florida, Gainesville, 1983.

Perris, C., & Rapp, W. Ambulatory activity during treatment with fluspirilene in chronic schizophrenics. *Acta Psychiatrica Scandanavica (Supplement)*, 1974, *249*, 117–122.

Saris, W. H. M., Snell, P., & Binkhorst, R. A. A portable heart rate distribution recorder for studying daily physical activity. *European Journal of Applied Psychology*, 1977, *37*, 17–25.

Saunders, K. J., Goldstein, M. K., & Stein, G. H. Automated measurement of patient activity on a hospital rehabilitation ward. *Archives of Physical Medicine and Rehabilitation*, 1978, *59*, 255–257.

Schang, S. J., Jr., & Pepine, C. J. Transient asymptomatic S-T segment depression during daily activity. *American Journal of Cardiology*, 1977, *39*, 396–402.

Smolen, D. M., Stein, G. H., Goldstein, M. K., & Rosenshein, J. S. NEW: An interactive data management system for monitoring ambulatory patients. *Computer Programs in Biomedicine*, 1978, *8*, 71–76.

Stunkard, A., & Pestka, J. The physical activity of obese girls. *American Journal of Diseases of Children*, 1962, *103*, 812–817.

6

Behavioral Assessment of Chronic Pain

Mary C. White, Laurence A. Bradley, and Charles K. Prokop

The International Association for the Study of Pain (IASP) has d veloped a definition of pain as "an unpleasant sensory and em tional experience associated with actual or potential tissue damag or described in terms of such damage" (IASP Subcommittee on Ta onomy, 1979, p. 250). The current authors accept this definiti of pain since it conveys the multidimensional and subjective natu of pain of diverse etiologies (Bradley, Prokop, Gentry, Van d Heide, & Prieto, 1981). Given that pain is a subjective experienc however, there is a great deal of disagreement among behavior medicine specialists with regard to the most appropriate metho with which to assess chronic pain.

The present chapter provides a representative and critical r view of the empirical literature published within the past sever years regarding the assessment of chronic pain. Consistent wi the majority of other investigators (e.g., Grzesiak, 1984; Sternbac 1978a), chronic pain is defined as pain that has persisted for at lea 6 months. The chapter first discusses the need for multidimension measurements of chronic pain that encompass overt motor beha iors, cognitive responses, and physiological variables. Next, the literature concerning each of the assessment dimensions previously noted are examined; particular attention is devoted to the methodological difficulties associated with each assessment dimension. Finally, conclusions are offered concerning the current status of chronic pain assessment, and suggestions are provided for future research.

It should be noted that, in accord with the emphasis of this volume upon the measurement of observable behaviors and the physical consequences of those behaviors, the literature concerning the assessment of personality attributes, affective responses, and related factors that may influence the experience of chronic pain are not examined in the present chapter. A complete review of this literature can be found by examining several publications (Bradley & Prokop, 1982; Bradley et al., 1981; Keefe, 1982). The literature regarding assessment of patients' cognitions is included in the present chapter since the authors agree with Fordyce (1978) that pain behavior encompasses "all behavior generated by the individual commonly understood to reflect the presence of nociception" (p. 54). It is acknowledged, however, that subjective reports of pain and other cognitive variables may not always be consistent with behavioral pain indices.

Multidimensional Measurement of Chronic Pain

The assessment of any patient with chronic pain, regardless of whether it is benign or malignant, begins with the patient's presentation of one or more *pain complaints*. Pain complaints are defined as "the tendency to present in the clinical situation with pain as a symptom" (Sternbach, 1978b, p. 253). Thus, the patient's pain complaints are distinguished from the patient's subjective experience of pain. Although a number of psychological and social factors may influence the manner in which the pain experience is expressed, it is necessary to attempt to assess the patient's pain as objectively as possible. The following discussion examines the relatively objective techniques that have been developed to assess chronic pain.

As noted previously in this chapter, the IASP has recognized that the experience of pain is composed of both a sensory and an affective dimension. Some investigators, such as Melzack and Dennis (1978), have suggested that cognitive processes also interact with sensory and affective processes during the pain experience. Although there is some disagreement with respect to the number of components to the pain experience, several investigators have indicated that the multidimensional nature of pain makes it necessary to use multidimensional systems of pain assessment and measurement (e.g., Black & Chapman, 1976; Bradley et al., 1981; Duncan, Gregg, & Ghia, 1978; Grzesiak, 1984; Sanders, 1979). Indeed, Sanders (1979) has produced a framework for pain assessment that consolidates measures of patients' overt motor, cognitive, and physiological responses. Since the framework allows for the eventual integration of treatment approaches by the behavioral and biomedical sciences (cf. Sanders, 1979, p. 553), the following discussion of pain assessment techniques is organized according to the type of pain response associated with each technique.

Measurement of Overt Motor Behaviors

Fordyce and his colleagues (Fordyce, 1973, 1976, 1978; Fordyce, Fowler, DeLateur, Sand, & Trieschmann, 1973; Fordyce, Fowler, Lehmann, & DeLateur, 1968) have produced an influential series of papers that have demonstrated the benefit of using overt motor behaviors as measures of pain. These overt motor behaviors may include "well behaviors" (e.g., activity or physical exercise) and "pain behaviors" (e.g., medication intake, time spent reclining or sitting). The benefit associated with the measurement of these behaviors is that they provide the diagnostician or therapist with measures of disability displayed by patients in physical mobility and other activities that are directly related to functioning in vocational, social, and leisure endeavors. As noted by Bradley et al. (1981), these measures of disability are ideally suited for evaluation purposes in inpatient treatment programs (e.g., those described by Cairns, Thomas, Mooney, & Pace, 1976; Fordyce, 1976; Roberts & Reinhardt, 1980; Swanson, Maruta, & Swenson, 1979) in which the treatment goal of pain reduction is secondary to that of returning the patient to satisfying vocational and social endeavors.[1]

---

[1]It should be noted, however, that several outcome studies have demonstrated that increases in well behaviors among chronic pain patients are associated with reductions in verbal reports of pain as well as reductions in pain behaviors (e.g., Fordyce, McMahon, Rainwater, Jackins, Questal, Murphy, & DeLateur, 1981; Keefe, Block, Williams, & Surwit, 1981; Roberts & Reinhardt, 1980).

The measurement of overt motor behaviors may be accomplished by using: (1) direct behavioral observations, (2) self-monitored observations, and (3) automated measurement devices. The remainder of this discussion examines the literature concerning investigations of each of the previously noted approaches to the measurement of overt motor behaviors.

Direct Behavioral Observations

Fordyce and his colleagues have made the most notable contributions to the development of direct observation methods for the measurement of overt motor behaviors. These investigators have relied primarily upon nurses, physical therapists, and other health care personnel to record patients' behaviors on an intermittent basis in terms of "movement cycles" (Fordyce, 1976, p. 80). A movement cycle is defined as beginning when a patient starts a particular behavior and ending when the patient is capable of repeating the behavior. The counting of movement cycles within specific time periods provides information concerning the rate of behavior that is observed. For example, Fordyce et al. (1973) evaluated the effectiveness of an inpatient treatment program in part by quantifying several well behaviors (i.e., walking, weaving, and sit-ups) as movement cycles within specific time periods (see Fordyce, 1976, for a complete discussion of the use of direct behavioral observations of well and pain behaviors).

The influence of Fordyce's approach to behavioral measurement may be found in several other investigations. These include investigations of the behaviors shown by patients with chronic benign pain (Brena & Unikel, 1976; Cairns & Pasino, 1977; Rybstein-Blinchik, 1979), pain due to cancer (Bourhis, Boudouresque, Pellet, Fondarai, Ponzio, & Spitalier, 1978), and pain due to burns (Klein & Charlton, 1980). It should be noted, however, that in order for direct observations of overt motor behavior to be useful, it is necessary to ensure that the observations are accurately and reliably recorded. For example, Rybstein-Blinchik (1979) compared the effects of three treatment strategies upon chronic pain patients' scores on the McGill Pain Questionnaire (Melzack, 1975; see "Measurement of Patients' Pain Perceptions"), direct observations of patients' pain behaviors during treatment sessions, and nurses' observations of patient recidivism and disturbances in patients' sleeping, eating, and medication intake. It was found that the most effective treatment produced relatively greater positive changes on all outcome measures except those based on nurses' observations. Rybstein-Blinchik (1979) attributed the lack of concordance between the nurse observation measures and the other outcome measures to inadequate training of nurses in defining the criterion measures.

Keefe and Block (1982) have developed a direct observation method for performing reliable and valid measurements of five pain behaviors. Ten-minute videotape recordings were made of 27 chronic low back pain patients as they engaged in sitting, reclining, standing, walking, and shifting from one position to another. Two trained observers independently viewed the videotapes and recorded the frequency of guarding, bracing, rubbing, grimacing, and sighing behavior during 20-sec observation periods. It was found that (1) the percentage of agreements between observers for each of the five pain behaviors ranged from 80% to 96%, (2) there was a significant and positive correlation between pain behaviors observed and patients' self-reports of pain intensity, (3) patients displayed significantly more pain behaviors during intervals involving movement relative to nonmovement intervals, (4) patients showed significant decreases in guarding and rubbing during the course of a behaviorally oriented inpatient treatment program, (5) there was a significant and positive correlation between naive observers' global ratings of patients' pain levels and the frequency of patients' pain behaviors across the five behavior categories, and (6) patients displayed the five pain behaviors significantly more often than did pain-free normal volunteers and depressed patients who participated in videorecording sessions identical to those originally engaged in by the chronic pain patients. Thus, the behavioral observation system developed by Keefe and Block (1982) may allow investigators to accurately and reliably record the frequency of several behaviors associated with chronic low back pain and use these recordings as a measure of treatment efficacy. It should be noted, however, that the use of the Keefe and Block behavioral observation system, as with all direct observation methods, requires the careful training of observers to ensure maximum utility of the system.

In summary, direct observation of patients' pain and well behaviors represents a practical method of assessment that provides important information regarding patients' disabilities in activities of daily living. The behavioral observation system developed by Keefe and Block (1982) represents a major advance in the assessment literature for two reasons. First, unlike the direct observation of patient behavior in the hospital setting, the system requires relatively little observer time or expense. The system also provides a videotape record of patient behavior that may be reused if observers should disagree with one another during observation periods. Nonetheless, proper use of the behavioral observation system and all other methods of direct observation requires investigators and clinicians to provide evidence concerning the accuracy and reliability of their behavioral measures (Bradley & Prokop, 1982; Bradley et al., 1981). Investigators who have examined the reliability of direct observation measures usually have employed multiple observers to record target behaviors and have presented various indices of the extent of agreement among observers. These indices often have consisted of the ratio of the sum of agreements produced by the observers to the total number of observations (Mitchell, 1979). It has been recommended, however, that investigators assess interobserver reliability by means of the kappa coefficient (Cohen, 1960) or the phi coefficient in order to correct for the occurrence of chance agreements (e.g., Conger, 1980). Mitchell (1979) also has recommended the use of several statistical procedures, based upon generalizability theory (Cronbach, Gleser, Nanda, & Rajaratnam, 1972), to obtain estimates of the proportion of variance in subject behavior that may be attributed to observers relative to that which may be attributed to subjects. Bradley et al. (1981) also have suggested that once adequate interobserver reliability is achieved, it may be desirable to perform reliability checks at random intervals in order to detect and correct possible sources of observer unreliability such as "drift" (Kent & Foster, 1977).

Self-Monitored Observations

Patient self-monitoring of their pain and well behaviors is a commonly used method of assessment in the chronic pain literature (Bradley & Prokop, 1982). It is likely that many investigators have chosen to use self-monitored observations of patient behavior because (1) it does not require additional training of health care staff members, and (2) it allows for the continuous recording of patient behavior in environments other than the hospital.

Fordyce (1976) advocated the use of a daily activity diary as a self-monitoring assessment instrument. The diary consists of a standard form on which an outpatient records on an hourly basis the amount of time spent reclining, sleeping, sitting, and walking or standing as well as medication intake. The amount of time recorded in each behavioral category and the amount of medication intake can be derived at the end of the assessment period in order to help formulate an appropriate treatment plan (Keefe, 1982). In addition, the patient may be asked to continue self-monitoring during treatment and follow-up periods in order to assess the effectiveness of treatment.

The major difficulty associated with the use of chronic pain patients' self-monitored observations is that, despite training, patients may not accurately or reliably record their behaviors. For example, Taylor, Zlutnick, Corley, and Flora (1980) performed a 6-month follow-up study on a brief, inpatient treatment intervention for several chronic-pain patients. One assessment measure consisted of patients' self-monitored records of medication intake during a 1-week period. Five patients reported taking some kind of analgesic or hypnosedative medication at follow-up; however, only three patients' reports concerning their medication use were consistent with the results of urine tests that also were performed at follow-up. Similar results were reported by Kremer, Block, and Gaylor (1981b) regarding inpatients' self-monitoring of their activity levels and social behavior, and by Ready, Sarkis, and Turner (1982) concerning inpatients' reports of their medication intake.

In summary, there are two advantages associated with the use of self-monitored observations relative to the use of direct observations of patient behavior. First, self-monitored observations may be derived on a continual basis, whereas direct observations may be produced only at specific time periods. In addition, the use of self-monitored observations allows for the assessment of patient behavior in the natural environment (e.g., home, place of work) or the treatment setting, while the use of direct observations of patient behavior generally can be performed only in the treatment setting. Unfortunately, despite early optimism regarding the accuracy and reliability of chronic pain patients' self-monitored observations (cf. Sternbach, 1974), the results of later investigations (Kremer et al., 1981b; Ready et al., 1982; Taylor et al., 1980) make it clear that self-monitored observations must be compared with some external criterion (e.g., direct observations produced by treatment staff or family members) before they can be accepted as accurate and reliable.

Automated Measurement Devices

The difficulties that are described in the preceding section with regard to the use of direct and self-monitored observations of chronic pain patient behavior have led some investigators to produce devices for the automated measurement of behavior. The first automated device was developed by Cairns and his colleagues (Cairns et al., 1976) as a means by which to automatically measure a patient's "uptime." The uptime recorder, which is similar in appearance to a large clock, may be mounted on a patient's bed; it automatically records and graphically displays to the patient the amount of time spent out of bed each day. The disadvantage associated with this device, however, is that in both inpatient and outpatient settings, patients may sit or recline in areas other than their bedrooms.

Sanders (1980) has attempted to overcome the limitations of the previously described recording device by developing an inexpensive, portable automatic device for recording daily uptime. The device consists of a miniature electronic calculator that is modified to interface with a mercury tilt switch mounted on a patient's thigh with an elastic bandage. The calculator may be worn in a relatively unobtrusive manner in its carrying case on a patient's belt. Sanders (1980) has presented a series of investigations that have provided positive evidence regarding the reliability and concurrent validity of uptime measurements produced by the automatic recording device. Two important benefits of Sanders's recording device are that it allows for continuous monitoring of patient behavior and that it provides data that may be used as criteria against which to compare patients' self-monitored observations of their uptime. However, as noted by Keefe (1982), a major limitation of the device is that it can record only the length of uptime activities each day. Thus, criteria against which to compare patients' reports concerning their performance of specific uptime behaviors must be derived from direct observations produced by health care staff or family members. Also, there currently exists no evidence that outpatients can use the device in their home environments without close supervision.

In summary, little attention has been directed toward the development of automated measurement devices relative to the development of direct observation and self-monitoring assessment techniques. Sanders's (1980) portable uptime calculator represents a major improvement relative to the stationary uptime recorder developed by Cairns et al. (1976). Moreover, it can be used to generate data that may serve as criteria against which to validate patients' self-monitored reports of uptime. At the present time, however, the uptime calculator can be used with confidence only in inpatient settings. The present authors suggest that the calculator should be employed only in combination with other direct observation or self-monitoring assessment techniques. This suggestion is based on the fact that sole reliance upon the uptime calculator would result in the loss of valuable information regarding the types of uptime activities engaged in by patients and the manner in which these activities are performed. For example, without the use of adjunct assessment techniques, it would be impossible to determine if patients (1) appropriately pace their activities, (2) engage in a variety of uptime activities with other persons or perform a small number of uptime activities in isolation from others, or (3) engage in uptime activities that may be too strenuous or excessively restricted given the status of their physical injuries.

Conclusions on Overt Motor Behaviors

The measurement of overt motor behaviors represents a very practical approach to chronic pain assessment given that it provides the investigator or clinician with measures of patients' functional disabilities that may be repeatedly assessed during treatment and follow-up periods. Furthermore, the use of behavioral measurements also avoids the difficulties associated with reliance upon subjective, global pain reports obtained during diagnostic interviews (Bradley et al., 1981). There are, however, several inadequacies associated with behavioral measurements. First, the measurement of behavior cannot provide information regarding the presence of some underlying pathology such as the locus, temporal quality, and sensory and affective aspects of the pain experience (Bradley et al., 1981; Sternbach, 1978a). This limitation of behavioral measurement may be of crucial importance in the case of pain patients who suffer from physical disorders that have remained undetected prior to behavioral assessment.

The second inadequacy is that, with the exception of automated measurement devices, the reliability of all of the behavioral measurement techniques described here must be reexamined at various intervals in order to ensure that observers or patients accurately and consistently record their data. The Rybstein-Blinchik (1979) and Taylor et al. (1980) investigations provide excellent examples of the need to assess the reliability of direct behavioral observations and self-monitored behavioral recordings if investigators and clinicians are to avoid making errors concerning the effectiveness of treatment interventions.

The final inadequacy associated with behavioral measurements is that it currently is unknown to what extent reactivity affects direct observations, self-monitored assessments, and automated recordings of patient behavior (see Bradley et al., 1981). *Reactivity* refers to patient initiation of behavior change due to the assessment procedure alone. It is highly likely that reactivity will occur when self-monitoring or automated assessment techniques are employed. In addition, reactivity is likely to occur in inpatient settings when health care personnel must record patient exercise and activity levels or when assessment systems such as that developed by Keefe and Block (1982) are implemented.

Measurement of Cognitive Responses

A great deal of research has been published concerning the assessment of patients' cognitions concerning their pain experiences (e.g., Bradley & Prokop, 1982). The increased interest in patients' cognitions may be attributed to the recent acknowledgment of the subjective aspect of the pain experience (IASP Subcommittee on Taxonomy, 1979) and the growing acceptance of the hypothesis that patients' appraisals of their self-efficacy mediate changes in their behavior during behaviorally oriented treatment (Bradley & Prokop, 1982; Keefe, 1982).

The great majority of the literature regarding the cognitive activity of chronic pain patients is devoted to the development of procedures with which to measure patients' subjective estimations of various dimensions of their pain experiences. The only systematic examinations of the role of cognitive activity in the modification of pain behaviors can be found in the laboratory-based, experimental pain literature (e.g., Leventhal, Brown, Shacham, & Engquist, 1979; Price, Barrell, & Gracely, 1980; Spanos, Radtke-Bodorik, Ferguson, & Jones, 1979; White, Bradley, & Moore, 1982). These studies, however, have prompted a small number of investigators to examine patterns of chronic pain patients' cognitive activity that may affect treatment outcome.

The following discussion examines the small literature concerning the assessment of cognitive activity of patients with chronic pain. It then reviews the relatively substantial literature regarding the measurement of patients' pain perceptions.

Assessment of Cognitive Activity
Relevant to Treatment Outcome

Genest and Turk (1979) have proposed that the four major models for the treatment of chronic pain — cognitive-behavioral therapy (Turk, 1978), operant conditioning (Fordyce, 1976), trans-

actional analysis (Sternbach, 1974), and multimodal rehabilitation (Gottlieb, Strite, Koller, Madorsky, Hockersmith, Kleeman,
& Wagner, 1977) — all share several characteristics. That is, all of
the models involve (1) the assessment and alteration of patients'
cognitions regarding their pain problems; (2) the development, acquisition, and rehearsal of new cognitive and behavioral skills for
coping with pain and the subsequent enhancement of patients' expectations of personal efficacy with regard to pain control; and
(3) techniques for the maintenance and generalization of positive
therapeutic change. Genest and Turk (1979) therefore have advocated the use of several assessment procedures that rely upon patients' self-reports of their cognitions (i.e., "think aloud" [Genest
& Turk, 1981] or "self-referent speech" [Kendall & Hollon, 1981]
procedures). However, only a small number of investigators actually have attempted to perform empirical examinations of patients' cognitions that may be related to treatment outcome.[2] These
investigators have not attempted to examine the utility of the assessment methods noted earlier. Instead, they appear to have been influenced by the laboratory-based experimental pain literature.
These investigators have attempted to develop psychometric instruments for the measurement of cognitions that may direct patients' attention toward or away from their painful perceptions and
thus either exacerbate or reduce their pain experiences.

Lefebvre (1981) has produced two questionnaires that measure cognitive errors that may be made by depressed, low back pain
patients. The reliability of the questionnaires is sufficiently high.
The validity studies reported by Lefebvre (1981) suggest that depressed, low back pain patients tend to produce cognitive errors
with regard to both general life experiences and specific experiences associated with chronic low back pain.

Rosenstiel and Keefe (1980) developed a questionnaire for the
assessment of patients' use of various cognitive and behavioral coping strategies. The internal reliability of the questionnaire was sufficiently high. Therefore, a factor analysis of chronic low back pain
patients' responses to the questionnaire was performed. Three factors emerged from the analysis. These were: (1) cognitive coping
and suppression, (2) helplessness, and (3) praying and distraction.

---

[2]Indeed, only one (Grzesiak, 1984) of three reviews of cognitive-behavioral
treatments for the control of pain (cf. Tan, 1982; Turner & Chapman, 1982) includes a substantial discussion of the assessment of patients' cognitions during
treatment.

It was found that patients with high scores on the cognitive coping and suppression or the praying and distraction factors tended to show high levels of functional impairment. Patients who produced high scores on the helplessness factor tended to display high levels of anxiety and depression. It should be noted, however, that the factor structure of the questionnaire may be somewhat unstable given the relatively low ratio of respondents to items associated with the analysis (cf. Gorsuch, 1974). Nonetheless, the Rosenstiel and Keefe (1980) investigation does provide some empirical evidence that use of the primarily cognitive coping strategies may not adequately direct patients' attention from their perceptions of pain and thus may be associated with high levels of functional impairment or depression and anxiety.

In summary, despite the surge of interest in the cognitive activity of chronic pain patients, little empirical work has been performed concerning the systematic assessment of patients' cognitions. The two investigations (Lefebvre, 1981; Rosenstiel & Keefe, 1980) reviewed here have provided evidence suggesting that some chronic low back pain patients are likely to suffer from cognitive distortions regarding their life experiences or may attempt to use cognitive coping strategies that may be related to poor functional adjustment. The results of these investigations should prompt other researchers to develop more refined psychometric instruments and verbal self-report measures for the assessment of patients' cognitions. It would be particularly important to further examine the assessment and efficacy of the cognitive coping and suppression strategy derived by Rosenstiel and Keefe (1980), given that the responses associated with this strategy (e.g., reinterpretation of painful perceptions, producing positive self-statements) are quite similar to those taught to chronic pain patients by therapists with cognitive-behavioral orientations (e.g., Hartman & Ainsworth, 1980; Herman & Baptiste, 1981; Rybstein-Blinchik, 1979; Turk, 1978; Turner, 1982).

Measurement of Patients' Pain Perceptions

One of the most difficult tasks facing investigators and clinicians is the measurement of patients' subjective pain experiences (Bradley & Prokop, 1982). Despite the multidimensional nature of the subjective pain experience, investigators and clinicians usually ask patients to rate the intensity of their pain along numerical or verbal category scales. Although these scales are easily administered and scored, they do suffer from a lack of sensitivity (Huskisson, 1974; Wolff, 1978). This lack of sensitivity is due to the fact that the number of scale categories must be limited (e.g., 0-6) since human sensory information processing is restricted to effective discrimination of approximately seven categories (Bradley et al., 1981). In addition, it cannot be assumed that the differences between scale categories (e.g., mild vs moderate; moderate vs severe) are equal to one another (Gracely, 1979).

Given the difficulties associated with numerical and verbal category scales, a number of investigators and clinicians have begun to use visual analogue scales. A visual analogue scale (VAS) consists of a 10-cm line labeled "no pain" at one end and "unbearable pain" at the other. The subject or patient is required to place a perpendicular mark at the point along the line that best represents the perceived intensity of pain (Merskey, 1973). Several investigations have produced high and consistent correlations between patients' pain intensity ratings on visual analogue and verbal category scales (Kremer, Atkinson, & Ignelzi, 1981a; Scott & Huskisson, 1976; Woodforde & Merskey, 1972). It also has been demonstrated that patients' pain intensity ratings on visual analogue and numerical category scales are highly associated with one another (Kremer et al., 1981a; Reading, 1979a). Two advantages of the use of visual analogue scales relative to numerical and verbal category scales have been identified. First, the simplicity of the VAS procedure allows it to be used with children as young as 5 years with no greater incidence of failure than that associated with adults (Scott, Ansell, & Huskisson, 1977). Furthermore, there is some evidence that visual analogue scales are sensitive to small changes in perceived pain intensity following analgesic treatment (Scott & Huskisson, 1976; Twycross, 1976). Gracely (1979), however, has questioned the sensitivity of visual analogue scales. Two empirical studies also have provided evidence that persons tend to be unable to reproduce VAS scores (Dixon & Bird, 1981; Scott & Huskisson, 1979). Dixon and Bird (1981) found that VAS ratings within ±2 cm of the midpoint were most difficult for persons to reproduce, while Scott and Huskisson (1979) found that patients tended to overestimate pain intensity when their initial VAS ratings were unavailable to them. These reproduction errors have been attributed to poor instructions, patient noncompliance, and patients' attempts to present what they believe they ought to feel rather than what they actually experience (Dixon & Bird, 1981). Kremer and his colleagues (1981a) have reported that patient age is positively correlated with failure to complete a VAS measure of pain intensity. These investigators have suggested that the greater cognitive activity required by visual analogue scales relative to numerical and verbal category scales may lead to failure among the elderly or those who are prone to be noncompliant. Nonetheless, numerous investigators continue to use visual analogue scales to assess pain intensity as well as various other experiences associated with pain (e.g., stiffness, interference with work, analgesic effectiveness) (Million, Hall, Nilsen, Baker, & Jayson, 1982).

The measurement techniques described in the preceding paragraphs are similar to one another in that they all were developed to assess only one dimension of pain. None of these techniques, therefore, may be used to fully evaluate the multidimensional nature of patients' pain states. As a result, there has been considerable effort directed toward the development of verbal descriptor scales that measure various dimensions of pain (Bradley et al., 1981). The verbal descriptor scale that is most frequently used by investigators and clinicians is the McGill Pain Questionnaire (Melzack, 1975; MPQ). The MPQ consists of 20 category scales of verbal descriptors; the descriptors within each category scale are rank ordered in terms of pain intensity. Thirteen of the category scales are considered to be representative of the *sensory qualities* of pain (e.g., temporal, spatial). The *affective dimension* of pain (e.g., tension, fear) is represented by six category scales, while the *evaluative dimension* (i.e., overall subjective intensity) is represented by one scale. The patient or subject is required to choose one word from a five-category, verbal- and numerical-interval scale of pain intensity (Melzack & Torgerson, 1971) that best describes the subjective pain experience at that moment. The patient or subject then must examine each category scale and choose one word from each relevant scale that best describes the subjective pain experience. Three different pain measures may be derived. These measures are the: (1) Present Pain Intensity (PPI), or the estimate of pain intensity on the five-category interval scale developed by Melzack and Torgerson (1971); (2) Number of Words Chosen (NWC) from among the 20 category scales; and (3) Pain Rating Index (PRI), which may be the sum of the rank values of descriptors chosen from each of the three pain dimensions or across all dimensions.

Data regarding the psychometric properties of the MPQ have not been produced as rapidly as have investigations that have used the MPQ as a measure of treatment efficacy (Bradley & Prokop,

1982). For example, only two investigations of the reliability of patients' choices of category scales have been performed (Graham, Bond, Gerkovich, & Cook, 1980; Melzack, 1975). Both of these investigations, however, have produced positive results.

The validity of the MPQ has been examined by several investigators who generally have used different experimental methods. First, some investigators have examined the construct validity of the MPQ by assessing changes in the descriptor choices made by patients following the administration of an analgesic or algesic treatment intervention (Fox & Melzack, 1976; Melzack & Perry, 1975; VanBuren & Kleinknecht, 1979). The results of all three studies have indicated that the PPI and PRI measures of the MPQ are sensitive to changes in patients' pain experiences following the administration of various interventions. Similar results have been obtained in a laboratory setting by Klepac, Dowling, and Hauge (1981).

Another group of investigators have examined the construct validity of the MPQ by performing factor analyses of patients' responses. These investigators have sought to delineate relatively independent factors composed of sensory, affective, and evaluative descriptors or category scales. The results of two early investigations (Crockett, Prkachin, & Craig, 1977; Leavitt, Garron, Whisler, & Sheinkop, 1978) suggested that there were five and seven dimensions, respectively, underlying subjects' MPQ responses. These results must be viewed with caution due to methodological deficiencies with both the Crockett et al. and Leavitt et al. investigations (Bradley et al., 1981; Prieto & Geisinger, in press). Several relatively sophisticated factor analytic investigations have provided strong evidence regarding the construct validity of the MPQ (McCreary, Turner, & Dawson, 1981; Prieto, Hopson, Bradley, Byrne, Geisinger, Midax, & Marchisello, 1980; Reading, 1979b). Each of these investigations differed from the others with respect to either subjects (back pain clinic patients vs gynecology clinic patients) or factor analytic methods (e.g., orthogonal vs oblique rotation solutions). Nonetheless, four-factor solutions were derived in each investigation. Furthermore, factors comprised solely of sensory and affective category scales, respectively, were derived from each investigation. The Prieto et al. (1980) study was particularly significant given that the analysis produced three factors composed entirely of sensory, affective, and evaluative category scales as well as a fourth factor that was defined by both sensory and affective scales. A cross-validation study (Byrne, Troy,

Bradley, Marchisello, Geisinger, Van der Heide, & Prieto, 1982) produced three factors that were highly associated with the sensory, evaluative, and affective-sensory factors derived by Prieto et al. (1980). Unfortunately, the affective factor previously found by Prieto et al. was not successfully cross-validated.

Despite the somewhat disappointing results of the Byrne et al. (1982) investigation, a final group of investigators have provided independent evidence concerning the construct validity of the affective dimension of the MPQ. Kremer and Atkinson (1981), for example, reported that chronic pain inpatients with relatively high affective PRI scores produced significantly higher scores on the Somatization, Depression, and Anxiety Scales of the Brief Symptom Inventory than did those with relatively low affective PRI scores. McCreary et al. (1981) found that a sample of outpatients attending a back clinic produced affective MPQ responses that were significantly associated with their scores on the Hypochondriasis, Depression, and Hysteria Scales of the MMPI independent of their pain intensity ratings. Similarly, Hunter and Philips (1981) showed that there were significant correlations between the affective PRI and Wakefield Depression Scale scores of psychiatric patients with tension headaches. In an examination of the concurrent validity of the MPQ, Mendelson and Selwood (1981) correlated the VAS pain intensity ratings and PRI scores produced by chronic pain patients at three different times during a double-blind, crossover trial of acupuncture effectiveness. Significant correlations between VAS ratings and all PRI scores were found at each assessment. Among the PRI scores, however, the affective scores showed the lowest association with the VAS ratings at two of the three assessments.

Reading, Everitt, and Sledmere (1981) have produced the most ambitious study of the construct validity of the MPQ. These investigators attempted to replicate the MPQ's 20-category scale structure and determine the intensity distribution of the verbal descriptors in each scale using methodological and statistical procedures different from those used by Melzack (1975; Melzack & Torgerson, 1971). Ninety subjects' naive sortings of MPQ descriptors into pain quality categories were transformed into a similarity matrix and subjected to cluster analysis procedures. Although a 20-category solution showed "considerable similarity" (Reading et al., 1981, p. 343) to the MPQ structure, a solution comprised of 16 categories (13 sensory and 3 affective) appeared to be most appropriate. The similarity of 20 additional subjects' ratings of descriptor intensity within each category was examined using Kendall's W statistic. Subjects' ratings on 13 categories were significantly associated with one another although the W statistic was greater than 0.50 on only six categories. It may be concluded that the Reading et al. (1981) investigation provided positive evidence regarding the construct validity of the sensory and affective dimensions of the MPQ. Similar to the results of the majority of the factor analytic investigations, evidence for the validity of the evaluative dimension was not found. The results of the Reading et al. study also suggested that there may be large interindividual differences in subjects' perceptions of the intensities of the MPQ descriptors.

The evidence reviewed here suggests that the reliability and validity of the MPQ are acceptable. In addition, the MPQ provides a unique, multidimensional assessment of the pain experience that is in accord with current pain taxonomy and theories of pain perception (Bradley et al., 1981). It should be noted, however, that Klepac and his colleagues (Klepac, Dowling, Rokke, Dodge, & Schaffer, 1981) have shown that differences in the administration of the instrument may produce significantly different scores on all of the PRI and NWC measures. Thus, refinements in the instructions, structure, and scoring of the MPQ may well be performed in the future as additional construct validity studies are performed and replicated.

As noted in the preceding discussion, the development of the MPQ represents a major advance in the assessment of pain. However, the scaling techniques used to construct the MPQ yield only ordinal data. The scaling techniques, then, are rather unsophisticated compared to the psychophysical scaling procedures of magnitude estimation and cross-modality matching that have been used by a small number of investigators to develop relatively bias-free ratio scales of verbal pain descriptors (cf. Bradley et al., 1981; Keefe, 1982). Gracely and his colleagues at the National Institute of Dental Research have produced the most voluminous research in this area (Gracely, Dubner, & McGrath, 1979; Gracely, Mc-Grath, & Dubner, 1978b, 1978c). These investigators have provided impressive evidence concerning the reliability, objectivity, and validity of relatively bias-free ratio scales of sensory intensity and affect (see Gracely and Dubner [1981] for an excellent summary of this research program). In addition, they also have produced some preliminary evidence that the scales may permit valid evaluations of clinical as well as experimental pain (Gracely, Dubner, McGrath, & Heft, 1978a; Heft, Gracely, Dubner, & McGrath,

1980). For example, Heft et al. (1980) found that college-educated subjects' judgments of sensory intensity and affect (unpleasantness) associated with "clinical" noxious stimulation (i.e., ethyl chloride applied for 1 sec to the exposed dentin of an excavated cavity preparation) could be reliably predicted from (1) matches between "clinical" and experimental stimulation (i.e., electrical stimulation of tooth pulp) and the judgments of sensory intensity and affect; and (2) the psychophysical power function relating intensity or affect judgments of the experimental stimulation with stimulation intensity. It should be noted, however, that both the Gracely et al. (1978a) and the Heft et al. (1980) investigations used small numbers of well-educated and presumably highly motivated subjects who were capable of performing the scaling procedures without difficulty. It therefore is necessary to perform further investigations with large numbers of persons suffering clinical pain before the ratio scales of sensory intensity and affect may be accepted as useful clinical instruments.

In summary, there are several techniques available for the measurement of patients' pain perceptions. Techniques such as numerical and verbal category scales and visual analogue scales have been used by a large number of investigators and clinicians to measure perceptions of pain intensity. Although these scales can be administered to most persons with relative ease, many have serious deficiencies with regard to (1) the use of limited response categories, (2) sensitivity, and (3) the provision of unidimensional judgments.

The MPQ is a multidimensional measure of pain that is free from many of the difficulties associated with the other scales described here. Several investigators have produced encouraging evidence regarding the reliability and validity of the instrument. However, the MPQ may be criticized with respect to its (1) reliance upon category scaling procedures, (2) inclusion of verbal descriptors that may not be easily used by patients from low socioeconomic backgrounds or who are unfamiliar with the English language (Bradley et al., 1981; Wolff, 1978), and (3) tendency to generate different PRI and NWC scores as a function of mode of administration.

Conclusions on Cognition

The majority of investigations devoted to the assessment of chronic pain patients' cognitions have involved the measurement of patients' pain perceptions. Two very important advances have been made in the measurement of pain perceptions (see Bradley et al., 1981). First, there has been the acknowledgment among investigators and many clinicians that the use of unidimensional category scales or visual analogue scales is not sufficient to adequately measure pain perceptions. The second advance has been the attempt to develop verbal descriptor scales of the multiple dimensions of pain (e.g., Gracely et al., 1978b, 1978c; Melzack, 1975). Although these verbal descriptor scales provide reliable and valid measures of pain perceptions, their use with chronic pain patients may be limited by the level of verbal sophistication required by the instruments.

Given that all of the pain perception measures described in this section have various advantages and shortcomings, it may be necessary for investigators and clinicians to administer several pain measurement instruments to their subjects and patients in order to establish the levels of correspondence between the instruments. Thus, if different measures of the same pain dimension are found to be highly associated with one another, the instruments may be used with confidence (see Reading, 1979a).

The remainder of the research concerning chronic pain patients' cognitions has been devoted to the development of psychometric instruments for the assessment of cognitions that may be related to treatment outcome. These instruments include measures of (1) cognitive errors regarding chronic back pain and general life experiences (Lefebvre, 1981) and (2) cognitive and behavioral coping strategies (Rosenstiel & Keefe, 1980). Although the psychometric properties of these instruments are adequate, it will be necessary for future investigators to determine their clinical utility (e.g., predictive validity with respect to outcome).

Measurement of Physiological Variables

The measurement of physiological variables has not received a great deal of attention among chronic pain investigators with the exception of those interested in applying biofeedback technology in the treatment of stress-related disorders such as tension and migraine headaches and Raynaud's disease (see Bradley and Prokop [1982] for a complete review of this literature). Thus, for example, the stress-related disorder literature contains many studies that include measurements of frontal EMG levels (i.e., a purported measure of tension headache activity) and peripheral skin temperature (i.e., an indirect measure of peripheral blood volume used in studies of migraine headaches and Raynaud's disease activity). The difficulty with this literature is that the evidence indicates that there are not necessarily direct relationships between measurements of the physiological variables noted and episodes of or improvements in the disorders with which they are associated (see Andrasik & Holroyd, 1980; Bradley & Prokop, 1982; Burish, 1981; Holmes, 1981; Scott, 1979).

Investigations regarding chronic pain problems other than those usually identified as stress related often have included measures of EMG activity from various muscle sites. This emphasis upon measurement of EMG activity stems from the widely held belief that many patients who experience chronic pain tend to restrict their spinal motion and other movements, and thus alter their muscle activity levels for prolonged periods. These changes lead to a vicious cycle in which normal activities of daily living elicit increased muscle pain, which, in turn, produces further restriction of motion (e.g., Keefe, 1982; Pope, Rosen, Wilder, & Frymoyer, 1980). However, as in the case of the stress-related disorders, the relationship between EMG activity at various muscle sites and the experience of pain or muscle spasm is not necessarily direct (Keefe, 1982).

Wolf and his colleagues, (Wolf, 1982; Wolf, Nacht, & Kelly, 1982) recently have attempted to resolve some of the inconsistencies in the physiological assessment literature by studying patterns rather than absolute levels of EMG activity in lumbar muscle sites among chronic pain patients. It was found, for example, that during static and dynamic activities, normal persons tend to produce low and symmetrical levels of EMG activity from electrode placements on both sides of the lumbar spine. However, chronic back pain patients tend to show abnormal EMG patterns (e.g., asymmetry of right and left lumbar spine EMG levels) during static and dynamic activities. It also was reported that patients who were trained to produce more normal EMG patterns tended to report reduced perceptions of pain and to display increased activity levels (Wolf, 1982; Wolf et al., 1982).

Another group of investigators have attempted to use cerebrospinal fluid (CSF) levels of endorphins and related physiological measures as biological markers of patients' pain experiences. Terenius and his colleagues have performed several investigations in which it was demonstrated that CSF concentrations of Fraction I endorphins were related to subjects' pain thresholds (Von Knor-

ring, Almay, Johansson, & Terenius, 1978) and to patients' repc
of decreased pain perception following low-frequency, high-int
sity, transcutaneous nerve stimulation (Terenius, 1979). Teren
also has found significantly higher levels of Fraction I endorph
among patients with pain judged by physicians as organic (p
ticularly neurogenic pain) than among healthy volunteers or
tients with pain classified as psychogenic (Terenius, 1979). Sim
to the results already noted, Anselmi and his colleagues (Ansel
Baldi, Cassacci, & Salmin, 1980) have found significant reducti
in CSF enkephalins among migraine headache patients during
graine episodes.

These studies are of interest since they all have demonstra
consistent relationships between CSF levels of endorphins or
kephalins and patients' perceptions of pain. The results of th
studies, however, do not possess a great deal of clinical utility gi
that it is unfeasible, both with regard to clinical risks and fin
cial costs, to routinely perform assays of CSF endorphin lev
among chronic pain patients.

Unlike the investigations concerning CSF endorphin and
kephalin levels, a series of studies regarding the use of seroto
or its precursor, blood plasma L-tryptophan, as a biological mar
for chronic pain have produced results with some clinical utili
It should be noted that several laboratory investigations with a
mals have shown that descending serotonergic pathways in the c
tral nervous system are involved in the modulation of nocicept
transmission (Carstens, Fraunhoffer, & Zimmerman, 1981; H
vey, Schlosberg, & Yunger, 1975; Messing & Lytle, 1977; Yal
& Wilson, 1979). A number of studies with human subjects ha
indicated that persons' pain perceptions are associated with lev
of serotonin or L-tryptophan. For example, Mao and his colleag
(Mao, Ghia, Scott, Duncan, & Gregg, 1980) reported that chro
pain patients who were given high-intensity electroacupunct
treatments showed significant decreases in global pain estimat
significant and positive changes in their self-reports of vari
activities of daily living, and significant increases in blood seroto
levels. Similarly, Hosobuchi (1978, 1980) demonstrated that tol
ance to analgesia produced by periaqueductal gray stimulati
(PAGS) was reversed by loading subjects' diets with L-tryptoph
These studies at first may suggest that levels of serotonin or
tryptophan might constitute promising and relatively object
markers of the chronic pain experience. It should be noted, ho
ever, that serotonin levels also have been shown to be associat

with patients' reports of depression (e.g., Coppen, 1972; Lapin & Oxenburg, 1969; Sarai & Kayano, 1968). Given that serotonin levels are linked to depression and that depression tends to accompany chronic pain conditions (Sternbach, 1974), it may be that serotonin levels serve primarily as markers of depression among chronic pain patients. Nonetheless, the serotonin investigations have been shown to have some clinical significance. Hosobuchi, Lamb, and Bascom (1980) found that five chronic pain patients with arachnoiditis who were morphine tolerant showed complete or nearly complete relief of pain with morphine administration following dietary loading with L-tryptophan. Patients' self-reports of pain relief were validated by patients' endurance of straight leg raising to normal limits. Thus, despite the fact that serotonin levels may not represent truly objective measures of perceptions of chronic pain, preliminary investigations (Hosobuchi, 1978, 1980; Hosobuchi et al., 1980) suggest that dietary manipulations involving L-tryptophan may be useful as adjunct treatments for some chronic pain conditions (for a complete review, see Seltzer, Marcus, & Stock [1981]).

In conclusion, the assessment of physiological variables poses two important problems for both investigators and clinicians. First, although there are some physiological variables that are assumed to be associated with the occurrence of several stress-related disorders (e.g., frontal EMG levels as markers of tension headache activity), there are not necessarily direct relationships between these variables and episodes of the various disorders. The validity of the assessment of physiological variables, therefore, has not been adequately established. The second problem posed by the physiological variables is their clinical utility. For example, Terenius (1979) and other investigators have demonstrated that CSF endorphin and enkephalin levels tend to be associated with patients' reports of pain. Although assessment of endorphin and enkephalin levels may represent a valid measure of the pain experience, it would not be useful to routinely perform assays on chronic pain patients due to the clinical risks and expenses involved with the assay procedures.

The measurement of serotonin or L-tryptophan levels appears to be a promising physiological assessment technique. Although it is unclear to what extent these physiological variables reflect levels of depression or chronic pain, the assessment of these variables is inexpensive and safe relative to that of CSF endorphin and enkephalin levels (e.g., Mao et al., [1980] drew 5 ml of venous blood from each subject to perform their serotonin assay). Preliminary investigations (Hosobuchi, 1978, 1980; Hosobuchi et al., 1980) have indicated that increases in chronic pain patients' L-tryptophan levels are positively associated with their responses to various analgesic interventions (i.e., PAGS, administration of morphine).

Another promising assessment technique appears to be the measurement of patterns of lumbar EMG activity described by Wolf and his colleagues. Despite the fact that this assessment technique is relatively new, preliminary evidence suggests that changes in lumbar EMG patterns are associated with changes in pain perceptions and improved functional abilities (Wolf, 1982).

In summary, a large number of physiological variables have been used to aid in the assessment of chronic pain. The results of the literature performed to date, however, suggest that measurement of physiological variables represents an imprecise and inadequate means with which to assess chronic pain. It is hoped that future research concerning the relatively promising physiological assessment techniques will produce more valid and clinically useful assessment procedures.

Current Status of Behavioral Assessment of Chronic Pain and Suggestions for Future Research

The current chapter presents a critical review of the empirical literature regarding the assessment of overt motor behaviors, cognitive responses, and physiological variables associated with chronic pain. It is not possible to describe the current status of the assessment literature as a single entity. Given that the relationships among overt motor, cognitive, and physiological variables have not been studied sufficiently, it is best to describe the assessment literature as consisting of three relatively independent content areas, each of which is associated with various strengths and weaknesses.

The literature concerning the assessment of overt motor behavior is more fully developed relative to that regarding the assessment of cognitive and physiological variables. The results of the investigations utilizing direct observation methods indicate that well-trained observers can provide reliable data regarding patients' disabilities in activities of daily living. The behavioral observation system developed by Keefe and Block (1982) represents a particularly useful assessment technique. Although this system and other methods of direct monitoring are susceptible to reactivity effects, they tend to produce data with greater accuracy and reliability than do the self-monitoring methods such as the daily activity diary. The development of automated devices for the measurement of patient uptime, such as that produced by Sanders (1980), represents a means by which to continuously record patient behavior in a highly reliable fashion. These automated devices also produce data that may serve as criteria against which to validate patients' self-monitored observations of their uptime behavior. However, automated uptime measurement is limited in that (1) it cannot assess the performance of specific uptime behaviors, (2) it is susceptible to reactivity effects, and (3) there is no evidence to suggest that outpatients can use automated devices in a reliable fashion in their home environments.

The majority of research concerning the assessment of patients' cognitions has been devoted to the development of reliable and valid measures of patients' pain perceptions. The most significant work in the area of cognitive assessment has been the development of multidimensional, verbal descriptor measures of pain perceptions. These measures, unlike the overt motor assessment techniques previously described, provide clinicians with information regarding the sensory and affective qualities of pain that may be useful in determining the etiology of the perceived pain. Nevertheless, the utility of the verbal descriptor scales is dependent upon patients' facility with the English language. It also should be noted that there are unique advantages and disadvantages associated with the two verbal descriptor measures that are currently available. That is, the MPQ appears to provide reliable and valid data but suffers from its (1) reliance upon category scales and (2) sensitivity to differences between modes of administration (e.g., Klepac et al., 1981). The verbal descriptor scales developed by Gracely et al. (1978b, 1978c) are products of sophisticated psychophysical scaling techniques. However, the clinical utility of these scales has not been established.

The assessment of physiological variables is a very new area of investigation in the chronic pain literature. Although a few promising assessment techniques do exist (e.g., Mao et al., 1980; Wolf et al., 1982), no single physiological measure can currently be used as a marker of the pain experience.

The preceding discussion indicates that none of the assessment techniques described in this chapter provides a complete assessment of patients' pain experiences. As a result, many clinicians and investigators use multiple measures of overt motor behavior, cognitive responses, and physiological variables to evaluate chronic pain patients and their treatment outcomes. For example, Keefe et al. (1981) published an evaluation of the efficacy of an inpatient treatment program that reported patient changes with respect to (1) VAS ratings of subjective tension and pain intensity (cognitive variables), (2) frontal EMG activity levels (physiological variables), and (3) medication intake and activity level (overt motor behaviors). Although the use of multiple assessment measures is desirable, it is necessary for future investigators to determine the relationships among various pain assessment measures within specific patient groups. Both Bradley et al. (1981) and Keefe (1982) have encouraged investigators to perform multivariate studies with large patient samples in order to help behavioral medicine specialists make optimal judgments regarding diagnosis and treatment on the basis of assessment data.

A second task for future investigators is to devote greater attention to the behavior of family members and other significant persons who may influence the pain behaviors shown by patients prior to, during, and following treatment. Although Fordyce (1976) and Sternbach (1974) acknowledged the importance of family members in patients' chronic pain problems in the mid-1970s, considerable time elapsed before the assessment of family members received substantial attention from investigators (e.g., Blumer & Heilbronn, 1980; Maruta & Osborne, 1978; Maruta, Osborne, Swanson, & Halling, 1981). Three important findings have emerged from the small literature that is available. First, there appears to be a tendency among a subgroup of chronic pain patients and their spouses (who may be especially difficult to successfully treat) to share symptoms or beliefs regarding pain (see Mohamed, Weisz, & Waring, 1978; Shanfield, Herman, Cope, & Jones, 1979; Swanson & Maruta, 1980). Second, patients' pain experiences and pain behaviors are influenced by their relationships with their spouses and other family members (Block, Kremer, & Gaylor, 1980; Richards, Meredith, Nepomuceno, Fine, & Bennett, 1980; Swanson & Maruta, 1980). Finally, one investigation (Block, 1981) has demonstrated that spouses of chronic pain patients who report relatively high levels of marital satisfaction show greater skin conductance responses when viewing facial pain displays of their marital partners than do spouses who report relatively low levels of marital satisfaction. The spouses who reported high and low levels of satisfaction (1) did not differ with respect to their ratings of the intensity of their partners' pain displays and (2) did not produce different skin conductance responses when viewing the pain displays of unfamiliar persons who were described as chronic pain patients. These results suggest that future investigators should attempt to develop methods for the assessment of spouses and other family members that might be useful in treatment planning or in the prediction of treatment outcome.

A final task for future investigators is to develop methods of behavioral assessment that might be used by physicians (e.g., family practitioners) and other health care personnel (e.g., physician assistants) who often must treat chronic pain patients without having the services of a skilled psychologist available to them. Pope et al. (1980) described the use of several automatic recording devices that provide accurate and reliable measurements of patient behaviors that are of interest to orthopedic surgeons. For example, in order to measure straight leg raising (SLR), light-emitting diodes (LEDs) were fixed to a patient's ankles, knees, and upper thighs; the thigh LEDs would flash only when the patient turned a switch to signal the onset of perceived pain. As the orthopedic surgeon lifted the patient's ankle to begin the SLR procedure, a camera shutter opened and a pathway of dots was recorded on film. The automatic recording device permitted the measurement and recording of the patient's performance on the SLR procedure and the point at which the patient experienced pain. Although this device might be expensive or cumbersome, it would be expected to increase the reliability of physicians' judgments concerning patients' SLR performance. Similarly, the use of automated uptime recorders among physicians might help them to better evaluate inpatients' reports of functional disabilities. It may be that further development and refinement of behavioral assessment techniques, particularly those that automatically record patient behavior, could be beneficial both to psychologists interested in the assessment of chronic pain and to physicians and other health care personnel who often must treat chronic pain patients without the benefit of consultation with psychologists.

References

Andrasik, F., & Holroyd, K. A test of specific and nonspecific effects in the biofeedback treatment of tension headache. *Journal of Consulting and Clinical Psychology*, 1980, 48, 575–586.

Anselmi, B., Baldi, E., Cassacci, F., & Salmin, S. Endogenous opioids in cerebrospinal fluid and blood in idiopathic headache sufferers. *Headache*, 1980, *20*, 294–299.

Black, R. G., & Chapman, C. R. The SAD index for clinical assessment of pain. In J. J. Bonica & D. Albe-Fessard (Eds.), *Advances in pain research and therapy* (Vol. 1). New York: Raven Press, 1976.

Block, A. R. An investigation of the response of the spouse to chronic pain behavior. *Psychosomatic Medicine*, 1981, *43*, 415–442.

Block, A. R., Kremer, E. F., & Gaylor, M. Behavioral treatment of chronic pain: The spouse as a discriminative cue for pain behavior. *Pain*, 1980, *9*, 243–252.

Blumer, D., & Heilbronn, M. The pain-prone disorder: A clinical and psychological profile. *Psychosomatics*, 1980, *22*, 395–402.

Bourhis, A., Boudouresque, G., Pellet, W. P., Fondarai, J., Ponzio, J., & Spitalier, J. M. Pain infirmity and psychotropic drugs in oncology. *Pain*, 1978, *5*, 263–274.

Bradley, L. A., & Prokop, C. K. Research methods in contemporary medical psychology. In P. C. Kendall & J. N. Butcher (Eds.), *Handbook of research methods in clinical psychology*. New York: Wiley, 1982.

Bradley, L. A., Prokop, C. K., Gentry, W. D., Van der Heide, L. H., & Prieto, E. J. Assessment of chronic pain. In C. K. Prokop and L. A. Bradley (Eds.), *Medical psychology: Contributions to behavioral medicine*. New York: Academic Press, 1981.

Brena, S. F., & Unikel, I. P. Nerve blocks and contingency management in chronic pain states. In J. J. Bonica & D. Albe-Fessard (Eds.), *Advances in pain research and therapy* (Vol. 1). New York: Raven Press, 1976.

Burish, T. G. EMG biofeedback in the treatment of stress-related disorders. In C. K. Prokop & L. A. Bradley (Eds.), *Medical psychology: Contributions to behavioral medicine*. New York: Academic Press, 1981.

Byrne, M., Troy, A., Bradley, L. A., Marchisello, P. J., Geisinger, K. F., Van der Heide, L. H., & Prieto, E. J. Cross-validation of the factor structure of the McGill Pain Questionnaire. *Pain*, 1982, *13*, 193–201.

Cairns, D., & Pasino, J. A. Comparison of verbal reinforcement and feedback in the operant treatment of disability due to chronic low back pain. *Behavior Therapy*, 1977, *8*, 621–630.

Cairns, D., Thomas, L., Mooney, B., & Pace, J. B. A comprehensive treatment approach to chronic low back pain. *Pain*, 1976, *2*, 301–308.

Carstens, E., Fraunhoffer, M., & Zimmermann, M. Serotonergic mediation of descending inhibition from midbrain periaqueductal gray, but not reticular formation, of spinal nociceptive transmission in the cat. *Pain*, 1981, *10*, 149–167.

Cohen, J. A. A coefficient of agreement for nominal scales. *Educational and Psychological Measurement*, 1960, *20*, 37–46.

Conger, A. J. Integration and generalization of kappas for multiple raters. *Psychological Bulletin*, 1980, *88*, 322–328.

Coppen, A. Serotonin in the affective disorders. *Journal of Psychosomatic Research*, 1972, *9*, 163–172.

Crockett, D. J., Prkachin, K. M., & Craig, K. D. Factors of the language of pain in patient and volunteer groups. *Pain*, 1977, *4*, 175–183.

Cronbach, L. J., Gleser, G. C., Nanda, H., & Rajaratnam, M. *The dependability of behavioral measurements: Theory of generalizability for scores and profiles*. New York: Wiley, 1972.

Dixon, J. S., & Bird, H. A. Reproducibility along a 10 cm vertical visual analogue scale. *Annals of the Rheumatic Diseases*, 1981, *40*, 87–89.

Duncan, G. H., Gregg, J. M., & Ghia, J. N. The pain profile: A computerized system for assessment of chronic pain. *Pain*, 1978, *5*, 275–284.

Fordyce, W. E. An operant conditioning method for managing chronic pain. *Postgraduate Medicine*, 1973, *53*, 123–128.

Fordyce, W. E. *Behavioral methods for chronic pain and illness*. St. Louis: C. V. Mosby, 1976.

Fordyce, W. E. Learning processes in pain. In R. Sternbach (Ed.), *The psychology of pain*. New York: Raven Press, 1978.

Fordyce, W. E., Fowler, R. S., DeLateur, B. J., Sand, P. L., & Trieschmann, R. B. Operant conditioning in the treatment of chronic pain. *Archives of Physical Medicine and Rehabilitation*, 1973, *54*, 399–408.

Fordyce, W. E., Fowler, R. S., Lehmann, J. F., & DeLateur, B. J. Some implications of learning in problems of chronic pain. *Journal of Chronic Diseases*, 1968, *21*, 179–190.

Fordyce, W., McMahon, R., Rainwater, G., Jackins, S., Questal, K., Murphy, T., & DeLateur, B. Pain complaint: Exercise performance relationship in chronic pain. *Pain*, 1981, *10*, 311–321.

Fox, E. J., & Melzack, R. Transcutaneous electrical stimulation and acupuncture: Comparison of treatment for low back pain. *Pain*, 1976, *2*, 141–148.

Genest, M., & Turk, D. C. A proposed model for behavioral group therapy with pain patients. In D. Upper & S. M. Ross (Eds.), *Behavioral group therapy: An annual review*. Champaign, IL: Research Press, 1979.

Genest, M., & Turk, D. C. Think-aloud approaches to cognitive assessment. In T. Merluzzi, C. Glass, & M. Genest (Eds.), *Cognitive assessment*. New York: Guilford Press, 1981.

Gorsuch, R. L. *Factor analysis*. Philadelphia: W. B. Saunders, 1974.

Gottlieb, H., Strite, L. C., Koller, R., Madorsky, A., Hockersmith, V., Kleeman, M., & Wagner, J. Comprehensive rehabilitation of patients having chronic low back pain. *Archives of Physical Medicine and Rehabilitation*, 1977, *58*, 101–108.

Gracely, R. H. Psychophysical assessment of human pain. In J. J. Bonica, J. C. Liebeskind, & D. Albe-Fessard (Eds.), *Advances in pain research and therapy* (Vol. 3). New York: Raven Press, 1979.

Gracely, R. H., & Dubner, R. Pain assessment in humans — A reply to Hall. *Pain*, 1981, *11*, 109–120.

Gracely, R. H., Dubner, R., & McGrath, P. Narcotic analgesia: Fentanyl reduces the intensity but not the unpleasantness of painful tooth pulp sensations. *Science*, 1979, *203*, 1261–1263.

Gracely, R. H., Dubner, R., McGrath, P., & Heft, M. New methods for pain measurement and their application to pain control. *International Dental Journal*, 1978, *28*, 52–65. (a)

Gracely, R. H., McGrath, P., & Dubner, R. Ratio scales of sensory and affective pain descriptors. *Pain*, 1978, *5*, 5–18. (b)

Gracely, R. H., McGrath, P., & Dubner, R. Validity and sensitivity of ratio scales of sensory and affective verbal pain descriptors: Manipulation of affect by diazpam. *Pain*, 1978, *5*, 19–29. (c)

Graham, C., Bond, S., Gerkovich, M. N., & Cook, M. R. Use of the McGill Pain Questionnaire in the assessment of cancer pain: Replicability and consistency. *Pain*, 1980, *8*, 377–387.

Grzesiak, R. C. Rehabilitation of chronic pain syndromes. In C. J. Golden (Ed.), *Current topics in rehabilitation psychology*. New York: Grune & Stratton, 1984.

Harvey, J. A., Schlosberg, A. J., & Yunger, L. N. Behavioral correlates of serotonin depletion. *Federation Proceedings*, 1975, *34*, 1796–1801.

Hartman, L. N., & Ainsworth, K. D. Self-regulation of chronic pain. *Canadian Journal of Psychiatry*, 1980, *25*, 38–43.

Heft, M. W., Gracely, R. H., Dubner, R., & McGrath, P. A. A validation model for verbal descriptor scaling of human clinical pain. *Pain*, 1980, *9*, 363–373.

Herman, E., & Baptiste, S. Pain control: Mastery through group experience. *Pain*, 1981, *10*, 79–86.

Holmes, D. S. The use of biofeedback for treating patients with migraine headaches, Raynaud's disease and hypertension: A critical evaluation. In C. K. Prokop & L. A. Bradley (Eds.), *Medical psychology: Contributions to behavioral medicine*. New York: Academic Press, 1981.

Hosobuchi, Y. L-Tryptophan reversal of tolerance to analgesia induced by central gray stimulation. *Lancet*, 1978, *2*, 47.

Hosobuchi, Y. Dietary supplementation with L-tryptophan reverses tolerance to analgesia induced by periaqueductal gray stimulation in humans. In E. L. Way (Ed.), *Endogenous and exogenous opiate agonists and antagonists*. Elmsford, NY: Pergamon Press, 1980.

Hosobuchi, Y., Lamb, S., & Bascom, D. Tryptophan loading may reverse tolerance to opiate analgesics in humans: A preliminary report. *Pain*, 1980, *9*, 161–169.

Hunter, M., & Philips, C. The experience of headache: An assessment of the qualities of tension headache pain. *Pain*, 1981, *10*, 209–219.

Huskisson, E. C. Measurement of pain. *Lancet*, 1974, *2*, 1127–1131.

IASP Subcommittee on Taxonomy. Pain terms: A list with definitions and notes on usage. *Pain*, 1979, *6*, 249–252.

Keefe, F. J. Behavioral assessment and treatment of chronic pain: Current status and future directions. *Journal of Consulting and Clinical Psychology*, 1982.

Keefe, F. J., & Block, A. R. Development of an observation method for assessing pain behavior in chronic low back pain patients. *Behavior Therapy*, 1982.

Keefe, F. J., Block, A. R., Williams, R. B., & Surwit, R. S. Behavioral treatment of chronic low back pain: Clinical outcomes and individual differences in pain relief. *Pain*, 1981, *11*, 221–231.

Kendall, P. C., & Hollon, S. D. Assessing self-referent speech: Methods in the measurement of self-statements. In P. C. Kendall & S. D. Hollon (Eds.), *Assessment strategies for cognitive-behavioral interventions*. New York: Academic Press, 1981.

Kent, R. N., & Foster, S. L. Direct observational procedures: Methodological issues in naturalistic settings. In A. R. Ciminero, K. S. Calhoun, & H. E. Adams (Eds.), *Handbook of behavioral assessment*. New York: Wiley, 1977.

Klein, R. N., & Charlton, J. E. Behavioral observation and analysis of pain behavior in critically burned patients. *Pain*, 1980, *9*, 27–40.

Klepac, R. K., Dowling, J., & Hauge, G. Sensitivity of the McGill Pain Questionnaire to intensity and quality of laboratory pain. *Pain*, 1981, *10*, 199–207.

Klepac, R. K., Dowling, J., Rokke, P., Dodge, L., & Schaffer, L. Interview vs. paper-and-pencil administration of the McGill Pain Questionnaire. *Pain*, 1981, *11*, 241–246.

Kremer, E., & Atkinson, J. H. Pain measurement: Construct validity of the affective dimension of the McGill Pain Questionnaire with chronic benign pain patients. *Pain*, 1981, *11*, 93–100.

Kremer, E., Atkinson, J. H., & Ignelzi, R. J. Measurement of pain: Patient preference does not confound pain measurement. *Pain*, 1981, *10*, 241–248. (a)

Kremer, E. F., Block, A., & Gaylor, M. S. Behavioral approaches to treatment of chronic pain: The inaccuracy of patient self-report measures. *Archives of Physical Medicine and Rehabilitation*, 1981, *62*, 188–191. (b)

Lapin, I. P., & Oxenburg, G. F. Intensification of the central serotonergic processes as a possible determinant of the thymoleptic effect. *Lancet*, 1969, *1*, 132.

Leavitt, F., Garron, D. C., Whisler, W., & Sheinkop, M. B. Affective and sensory dimensions of back pain. *Pain*, 1978, *4*, 273–281.

Lefebvre, M. F. Cognitive distortion and cognitive errors in depressed psychiatric and low back pain patients. *Journal of Consulting and Clinical Psychology*, 1981, *49*, 517–525.

Leventhal, H., Brown, D., Shacham, S., & Engquist, G. Effects of preparatory information about sensations, threat of pain, and attention on cold pressor distress. *Journal of Personality and Social Psychology*, 1979, *37*, 688–714.

Mao, W., Ghia, J. N., Scott, D. S., Duncan, G. H., & Gregg, J. M. High versus low intensity acupuncture analgesia for treatment of chronic pain: Effects on platelet serotonin. *Pain*, 1980, *8*, 331–342.

Maruta, T., & Osborne, D. Sexual activity in chronic pain patients. *Psychosomatics*, 1978, *19*, 531–537.

Maruta, T., Osborne, D., Swanson, D. W., & Halling, J. M. Chronic pain patients and spouses: Marital and sexual adjustment. *Mayo Clinic Proceedings*, 1981, *56*, 307–310.

McCreary, C., Turner, J., & Dawson, E. Principal dimensions of the pain experience and psychological disturbance in chronic low back pain patients. *Pain*, 1981, *11*, 85–92.

Melzack, R. The McGill Pain Questionnaire: Major properties and scoring methods. *Pain*, 1975, *1*, 277–299.

Melzack, R., & Dennis, S. G. Neurophysiological foundations of pain. In R. Sternbach (Ed.), *The psychology of pain*. New York: Raven Press, 1978.

Melzack, R., & Perry, C. Self-regulation of pain: The use of alpha-feedback and hypnotic training for the control of chronic pain. *Experimental Neurology*, 1975, *46*, 452–469.

Melzack, R., & Torgerson, W. S. On the language of pain. *Anesthesiology*, 1971, *34*, 50–59.

Mendelson, G., & Selwood, T. S. Measurement of chronic pain: A correlation study of verbal and nonverbal scales. *Journal of Behavioral Assessment*, 1981, *3*, 263–269.

Mersky, H. The perception and measurement of pain. *Journal of Psychosomatic Research*, 1973, *17*, 251–255.

Messing, R. B., & Lytle, L. D. Serotonin-containing neurons: Their possible role in pain and analgesia. *Pain*, 1977, *4*, 1–21.

Million, R., Hall, W., Nilsen, K. H., Baker, R. D., & Jayson, I. V. Assessment of the progress of the back-pain patient. *Spine*, 1982, *7*, 204–212.

Mitchell, S. K. Interobserver agreement, reliability, and generalizability of data collected in observational studies. *Psychological Bulletin*, 1979, *86*, 376–390.

Mohamed, S. N., Weisz, G. M., & Waring, E. M. The relationship of chronic pain to depression, marital adjustment, and family dynamics. *Pain*, 1978, *5*, 285–292.

Pope, M. H., Rosen, J. C., Wilder, D. G., & Frymoyer, J. W. The relation between biochemical and psychological factors in patients with low-back pain. *Spine*, 1980, *5*, 173–178.

Price, D. D., Barrell, J. J., & Gracely, R. H. A psychophysical analysis of experiential factors that selectively influence the affective dimension of pain. *Pain*, 1980, *8*, 137–149.

Prieto, E. J., & Geisinger, K. F. Factor analytic studies of the McGill Pain Questionnaire. In R. Melzack (Ed.), *Pain measurement and assessment*. New York: Raven Press, 1983.

Prieto, E. J., Hopson, L., Bradley, L. A., Byrne, M., Geisinger, K. F., Midax, D., & Marchisello, P. J. The language of low back pain: Factor structure of the McGill Pain Questionnaire. *Pain*, 1980, *8*, 11–19.

Reading, A. E. A comparison of pain rating scales. *Journal of Psychosomatic Research*, 1979, *24*, 119–124. (a)

Reading, A. E. The internal structure of the McGill Pain Questionnaire in dysmenorrhea patients. *Pain*, 1979, *7*, 353–358. (b)

Reading, A. E., Everitt, B. S., & Sledmere, Z. M. The McGill Pain Questionnaire: A replication of its construction. *British Journal of Clinical Psychology*, 1982, *21*, 339–349.

Ready, L. B., Sarkis, E., & Turner, J. A. Self-reported vs. actual use of medications in chronic pain patients. *Pain*, 1982, *12*, 285–294.

Richards, J. S., Meredith, R. L., Nepomuceno, C., Fine, P. R., & Bennett, G. Psycho-social aspects of chronic pain in spinal cord injury. *Pain*, 1980, *8*, 355–366.

Roberts, A. H., & Reinhardt, L. The behavioral management of chronic pain: Long-term follow-up with comparison groups. *Pain*, 1980, *8*, 151–162.

Rosenstiel, A. K., & Keefe, F. J. The use of coping strategies in chronic low back pain patients: Relationship to patient characteristics and current adjustment. *Pain*, 1983, *17*, 33–44.

Rybstein-Blinchik, E. Effects of different cognitive strategies on chronic pain experience. *Journal of Behavioral Medicine*, 1979, *2*, 93–101.

Sanders, S. H. Behavioral assessment and treatment of clinical pain: Appraisal of current status. In M. Hersen, R. M. Eisler, & P. M. Miller (Eds.), *Progress in behavior modification* (Vol. 8). New York: Academic Press, 1979.

Sanders, S. H. Toward a practical instrument system for the automatic measurement of "uptime" in chronic pain patients. *Pain*, 1980, *9*, 103–109.

Sarai, K., & Kayano, M. The level and diurnal rhythm of serum serotonin in manic-depressive patients. *Folia Psychiatrica et Neurologica Japonica*, 1968, *22*, 271–278.

Scott, D. S. A comprehensive treatment strategy for muscle contraction headaches. *Journal of Behavior Therapy and Experimental Psychiatry*, 1979, *10*, 35–40.

Scott, P. J., Ansell, B. M., & Huskisson, E. C. Measurement of pain in juvenile chronic polyarthritis. *Annals of the Rheumatic Diseases,* 1977, *36,* 186–187.

Scott, P. J., & Huskisson, E. C. Graphic representation of pain. *Pain,* 1976, *2,* 175–184.

Scott, P. J., & Huskisson, E. C. Accuracy of subjective measurements made with or without previous scores: An important source of error in serial measurement of subjective states. *Annals of the Rheumatic Diseases,* 1979, *38,* 558–559.

Seltzer, S., Marcus, R., & Stock, R. Perspectives in the control of chronic pain by nutritional manipulation. *Pain,* 1981, *11,* 141–148.

Shanfield, S. B., Heiman, E. M., Cope, D. N., & Jones, J. R. Pain and the marital relationship: Psychiatric distress. *Pain,* 1979, *7,* 343–351.

Spanos, N. P., Radtke-Bodorik, L., Ferguson, J. D., & Jones, B. The effects of hypnotic susceptibility, suggestions for analgesia, and the utilization of cognitive strategies on the reduction of pain. *Journal of Abnormal Psychology,* 1979, *88,* 282–292.

Sternbach, R. A. *Pain patients: Traits and treatment.* New York: Academic Press, 1974.

Sternbach, R. A. Clinical aspects of pain. In R. A. Sternbach (Ed.), *The psychology of pain.* New York: Raven Press, 1978. (a)

Sternbach, R. A. Psychological dimensions and perceptual analyses, including pathologies of pain. In E. C. Carterette & M. P. Friedman (Eds.), *Handbook of perception* (Vol. 6B). New York: Academic Press, 1978. (b)

Swanson, D. W., & Maruta, T. The family's viewpoint of chronic pain. *Pain,* 1980, *8,* 163–166.

Swanson, D. W., Maruta, T., & Swenson, W. M. Results of behavior modification in the treatment of chronic pain. *Psychosomatic Medicine,* 1979, *41,* 55–61.

Tan, S-Y. Cognitive and cognitive-behavioral methods for pain control: A selective review. *Pain,* 1982, *12,* 201–228.

Taylor, C. B., Zlutnick, S. I., Corley, M. J., & Flora, J. The effects of detoxification, relaxation, and brief supportive therapy on chronic pain. *Pain,* 1980, *8,* 319–329.

Terenius, L. Endorphins in chronic pain. In J. J. Bonica, J. C. Liebeskind, & D. Albe-Fessard (Eds.), *Advances in pain research and therapy* (Vol. 3). New York: Raven Press, 1979.

Turk, D. C. Cognitive behavioral techniques in the management of pain. In J. P. Foreyt & D. P. Rathjen (Eds.), *Cognitive behavior therapy.* New York: Plenum Press, 1978.

Turner, J. A. Comparison of group progressive-relaxation training and cognitive-behavioral group therapy for chronic low back pain. *Journal of Consulting and Clinical Psychology,* 1982, *50,* 757–765.

Turner, J. A., & Chapman, C. R. The psychological interventions for chronic pain: A critical review. II. Operant conditioning, hypnosis, and cognitive-behavioral therapy. *Pain,* 1982, *12,* 23–46.

Twycross, R. G. The measurement of pain in terminal carcinoma. *Journal of International Medical Research*, 1976, *4*, 58–67.

VanBuren, J., & Kleinknecht, R. A. An evaluation of the McGill Pain Questionnaire for use in dental pain assessment. *Pain*, 1979, *6*, 23–33.

Von Knorring, L., Almay, B. G. L., Johansson, F., & Terenius, L. Pain perception and endorphin levels in cerebrospinal fluid. *Pain*, 1978, *5*, 359–365.

White, M. C., Bradley, L. A., & Moore, R. *Effects of choice of coping strategies and locus of control orientation in stress innoculation training for pain control.* Manuscript submitted for publication, 1982.

Wolf, S. L. *EMG feedback training during dynamic movement for low back pain patients.* Paper presented at the Duke-UNC Pain Study Group, May 1982.

Wolf, S. L., Nacht, M., & Kelly, J. L. EMG feedback training during dynamic movement for low back pain patients. *Behavior Therapy*, 1982, *13*, 395–406.

Wolff, B. B. Behavioral measurement of human pain. In R. A. Sternbach (Ed.), *The psychology of pain.* New York: Raven Press, 1978.

Woodforde, J. M., & Merskey, H. Some relationships between subjective measures of pain. *Journal of Psychosomatic Research*, 1972, *16*, 173–178.

Yaksh, T. L., & Wilson, T. R. Spinal serotonin terminal system mediates antinociception. *Journal of Pharmacology and Experimental Therapeutics*, 1979, *208*, 446–453.

7

Measurement of Human Activity

Warren W. Tryon

The purpose of this chapter is to introduce the reader to the broad range of issues surrounding the measurement of human activity. The first question I am often asked regarding this subject is "Why do you want to measure activity?" Some of my reasons pertain to normal behavior and others pertain to behavioral abnormalities. This chapter discusses both types of reasons for studying human activity.

People talk about activity as though it were a monolithic unifactorial quantity, which, we will later see, it is not. This discussion explores three different ways in which activity has been defined and measured. The last of these approaches introduces us to the topic of *behavioral physics*, which concerns itself with transducing the physical forces associated with the emission and omission of behavior. This brings the realization that mechanical instruments, constructed in accordance with different physical principles, respond to different aspects of what is generally called *activity*. Hence, investigators using different instruments will "see" different aspects of what is taking place.

The chapter finally considers the operating characteristics of available activity transducers. We see how the issues of instrument validity and reliability are both subsumed under the topic of *in-*

strument accuracy. Then the discussion proceeds to the units of measure issue and shows how some arbitrary units can be converted into standard units commonly employed within the natural sciences.

Why Study Human Activity?

Many reasons exist for studying human activity; some are obvious and others less so. Some reasons can be articulated today, and others involve faith that new methods of measurement will open up new frontiers of knowledge.

Normal Behavior

The first, and perhaps most profound, reason for studying human activity is that it is an integral and universal aspect of behavior itself. To say that an organism behaves is to say that it moves. Active behavior implies much movement while passive behavior implies little movement. Obtaining quantitative measurements concerning the magnitude of movements typically found under interesting circumstances is a legitimate enterprise for behavioral scientists. Quantitative articles describing human activity should be published in order to provide a data base for other investigators. New fact patterns expressing quantitative relationships among environmental conditions and activity could then be elucidated. In sum, if behavior is to be studied as a subject matter unto itself, rather than as an index of something else, and if movement is an integral aspect of behavior, then it follows that basic measurements of human activity are to be encouraged in their own right as an important aspect of behavioral science.

Another reason for studying human activity is that various theorists and investigators have emphasized its role in explaining human behavior. Hall and Lindzey (1957) describe Gardner Murphy's personality theory as giving prominence to activity needs called "organic traits" (p. 511). Thomas, Chess, and Birch (1968, 1970) maintain that temperament is the core of personality and that two of the nine components of temperament involve activity. Buss and Plomin (1975) also theorize that temperament is the basis of all personality. The authors clearly state their position: "Level of activity refers to total energy output" (p. 7). "Activity level has already been defined in general terms as energy output: an active person moves around more, tends to be in motion, hurries more than others, and keeps busier than those around him" (p. 30). "Activity is equivalent to movement: the person who moves more is called more active" (p. 32). Werry (1978) takes a similar position when defining activity.

Sleep

We usually think of activity as a correlate of the waking state. However, people move even when sleeping (Cox & Marley, 1959; Hobson, Spagna, & Malenka, 1978; Kleitman, 1963; Monroe, 1967; Oswald, Berger, Jaramillo, Keddie, Olley, & Plunkett, 1963; Stonehill & Crisp, 1971). "Measuring body motility was one of the first objective methods used in sleep research" (Johns, 1971, p. 489).

It is a well-known clinical fact that pathology disturbs sleep. Foster and Kupfer (1975) provided evidence of this by showing that depressives have significantly higher levels of nocturnal activity than control subjects. They also displayed greater sleep discontinuity than did control subjects. Reich, Kupfer, Weiss, McPartland, Foster, Detre, and Delgado (1974) reported: "The findings indicate that the recording of psychomotor activity during the first 2 hr of bedtime provides reliable data with regard to the efficiency of the entire night's sleep" (p. 255).

In sum, activity measures taken during sleep are as interesting as those taken when the person is awake. The fact that sleep activity readings can be taken easily while the persons sleep in their own beds means that ecologically valid behavioral sleep studies are clearly possible to conduct. The tremendous importance of such data for studying sleep disorders such as insomnia and those related to various medical diseases and psychopathology means that much exciting research awaits investigators who would make behavioral measures of activity during sleep.

Abnormal Behavior

Since activity is an integral part of all behavior, it follows that aberrant levels of activity will be present in abnormal behavior and in medical conditions that influence behavior. In fact, measurements of activity should play a central role in diagnosing the presence of abnormal behavior. The latest edition of the *Diagnostic and Statistical Manual of Mental Disorders* (American Psychiatric Association, 1980), known as the DSM-III, has acknowledged the central role that activity measurements play in diagnosing abnormal behavior.

The DSM-III section on affective disorders begins with a discussion of the criteria by which one diagnoses a *manic episode*. The first criterion mentioned is an "increase in activity" (p. 208). This abnormal condition must either persist for 1 week or be sufficiently severe as to require hospitalization. The 1-week period means that brief, laboratory-type measurements are unacceptable. The data must reflect the person's normal behavior over at least 7 consecutive days.

Next the criteria for diagnosing a *depressive episode* are given. Among them is "psychomotor agitation or retardation (but not merely subjective feelings of restlessness or being slowed down) (in children under six, hypoactivity)" (p. 214). This condition must persist for at least 2 weeks. Activity may either increase or decrease, but the result must persist for a 2-week period. It is especially noteworthy that subjective feelings about being slowed down are explicitly rejected as a valid basis for diagnosing a depressive episode. This emphasizes the need for a protracted naturalistic measurement of the magnitude of activity.

Behavioral Medicine

Chapters 2, 5 and 8 of this volume show that obesity influences activity. Chapter 5 shows that various chronic diseases influence activity. Chapter 6 argues that chronic pain influences activity. Chapter 1 makes the point that — since smoking influences pulmonary function, which influences activity — chronic heavy smoking may decrease activity (see Chapter 3). Chapter 1 also makes the point that — since excessive alcohol consumption affects liver function, which influences activity — prolonged heavy alcohol consumption may decrease activity (see Chapter 4). In sum, many topics traditionally associated with behavioral medicine relate to activity. Yet activity research is underrepresented in contemporary research. The major objective of this chapter is to orient the reader regarding basic issues in activity research. Chapter 8 extends this orientation by reviewing quantitative results obtained to date.

Basic Issues in Activity Measurement

Several basic issues are covered in this section. The first issue concerns definition and measurement. Three rather different orientations exist regarding the definition and measurement of what has long been called *activity*. These perspectives, like scientific paradigms, almost completely govern one's subsequent actions. Here we conclude in favor of the approach called *behavioral measurement*, which means that physical measures of activity provide the basic data. This choice raises another basic issue: the operating characteristics of the instruments used to measure human activity. From this perspective we are able to examine properties of our data collection devices independent of the behavior we wish to study — a novel and refreshing position for psychologists to be in. We can see how the traditional issues of validity and reliability are subsumed under the broader issue of instrument accuracy. We then take up a discussion of the units of measure related to the available devices. Then we describe problems created by arbitrary units of measure and discuss methods for converting them into standard units employed by the natural sciences. Finally, we discuss the specific operational characteristics of currently available activity measurement devices.

Definitions and Methods of Measurement

"Measurement is the cornerstone of all scientific activity. The history of science is co-extensive with the history of measurement of natural phenomena . . . " (Johnston & Pennypacker, 1980, p. 55). Human activity has been defined and measured on three levels of inference (Tryon, 1976). Each of these approaches gives rise to different data such that the results of one approach cannot be directly compared with data collected using the other approaches.

Ratings

The method characterized by the greatest amount of inference and therefore the least precise definition of activity involves ratings. Parents, teachers, and therapists are often asked to rate how active a child or adult is. This approach assumes that we all know what activity is; this view is consistent with the intuition of many people. Moreover, this approach assumes that people can informally observe human activity and correctly report its magnitude using a rating scale provided by the investigator. It is beyond the scope of the present discussion to evaluate the validity of these assumptions in any detailed way. Let it suffice to say that these assumptions represent an exceedingly optimistic and naive view of human behavior. The literature on eyewitness testimony (see Buckout, 1974) is particularly instructive concerning how much inference characterizes observations made while people go about their daily routines. Ratings represent a global impression of largely inaccurate observations.

Behavioral Observations

The notion that behavior could be directly observed and recorded was a great intellectual departure and leap forward for the natural science of behavior in general and for behavioral assessment in particular.

The initial excitement with this new technology of behavioral observation gradually gave way to a more sober view. Reid (1970) reported that observers "drift," meaning that their operational definitions of the behaviors under observation change within relatively short periods of time. Hence, continual retraining of the observers is necessary. Continual reliability checks are also necessary to ensure quality control. This implies that behavioral observation is an expensive and time-consuming process not easily afforded by most clinics and institutions.

Questions arose concerning the best way to establish and report observer reliability (e.g., S. M. Johnson & Bolstad, 1973; Jones, Reid, & Patterson, 1975). Cone (1977, 1981) and Tryon (1984) both noticed that behavioral observations can be reliable and valid but inaccurate! This is due to the nature of the psychometric concepts of reliability and validity that have been adopted by behavioral observers. Let us examine these matters more closely. The relevant points are best illustrated with an example that is unencumbered with the surplus meaning that often accompanies behavioral phenomena: the measurement of temperature. Suppose that we took several different glass tubes, filled them with mercury, and sealed them. Next we would etch numbers, probably at equal intervals, along each glass tube. Repeated insertion of each "thermometer" into a particular medium would yield very similar readings; hence, each "thermometer" would be reliable by psychometric standards. A test–retest reliability (i.e., correlation) coef-

ficient calculated over, say, 20 media exposed to a standard flame
for various times would probably approach unity. The rank order
correlation between temperature readings of media exposed to a
standard flame for increasingly longer periods of time and the
duration of their exposure would also approach unity. The fact
that the higher readings were always associated with the "hotter"
media would be proof positive of the validity of each "thermometer." The paradox is completed by simultaneously inserting all
"thermometers" into any of the media and observing different numbers. If the "thermometers" are both reliable and valid, how can
they all give different readings regarding the temperature of any
particular medium? How can the readings be inaccurate if they
are both reliable and valid?[1] The answer lies in the fact that the
"thermometers" were not based upon any standard unit of measure. I have dubbed this the *units problem*.

Behavioral Measurement

The method of behavioral measurement uses electronic/me-
chanical devices to transduce (i.e., sense), quantify, and record
the physical forces or biological consequences associated with the
emission/omission of behavior. Let us examine this rather lengthy
definition more closely. We first note that this approach derives
data from an instrument of some kind, which may be partly or
wholly electronic or mechanical in nature. This characteristic alone
is sufficient to separate it from behavioral observations, which always involve a person as the observer. The term *measurement* is
used here to explicitly denote the presence of an inanimate device
for data acquisition. Such instruments are generally characterized
by high levels of accuracy, which makes them both reliable and
valid monitors of the physical properties they were designed and
calibrated to measure. (This topic is expanded upon under the
heading Construction Validity in the discussion of each device.)
Corollaries are that the devices remain accurate for much longer
periods of time than do human observers, they can monitor behavior over protracted periods of time, they do not invade the person's privacy, and they are often far less expensive in the long run
than are trained observers. These qualities mean that protracted

---

[1]The possibility exists that one or more of each set of measurements could be precisely accurate. This trivial exception has no programmatic consequences for developing accurate behavioral measurements.

naturalistic samples of human activity are now available at a reasonable cost to clinics and other institutions that cannot afford to obtain behavioral observations.

The second significant aspect of the definition is that one is transducing, quantifying, and recording either the physical forces or the biological consequences associated with either the emission or omission of behavior, and not the behavior itself. The important point here is that one has abandoned the traditional qualitative definition of behavior in favor of a quantitative physical measure of its correlates. One no longer talks about standing, walking, and running behaviors. Rather, one measures velocity, acceleration, or kinetic energy. These are physical measures of the correlates of behavior such as standing, walking, and running. These physical measures pertain to all possible behaviors because movement in time and space is an integral and universal aspect of behaving! Instead of talking about drinking behavior we would discuss blood alcohol levels as they represent a biological consequence of ingesting alcoholic beverages. Instead of talking about smoking behavior we would discuss levels of saliva thiocyanate as they index the volume and density of inhaled smoke.

This transition away from qualitative definitions of individual behaviors to quantitative measures of the physical forces and biological consequences of behaviors has profound theoretical and practical implications for the natural science of behavior in general and behavioral assessment in particular, with special relevance to behavioral medicine. We initially lose many definitions of specific behaviors that we have grown comfortable with over the years. We are now dealing with data that are not so directly available to the senses of vision and hearing. We may see people smoking, but we do not see their saliva thiocyanate levels. We may see people walking and running, but we cannot so readily guess the kinetic energy levels associated with these behaviors. Hence, behavioral measurement represents a novel approach that may intimidate some investigators, especially those who are not very comfortable with measurements used in the natural sciences.

There are many advantages and benefits to behavioral measurements. We will have finally solved the age-old question regarding the proper units of behavior. This will be done by adopting the units of measurement that have been standardized within the natural sciences. This step alone will do much to unite behavioral science with the other natural or physical sciences, for it will mean that we will all speak a common scientific language. Moreover,

we will finally have accurate measurements that will not be subject to the same intense debate as our current methods incur. This
means that the results of experiments will be far less ambiguous
than is presently the case. We will also be able to collect protracted
naturalistic records that will do much to facilitate the urgent need
for ecologically valid research. Perhaps most importantly, behavioral measurements will offer us a new perspective from which to
view behavioral science. This may just be the view that allows behavioral science to emerge from its preparadigmatic state (see
Kuhn, 1970) and finally achieve the long-hoped-for state as a
mature natural science. The presently available and clearly possible positive consequences of adopting the method of behavioral
measurement make it extremely attractive and well worth the difficulties associated with achieving the necessary conceptual shift.

Behavioral Physics

The branch of behavioral measurement that assesses the physical forces associated with the emission and omission of overt behavior is behavioral physics. I limit my remarks here to the measurement of human activity, though the principles involved are truly
general and can be applied to other aspects of human and animal
behavior.

The first issue one confronts when attempting to measure the
physical forces associated with behavior is where to place the sensor. To which part of the anatomy should the device be attached?
I refer to this as the *site of attachment issue*. When we think in
terms of specific behaviors we make reference to the organism as
a whole. When we think in terms of behavioral physics we think
of placing a sensor somewhere on the organism. A moment's reflection reveals that the physical forces associated with behaviors
are not equal over all possible sites of attachment. A sensor placed
on the shoulder will record lower values of acceleration than will
a sensor placed on the elbow, which in turn will record lower
values of acceleration than a sensor placed on the wrist. Hence,
one must be careful to report the site of attachment as part of the
measurement. This is analogous to reporting the city one is in when
reporting the daily temperature to the weather bureau. Temperature values alone cannot be interpreted until one knows where they
have been taken. Let us say that we have chosen the wrist and
ankle as the two sites that we will monitor.

The next issue relates to how the sensors are to be attached to the selected site so that they will transduce the majority of the physical forces impinging upon this locus. For example, an actometer is a modified man's calendar wristwatch whose self-winding rotor is used to drive the minute and hour hands plus the calendar date rather than to wind the mainspring, which has been removed. This type of device is sensitive to movement in two of the three possible planes. This is because the self-winding rotor is a pie-shaped element that rotates about a pin. Therefore it is responsive to movements in both the north–south and east–west planes, but not in the up–down plane. Hence, one would attach it to either the inside or outside of the wrist or ankle rather than to either the front or back of the wrist or ankle. Rotational movements will have vector components in all three planes. The vectors in the north–south and east–west planes will be recorded but not those in the up–down plane. Hence, something less than 100 % of the physical forces associated with the ankle and wrist sites of attachment will be transduced by the actometer.

We now take our initial reading, note the time of day it was taken, and let the individual return to his natural environment. Almost all of the person's limb movements will be sufficient to cause the actometer to increment. Twenty-four hours later the actometer will be removed and a post reading taken. The results will initially be reported in terms of actometer units per minute of wearing time. One actometer unit (AU) is defined as the energy required to cause the self-winding rotor to move enough to advance the "minute" hand by a 1-min marking on the face of the dial. We subsequently talk about how such arbitrary units of measure can be converted into standard physical units, but this would divert us from the main point here, which is how to interpret our results.

Most people who first encounter AU/minute data ask questions about what behaviors the people were engaged in at the time the activity readings were obtained. This is like telling a person the current temperature in degrees centigrade and then having him ask you how hot it is. A conversion is being requested: Please express your unfamiliar units in terms of units that I understand. Such a request reveals the absence of the paradigmatic shift that is at the heart of behavioral measurement. A more enlightened question would have made reference to the clinical status of the person who accumulated that many AUs/minute. Are these levels within normal limits for the person's age, sex, and environmental circumstance? Were the AU/minute readings associated with class time less than the AU/minute readings associated with recess? Note that this discussion does not make reference to specific behaviors engaged in during class or recess. Rather, actometer readings are being associated with clinical status and ecologically valid circumstances. The preceding reference to normal limits means that many initial measurements must be made with regard to "normal" behavior in clinically relevant circumstances under naturalistic conditions. Only then will we have a proper context for interpreting data collected from persons who seek professional assistance for behavior disorders.

Another question often asked by persons who are new to behavioral measurement concerns the reliability of the obtained data. The typical response of such people is to investigate the reliability of the apparatus by attaching it to people on two occasions and then correlating the results. (We review this matter in greater detail later, when we review the literature associated with the reliability of actometers.) Such behavior is consistent with the psychometric tradition where the reliability of test scores is always confounded with the behavior under study. One cannot study the properties of a psychological test independent of the human behavior it purports to measure. Such confounding is not only unnecessary but undesirable from the behavioral measurement perspective. Here we have physical instruments with their own response characteristics that can be evaluated under laboratory conditions that are totally independent of the behavior of all subject populations. The only certain method of evaluating the reliability of the data collected by these devices is to repeatedly submit them to exactly the same physical conditions. Far greater control over the physical conditions is possible through the use of mechanical devices than by attaching the devices to people and instructing them to behave in certain ways. Later in this discussion we see how the reliability of actometers was rigorously established by attaching them to a motorized pendulum capable of creating various well-defined levels of acceleration and deceleration. No set of human beings could ever create such systematic and well-controlled physical forces. The correlation, or lack thereof, between actometer readings on two occasions says nothing directly about the reliability of the actometer as an instrument for measuring human activity. Rather, it may be a comment upon actual changes in behavior when no obvious reason exists for the difference; for example, consider two play sessions separated by 1 week's time. Such data comment much more directly upon the presence or absence of trait-like stability in human activity than upon the reliability of the actometer. We subsequently see how this distinction has eluded most previous investigators.

Behavioral Physiology

It is sometimes more fruitful to measure the physiological consequences of behavior than it is to measure either the behavior per se or even the physical forces associated with the emission of that behavior. Take smoking, for example. The typical approach is to measure the number of cigarettes smoked per day. This is really the number of cigarettes disposed of in one way or another per day. Perhaps the person lit the cigarette, took one puff, and then placed it in an ashtray until it burned up. This person is said to have smoked one cigarette just as the person who puffed and puffed and puffed is said to have smoked one cigarette. The problem is further complicated by the nicotine and tar contents of the various brands of cigarettes that might have been smoked. Passive smoking refers to the biological consequences of being in the presence of a smoker but not smoking directly. Hence, zero cigarettes a day can be associated with measurable biological effects that depend upon the smoking behavior of other people. In short, records of smoking behavior tell us little about the biological consequences that produce the health hazards that gave rise to the interest in smoking behavior in the first place. Attaching an actometer to the dominant or preferred wrist will also be uninformative about smoking behavior. The forces associated with the behaviors of lighting cigarettes and repeatedly bringing them to the mouth will not be registered separately from the forces generated by all other behavior. A much better approach would be to obtain saliva samples and evaluate them for their thiocyanate content. This measure is directly related to the quantity and density of cigarette-related gases inhaled by the smoker. It is a direct measure of the health risk that the subject is running regardless of the specific series of particular behaviors that led to such levels of ingestion, including passive smoking.

Analogous arguments can be made with regard to drinking behavior. Counting drinks taken does not control for the alcoholic content of the drink or the quantity of each drink. Measures of wrist activity associated with drinking alcohol will not be recorded separately from the activity of drinking milk or any other beverage, or engaging in any other behavior. However, measures of alcohol in the breath are directly related to the amount of alcohol ingested by whatever means. If we are to shape problem drinkers into being social drinkers then we should shape them to maintain reasonable breath, and therefore blood, alcohol levels.

Behavioral and physiologic measures are useful in part because they require only minimal cooperation to be accurate. The measurement of obesity illustrates this point well. No amount of forgetting to record calories consumed or inaccuracies about portions eaten, and no amount of secret eating can escape weight or skinfold density measurements. No amount of smoking other people's cigarettes can artificially reduce saliva thiocyanate levels. Nor is it necessary to trust the self-reports of an alcoholic concerning his drinking behavior or enlist a substantial number of friends and relatives to obtain accurate measures of breath alcohol. Such assurances concerning the accuracy of one's data does much to persuade others regarding the veracity of the obtained findings. Critics cannot dismiss behavioral measurement data as easily as other forms of assessment on the basis of measurement inadequacies. This fact alone will do much to increase the contribution of behavioral investigators.

Motor activity increases heart rate, body temperature, and oxygen consumption. Stott (1977) and Wade, Ellis, and Bohrer (1973) described methods of measuring heart rate in mobile subjects. Romanczyk, Crimmins, Gordon, and Kashinsky (1977) described methods for recording body temperature, and Schulman, Kaspar, and Throne (1965) described the use of a portable oxygen consumption device.

Instrument Operating Characteristics

It is rare in psychological research that one can examine the response characteristics of their data acquisition procedures independent of the phenomenon under study. This is not possiible with psychological tests because their validity and reliability cannot be evaluated apart from administering them to people. For example, one cannot assess either the reliability or validity of an intelligence test apart from administering it to people. The best one can do is to use separate groups of people to establish the test's reliability and validity, and then proceed to study the phenomenon in question. Nevertheless, variation in the phenomenon under study is totally confounded with the test's characteristics. Said otherwise, it is meaningless to talk about the test's characteristics apart from human behavior.

The situation is very similar with regard to behavioral observation. People are trained to observe the behavior of other people until they reach some performance criterion. It is interesting to note that few, if any, investigators report the types of behaviors emitted during the training session. This means that it is possible for the training situation to involve simple behavioral sequences while the actual experiments involve much more complex behavioral sequences. In either case, the operating characteristics of human observers are not being assessed independent of the phenomenon under study. This means that unknown interactions may exist between the observation procedures and the behaviors being observed. The best that can be done is to have people observe stimulus events that do not involve human behavior, such as lights and/or sounds of various kinds or patterns. This would provide a much more rigorous context for evaluating the operating characteristics of human observers.

The types of questions one asks when studying the operating characteristics of an instrument are, in some ways, substantially different than the questions psychologists have been trained to ask. Hence, a few words are in order concerning these questions, as they provide the logic underlying this section.

Two types of questions exist with regard to instruments. The first question concerns what the instrument measures. Here we will want to know how the instrument is constructed and what physical principles govern its operation. These matters determine what the device will and will not respond to. A comprehensive understanding of these matters is crucial to properly attaching the device to the subject and properly interpreting the data collected by the instrument. I refer to the geometry of the device as the instrument's *construction validity* because how the instrument is constructed determines what it can and cannot be expected to measure. Construction validity is very similar to face validity. The latter is determined by inspecting the content of the items; the former is determined by inspecting the construction (i.e., physical content) of the instrument. A related matter concerns the units of measure associated with the instrument. To say that a reading of 5 was obtained is totally meaningless until the units of measure are specified. Five millimeters and 5 km are rather different distances, as are 5° centigrade and 5° kelvin (equal to $-268.16°C$). The units of measure associated with an instrument are a function of the way it is constructed.

The second line of questioning relates to the accuracy with which the instrument measures what it was designed and constructed to measure. We will want to know how reliably or consistently the device measures a constant physical entity. This fact can be determined by repeatedly measuring a standard quantity. The standard deviation of these measurements can then be divided by their mean and the resultant value multiplied by 100 to obtain the coefficient of variation (CV) (Winn & Johnson, 1978). This statistic indicates the percentage of error associated with some magnitude of measure. For example, a CV of 5.0 indicates 5% error. This means that 5 parts of error exist for each 100 parts of magnitude. This is equivalent to an accuracy of 1 part in 20. A corollary issue again involves us with the units of measurement. Accurate measures imply the use of standard units of measure. Accurate measures of temperature are possible only because incontrovertible definitions of the centigrade, fahrenheit, and kelvin degrees exist. We would lack a direct basis for comparing the obtained readings with the expected readings if we did not have standard units. In short, it is not possible to talk about an instrument's accuracy unless one has both a standard or definitional quantity and a standard unit of measure.

If our instrument does not initially provide readings that equal the standard quantities, then we will want to know if the device can be altered so that it does give readings that agree with the standard quantities. This process is known as *calibration*. Some instruments are either unalterable or give readings based upon arbitrary units. In this latter case we will want to have either a mathematical equation or an empirically derived table for the purpose of transforming or converting the incorrect values or arbitrary units into standard units such that the device accurately measures standard quantities.

In sum, we want to know what an instrument measures, the unit of that measure, and how accurate the device is. This information should be established apart from the particular study in question in such a manner that the operating characteristics of the instrument are well known.

Actometers

Construction Validity

Nature of measure
The actometer was first described by Schulman and Reisman (1959). It is a modified man's calendar wristwatch. The self-winding mechanism has been altered such that it drives the minute

hand, which drives both the hour hand and the calendar date in the usual manner. The first actometer was an Omega watch that was modified by a jeweler. Bell (1968) reported that the Engineering Department of Timex Industries would modify Timex watches in the same way. Timex calls these devices Motion Recorders.[2] I made a detailed study of how actometers are constructed because I use them in my own research. The self-winding counterweight, called a rotor, is pie shaped and weighs 4.49 g on average (range = 4.4 to 4.6 g). It revolves in a plane parallel to the face of the device around an axis located 0.562 ($\pm$0.002) in. from the edge of the rotor. One complete revolution of the rotor advances a ratchet wheel 6 of its 85 teeth through a cam-rocker arm-click assembly. One revolution of the ratchet wheel advances an 89-tooth barrel 1/7.333 of a revolution. The barrel engages a pinion having 15 teeth, and the minute hand is attached to this pinion. Hence, $(85/6) \times 7.33 \times (15/89) = 17.5$, the number of rotor revolutions required to produce one revolution of the minute hand.

The self-winding mechanism also responds partially to movements insufficient to produce an entire revolution of the rotor. However, this type of movement increments the minute hand less efficiently. Part of the problem is that the cam-rocker is heart shaped rather than circular, resulting in a maximum diameter of 0.0782 in. and a minimum diameter of 0.0290 ($\pm$0.0002) in. The amount of movement in the minute hand is directly proportional to the radius of this cam-rocker when the rotor begins to move. Moreover, the rotor activates the minute hand only when the arm-click is ascending a ratchet wheel tooth. Hence, if a click ends its stroke on the high point of a ratchet wheel tooth, no motion will be recorded until the click advances to the root of the next tooth to push it forward. Up to 30° of rotor motion can be lost in this way.

In summary, the energy contained in full revolutions of the rotor is more completely and consistently registered by the actometer than is energy associated with oscillations of the rotor. However, a monotonic relationship exists in that greater kinetic energy will always be associated with larger actometer readings down to a threshold point.

This physical design means that actometers will respond in direct proportion to the forces of acceleration that are parallel to

[2]Model 108 Motion Recorders can be purchased from the Engineering Department, Timex Industries, Waterbury, Connecticut 06720.

the two spatial planes that are parallel to its face, and not at all to the spatial plane that is perpendicular to its face. Said otherwise, the east–west and north–south acceleration vectors of all movements will be recorded in monotonic fashion by the actometer. The vertical (up–down) vector component of all movements will go undetected. This analysis presumes that the actometer is horizontal and parallel with the ground.

Unit of measure

An Actometer unit (AU) is defined as the average kinetic energy sufficient to move the self-winding rotor just enough to advance the minute hand from one minute marking to another on the face of the modified watch. One typically records the number of minutes of wearing time so that AU/minute calculations can be made. This allows one to compare measurements across unequal wearing intervals. The easiest method of collecting data in naturalistic settings is to obtain one reading at the same time each day or to obtain one reading for waking hours and another reading for sleeping hours. Hence, data over the entire 24-hr day is obtained.

Accuracy

Reliability

The validity and accuracy of actometers are limited by the reliability (i.e., consistency) with which they measure the same physical forces. Most previous studies of actometer reliability have confounded the instrument's operating characteristics with the behavioral stability of the subjects under investigation, as indicated in the following.

TEST–RETEST STUDIES.   The most popular method of reporting actometer reliability data uses the test–retest procedure. For example, Maccoby, Dowley, Hagen, and Dergman (1965) correlated the activity of a group of children on two occasions 7 to 14 days apart. They reported correlations of $r(11) = 0.31$ for females and $r(11) = 0.76$ for males with respect to wrist movements, and $r(11) = 0.22$ for females and $r(13) = 0.44$ for males with respect to ankle movements. Schulman et al., (1965) reported a Spearman rank-order correlation coefficient of $rho(25) = 0.67$ after testing 27 retarded boys twice, with anywhere from 1 to 3 weeks intervening between the two tests. Massey, Lieberman, and Batarseh (1971) reported a correlation of $r(31) = 0.798$ with 1 week intervening between the two tests.

A related procedure is the odd–even method of establishing reliability employed by psychometricians. Bell (1968) correlated the odd and even data points for 31 females over time and reported correlations of $r(29) = 0.55$ for foot measures and $r(29) = 0.56$ for jacket measures.

Both the test–retest and the odd–even procedures are entirely unsatisfactory methods of estimating the reliability of actometers because they confound variability due to the actometer with variability due to the subject. These analyses presume that the movements executed during both the test and retest or on odd and even days were identical in all respects. This absurd assumption of zero intra- and intersubject variability causes a substantial underestimate of the actometer's reliability. Data are shortly presented showing that the reliability of actometers almost always corresponds to correlation coefficients above 0.90 and sometimes above 0.99.

MECHANICAL ASSESSMENT. The only adequate method of ensuring that the same, or very nearly the same, physical conditions exist from trial to trial is to construct a device that produces known levels of acceleration. Schulman and Reisman (1959) placed modified Omega self-winding calendar watches at points from 4 in. (10.16 cm) to 7 in. (17.78 cm) from the center of a device that rotated in a vertical plane at a uniform rate of two revolutions per minute (0.2094 rad/sec). The actometers were then attached such that their faces were parallel to the plane of rotation. The actometers were then tested an unreported number of times for an unspecified duration. However, results were reported for two of the trials. One actometer recorded 499 AU/hr and the other actometer recorded 500 AU/hr, resulting in 1 part error for every 499 actometer units, which equals 99.8% reliability.

Two major problems exist with this study. First, rotary movement was used; people's arms and legs simply do not revolve in a circular fashion. Rotary movement is therefore unrepresentative of human movement. The second major problem is that an extremely low, and therefore unrepresentative, acceleration was applied.

C. F. Johnson (1971) replicated the vertical plane rotation experiment published earlier by Schulman and Reisman (1959) and reported average values of 305.6 AU for the first actometer and 295.7 AU for the second actometer after being rotated for 24 5-min trials. This equals 61.12 and 59.14 AU/min, respectively. Associated reliability rates were 98.2% and 98.4%. Johnson then reported the results for rotating the actometers in a horizontal plane. The average AU value dropped to 35.5 for 24 5-min trials (7.1 AU/min) for both devices, with associated reliability estimates of 84.2% and 85.0%. The fact that Johnson used extremely low levels of acceleration in conjunction with rotary motion makes these results unrepresentative of human activity. Johnson then attached the actometers to an IBM electric typewriter and pressed the tab button such that the carriage moved 12.4 in. in an unknown time and therefore with an unknown acceleration. Ten trials yielded reliability estimates for the two actometers of 90.1% and 92.4%. Additional to the unknown level of acceleration is the fact that linear acceleration was used, which is unrepresentative of human movement.

Saris and Binkhorst (1977) modified 10 Swiss-made Tussot watches into actometers and exposed them to two types of standard movement. The first testing device rotated the actometers at a rate that I assume to be 0.965 rpm for five 1-hr periods. No description of the test machine was given. The means and standard deviations over the five trials for each of the 10 actometers were reported. The means ranged from 57.8 to 58.0 AU/hr, which equals approximately 57.798 to 58.002 AU/hr. The standard deviations ranged from 0.03 to 0.09 AU/hr. This led to coefficients of variation ranging from 0.052 to 0.155, demonstrating that the measurement error ranges from 1/20th to 1/7th of 1%. This incredibly low measurement error is due to the fact that slow rotational movement of the testing machine caused the actometer's counterweight (rotor) to make one revolution for every revolution of the testing machine.

The 10 actometers were then attached to another undescribed device that moved them "to and fro" an unreported distance at an unreported rate. They were again studied for five 1-hr trials. The means and standard deviations over the five trials for each of the 10 actometers were reported. The means ranged from 396.6 AU/hr to 700.3 AU/hr. The standard deviations ranged from 8.7 to 136.7 AU/hr. Omitting the 136.7 reading would reduce the range of standard deviations to 8.7 to 18.4 AU/hr. The range of coefficients of variation within this more reasonable range of standard deviations was 1.24 to 2.57, indicating a measurement error of approximately 1% to 3% under these conditions.

NEW STUDY. The inadequacy of existing data concerning the reliability of actometers prompted the following study conducted by the author and G. M. Klemuk (see Tryon & Klemuk, 1982). Our source of well-defined motion was a motorized pendulum that

I previously designed; this is described in a later section where we discuss converting arbitrary AU/minute data into units of kinetic energy. I also wrote a computer program to calculate the radial, tangential, and total vector forces of acceleration associated with many positions during each oscillation of the motorized pendulum. This allowed us to select our stimulus values of motor speeds, pendulum distances, and therefore rates of acceleration to produce specified average levels of acceleration. Although the radial or tangential components of acceleration could have been used, we decided to use the total acceleration vector, which would be more representative of normal human movement. The eight particular combinations of drive motor speeds and pendulum radii to produce the specified values of total acceleration ($1G = 9.8$ m/s/s) were: 0.05 G (1.417 rad/sec, 28.3 cm), 0.25 G (3.243 rad/sec, 35.3 cm), 0.35 G (3.243 rad/sec, 49.5 cm), 0.45 G (3.243 rad/sec, 63.6 cm), 0.50 G (3.243 rad/sec, 70.7 cm), 0.55 G (3.243 rad/sec, 77.7 cm), 0.65 G (3.243 rad/sec, 91.9 cm), and 0.85 G (4.245 rad/sec, 77.8 cm). These eight activity levels equal 0.3216, 2.6210, 5.1539, 8.5082, 10.5139, 12.6989, 17.7646, and 21.8145 watts of kinetic energy, respectively, assuming a 1-kg mass for the site of attachment [see Eq. (25)]. The actometers were placed with their backs against the meter stick in order for the face of the device to be parallel to both the radial and tangential acceleration vectors. All distances were measured to the center of the actometer, which is the locus of rotation for the rotor portion of the self-winding mechanism.

PROCEDURES. The following procedures refer to the testing sessions proper. First, each of the actometers was reset by pulling out the stem and turning it until a new date appeared. The stem was then pushed back in and the sensor tapped or shaken to make certain that it was responding properly. Second, the wooden platform was moved to a point 1.8 cm beyond the previously mentioned values. This was done to compensate for the 1.8-cm difference between the edge of the actometer, which rested on the platform, and the center of the device, which served as the axis of rotation for the self-winding rotor. The drive motor speed was then selected. Third, the actometers were attached to the pendulum. One pair of actometers was mounted with their backs resting firmly against the meter stick, while the backs of the second pair rested firmly against the crystals of the first pair. The "day," "hour," and "minute" readings were taken after each pair was attached. Fourth, the revolution counter was set to zero. Alligator clips were used to secure the watch bands of the inner and outer pairs to one another. Specially designed pieces of styrofoam were inserted between the actometers to take up any slack space such that all four actometers were firmly connected to the meter stick with the 3 o'clock portion of the dial facing up. A C-clamp underneath the wooden platform prevented the sensors from sliding past the designated position. Fifth, a stop watch was started at the same time that the drive motor was activated, and each trial lasted 10 min.

In order to achieve the theoretically predicted number of pendulum oscillations in the 10-min time interval, small voltage adjustments were necessary. A schedule of pendulum oscillations was established specifying the desired counter readings at 30-sec intervals throughout the 10-min period. The experimenter altered the dial on the voltage regulator to produce the voltage changes. A 1-V AC change produced a 0.1-V DC change. Sixth, the number of pendulum revolutions was recorded from the counter, and a new number of "days," "hours," and "minutes" associated with each of the four actometers was recorded at the end of each 10-min trial. Seventh, the total number of "minutes" between the two readings for each actometer was determined and labeled as actometer units (AU). This number was divided by 10 to obtain the actometer units per minute. A total of 10 trials were conducted at each of eight average G forces. All 10 trials at a particular average G force were conducted in one session.

RESULTS.   Table 7.1 contains the means, standard deviations, coefficients of variation (CV) and their correlational equivalents. (The correlational equivalent of a CV is the value of r such that squaring it and subtracting from 1.0 gives the CV.) The CV is the percentage of error variance. It expresses the error of measurement as a percentage of the magnitude of the measurement since it equals 100 times the ratio of the standard deviation divided by the mean. The main result in Table 7.1 of present interest is the relatively low values of the CVs and their correspondingly large correlational equivalents (based on N = 10 trials − 2 = 8 df). The greatest CV was 22.45, associated with $r(8) = 0.99$. The lowest CV was 2.36, associated with $r = 0.99$. With one exception, all of the correlation equivalents equaled or exceeded $r(8) = 0.90$. In sum, actometers are exceptionally reliable by psychometric standards over the rather broad range of acceleration–deceleration forces studied.

Actometers are not equally reliable at all G force levels. Inspection of Table 7.1 reveals a curvilinear relationship between the CV and G force levels. The average CV associated with the

Table 7.1. Means, Standard Deviations, Coefficients of Variation, Correlation Equivalents, and Analyses of Variance for Four Actometers Under Eight Levels of Accelerated Movement

G Force	Stats	Sensor 1	Sensor 2	Sensor 3	Sensor 4	F(3, 36)
0.05	M	8.78	13.76	11.59	8.58	27.28**
	SD	0.29	2.55	0.96	1.21	
	CV[a]	3.30	18.53	8.28	14.10	
	r[b]	0.98	0.90	0.96	0.93	
0.25	M	25.34	31.43	35.69	23.83	9.64**
	SD	4.54	5.84	6.49	5.35	
	CV	17.92	18.58	18.18	22.45	
	r	0.91	0.90	0.90	0.88	
0.35	M	119.10	106.80	114.90	125.10	1.99
	SD	23.59	12.22	13.41	17.21	
	CV	19.81	11.44	11.67	13.76	
	r	0.90	0.94	0.94	0.93	
0.45	M	307.79	353.42	322.10	322.97	1.44
	SD	54.39	40.75	56.01	50.22	
	CV	17.67	11.53	17.39	15.55	
	r	0.91	0.94	0.91	0.92	
0.50	M	526.43	570.55	542.75	545.45	3.26*
	SD	36.23	26.04	31.30	33.27	
	CV	6.88	4.56	5.77	6.10	
	r	0.97	0.98	0.97	0.97	
0.55	M	612.30	639.08	654.37	612.91	1.56
	SD	48.21	56.60	42.63	58.46	
	CV	7.87	8.86	6.51	9.54	
	r	0.96	0.95	0.97	0.95	
0.65	M	683.83	718.88	705.83	693.78	5.67**
	SD	16.12	17.01	20.16	25.77	
	CV	2.36	2.37	2.86	3.71	
	r	0.99	0.99	0.99	0.98	
0.85	M	803.63	827.73	816.62	797.13	1.46
	SD	33.82	35.64	32.19	40.67	
	CV	4.21	4.31	3.94	5.10	
	r	0.98	0.98	0.98	0.97	

[a]The coefficient of variation CV= $(SD/M) \times 100$. It represents the parts of error per 100 units of measurement, or the percent error.
[b]The correlation coefficient equivalent of the CV indicates the magnitude of correlation necessary to reduce error variance to the level indicated by the CV.
*$p < 0.05$.
**$p < 0.01$.

eight G force values from 0.05 G to 0.85 G are: 11.08, 19.28, 14.17, 15.54, 5.83, 8.20, 2.83, and 4.39, respectively. The mean (and standard deviation) of the first four CV values ($M = 15.02$, $SD = 3.40$) is greater than the mean of the second four CV values ($M = 5.31$, $SD = 2.28$). The general implication is that reliability was substantially greater when the actometers were exposed to larger (i.e., greater than 0.5 G) acceleration–deceleration forces. Said otherwise, the acceleration–deceleration forces associated with behavior are more reliably measured when they equal or exceed one-half the force of acceleration due to gravity.

We now turn to the matter of actometer accuracy, which partly concerns the consistency across actometers. Table 7.1 again contains the relevant information. The four actometers gave significantly different readings when tested at 0.05, 0.25, 0.50, and 0.65 G. The simplest explanation for such a result would be that an actometer ran consistently slow or fast in response to various G forces. The data do not support such an interpretation. Sensors 2 and 4 were slowest at some G forces and fastest at others. Sensors 1 and 3 spread across three of the four possible rankings, responding faster at some G force levels and slower at others. A complete explanation of these data eludes the present author. Most likely, they are due to resonance differences caused by small variations in their construction. This problem is addressed again later when we consider converting the arbitrary AU/minute units into standard physical units of kinetic energy to remove interdevice variability and thereby equate accuracy with reliability.

Standard quantities

An actometer unit (AU) is an arbitrary unit of measure. It is equivalent to the average acceleration necessary to move the self-winding rotor just enough to increment the minute hand one minute marking on the dial. We have seen that this value is not the same at all acceleration–deceleration values; nor is it constant across actometers. However, we shall shortly see that AUs for each actometer are definitely a function of G forces, and therefore it is possible to convert these arbitrary units into standard units of acceleration.

RESPONSE TO G FORCES.   Table 7.2 is a different version of Table 7.1. It gives the mean AU/minute values associated with the 10 trials that each of the four actometers underwent. An outstanding feature of these data is that the standard deviations are highly correlated with the means over the first six values (0.05 to 0.55

Table 7.2. Condensed and Extended Version of Table 7.1 Showing The AU/ minute Values for Four Actometers at Eight *G* Force Levels Over 10 Trials, Plus the Mean, Standard Deviation, and Coefficient of Variation at Each *G* Force Level

| G | Sensor | | | | | | |
	1	*2*	*3*	*4*	*av*	SD	CV
0.05	8.78	13.76	11.59	8.58	10.67	2.48	23.24
0.25	25.34	31.43	35.69	23.83	29.07	5.50	18.92
0.35	119.10	106.80	114.90	125.10	116.48	7.69	6.60
0.45	307.79	353.42	322.10	322.97	326.57	19.21	5.88
0.50	526.43	570.55	542.75	545.45	546.30	18.22	3.34
0.55	612.30	639.08	654.37	612.91	629.67	20.67	3.28
0.65	683.83	718.88	705.83	693.78	700.58	15.16	2.16
0.85	803.63	827.73	816.62	797.13	811.28	13.64	1.68

G). The remaining two values were not considered in the following analyses because they were obtained under conditions where the motorized pendulum was driven sufficiently hard so as to introduce a vibrational artifact. The correlation between the standard deviations and the means for the first six activity levels was $r(4) = 0.9331$, $p < 0.01$. The regression equation is:

$$SD = 0.0278 \ (\text{Av AU/min}) + 4.6165 \tag{1}$$

Inspection of Table 7.2 reveals that the standard deviations were bimodal; they ranged either from 2.48 to 7.69 or from 18.22 to 20.67. This suggests that a critical activity level exists associated with a quantum shift in the consistency of measurement. This level appears to be near an acceleration value of 0.4 *G* (*G* = 9.8 m/s/s) or 3.92 m/s/s. Another perspective on this issue is provided by the coefficient of variation (CV). A sharp decrease in the CV occurs at approximately 0.3 *G* = 2.94 m/s/s. The correlation coefficient between the CV and the average AU/minute is $r(4) = -0.8282$, $p < 0.05$.

It was possible to accurately predict the AU/minute results for the four sensors over the first six *G* force levels (0.05 to 0.55 *G*). The two remaining values were omitted because they appeared to contain artifacts due to overloading the motorized pendulum. Equations (2) through (5) describe the empirical relationship between AU/minute values as a function of G force values for Sensors 1 through 4, respectively.

$$\log 10 \ (AU/min) = 3.9951 \ (G) + 0.6384 \qquad (\ 2)$$
$$\log 10 \ (AU/min) = 3.6704 \ (G) + 0.8139 \qquad (\ 3)$$
$$\log 10 \ (AU/min) = 3.7397 \ (G) + 0.7825 \qquad (\ 4)$$
$$\log 10 \ (AU/min) = 4.0531 \ (G) + 0.6212 \qquad (\ 5)$$

Notice that the values for the slope and intercept in these four equations are very similar. This indicates that the functional characteristics of the four actometers are quite similar. These functions fit the data very well. The correlation coefficients associated with Eqs. (2) through (5) are $r(4) = 0.9858$, 0.9794, 0.9905, and 0.9832, respectively, $p < 0.01$.

A more accurate functional relationship between AUs and G forces is afforded by averaging the mean AU readings over the four actometers at each of the eight G force levels. These data are provided in Table 7.2 under the heading Average. Equation (6) predicts the average AU/minute values across all four actometers as a function of G.

$$\log 10 \ (Av \ AU/min) \ U/min) = 3.8468 \ (G) + 0.7230 \qquad (\ 6)$$

The correlation for this function is $r(4) = 0.9856$, $p < 0.01$, indicating an excellent fit to the data.

CONVERSION TO STANDARD UNITS.   The preceding functions clearly establish that the arbitrary AU/minute units are related to the standard G force units. However, they do not allow one to transform AU/minute units into G force units. Equations (7) through (10) have the proper form to make the desired conversion from one set of units to another for Sensors 1 through 4, respectively:

$$G = 0.2433 \ (\log 10 \ AU/min) - 0.1452 \qquad (\ 7)$$
$$G = 0.2613 \ (\log 10 \ AU/min) - 0.1981 \qquad (\ 8)$$
$$G = 0.2624 \ (\log 10 \ AU/min) - 0.1985 \qquad (\ 9)$$
$$G = 0.2385 \ (\log 10 \ AU/min) - 0.1362 \qquad (10)$$

Again notice that all four slope values are very similar to one another, as are all four intercept values. This is, of course, simply a corollary of agreement existing across Eqs. (2) through (5). It follows that these functions also fit the data very well. This view is corroborated by the correlation coefficients of $r(4) = 0.9858$,

0.9794, 0.9905, and 0.9832 associated with Eqs. (7) through (10), respectively.

A more general equation for converting AU/minute units into G force units is obtained by fitting a curve to the average AU/minute values. The resulting relationship is:

$$G = 0.2525 \ (\log 10 \ \text{Av AU/min}) - 0.1723 \qquad (11)$$

The correlation coefficient associated with Eq. (11) is $r(4) = 0.9856$, indicating an excellent fit to the data. This function glosses over the previous finding that the four actometers gave significantly different AU/minute readings when exposed to 0.05, 0.25, 0.50, and 0.65 G. This suggests that individual conversion coefficients associated with each actometer will likely give a more accurate transformation from arbitrary to standard units than will Eq. (11). The use of empirically determined conversion constants for each actometer will also help remove some interdevice variability from the data.

Mechanical Oscillator

One must have a well-defined source of movement in order to convert the arbitrary AU/minute units into standard G force units. It is helpful if this source of controlled motion is similar to the general type of movement characteristic of the behavior under study. The purpose of this section is to describe a mechanical oscillator that meets these criteria.

Figure 7.1 presents a diagram of the more important geometrical features of the mechanical oscillator. Point O represents the end-on view of the shaft of the electric motor (I used a Mazda RX2 electric windshield wiper motor having a 68 : 1 gear ratio). Segment OA represents a drive arm attached at right angles to the motor's drive shaft such that one revolution of the motor shaft provides one revolution of the drive arm OA. This drive arm is attached to the vertical bar BIC, which is connected to horizontal tracks DE and FG by ball bearing slides. As the drive arm OA of radius r revolves in a circular fashion, point I moves left and right at a rate equal to the radius r times the cosine of the drive angle a, according to Eq. (12).

$$OI = x = r \ \cos(a) \qquad (12)$$

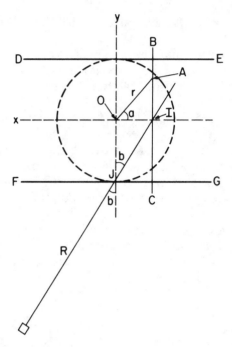

Figure 7.1. Schematic diagram of the more important geometrical features of the mechanical oscillator.

The distance $x = OI$ is positive and maximum when $a = 0$, and minimum and equal to 0 when $a = 90°$. The x distance then increases negatively to a maximum when $a = 180°$, and the process reverses itself while a increases to $360°$. The angle b is defined by the legs OI and OJ of triangle OIJ, in accordance with

$$b = \text{arc } \tan(OI/OJ) \tag{13}$$

If we let $y = OJ$, then by Eq. (12) we can write Eq. (14):

$$b = \text{arc } \tan[r \cos(a)/y] \tag{14}$$

When $y = r$, then Eq. (14) becomes

$$b = \text{arc } \tan[\cos(a)] \tag{15}$$

and the pendulum will swing through a $90°$ arc that is centered about the vertical axis such that it moves $45°$ to either side. Since angle a equals the angular velocity of angle a, symbolized by ωa, times time (t), we can write Eq. (16), which expresses angle b as a function of time, given that the angular velocity of the drive shaft remains constant.

$$b = \text{arc } \tan[\cos(\omega a \cdot t)] \tag{16}$$

It should be noted that the absolute units of the apparatus are irrelevant to the previous relationships and are therefore not presented.

Figure 7.2 presents an analysis of the acceleration forces impinging upon the activity sensor placed at distance R on the motorized pendulum. The radial, or centripital (center-seeking) component of acceleration is always parallel to the pendulum. The tangential component of acceleration is always at right angles to the pendulum. The total force due to acceleration is the vector sum of the tangential and radial components, and can be calculated by the Pythagorean theorem.

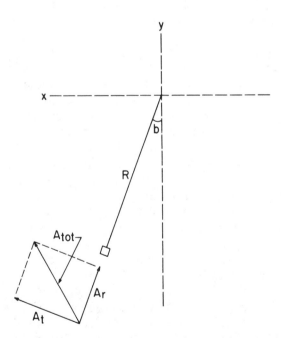

Figure 7.2. Schematic diagram of the radial, tangential, and total forces of acceleration impinging on an actometer moving at distance R on the mechanical oscillator.

The rate of change of angle b with respect to time is called the *angular velocity* of b and is symbolized by ωb. The radial component of acceleration equals the length of the pendulum (R) times the square of the angular velocity of b as per Eq. (17):

$$Ar = \omega b^2 \cdot R \qquad (17)$$

The tangential component of acceleration equals the derivative of ωb with respect to time multiplied by the length of the pendulum (R) as per Eq. (18). The total acceleration can be calculated at each of N points during one oscillation and then summed according to Eq. (19):

$$At = [d(\omega b)/dt]R \qquad (18)$$
$$A\text{tot}^2 = Ar^2 + At^2 \qquad (19)$$

These relationships make it possible to select motor speeds and pendulum radii for producing known integrals of total acceleration expressed in meters/second/second. Or, the units can be expressed in terms of the force of gravity (G force) knowing that 1 $G = 9.8$ m/s/s.

An empirical table for converting arbitrary units of measure into standardized ones can be constructed as follows. First, select settings for creating the desired acceleration–deceleration integrals that are representative of the movement to be studied. Then attach the movement sensors to the motorized pendulum and oscillate them for at least 10–20 min. Record the average arbitrary units reported by each sensor for each acceleration integral. The empirical conversion table is now complete. When future data are collected, one can convert them from arbitrary to standard units as follows. Find where each reading would belong in the arbitrary units column of the empirical conversion table; interpolation may be necessary. Then determine the corresponding standardized units value; interpolation may again be necessary.

Table 7.3 provides conversion constants for 59 actometers that have been studied under six G force levels. Values of G in excess of 0.55 were not studied because they were not needed for ongoing research. The AU/minute values associated with long wearing times are rather low despite short periods of intense activity. Hence, only the lower G force values are required. The observations of greatest interest relate to the average AU/minute values and the associated standard deviations and CVs at the bottom of

Table 7.3. Conversion Constants for a Sample of 59 Actometers at Six *G* Force Levels

0.05 G	*0.25* G	*0.35* G	*0.45* G	*0.50* G	*0.55* G
8.45	31.30	102.45	246.30	543.15	676.60
7.10	41.85	88.50	354.15	513.20	660.05
7.35	94.70	103.60	272.40	388.40	431.90
38.00	69.95	93.40	275.50	313.00	528.10
13.25	42.70	109.55	217.85	238.70	463.10
8.40	15.25	50.75	243.50	444.65	475.35
14.35	38.35	66.25	289.35	514.75	525.50
14.25	42.50	70.70	309.10	401.65	557.60
14.60	36.50	87.75	213.05	428.50	473.50
9.10	60.10	76.45	299.55	443.05	522.40
16.45	43.65	80.50	297.05	331.15	701.55
57.50	61.60	113.55	300.40	391.60	517.70
24.60	64.50	141.65	245.00	324.75	491.75
10.75	53.80	112.40	315.70	670.50	736.55
10.50	74.50	143.20	314.00	416.25	630.50
47.50	81.60	251.75	499.70	582.30	708.95
7.90	25.15	177.90	467.05	523.35	596.10
6.25	37.50	152.00	289.50	812.50	911.75
44.60	65.25	91.80	346.45	448.10	464.35
10.35	32.70	99.55	349.80	505.25	656.05
9.75	32.25	106.00	246.00	567.50	616.00
26.30	53.80	76.70	383.15	578.75	596.50
8.90	36.15	129.40	259.10	307.85	523.90
10.60	52.45	131.90	223.80	453.35	543.90
44.10	57.60	104.55	245.50	345.10	438.80
9.55	22.45	97.80	360.90	429.25	690.75
9.00	51.95	130.90	333.00	443.25	576.00
8.00	40.35	66.15	453.50	523.95	529.90
7.55	20.35	111.05	305.40	539.35	594.15
13.80	65.70	142.80	439.35	525.40	615.40
10.75	54.25	80.40	265.40	582.50	789.15
8.70	19.90	42.05	273.60	317.20	500.55
3.55	23.70	82.65	306.50	327.85	573.55
10.55	64.60	139.90	549.90	551.05	719.70
0.25	70.30	124.85	425.80	483.20	626.15
8.50	27.25	52.50	139.75	510.75	656.00
8.75	36.55	56.25	367.95	608.65	513.25
6.00	68.25	101.15	336.60	446.50	620.75
7.60	26.50	77.00	222.65	389.95	577.30
9.95	30.10	52.55	410.15	508.90	609.55

(continued)

Table 7.3. (continued)

	0.05 G	0.25 G	0.35 G	0.45 G	0.50 G	0.55 G
	13.25	32.50	86.50	288.25	513.25	692.50
	13.40	30.60	96.00	407.75	594.15	712.60
	10.75	26.00	141.50	215.25	629.00	719.75
	45.00	48.15	130.90	385.50	477.25	563.50
	7.25	60.65	82.55	222.25	439.25	700.85
	6.75	26.75	97.80	202.00	569.75	713.50
	13.00	68.10	84.95	185.65	348.50	617.15
	4.50	138.35	205.50	268.75	393.55	598.75
	62.75	79.25	151.90	353.25	372.35	711.95
	13.60	126.45	162.95	411.45	592.10	675.00
	9.50	52.90	108.00	548.00	627.25	683.35
	48.85	57.05	126.50	464.90	648.50	726.90
	8.95	27.25	183.00	534.80	669.00	788.10
	8.00	62.15	87.20	510.25	604.80	712.05
	11.60	41.40	179.10	200.80	225.15	515.75
	13.30	23.85	101.90	214.90	301.05	506.30
	11.80	35.35	139.40	260.45	329.15	471.40
	15.35	47.85	128.65	288.70	310.45	525.25
	8.15	38.60	87.75	204.55	218.80	468.75
Mean	15.58	49.00	110.21	319.68	466.75	605.83
SD	14.05	23.91	40.04	98.54	124.85	102.59
CV	90.21	48.40	36.33	30.83	26.75	16.93

the table. Equation (20) shows that these average AU/minute units are clearly a function of the G force stimulus values:

$$\log 10 \text{ (Av AU/min)} = 3.3308 \ (G) + 0.9533 \tag{20}$$

The correlation coefficient associated with Eq. (20) is $r(4) = 0.9933$, indicating an excellent fit to the data. Equation (21) reiterates another earlier point, which is that the errors of prediction are also a function of the G force stimulus values:

$$\log 10 \text{ (CV)} = -1.3029 \ (G) + 2.0244 \tag{21}$$

The correlation coefficient associated with Eq. (21) is $r(4) = -0.9799$, indicating an excellent fit to the data. Equation (22) provides a method of converting average AU/minute units into G units:

$$G = 0.2962 \log 10 \ (\text{Av AU/min}) - 0.2777 \qquad (22)$$

The correlation coefficient associated with Eq. (22) is $r(4) =$ 0.9933, indicating an excellent fit to the data.

Investigators are more typically concerned with converting AU/minute data from a single actometer into G units. The data in Table 7.3 were used to correlate the 354 individual G and AU/minute values resulting in Eq. (23) for converting individual AU/minute values into G units.

$$G = 0.2528 \log 10 \ (\text{AU/min}) - 0.1741 \qquad (23)$$

The correlation coefficient associated with Eq. (23) is $r(352) =$ 0.9490, indicating an excellent fit to the data. Investigators who wish to convert data presented in G units back into AU/minute units may use Eq. (24).

$$\log 10 \ (\text{AU/min}) = 3.5616 \ (G) + 0.8297 \qquad (24)$$

The correlation coefficient associated with Eq. (24) also equals $r(352) = 0.9490$ since Eq. 24 is the inverse of Eq. (23).

The mechanical oscillator described earlier produces known levels of acceleration and deceleration. It is probably a safe assumption that most people do not intuitively think of activity in these terms. It is more intuitive to think of the energy associated with behavior; we even describe very active people as energetic. The kinetic energy (KE) associated with one quarter-cycle of the motorized pendulum is given by Eq. (25), where M equals the mass of the oscillating object, R equals the effective radius of the pendulum, and Ω (omega) is the radians of angular change per second (angular velocity) associated with the moving pendulum (1 radian = 57.296°). The value of M is set to 1 kg since no more satisfactory procedure is apparent for calculating the mass of the site of attachment regarding actometers. This decision allows other investigators to scale the resulting KE values up or down depending upon their value for M.

$$\text{KE} = \frac{MR^2\Omega^2}{2} \qquad (25)$$

The result of Eq. (25) is multiplied by 4 to obtain the kinetic energy expended during one complete oscillation. Kinetic energy is measured in joules and is a measure of work. Power refers to the rate with which energy is expended. One watt equals the expenditure of 1 joule per second. The average power expended during each oscillation of the pendulum equals the total expended kinetic energy in joules divided by the total time in seconds to complete one oscillation. Power is a rate measure just as AU/minute is a rate measure. Hence, it seems natural to convert AU/minute readings into watts (W) rather than G forces when converting to standard physical units. Equations (26) through (29) describe the empirical relationship between average power in joules/second — that is, watts and AU/minute units — based on the four actometers studied.

$$W = 6.1693 \log 10 \ (AU/min) - 6.1340 \qquad (26)$$
$$W = 6.7267 \log 10 \ (AU/min) - 7.6856 \qquad (27)$$
$$W = 6.6683 \log 10 \ (AU/min) - 7.5168 \qquad (28)$$
$$W = 6.0439 \log 10 \ (AU/min) - 5.8959 \qquad (29)$$

The correlation coefficients associated with Eqs. (26) through (29) are $r(4) = 0.9735, 0.9816, 0.9807$, and 0.9702, respectively. Equation (30) is a general one for converting average AU/minute values into watts:

$$W = 6.4309 \log 10 \ (Av \ AU/min) - 6.8776 \qquad (30)$$

The correlation coefficient associated with Eq. (30) is $r(4) = 0.9744$, indicating an excellent fit to the data.

The preceding functional relationships are based upon only six points, where each data point represents the average of repeated measurements for a particular actometer and over four actometers. The resulting regression equations do not allow one to convert a single reading from a single actometer into watts of kinetic energy. Therefore the data in Table 7.3 were used to determine the quantitative relationship between 354 pairs of watt and AU/minute values obtained from 59 actometers to enable investigators to convert individual AU/minute values into watt values using Eq. (31):

$$W = 6.3793 \log 10 \ (AU/min) - 6.7985 \qquad (31)$$

The correlation coefficient associated with Eq. (31) is $r(352) = 0.9323, \ p < 0.001$.

I routinely convert the AU/minute values of each actometer into either a watt or *G* value using the empirically derived coefficients in Table 7.3 and then present group statistics in terms of watts or *G* units. This procedure has the advantage of considering the individual operating characteristics of each actometer within the conversion process. A disadvantage of this procedure is that the watt units cannot be directly compared with the AU/minute units reported by other investigators. Hence, it is desirable to have a method of reconverting watt units back into AU/minute units for the purpose of fostering communication among investigators still using nonstandard units of measure. Equation (32) provides the desired inverse regression equation.

$$\log 10 \ \text{AU/min} = 0.1363(W) + 1.2017 \qquad (32)$$

The correlation coefficient associated with Eq. (32) is the same as for Eq. (31) since it is the inverse regression from that of Eq. (31).

Counters

Construction Validity

Nature of measure
Motor activity involves changes in limb position with respect to time, and investigators have considered a count of these position changes to be an index of activity. McPartland, Foster, Kupfer, and Weiss (1976) described a device built for this purpose. The sensor consisted of a small tube, sealed at both ends and wrapped with many turns of fine copper wire. Inside the tube was a small ferromagnetic ball that would roll when the tube was tilted 5° or more off of the horizontal plane. The rolling ball altered the inductance of the tube, which occasioned a signal that a movement had just occurred. An FM transmitter sent a pulse to a receiver located within several hundred feet, which then activated a movement counter.

It is particularly important to realize that this type of device responds to movements that either begin in a horizontal position or move through a horizontal position. All other movements go undetected. For example, if the device is attached to the wrist while the arm is outstretched, a signal will be sent when the arm is rotated 5° or more off of the horizontal plane. Let us say that a 5° movement was executed to produce the first signal via the ball roll-

ing to one end of the tube. Further movement will not produce
a second count because the ball has already rolled to the end of
the tube. Only when the limb is rotated to a point 5° the other
side of the horizontal plane will the ball roll to the other end of
the tube, thereby causing a second signal to be sent and counted.
Hence, this device counts the number of times that the site of attachment deviates more than 5° from the horizontal plane. It is
very important that the investigator keep this fact in mind when
measuring activity. Such a device may give highly accurate counts
of certain stereotypic movements, such as body rocking, but may
give very inaccurate estimates of other types of behaviors. The investigators may operate on the assumption that most human behaviors involve rotations through the horizontal plane, though this
remains to be empirically demonstrated. Moreover, the magnitude
of the movement is irrelevant. A vigorous displacement from the
horizontal plane will be treated equally with a very slow one.
Hence, this type of counter should not be used to measure the force-
fulness of behavior.

A more popular type of counting device (Stevens, 1971) is
based upon a mercury switch that closes when tilted 5° or more
off of the horizontal plane. It contains a small ball of mercury that
is free to move when the switch is rotated, thereby opening and
closing an electric circuit. This apparatus is limited in the same
functional ways as is the ferromagnetic ball within the tube. The
small size of these switches allowed Schulman, Stevens, and Kupst
(1977) to mount three of them at 120° angles to each other. This
ensures that a 5° tilt in any of the three planes will be counted,
which does much to increase the sensitivity of the device. However,
the device is still totally insensitive to the intensity or magnitude
of the movement.

Unit of measure
The unit of measure is ±5° from the horizontal plane in the
case of the one-dimensional sensor. The unit of measure is ±5°
from any of the three orthogonal spatial planes in the case of the
three-dimensional sensor.

Accuracy

Reliability
Williamson, Calpin, DiLorenzo, Garris, and Petti (1981)
studied the reliability of mercury switches by attaching them to
an unspecified mechanical device that "mechanically closed the

mercury switches" (p. 405), presumably by rotating them back and forth an unspecified number of times. Perfect reliability was reported for all tests.

Standard quantities

The unit of ± 5° of tilt is not a standard quantity found in the natural sciences. Degrees per se is a standard unit. If one knew the total number of degrees that the site of attachment was rotated, then standard units would be available. Movement could also be expressed in terms of degrees of rotation per second or minute of wearing time. However, we have only the number of times the site of attachment rotated through the horizontal plane. In sum, the instrument does not read in standard units nor can it be calibrated to do so. The only hope of achieving standard units is to find an empirical relationship between the number of counts per minute and some other measure of activity already expressed in terms of standard units. An empirical conversion table or equation could then be constructed to allow investigators to transform the arbitrary counts-per-minute data into data having standard units of measure.

Pedometers

Construction Validity

Nature of measure

The typical mechanical pedometer contains a delicate arm that is balanced in the horizontal plane. Small vertical movements, like those associated with walking, are sufficient to displace this horizontal arm. Such action causes a system of gears to operate; this influences the dial from which the readings are taken. The stride adjustment governs the extent to which each vertical displacement of the horizontal arm advances the gears. In sum, the pedometer is a vertical movement counter that also contains a multiplier (stride adjustment).

While the pedometer was constructed to respond to the vertical movements associated with walking, it should be remembered that all behaviors having a vertical movement above that of the device's threshold sensitivity will activate it. Behaviors like hopping, jumping, kneeling, and bending will also displace the horizontal balance arm and be multiplied by the stride adjustment.

The stride adjustment is usually set such that walking a pre-

scribed distance will yield a corresponding distance on the pedometer. If a person has a large stride then the stride adjustment will
be set such that fewer counts equal a mile. This means that behaviors such as kneeling will increment the pedometer more for
the person with a long stride than for the person with a short stride.
This situation may not necessarily be undesirable since the person with the longer stride may be taller and thus have farther to
go when kneeling. The point is that the stride adjustment multi-
plies the results of all behaviors having a measurable vertical component, and not just walking behaviors.

Unit of measure

Pedometers typically give data in terms of miles walked. It
is expected that the wearer will walk a measured distance (e.g.,
1 mile), adjust the stride index, and walk the distance over again
until the stride adjustment is such that the pedometer reads 1 mile
after having walked a measured mile.

Accuracy

Reliability

Stunkard (1960) reported that calibrated pedometers are associated with an instrument error of 15% or less. This means that
when people repeatedly walk a measured mile, the pedometer can
show a number that varies up to 15% from the measured distance.
Gayle, Montoye, and Philpot (1977) published data that are in
good agreement with Stunkard's findings. These investigators studied three watch-type (analog) and three digital pedometers during a series of controlled walks by eight males. Each subject walked
a measured distance of 1 mile at 3 mph on a 0% grade on six different occasions. Each subject wore four pedometers during each
walk, two on the left hip and two on the right hip. The stride adjustment was set to 66 cm on all pedometers. The overall reproducibility error for all six pedometers was 11%. This error was reduced by recording the pedometer reading for each subject at the
end of the measured walk and calculating a conversion constant
for each subject. If 0.9 miles were recorded from the pedometer
after a 1-mile walk, then the conversion factor would be $1/0.9 =$
1.1. Hence, all future readings for that pedometer worn by that
person would be multiplied by 1.1. This procedure resulted in an
average reproducibility error of 5.9% for the digital pedometers

and 13.2% for the watch- , or analog-type pedometers, for an overall reproducibility error of 9.55%. It is noteworthy that the digital pedometers have less than half the error associated with them than do the analog pedometers.

Gayle, Montoye, and Philpot (1977) also reported significant differences in pedometer readings depending upon the site of attachment — left or right hip. The pedometer is activated by the impact of the foot against the ground, and these forces are apparently unequal for the right and left legs. However, the authors reported no significant relationships between pedometer performance and stride length, leg length, height, or body weight.

Marsden and Montgomery (1972) developed an electromechanical step counter that is placed in the heel of one's shoe. They also had subjects wear pedometers. The authors reported that "differences of fifty percent [in pedometer readings] were found during walking sessions involving the same number of counted steps" (p. 491). This study demonstrates that the act of stepping does not have uniform effects upon pedometers.

These approaches to assessing the reliability of pedometers have confounded the operating characteristics of the pedometers and the behavioral physics of locomotion. Saunders, Goldstein, and Stein (1978) vibrated approximately 36 digital pedometers on an Eberbach single-speed reciprocating power unit for 30 min (see Figure 5.1 in Chapter 5). They adjusted the stride index and retested the pedometers for another 30 min until all of the pedometers read to within ±0.5 miles of each other. The average reading was 37.5 miles, which was more than three times the highest reading ever reported by a patient in a rehabilitation setting. This means that the digital pedometers had a reproducibility error of $0.5/37.5 = 0.0133$, or 1.3%.

Heiser, Epstein, and Wing (1981) conducted a similar study using 55 digital pedometers. They vibrated these pedometers for 30 or 60 min on an Eberbach Lateral Shaker. During Experiment I the stride adjustment was set at 1 ft on all pedometers, and then they were vibrated for two 60-min periods. The results were that 85% of the pedometers gave readings of ±5% of 3 miles (range = 2.85–3.15) on both trials. The 3-mile mark was chosen because it was the modal value achieved by 67% of the pedometers. Experiment II began by resetting the stride adjustment to 2 ft. The pedometers were then vibrated for 30 min, readings were taken, the pedometers were vibrated for another 30 min, and the final readings were taken. The modal value was 3 miles after 30 min and

5.9 miles after 60 min of vibration. A total of 91 % of the pedometers were within ± 5 % of 6 miles (range = 5.7–6.3) after 60 min of shaking.

The preceding data show that pedometers per se have approximately 1.3 % to 5 % error when examined under laboratory conditions. The variability associated with measuring behavior on two occasions inflates the apparent pedometer error to approximately 5 % to 15 % error depending upon the type of pedometer used and whether conversion procedures are used.

Standard quantities

The naturalistic and laboratory methods for establishing the reliability of pedometers have distinctly different effects upon the unit of measurement. The first method requires subjects to walk a measured distance, such as a mile or kilometer; this means that subsequent readings will be in miles or kilometers. These are standard units of measure that have a long history in the natural or physical sciences. The second method of establishing the reliability of pedometers vibrates them a fixed number of times per minute, which is to say a fixed number of times over the selected interval (e.g., 30 min). This means that the pedometer no longer measures distance walked but counts the number of times the foot came in contact with the ground with enough force to be detected by the pedometer. However, it would still be possible to convert these counts into miles walked by having the person walk a measured mile, record the pedometer reading, and then adjust all future data by this conversion factor. For example, let us say that the pedometer reads 1.5 miles when attached to Person X and the individual has finished walking a measured mile. We now know that there is a 1.5 : 1 ratio between what the pedometer reads and the distance walked. Hence, a future reading of 5 miles would be multiplied by 1/1.5 (divided by 1.5) to obtain a transformed value of 3.3 miles.

The basic issue here is: How many steps did the person take and what was the average length of each step? Data on the number of steps taken are rather easy to come by (see Marsden & Montgomery, 1972). Data regarding the average distance or stride associated with these steps will be a function of the particular behavior under study. Running is associated with longer strides than is walking. Behaviors such as kneeling and bending do not have a stride length and therefore are problematic. Variability in stride length probably accounts for a large proportion of variation in pedometer data including most of the measurement error associated with reliability studies.

One solution to the present problem is to measure acceleration regarding the vertical component of motor behaviors, as discussed in the section on accelerometers (see Wong, Webster, Montoye, & Washburn, 1981). Such measurements can be multiplied by the person's body mass to obtain kinetic energy measures.

Stabilimeters

Construction Validity

Nature of measure

I am using the term *stabilimeter* in its generic sense to refer to devices that the individual sits or lies on in order to have their activity measured. The ballistographic chair described by Foshee (1958) consists of a deskchair mounted on a platform supported by a rubber stopper at each corner. A lever was attached to the back of the platform, which mechanically amplified all longitudinal movements. A bar magnet attached to the free end of the lever moved through a steel core wound with 4,000 turns of copper wire. Hence, changes in position of the subject produced platform movements, which caused the bar magnet to move within a coil, which made voltage changes take place, which were integrated and caused a certain number of condensor discharges per unit time.

Cromwell, Palk, and Foshee's (1961) ballistographic chair was slightly different. The platform was suspended from above by cables. A pendulum was attached to the platform, and a bar magnet was attached to the free end of the pendulum, which worked in the manner described previously.

Sprague and Toppe (1966) succinctly described the construction of their stabilimetric chair, which "was mounted on a platform in such a way that it tilted about ¼ inch when S moved forward–backward or when he moved right–left. The weight of the S was supported by a large bolt which projected from the floor of the platform and was inserted into a counter-sunk hole which had been drilled in a plate welded to the legs of the chair. Under each leg, small springs were placed. Sensitive switches were placed under the front leg (to record anterior–posterior movements) and under the right leg (to record lateral movement) and pairs of counters were connected to those switches" (p. 392).

A stabilimetric cushion (see Christensen, 1975; Edelson & Sprague, 1974; Juliano, 1974; Montagu & Swarbrick, 1975) is available that contains microswitches. The person sits on this cushion, and subsequent movements that exceed the sensitivity of the microswitches are counted. Every change in posture will produce as many counts as switches it closes. The total counts thereby depend directly upon the density of the switches within the cushion, in addition to the degree of movement. Two investigators using cushions having different sensor densities could easily obtain different counts per minute from the same person behaving in the same way.

Behavioral sleep studies have typically turned the subject's bed into a stabilimeter (Cox & Marley, 1959; Hobson et al., 1978; Kleitman, 1963; Monroe, 1967; Oswald et al., 1963; Stonehill & Crisp, 1971). Cairns, Thomas, Mooney, and Pace (1976) placed a microswitch under the subject's mattress such that lying or sitting on the bed turned off an "uptime" clock.

All of these stabilimetric devices measure changes in weight distribution. The investigator must then ask to what extent such an apparatus will accurately detect the type of behavior under study. Changing position of the torso will lead to clear changes in weight distribution on the stabilimetric platform or chair.[3] Changes in limb position, especially in small persons, might not give rise to sufficient weight redistribution to be detected by the stabilimetric device. It should be noted that stabilimetric devices respond to position changes regardless of how rapidly they occur.

Unit of measure
The unit of measure associated with stabilimetric instruments is the amount of weight distribution sufficient to cause a single count to be registered. This information has not been provided in the reports I have reviewed. Hence, the counts involve units of unknown size. The exception is Cairns et al.'s (1976) use of a microswitch to turn on a clock. Here the unit of measurement is the second, minute, or hour, which are clearly standard units.

---

[3]The Wiggle Chair can be purchased from Farrall Instruments, P.O. Box 1037, Grand Island, Nebraska 68801. A similar device can be purchased from Lafayette Instrument Company, Box 1279, Lafayette, Indiana 47902.

Accuracy

Reliability
I am presently unaware of any laboratory-based studies that have investigated the reliability of stabilimetric devices. Such studies would be straightforward. Various weights would be repeatedly displaced selected distances from specified starting points. Such data would reveal if the stabilimetric device responded consistently to the same stimulus regardless of its point of origin. Consistency of response could also be related to the magnitude of the stimulus.

Standard quantities
Stabilimetric counts are arbitrary units of measure. Stabilimeters cannot be directly calibrated in any way that would provide standard units of measure. However, it is possible to convert these arbitrary units of measure into standard ones. This would require knowing the physical forces necessary to cause a switch to close. Such force might be expressed in terms of degrees of tilt of a standard weight on a stabilimetric platform or the distance a standard weight had to be displaced on the stabilimetric platform to increment the count by a value of 1. The use of microswitches to activate a device such as a clock (see Cairns et al., 1976) clearly yields data having standard units.

Photoelectric Cells

Construction Validity

Nature of measure
Photoelectric cells produce an electric current when illuminated via an adequate light source. Motor movements that cause some portion of the anatomy to occlude a critical portion of this illumination will cause the photoelectric cell to terminate or sufficiently reduce its electric output. This event causes a counter to be incremented.

Photoelectric cells are normally placed on one side of a room, with their corresponding light sources placed directly opposite along the other wall (see Ellis & Pryer, 1959). This divides the room into slices. If a similar arrangement is made on the other two walls, the room is divided into squares whose size depends upon the spacing of the sensors. If the sensors are placed near the floor, then they will be triggered by leg movements and not arm movements unless the subject is lying down. If the photoelectric cells and light sources are placed at waist level, then movements of both the torso and the limbs will cause them to respond. This issue is the inverse of the site of attachment issue. One must decide where the sensor should be placed in the room rather than where to place the sensor on the person.

Investigators usually assume that the counts they record measure movement from one area of the room to another. While this is true, many other types of behaviors can cause photoelectric cells to increment counters, depending upon how high the cells have been placed. Kicking or throwing movements that occlude one or more light sources will cause photoelectric cells to respond. Push-up-like behavior could also repeatedly interrupt one or more light sources. In short, any behavior or the movement of any object that occludes a light source is sufficient to cause a count to occur.

Unit of measure

The unit of measure associated with photoelectric cells equals the distance the cells are spaced apart, provided that they are equally spaced along two perpendicular walls. For example, if the cells are placed at 1-m intervals on two perpendicular walls then the counts refer to the number of times that the subject moved a distance of 1 m. If the cells were placed 2 m apart, then the counts would refer to the number of times that the subject moved a distance of approximately 2 m. The subject could move diagonally, in which case he might be able to move slightly more than 2 m depending upon his posture at the time. Investigators should avoid placements of the cells that demarcate rectangular areas because this makes the units of measure ambiguous. If the cells were placed 1 m apart on one wall and 2 m apart on the other wall, then the subject could move 1 or 2 m before a count was registered. One could say that the unit of measure equaled the average of the two distances, or 1.5 m, but this is not a very desirable solution.

Accuracy

Reliability

C. F. Johnson (1972) examined the response of photoelectric cells to two behaviors. The first behavior involved an adult subject walking a predefined course at a slow speed for 3 min. The number of counts per 15 sec was recorded, giving rise to 12 data points. Their mean value was 59.42, and their standard deviation was 3.78, giving a CV of 6.36. The second behavior involved sitting. Zero counts were recorded in 11 of the 12 15-sec intervals, and a count of 1 was recorded in the remaining interval. In sum, the photoelectric cell device studied by Johnson detected walking behavior with just over 6% error and almost perfectly detected the absence of locomotion that characterizes sitting behavior.

Standard quantities
It is possible to express photoelectric cell counts in terms of meters of displacement if the cells are placed in such a way that they demarcate 1-m squares of floor space. It is recognized that not all counts will have come about due to bodily displacement of 1 m. However, the advantages of expressing measurements in terms of standard units outweighs the possibility that some portion, hopefully small, of the data will be artifactual.

Ultrasound

Construction Validity

Nature of measure
Ultrasonic movement detectors flood the observation area with high-frequency audio waves, too high to hear, and create what is called a standing wave pattern. The specific form of this wave is governed by the position of all objects in the room as well as the types of materials the room is made of. Any change in position of objects within the room, including people, will change the nature of this standing wave pattern. Transducers are placed within the room to monitor these standing wave patterns and to detect changes in them. Peacock and Williams (1962) detailed the construction of an instrument that generated a 41-kHz standing wave pattern (see Crawford & Nicora, 1964; Montagu & Swarbrick, 1975; Ray, Shotick, & Peacock, 1977).
Dabbs and Clower (1973) published information concerning the operating characteristics of ultrasonic movement detectors. They concluded that the "highest . . . rates occurred when the movement was fast, close to, or directly toward or away from the motion detector" (p. 475). Hence, the counts appear to be directly proportional to the rate of the movement and inversely propor-

tional to the distance of the subject from the transducer. The direction of motion is also important. Movement parallel to the major axis of the transducer (toward or away from it) produced more counts than did movement that was perpendicular to the major axis of the transducer (left or right of it).

Such operating characteristics complicate interpretation of data collected with ultrasonic movement detectors. Small, slow movements made close to and toward the transducer may produce more counts than large, fast movements made far from and perpendicular to the transducer. In short, the counts reflect as much about the distance and direction of the movement as they do about the extent and rate of the movement.

Unit of measure

The unit of measure for ultrasonic movement detectors is the amount or rate of displacement that is sufficient to give rise to 1 count. However, we have already seen that the amount or rate of displacement sufficient to trigger the device varies as a function of the distance and direction of the movement. This means that no constant degree of movement is associated with each count.

Accuracy

Reliability

The most thorough laboratory-based investigation of the consistency with which ultrasonic devices record movement was reported by C. F. Johnson (1972). One source of well-defined movement was provided by a $10.2 \times 15.2 \times 1.3$-cm vane revolving at 2 rpm 30.5 cm above and parallel to the floor. The ultrasonic equipment rarely detected the presence of this rotating vane. Enlarging the vane to $15.2 \times 76.3 \times 1.3$ cm did not increase its detectability. Perhaps the primary reason for the lack of detectability is that the vane was rotating parallel to the floor. This is just the sort of movement produced by a large record player. The axis of rotation was stationary, and the surface of the circular vane remained constant while revolving. The failure to detect this type of movement is not problematic because it is so different from movement associated with human behavior.

The second source of well-defined movement was a walking device that had two 50.8-cm-long legs that oscillated a distance of 5.7 cm in opposite directions at a rate of 7 rpm. The ultrasonic device did detect the presence of the walker. However, the mean number of counts differed when the walker was placed in five different locations. These means were: 43.00, 88.29, 31.86, 104.67, and 57.71 for the five sites, respectively. The differences in these means agree with the observations reported by Dabbs and Clower (1973) regarding variability in counts as a function of distance and direction of movement relative to the transducer. The bigger surprise was the relative inconsistency with which the ultrasonic device responded to the mechanical walker in the five locations. The coefficients of variation (CV) for these five sites were reported to be 33.30, 22.05, 39.01, 14.86, and 35.90, respectively. In conclusion, the ultrasonic device studied by C. F. Johnson (1972) exhibited from 14.86% to 35.90% error when monitoring the behavior of a mechanical walker in five different places within the observation area.

Standard quantities
Ultrasonic devices do not report data in standard units. The fact that counts are proportional to both the distance and direction of the movement, in addition to its extent and rate, drastically complicates all attempts to convert the arbitrary counts per minute into a standard quantity.

Electronic Accelerometers

Construction Validity

Nature of measure
The typical electronic accelerometer contains a small amount of mass attached to a piezoelectric crystal. The forces of acceleration impinging upon this mass cause the piezoelectric crystal to become proportionately deformed (i.e., squeezed), which causes a corresponding voltage change. Hence, an electric signal is obtained that is directly proportional to the rate of acceleration (see Mundel & Malmo, 1979). Wong, Webster, Montoye, and Washburn (1981) reported using a modified monoaural phonocartridge to measure acceleration. They attached a 0.225-g ball bearing to the tip of the stylus to increase its sensitivity. The device is typically attached at the waist to measure vertical displacements, which were shown to be directly proportional to normalized oxygen consumption.

Most accelerometers are largely unidimensional. That is, they respond almost entirely to forces of acceleration in one spatial plane but not in the other two. This characteristic limits the extent to which such a device properly responds to the magnitude of all movements. An important exception is the fact that all movements have vector components that lie in all three spatial planes. The unidimensional accelerometer will record the vector component of all behaviors that are parallel to its major axis and exceed the inertial properties of the sensor. A possible improvement would be to mount three unidimensional accelerometers at 120° angles from one another. This would ensure that the major axis of an accelerometer would lie in each of the three spatial planes. Three complications are associated with this approach. First, three accelerometers are required, which triples the expense. Second, the size of the triaxial sensor will be three times as large as the unidimensional sensor. Third, the three voltages coming from the three accelerometers must be combined into one voltage. This can be accomplished by squaring each of the voltages, adding the three squares together, and taking the square root of their sum.

Unit of measure
Manufacturers of commercial accelerometers provide the voltage readings associated with known levels of acceleration expressed in terms of meters/second/second. The fact that these accelerometers are linear over a wide range of acceleration makes it possible for the investigator to calculate acceleration readings given voltage readings recorded during a measurement period. This means that the unit of measurement is meters/second/second. These data can be divided by 9.8 meters/second/second, which is the gravitational constant governing freely falling bodies, to convert them into G force or gravity units. A value of 1 G is the acceleration associated with a freely falling object. (A nonlinear accelerometer is described by Kripke, Mullaney, Messin, & Wyborney, 1978.)

Some investigators have chosen to convert these standard physical measures into arbitrary activity counts. This was probably done because it is easier to increment a counter than to store the values of the voltage readings. Colburn, Smith, Guarini, and Simons (1976) used an accelerometer to trigger a square wave generator when more than a preset amount of acceleration was present. The unit of measure in this case is the level of acceleration, in meters/second/second, that characterizes the threshold for the square wave generator. One then records the number of times that accelerations of this magnitude were equaled or exceeded. A similar approach was taken by Ball, Sibbach, Jones, Steele, and Frazier (1975), who used an accelerometer to activate a shock generator to control assaultive and self-destructive behaviors in retarded persons. An acceleration threshold was set, and shock was administered when it was exceeded. A counter could have kept track of the shocks administered. In this case the unit of measure would be the number of times that acceleration values exceeded threshold, expressed in meters/second/second, which would equal the number of shocks given.

Accuracy

Reliability
I am presently unaware of systematic laboratory studies of the reliability of accelerometers. Perhaps one reason for the dearth of reliability studies is that commercial manufacturers of accelerometers are concerned with their accuracy. An accurate instrument is a reliable instrument by definition.

Standard quantities
The results of commercial accelerometers are already in standard units of measure; that is, meters/second/second.

Load Transducers

Construction Validity

Nature of measure
Fentem, Fitton, and Hampton (1976) and Barber, Evans, Fentem, and Wilson (1973) have described a simple load transducer that can be built into the heel of a person's shoe for the purpose of monitoring activity. The sensor is composed of a pressure-sensitive resistor made from polyurethane foam impregnated with colloidal carbon. Pressure changes, due to walking and other motor behaviors, alter the sensor's electrical resistance, which is recorded on a one-channel tape recorder.

This device clearly responds to the pressure changes associated with walking or pottering (standing still and shifting weight from one foot to another). The rate with which these pressure changes occur over time can be used to discriminate walking from more stationary behaviors, as is discussed later.

Marsden and Montgomery's (1972) step counter consisted of two brass strips attached to both sides of a 0.125 in. thick foam pad. The pad had a hole cut in it such that heel pressure would cause a dimple on one brass strip to pass through the hole and touch the other brass strip, thereby closing an electric circuit that activated a counter.

Unit of measure

Load transducers of this type are associated with units of measure expressed in terms of kilo-ohms of resistance. This is because the pressure changes associated with walking and other behaviors change the resistance of the load sensor. Fentem, Fitton, and Hampton (1976) successfully distinguished walking and active behaviors from inactive behaviors by examining the duration of the pressure change cycles. They found that "inactive" behaviors were associated with longer pressure cycles than were "active" behaviors. This allowed them to start and stop a timer to obtain the number of hours that walking behavior was present. An alternative expression is to measure the duration of each pressure cycle and express the data in terms of a histogram giving the percentage of all pressure cycles as a function of the duration of each cycle in milliseconds.

The unit of measure of Marsden and Montgomery's (1972) step counter is the pressure per square unit of area (e.g., pounds/square inch) necessary to close the switch.

Accuracy

Reliability

Reliability data are unavailable for both the load transducer and the step counter. Such data should be easy to collect. The reliability of the pressure-sensitive resistor could be determined by repeatedly placing the same weight upon the sensor and recording the voltage emitted by the device. The reliability of the step counter could be determined by placing the same weight upon the sensor 100 times and recording the value of the step counter, which should read 100. This will clearly be the case if a heavy enough weight is used. The weight just heavy enough will be the weight that provides the required pressure per square area to close the switch. The step counter should be highly accurate and therefore both reliable and valid under these conditions.

Standard quantities

The unit of measure associated with load transducers is already standard. The kilo-ohms of resistance are standard units, as are hours of activity and milliseconds of duration associated with each pressure cycle. The unit of measure associated with the step counter would be the pressure per square area necessary to close the switch.

Autonomic Measures

It is well known that activity increases pulse rate, blood pressure, oxygen consumption, and body temperature. It is therefore possible to measure these physiological indices and interpret them as measures of activity. It should be realized that these are indirect measures of activity at best.

Construction Validity

Nature of measure

Stott (1977) described methods for recording heart rate and/or blood pressure on a miniature tape recorder for 24-hr periods. Wade, Ellis, and Bohrer (1973) described a telemetric procedure for recording the heart rates in kindergarten children during free play. Bradfield, Paulos, and Grossman (1971) used FM telemetry to measure heart rate in obese high school girls. This information was used to calculate their energy expenditure. Microelectronic technology has allowed portable and fairly inexpensive heart rate monitors to become available. Microcomputer Technology retails the Pulse Tach Watch capable of displaying heart rate.[4] An updated reading of heart rate is associated with each heart beat. Biosig retails a bar-shaped device called Insta-Pulse that one grabs with both hands.[5] Heart rate information is averaged over several beats, and the results are displayed by light-emitting diodes in the middle of the bar. Ambulatory Monitoring retails portable equipment for obtaining 24-hr electrocardiograms (EKGs) in computer-compatible format.[6]

---

[4]The Pulse Tach Watch can be purchased from Microcomputer Technology, Inc., 3304 West MacArthur, Santa Ana, California 92704.

[5]Insta-Pulse, from Biosig, Inc., can be purchased from the Sharper Image, 260 California Street, San Francisco, California 94111.

[6]Product information can be obtained by writing to: Ambulatory Monitoring, Inc., 731 Saw Mill River Road, Ardsley, New York 10502.

Romanczyk, Crimmins, Gordon, and Kashinsky (1977) described an inexpensive sensor suitable for taking measurements of body temperature over a protracted period of time. It amounts to a small thermistor that is taped under the armpit, with a lead that goes to a digital voltmeter. Ambulatory Monitoring retails portable equipment for obtaining 24-hr body temperature records in computer-compatible format.[6]

Oxygen consumption is a physiologic measure of energy expenditure and can be measured with portable devices (see Schulman, Kaspar, & Throne, 1965). Ambulatory Monitoring retails this type of equipment.[6] Waxman and Stunkard (1980) measured the oxygen consumption of obese boys while they walked or ran at specified rates on a laboratory treadmill to determine the caloric expenditures associated with the various walking and running rates.

Globus, Phoebus, Humphries, Boyd, and Sharp (1973) used integrated EMG data to measure the activity of male college students participating in a study of circadian rhythms.

The specific design and construction of these devices is such that they accurately measure the physiological parameters they were designed to measure. The assessment problems that arise with this technology involve data interpretation as physiological measures are only indirect measures of the movements associated with the limbs and torso.

Unit of measure

The units of measure are standard ones that are specific to the particular physiologic function being measured. Heart rate is usually measured in beats per minute. However, Khachaturian, Kerr, Kruger, and Schachter (1972) reported that a nonlinear relationship exists between the interbeat interval, measured in milliseconds, and its corresponding beats per minute transformation. This implies that a constant change in interbeat interval does not produce the same change in beats per minute. Two major consequences are associated with this nonlinear change in units of measure. First, phasic and evoked cardiac responses are more clearly demonstrated when expressed in terms of interbeat interval units. Second, data expressed in terms of interbeat interval units contain from 1.9 to 4.6 times less skewness than do data expressed in terms of beats per minute. Both of these consequences of the nonlinear relationships between the units of measure are more noticeable at higher heart rates like those associated with infants or extreme exertion or fear in adults. The authors concluded that heart rate should be expressed in interbeat interval units rather than in beats per minute units unless some particular reason existed for using the beats per minute unit in a specialized application. Body temperature is specified in degrees fahrenheit or centigrade. Oxygen consumption is indicated in liters per minute. EMG is indicated in microvolts per square centimeter.

Accuracy

Reliability
Information concerning the reliability of physiological monitoring devices is most likely available from the manufacturer rather than the scientific literature. This is because these types of measurements are sufficiently advanced that investigators no longer question the reliability of these instruments.

Standard quantities
All of the instruments discussed report data in standard units that have long been associated with the natural or physical sciences.

Summary

Behavioral assessment began by attempting to rate or judge behavior. This constituted a quantitative approach to assessment that transcended qualitative descriptions of behavior. Behavioral observation was the next major quantitative advancement in behavioral assessment. Global behavioral categories were abandoned in favor of selected, well-defined behaviors. The specific occurrence of each behavior over a modest but specified time interval replaced personal impressions. Behavioral measurement was the next step in this growth process. Sensors were attached to the person or the person was placed in a special environment, and the physical forces associated with his behavior were measured. An alternative approach was to obtain biological specimens and examine them for substances indicative of the target behavior, like smoking or drinking alcohol.

Behavioral measurement is more than a simple extension of behavioral observation. It is not currently possible for mechanical instruments to duplicate what human observers are asked to do.

This is because behavioral observations require rather extensive judgments that instruments are not yet capable of accomplishing. Behavioral measurements require that we give up our comfortable global notions about behavior in favor of specific quantitative measures of the physical forces associated with either the emission or omission of these behaviors. In short, a new orientation is involved similar to the paradigmatic shift associated with the dawn of modern medical science when diseases began to be thought of in terms of measurements integral to the natural or physical sciences. Global clinical observations were increasingly supplemented by laboratory tests. Diseases were increasingly described in terms of newly acquired measuring instruments, thereby bringing about a marked shift in clinical perspective and practice. I believe that behavioral medicine awaits a similar revolution that will be led by advances in behavioral measurement. This chapter attempts to raise some of the important theoretical and practical issues associated with behavioral measurement in general and the measurement of activity in particular. The next chapter extends these developments by providing initial quantitative benchmark values associated with activity using existing instruments. This information should begin to provide a clinical context for interpreting activity data that hopefully will become an ever more integral aspect of behavioral assessment in behavioral medicine.

References

American Psychiatric Association. *Diagnostic and statistical manual of mental disorders* (3rd ed.). Washington, DC: American Psychiatric Association, 1980.

Ball, T. S., Sibbach, L., Jones, R., Steele, B., & Frazier, L. An accelerometer activated device to control assaultive and self-destructive behaviors in retardes. *Journal of Behavior Therapy and Experimental Psychiatry*, 1975, *6*, 223–228.

Barber, C., Evans, D., Fentem, P. H., & Wilson, M. F. A simple load transducer suitable for long-term recording activity patterns in human subjects. *Journal of Physiology*, 1973, *231*, 94–95.

Bell, R. Q. Adaptation of small wristwatches for mechanical recording of activity in infants and children. *Journal of Experimental Child Psychology*, 1968, *6*, 302–305.

Bradfield, R. B., Paulos, J., & Grossman, L. Energy expenditure and heart rate of obese high school girls. *American Journal of Clinical Nutrition*, 1971, *24*, 1482–1488.

Buckout, R. Eyewitness testimony. *Scientific American*, 1974, *231*, 23–31.

Buss, A., & Plomin, R. *A temperament theory of personality*. New York: Wiley, 1975.

Cairns, D., Thomas, L., Mooney, V., & Pace, J. B. A comprehensive treatment approach to chronic low back pain. *Pain*, 1976, *2*, 301–308.

Christensen, D. E. Effects of combining methylphenidate and the classroom token system in modifying hyperactive behavior. *American Journal of Mental Deficiency*, 1975, *80*, 266–276.

Colburn, T. R., Smith, B. M., Guarini, J. J., & Simons, N. N. *An ambulatory activity monitor with solid state memory*. Paper presented at the 13th annual Rocky Mountain Bioengineering Symposium and the 13th International ISA Biomedical Sciences Symposium, Laramie, Wyoming, 1976.

Cone, J. D. The relevance of reliability and validity for behavioral assessment. *Behavior Therapy*, 1977, *8*, 411–426.

Cone, J. D. "Psychometric" considerations in behavioral assessment. In M. Hersen & A. S. Bellack (Eds.), *Behavioral assessment: A practical handbook* (2nd ed.). New York: Pergamon Press, 1981.

Cox, G. H., & Marley, E. The estimation of motility during rest or sleep. *Journal of Neurology, Neurosurgery, and Psychiatry*, 1959, *22*, 57–60.

Crawford, M. L. J., & Nicora, B. D. Measurement of human group activity. *Psychological Reports*, 1964, *15*, 227–231.

Cromwell, R. L., Palk, B. E., & Foshee, J. G. Studies in activity level. V. The relationships among eyelid conditioning, intelligence, activity level, and age. *American Journal of Mental Deficiency*, 1961, *65*, 744–748.

Dabbs, J. M., Jr., & Clower, B. J. An ultrasonic motion detector with data on stare, restriction of movement, and startle. *Behavior Research Methods and Instrumentation*, 1973, *5*, 475–476.

Edelson, R. I., & Sprague, R. L. Conditioning of activity level in a classroom with institutionalized retarded. *American Journal of Mental Deficiency*, 1974, *78*, 384–388.

Ellis, N. R., & Pryer, R. S. Quantification of gross bodily activity in children with severe neuropathology. *American Journal of Mental Deviance*, 1959, *63*, 1034–1037.

Fentem, P. H., Fitton, D. L., & Hampton, J. R. Long-term recording of activity patterns. *Postgraduate Medical Journal*, 1976, *52*, 163–166.

Foshee, J. G. Studies in activity level. I. Simple and complex task performance in defectives. *Journal of Mental Deficiency*, 1958, *62*, 882–886.

Foster, F. G., & Kupfer, D. J. Psychomotor activity as a correlate of depression and sleep in acutely disturbed psychiatric inpatients. *American Journal of Psychiatry*, 1975, *132*, 928–931.

Gayle, R., Montoye, H. J., & Philpot, J. Accuracy of pedometers for measuring distance walked. *Research Quarterly*, 1977, *48*, 632–636.

Globus, G. G., Phoebus, E. C., Humphries, J., Boyd, R., & Sharp, R. Ultraradian rhythms in humans telemetered gross motor activity. *Aerospace Medicine*, 1973, *44*, 882–887.

Hall, C. S., & Lindzey, G. *Theories of personality*. New York: Wiley, 1957.

Heiser, J. R., Epstein, L. H., & Wing, R. R. Mechanical reliability of pedometers. *Behavior Therapist*, 1981, *4*, 21–22.

Hobson, J. A., Spagna, T., & Malenka, R. Ethology of sleep studied with time-lapse photography: Postural immobility and sleep-cycle phase in humans. *Science*, 1978, *201*, 1251–1253.

Johns, M. W. Methods for assessing human sleep. *Archives of Internal Medicine*, 1971, *127*, 484–492.

Johnson, C. F. Hyperactivity and the machine: The actometer. *Child Development*, 1971, *42*, 2105–2110.

Johnson, C. F. Limits on the measurement of activity level in children using ultrasound and photoelectric cell. *American Journal of Mental Deficiency*, 1972, *77*, 301–310.

Johnson, S. M., & Bolstad, O. D. Methodological issues in naturalistic observation: Some problems and solutions for field research. In L. A. Hamerlynck, L. C. Handy, & E. J. Mash (Eds.), *Behavior change: Methodology, concepts, and practices*. Champaign, IL: Research Press, 1973.

Johnston, J. M., & Pennypacker, H. S. *Strategies and tactics of human behavioral research*. Hillsdale, NJ: Erlbaum, 1980.

Jones, R. A., Reid, J. B., & Patterson, G. R. Naturalistic observations in clinical assessment. In P. McReynolds (Ed.), *Advances in psychological assessment* (Vol. 3). San Francisco, CA: Jossey-Bass, 1975.

Juliano, D. B. Conceptual tempo activity and concept learning in hyperactive and normal children. *Journal of Abnormal Psychology*, 1974, *83*, 629–634.

Khachaturian, Z. S., Kerr, J., Kruger, R., & Schachter, J. A methodological note: Comparison between period and rate data in studies of cardiac function. *Psychophysiology*, 1972, *9*, 539–545.

Kleitman, N. *Sleep and wakefulness*. Chicago: University of Chicago Press, 1963.

Kripke, D., Mullaney, D., Messin, S., & Wyborney, J. Wrist actigraphic measures of sleep and rhythms. *Electroencephalography and Clinical Neurophysiology*, 1978, *44*, 674–676.

Kuhn, T. S. *The structure of scientific revolutions*. Chicago: University of Chicago Press, 1970.

Maccoby, E., Dowley, E., Hagen, J., & Dergman, R. Activity level and intellectual functioning in normal pre-school children. *Child Development*, 1965, *36*, 761–770.

Marsden, J. P., & Montgomery, S. R. A general survey of the walking habits of individuals. *Ergonomics*, 1972, *15*, 491–504.

Massey, P. S., Lieberman, A., & Batarseh, G. Measure of activity level in mentally retarded children and adolescents. *American Journal of Mental Deficiency*, 1971, *76*, 259–261.

McPartland, R. J., Foster, F. G., Kupfer, D. J., & Weiss, B. Activity sensors for use in psychiatric evaluation. *IEEE Transactions on Biomedica Engineering*, 1976, *23*, 175–178.

Monroe, L. J. Psychological and physiological differences between good and poor sleepers. *Journal of Abnormal Psychology*, 1967, *72*, 255–264.

Montagu, J. D., & Swarbrick, L. Effect of amphetamines in hyperkinetic children: Stimulant or sedative? A pilot study. *Developmental Medicine and Child Neurology*, 1975, *17*, 293–298.

Mundel, W. J., & Malmo, H. P. An accelerometer for recording head movement of laboratory animals. *Physiology and Behavior*, 1979, *23*, 391–393.

Oswald, I., Berger, R. J., Jaramillo, R. A., Keddie, K. M. G., Olley, P. C., & Plunkett, G. B. Melancholia and barbiturates: A controlled E.E.G., body and eye movement study of sleep. *British Journal of Psychiatry*, 1963, *109*, 66.

Peacock, L. J., & Williams, M. An ultrasonic device for recording activity. *American Journal of Psychology*, 1962, *75*, 648–652.

Ray, A. B., Jr., Shotick, A. L., & Peacock, L. J. Activity level of mentally retarded individuals: Do they reflect the circadian rhythm? *Australian Journal of Mental Retardation*, 1977, *4*, 18–21.

Reich, L. H., Kupfer, D. J., Weiss, B. L., McPartland, R. J., Foster, F. G., Detre, T., & Delgado, J. Psychomotor activity as a predictor of sleep efficiency. *Biological Psychiatry*, 1974, *8*, 253–256.

Reid, J. B. Reliability assessment of observation data: A possible methodological problem. *Child Development*, 1970, *41*, 1143–1150.

Romanczyk, R. G., Crimmins, D. B., Gordon, W. C., & Kashinsky, W. M. Measuring circadian cycles: A simple temperature recording preparation. *Behavior Research Methods and Instrumentation*, 1977, *9*, 393–394.

Saris, W. H. M., & Binkhorst, R. A. The use of pedometer and actometer in studying daily physical activity in man. Part I. Reliability and validity. *European Journal of Applied Physiology*, 1977, *37*, 219–228.

Saunders, K. J., Goldstein, M. K., & Stein, G. H. Automatic measurement of patient activity on a hospital rehabilitation ward. *Archives of Physical Medicine and Rehabilitation*, 1978, *59*, 255–257.

Schulman, J. L., Kaspar, J. C., & Throne, F. M. *Brain damage and behavior: A clinical experimental study*. Springfield, IL: C. C. Thomas, 1965.

Schulman, J. L., & Reisman, J. M. An objective measure of hyperactivity. *American Journal of Mental Deviance,* 1959, *64,* 455–456.

Schulman, J. L., Stevens, T. M., & Kupst, M. J. The biomotometer: A new device for the measurement and remediation of hyperactivity. *Child Development,* 1977, *48,* 1152–1154.

Sprague, R. L., & Toppe, L. K. Relationship between activity level and delay of reinforcement in the retarded. *Journal of Experimental Child Psychology,* 1966, *3,* 390–397.

Stevens, E. A. Some effects of tempo changes on stereotyped rocking movements of low-level mentally retarded subjects. *American Journal of Mental Deficiency,* 1971, *76,* 76–81.

Stonehill, E., & Crisp, A. H. Problems in the measurement of sleep with particular reference to the development of a motility bed. *Journal of Psychosomatic Research,* 1971, *15,* 495–499.

Stott, F. D. Ambulatory monitoring. *British Journal of Clinical Equipment,* 1977, *March,* 61–68.

Stunkard, A. A method of studying physical activity in man. *American Journal of Clinical Nutrition,* 1960, *8,* 595–601.

Thomas, A., Chess, S., & Birch, H. *Temperament and behavior disorders in children.* New York: New York University Press, 1968.

Thomas, A., Chess, S., & Birch, H. The origin of personality. *Scientific American,* 1970, *223,* 102–109.

Tryon, W. W. A system of behavioral diagnosis. *Professional Psychology,* 1976, *7,* 495–506.

Tryon, W. W. Principles and methods of mechanically measuring motor activity. *Behavioral Assessment,* 1984, *6,* 129–139.

Tryon, W. W., & Klemuk, G. M. The reliability and validity of actometers, (unpublished manuscript), 1982.

Wade, M. G., Ellis, M. J., & Bohrer, R. E. Biorhythms in the activity of children during free play. *Journal of the Experimental Analysis of Behavior,* 1973, *20,* 155–162.

Waxman, M., & Stunkard, A. J. Caloric intake and expenditure of obese boys. *Journal of Pediatrics,* 1980, *96,* 187–193.

Werry, J. Measures in pediatric psychopharmacology. In J. Werry (Ed.), *Pediatric psychopharmacology: The use of behavior modifying drugs in children.* New York: Brunner/Mazel, 1978.

Williamson, D. A., Calpin, J. P., DiLorenzo, T. M., Garris, R. P., & Petti, T. A. Treating hyperactivity with dexedrine and activity feedback. *Behavior Modification,* 1981, *5,* 399–416.

Winn, P. R., & Johnson, R. H. *Business statistics,* New York: Macmillan, 1978.

Wong, T. C., Webster, J. G., Montoye, H. J., & Washburn, R. Portable accelerometer device for measuring human energy expenditure. *IEEE Transactions on Biomedical Engineering,* 1981, *BME-28,* 467–471.

8

Human Activity: A Review of Quantitative Findings

Warren W. Tryon

Chapter 7 of this volume contains material that is preliminary to the considerations of this chapter. Chapter 7 provides the rationale for studying human activity. It then focuses upon a number of important conceptual reorientations that accompany the use of instruments for acquiring data on human activity. Chapter 7 also surveys the available devices for measuring human activity. Finally, it discusses methods for converting the arbitrary units of one device, the actometer, into standard units.

The purpose of the present chapter is to orient the reader regarding the typical data one might expect from instruments when measuring activity. This chapter is intended to provide "benchmark" values stemming from instruments used to record human activity. Of particular importance is the section on normal values. All studies were inspected to see if they contained data regarding normal behavior; often this information came from control groups and was not of central importance to the published study. The data from all of these normal subjects have been compiled under a single heading.

The organization of this chapter is particularly noteworthy. The major headings relate to different instruments such as actometers, pedometers, stabilimeters, etc. This was done for reasons extensively discussed in the sections on behavioral measurement and behavioral physics in Chapter 7. Basically, each mechanical device has its own operating characteristics. Different devices literally sense different aspects of the physical processes associated with the emission and omission of behavior. There is currently no means of converting one data set into another. Therefore, data obtained with different instruments represent qualitatively different data. This problem would not be so severe if human activity were a highly unitary phenomenon sufficient to cause very high intercorrelations among a wide range of different mechanical devices. Because this seems not to be the case, instrument selection becomes a critical matter. I have consequently organized the presently available quantitative information about human activity with respect to the type of device used to collect it. Such organization reflects the critical and central role that measurement occupies within this book.

Actometers

Schulman and Reisman (1959) were the first persons to describe actometers. They purchased Omega self-winding men's calendar wristwatches and paid a jeweler to modify them so that the self-winding rotor advanced the minute hand, which advanced the hour hand and calendar date in the usual manner. The investigators noted the "days," "hours," and "minutes," plus the real time both before and after each observational session. The total elapsed apparent "days," "hours," and "minutes" were all converted into "minutes" and labled *actometer units* (AU). This value was divided by the actual number of minutes the device was worn, resulting in the AU/minute metric. Timex presently retails their own version of this device as a Model 108 Motion Recorder.[1]

Normal Children

Psychologists all too frequently begin studying clinical populations without having any data on normal subjects. It is refreshing to see that some attempts have been made to study the activity of normal children. Table 8.1 provides a summary of findings.

[1]Model 108 Motion Recorders can be purchased from the Engineering Department, Timex Industries, Waterbury, Connecticut 06720.

Table 8.1. Descriptive Statistics for Normal Children Wearing Actometers

| | | | Data as Reported | | Wrist activity (AU/min) | |
Study no. and investigator	n	Age	Sex	Mean	SD	Range
1. Campbell et al. (1971)	30	4 wk	M			
	29		F			
2. Rose & Mayer (1968)	13	2 mo	M			
	16	2 mo	F			
3. Chapman (1975)	80	6-8 mo	M	179.61	103.36	34.00-577.00
	73	6-8	F	136.60	77.00	29.00-407.00
4. Kaspar et al. (1971)	48	5-8 yr	M	36.89	29.17	
Free activity	24		F	13.40	11.27	
Structured activity			M	5.69	3.73	
			F	5.78	5.61	
5. Shaffer et al. (1974)	8	5-8	M+F	189.37	75.28	
6. Schulman et al. (1965)	8	5-7	M	46.83	24.33	
	8	7-8	M	78.00	36.50	
	11	8-9	M	98.50	119.50	
	7	9-10	M	56.83	57.33	
	7	10-12	M	55.17	52.33	
	10	5-7	F	26.33	15.17	
	7	7-8	F	26.67	10.83	
	7	8-9	F	21.67	10.17	

(continued)

259

Table 8.1. (continued)

| | | | | Data as Reported | | |
| | | | | | Wrist activity (AU/min) | |
Study no. and investigator	n	Age	Sex	Mean	SD	Range
6. Schulman et al. (1965) (continued)	7	9–10	F	28.33	21.17	
	7	10–12	F	27.33	34.50	
7. Pope (1970)	19	7–11	M			
Free play				77.30	43.60	
Simple task				217.80	93.00	
Difficult task				70.90	39.80	
8. Barkley & Cunningham (1979b)	14	9	M	39.13	28.20	
9. Cunningham & Barkley (1979)	20	5–12	M	32.43		

| | | Comparison of Data | | | | |
| | Ankle activity (AU/min) | | | Wrist + ankle activity (AU/min) | | |
Study no.	Mean	SD	Range	Mean	SD	Range
1.	15.89	8.42		88.46	16.86	
2.				86.36	23.80	

(continued)

Table 8.1. (continued)

Comparison of Data

Study no.	Ankle activity (AU/min)			Wrist + ankle activity (AU/min)		
	Mean	SD	Range	Mean	SD	Range
3.	125.99	65.76	40–430	305.60	150.74	76–958
	101.63	49.17	38–290	238.23	112.31	109–615
4.	62.10	49.20				
	17.14	14.34				
	6.30	8.31				
	3.30	5.13				
5.	319.38	179.61				
6.	51.50	87.33		98.33		
	58.50	43.17		136.50		
	76.83	76.33		175.33		
	57.33	56.17		114.16		
	20.00	25.17		75.17		
	40.17	42.62				
	16.83	12.00				
	13.33	12.50				
	18.33	17.33				
	24.83	39.67				
7	39.90	39.60		117.20	77.70	
	333.70	212.50		555.50	289.00	
	49.70	29.30		120.70	66.10	
8.	120.43	54.77				
9.	33.60					

Campbell, Kuyek, Lang, and Partington (1971) placed actometers on the right ankle of 30 male and 29 female neonates for
the first 96 hr, or 4 consecutive days, of life. Conversion of their
activity scores into actometer units per minute reveals the following results.[2] The average AU/minute and standard deviations (in
parentheses) per day for the first 4 days of life were: 10.33 (4.33),
14.67 (7.35), 17.22 (8.16), and 21.35 (12.00) AU/min. A clear progression of increasing activity is evident. It is also apparent that
the standard deviations are large in relation to the mean; that is,
from 42% to 56% of the mean. This indicates much individual
variability in motility during the first 4 days of life. The authors
also reported a substantial decrease in activity during Weeks 2 and
3 of life, which were the first 2 weeks spent at home ($t[57] = 3.2$,
$p < 0.01$). The mean AU/minute dropped to 13.08. The mean activity for Weeks 4 and 5 increased to 15.02 AU/min, which increased to 21.35 AU/min for Weeks 6 and 7 and then further increased to 26.17 AU/min during Weeks 9 and 10. Hence, activity
normally increases in a monotonic fashion from birth and is substantially depressed upon removing the child from the hospital to
the home, whereupon further increases in activity are noted ($F[3,
88] = 8.29$, $p < 0.005$). No sex differences were reported, nor were
the data presented separately for each sex. Overall, it appears that
infants less than 4 days old exhibit an average ankle activity of
15.89 AU/min, with an average standard deviation of about 8.42
AU/min.

Mack and Kleinhenz (1974) placed actometers (modified Tis-
sot self-winding wristwatches) in cloth packets and attached them
to five Black female infants using rubber belts similar to those used
to fasten EKG electrodes. Activity was monitored 24 hr a day when
the infant was 8, 16, 28, and 56 days old. Actometers were placed
on both wrists (dorsal surfaces) and both ankles (lateral aspects).
The actometer units of all four devices over the 24-hr period were

---

[2]Campbell et al. (1971) presented their activity data in "decimal numbers.
'Days' shown on the calendar became integers, and 'time' shown by the hands
became the decimal. These quantities were then divided by the time during which
observations had been made and the results expressed as activity/hr" (p. 110).
Hence, I multiplied their values, say, 0.73, for example, by 24 hr = 17.52. I interpreted the 17 to mean "days" accumulated and the 52 to mean 5.2 hr rather
than 5 hr 2 min. This decision was made partly because all decimals contained
two places, and three or four places would result if hours and minutes were recorded. Perhaps future investigators will adopt standard units of measurement
to avoid possible inaccuracies arising over different methods of reporting.

added together to obtain a single score. The least active infant showed no increase in activity over time. She was found to produce 172 AU/24 hr over four sites of attachment on Day 56. This equals an average of 0.030 AU/min for each site of attachment. A second infant was slightly more active at each of the four measurement points but did not show any systematic increase in activity over time. This infant was found to produce 283 AU/24 hr over four sites of attachment on Day 56. This equals an average of 0.049 AU/min for each site of attachment. Two other infants showed moderate increases in activity over the four measurement periods. They evidenced 783 and 834 AU/24 hr, respectively, over four sites of attachment on Day 56. This equals an average of 0.136 and 0.145 AU/min, respectively. The fifth infant showed a dramatic increase in activity with age. Her activity increased in an almost perfectly linear fashion over the four measurement periods. She was found to produce 2,849 AU/24 hr over four sites of attachment on Day 56. This equals an average of 0.495 AU/min.

Rose and Mayer (1968) studied 4- to 6-month-old infants. They attached an actometer to the wrist and contralateral ankle for 2 consecutive 24-hr periods.[3] The site of attachment was counterbalanced such that if recording was begun with the right wrist, the actometer was placed on the left wrist during the second observation period. The authors added both wrist measurements to both ankle measurements and divided by 4 to obtain their published measurements. I multiplied these values by 2 to obtain the wrist-plus-ankle values in Table 8.1. Dividing these tabled values by 2 provides the following estimates of wrist or ankle activity: $M = 22.12$ AU/min and $SD = 4.21$ AU/min for males, and $M = 21.59$ AU/min and $SD = 5.95$ AU/min for females. The males studied by Rose and Mayer were significantly ($t[70] = 2.59$, $p < 0.01$) more active than the combined male and female group studied by Campbell et al. (1971). The Rose and Mayer female group was also significantly ($t[73] = 2.54$, $p < 0.05$) more active than was the Camp-

---

[3]Rose and Mayer (1968) reported activity units/day, where "each day registered on the meter was considered to be one unit of activity" (p. 200), symbolized as AUd. One AUd = 1,440 AU as defined here, where 1 "minute" equals 1 AU. Hence, 34 AUd = 34 × 1,440 = 47,960 AU. Since 34 AUd were collected over a 24-hr period containing 1,440 min, 34 AUd = 47,960/1,440 = 34 AU/min. The authors added the two wrist and two ankle measures and divided by 4 to give "activity in units per limb per day" (p. 20). I therefore doubled their values to get a wrist-plus-ankle value per day.

bell et al. combined group. These results support the observation that activity naturally increases with age during infancy.

Chapman (1975) studied 6- to 8-month-old infants but reported results very different from Rose and Mayer (1968). Chapman obtained two 24-hr recordings from either the left or right wrist and ankle (determined randomly). The mean (and standard deviation) ankle values for males of 125.99 (65.76) AU/min and for females of 101.63 (49.17) AU/min are several times larger than the values reported by Rose and Mayer.

Saris and Binkhorst (1977a) placed actometers (modified Tussot self-winding wristwatches) on the right wrist and ankle of nine children aged 5 to 6 years. The children walked for 10 min or ran for 5 min depending upon the velocity of the treadmill. Walking was associated with four treadmill speeds of 1, 2, 3, and 5 km/hr. Running was associated with two treadmill speeds of 5 and 7 km/hr. Their data were presented in graphic but not tabular form, necessitating estimation from the graph. Walking levels produced 1, 2, 3, and 8 AU/min, whereas running levels produced 13 and 15 AU/min, respectively.

Saris and Binkhorst (1977b) administered an activity questionnaire to an unspecified number of 4- to 6-year-old kindergarten children. The two children with the highest scores and the two children with the lowest scores were selected to wear an actometer on their right wrist and ankle from 9:00 A.M. to 12:00 during 1 week from Monday to Friday. The authors apparently added the activity units of the two actometers to obtain an overall score. The means (and standard deviations) for the wrist actometers for the two most and two least active subjects are 170 (48) AU/3 hr and 148 (49) AU/3 hr, respectively. This difference was reported to be statistically significant at the 5% level using a t test. The mean values correspond to averages of 0.47 AU/min and 0.41 AU/min per site. The means (and standard deviations) for the ankle actometers for the two most and two least active subjects are 204 (72) AU/3 hr and 140 (70) AU/3 hr, respectively. This difference was reported to be statistically significant at the 1% level using a t test. The mean values correspond to averages of 0.57 AU/min and 0.39 AU/min per site. The wrist and ankle actometers did not correlate beyond chance levels ($r[2] = .69$, NS), but the chances of a Type II error are exceedingly great with only two degrees of freedom.

Extending the developmental period to 5- to 8-year-old children, we come to the study by Kaspar, Millichap, Backus, Child, and Schulman (1971), who measured wrist and ankle activity during free play and a structured situation (taking psychological tests). The mean (and standard deviation) free play ankle activity was 62.10 (49.20) AU/min for males and 17.14 (14.34) AU/min for females. These measurements for males are significantly ($t[59] = 2.91$, $p < 0.01$) greater than the values reported by Rose and Mayer (1968) for males. However, the value for females is not significantly different from the value provided by Rose and Mayer. Hence, we now have the first evidence of a sex difference, where the free play wrist activity for males is significantly greater ($z = 4.86$, $p < 0.001$) than for females. The boys' mean free play ankle activity was also significantly greater ($z = 5.78$, $p < 0.001$) than that recorded for the girls. The boys' ankle activity was also significantly ($F[47, 23] = 11.77$, $p < 0.01$) more variable than the girls'. However, no significant sex differences were found to occur during the structured activity condition.

Shaffer, McNamara, and Pincus (1974) also studied 5- to 8-year-old males and females by having them wear an actometer on their dominant wrist and ankle for 10 min of free play and during a Continuous Attention Test of unspecified duration. Their combined averages (and standard deviations) for males and females of 189.37 (75.28) AU/min for wrist and 319.38 (179.61) AU/min for ankle activity are much larger than the values reported by Kaspar et al. (1971). It appears as though the Shaffer et al. (1974) free play situation occasioned very active behavior.

Schulman, Kaspar, and Throne (1965) provide data on the activity of 5- to 12-year-old males and females. Their data are based upon wrist and ankle measurements taken during 20 to 35 min of free playroom activity. The means and standard deviations of ankle activity for 5- to 7-year-old males ($M = 51.50$, $SD = 87.33$ AU/min) and 7- to 8-year-old males ($M = 62.50$, $SD = 43.17$ AU/min) correspond closely to the values for males published by Kaspar et al. (1971). Nonsignificant increases in ankle activity were reported up to age 8 to 9 ($M = 76.83$, $SD = 76.33$ AU/min), whereupon ankle activity began to decrease. By age 10 to 12 ankle activity had dropped dramatically ($M = 20.00$, $SD = 25.17$ AU/min) but not significantly due to the large amount of variation at each age level. A parallel form of development was reported with regard to wrist activity.

Females displayed a rather different development. The 5- to 7-year-old girls exhibited the highest levels of ankle activity ($M = 40.17$, $SD = 42.67$ AU/min). They then decreased in activity until age 8 to 9 ($M = 13.33$, $SD = 12.50$ AU/min), whereupon they began to increase in activity to the age of 10 to 12 ($M = 24.83$, $SD = 39.67$ AU/min). These changes were not statistically significant due to the large amount of variation at each age level. The wrist activity changed little from age 5 to 7 ($M = 26.33$, $SD = 15.17$ AU/min), to age 8 to 9 ($M = 21.67$, $SD = 10.17$ AU/min), and to age 10 to 12 ($M = 27.33$, $SD = 34.50$ AU/min). These developmental changes are emphasized in Table 8.2.

The boys were considerably more variable than the girls at almost every age. The ratio of the male/female variances for wrist activity was maximum at age 8 to 9 ($F[10, 6] = 138.07$, $p < 0.001$) and minimum at age 10 to 12 ($F[6, 6] = 2.30$, NS). The ankle activity was also significantly more variable in males than females at age 8 to 9 ($F[10, 6] = 37.29$, $p < 0.001$). By age 10 to 12, the girls were slightly, but not significantly, more variable than the boys ($F[6, 6] = 2.24$, NS).

The impact of the testing situation upon the activity readings is illustrated by the following two studies. Cunningham and Barkley (1979) attached actometers to the preferred wrist and ankle of 20 5- to 12-year-old boys who then engaged in 15 min of free play in a room measuring 4×6.1 m with normal ceilings. Their activity was then measured during a 15-min structured task period, resulting in a 30-min observation session altogether. The mean wrist activity was 32.43 AU/min, and the mean ankle activity was 33.60 AU/min. Barkley and Cunningham (1979b) attached actometers to the preferred wrist and ankle of 14 9-year-old boys who then

Table 8.2. Averages of Wrist Plus Ankle Activity Values for Normal Boys and Girls Aged 4 Months to 12 Years

Investigator	Age	Mean (AU/min)[a]	
		Male	Female
Rose & Mayer (1968)	4–6 mo	22.12	21.59
Kaspar et al. (1971)	5–8 yr	49.50	15.27
Schulman et al. (1965)	5–8 yr	58.71	28.51
	8–9 yr	87.40	17.50
	9–10 yr	57.08	23.33
	10–12 yr	37.59	26.08
	9–10 yr	57.08	23.33

[a]These values were obtained by dividing the reported total of wrist plus ankle by 2 if both measures were available.

engaged in 10 min of free play in a gymnasium measuring 17.7 ×
14.6 m with 12.8-m ceilings. The mean wrist activity was reported
to be 39.23 AU/min, which is not very different from the value
published by Cunningham and Barkley (1979). However, the mean
ankle activity was 120.43 AU/min, which is nearly four times the
value reported by Cunningham and Barkley. It appears that the
larger gymnasium occasioned much more running activity than
did the more modest-sized playroom. Hence, a careful description
of the conditions under which the activity measurements are taken
must be provided if seemingly incompatible data sets are to be
avoided.

It is noteworthy that the means and standard deviations for
the wrist data in Table 8.1 are highly correlated ($r[18] = 0.81$,
$p < 0.001$). The average standard deviation of the wrist data was
57.6% of the grand mean of the wrist data. The means and standard deviations for the ankle data are also highly correlated
($r[40] = 0.90$, $p < 0.001$). The average standard deviation for the
ankle data was 65.06% of the grand mean of the ankle data.

Normal Adults

Saris and Binkhorst (1977a) placed actometers (modified Tussot
self-winding wristwatches) on the right wrist and ankle of 15 adult
men aged 21 to 31 years. They were then asked to walk and run
on a treadmill for 10 min at the following speeds: 4, 6, 7, 9, and
10 km/hr. They ran for only 5 min at speeds of 13 and 15 km/hr.
The authors presented their data in graphic form, thereby necessitating estimation from the graph. Walking at 4, 6, 7, and 9 km/hr
produced approximately 3, 4, 5, and 7 AU/min. Running at 7, 9,
10, 13, and 15 km/hr produced approximately 12, 13, 13, 17, and
19 AU/min.

All of these studies have obtained brief samples of activity
under laboratory or clinic conditions. It was assumed that findings
obtained under these conditions would generalize to extended
measurements of activity obtained in the subjects' natural environments. The validity of this critical assumption can be tested
using small portable and unobtrusive mechanical devices such as
actometers, pedometers, and counters. Future studies should obtain such extended activity measurements to support the ecological
validity of their findings.

Brain-Injured Children

Strauss and Lehtinen (1947) popularized the hypothesis that hyperactivity in children results from brain injury. Their theory presumes that brain damage or dysfunction prevents the child from being able to ignore irrelevant stimuli. Consequently, children become overstimulated, and their activity is said to be "driven" at a high rate. An obvious method for studying this hypothesis would be to obtain a sample of brain-injured children and a normal control group, measure their activity level, and determine if the two groups are significantly different. Kaspar et al. (1971) provided such a test. The brain-injured group consisted of 24 boys and 12 girls aged 5 to 8 years who were judged to have brain injury by a board-eligible or certified pediatric neurologist after conducting an individually administered neurological examination. Another 24 boys and 12 girls who were also examined and found not to have brain injury served as control subjects. Each subject wore an actometer on the dominant wrist and ipsilateral ankle during the administration of four distractability tests (the structured situation) and subsequently for a free play period (the unstructured situation). The results are summarized in Table 8.3. The main effects for brain-injured children, as a group, demonstrated significantly more wrist ($F[1, 64] = 4.91$, $p < 0.05$) and ankle ($F[1, 64] = 5.52$, $p < 0.05$) activity than did the normal children. Most of this difference resulted from the brain-injured girls. The brain-injured children were about twice as active as the normal children during the structured task.

Further analysis of this data by the present author revealed that the brain-injured group was much more variable than the normal group. In all cases, the variances of the brain-injured group were larger than those of the normal group. The F ratios ranged from 1.01 to 27.99. Nine of the twelve F ratios were statistically significant. This fact is corollary to the prior observation that the means and standard deviations are highly correlated in actometer data. Eleven of the 12 means for the brain-injured children exceeded the corresponding means for the normal children, and these higher means were associated with higher standard deviations, which obviated significant mean differences. Said otherwise, brain damage appears to have a much more pronounced and general effect upon intersubject variability than it does upon mean activity level. Perhaps brain damage also increases the within-subject variability in the same proportion as it increases the intersubject variability.

Table 8.3. Means and Standard Deviations of Wrist and Ankle Actometer Data for Brain-Damaged Children, 24 Boys and 12 Girls; Normal Values in Parentheses[a]

	Wrist (AU/min)		Ankle (AU/min)	
	Free play	*Structured*	*Free play*	*Structured*
		Boys		
M	47.41	10.22	58.33	10.72
	(36.89)	(5.69)	(62.10)	(6.30)
SD	51.29	13.23	49.52	11.89
	(29.17)	(3.73)	(49.20)	(8.31)
F max	3.09**	12.58**	1.01	2.05*
		Girls		
M	50.80	11.78	61.68	10.15
	(13.40)	(5.78)	(17.14)	(3.30)
SD	59.62	11.20	50.27	8.47
	(11.27)	(5.61)	(14.34)	(5.13)
F max	27.99**	4.00*	12.29**	2.73
		Combined		
M	48.54	10.74	59.45	10.53
	(29.68)	(5.72)	(47.11)	(5.30)
SD	53.37	12.45	49.17	10.75
	(27.36)	(4.36)	(46.02)	(7.47)
F max	3.81**	8.15**	1.14	2.07*

[a] Data from Kaspar et al. (1971).
*$p < 0.05$.
**$p < 0.01$.

Pope (1969, 1970) reported a similar experiment on 19 boys, aged 7 to 11 years, carrying a diagnosis of brain injury or minimal cerebral dysfunction. Actometers were attached to the wrist of each boy's writing hand and to the ipsilateral ankle for a total of 30 min over four periods, the first three of which are discussed here. The first session involved 15 min of free play. The second session involved a simple Seguin Form Board task, while the third session involved a difficult Seguin Form Board task. These latter two sessions took 15 min to complete. The results of Pope's study are summarized in Table 8.4. Although five of the six means for the brain-damaged children exceeded the means for the normal con-

Table 8.4. Means and Standard Deviations of Wrist and Ankle Actometer Data for 19 Brain-Damaged Boys; Normal Values in Parentheses[a]

Stat	Free Play	Simple Task	Difficult Task
		Wrist (AU/min)	
M	106.9 (77.3)	231.8 (217.8)	103.2 (70.9)
SD	86.9 (43.6)	129.8 (93.0)	74.9 (39.8)
F max	3.97*	1.95	3.54*
		Ankle (AU/min)	
M	83.4 (39.9)	329.2 (337.7)	94.1 (49.7)
SD	81.5	167.1	87.7
F max	4.24**	1.62	8.96*

[a] Data on brain-damaged subjects from Pope (1969, 1970).
*$p < 0.01$.

trols, only two mean differences were significant and both of them concerned the ankle. The brain-injured children displayed significantly more ankle activity in the free play situation ($t[36] = 2.04$, $p < 0.05$) and when performing the difficult task ($t[36] = 2.04$, $p < 0.05$). It is noteworthy that all of the standard deviations for the brain-damaged children exceeded the standard deviations for the normal children. The F ratios ranged from 1.62 to 8.96, with four out of six being significant. Both the wrist and ankle measurements taken from the brain-damaged subjects are significantly more variable than normal in both the free play and difficult task situations. Hence, the mean squared value, or power, of the time series data for brain-injured subjects will exceed that for normal subjects. No such differences arose with regard to the simple task. It is again clear that brain damage has a greater impact upon inter-subject variability than upon mean activity level.

In sum, the effect of brain damage is to elevate mean activity and augment variability to an even larger degree. These effects are particularly pronounced in structured situations requiring the inhibition of motor movements. However, it should be noted that only very small samples of free play behavior have been taken. It would be informative to see consecutive 24-hr samples taken and broken down into sleep and waking periods. Perhaps differences exist between brain-injured and normal children during sleep and during longer free play periods. Investigations have yet to fully exploit such advantages of actometers.

Hyperactive Children

High-Stimulus Studies

One research strategy is to select children who are diagnosed as hyperactive and examine the extent to which they respond unfavorably to highly stimulating environments, as predicted by Strauss and Lehtinen (1947); Alabiso (1972); Wasserman, Asch, and Snyder (1972); and Haring (1974). Zentall and Zentall (1976) attached actometers to the dominant wrist and ipsilateral ankle of 16 hyperactive children between the ages of 7 and 11. These children were selected from 88 children enrolled in a private school for learning disabilities and emotional disorders. Selection was based on the Rating Scale for Hyperactivity (Davids, 1971) and the Connor Teacher Rating Scale (Connors, 1969). Two 20-min measurement sessions were held 48 hr apart. Each session was divided into two 10-min parts. The subjects were told to sit and wait for the experimenter during the first part of each session. They were then asked to circle certain letters on a printed page for the last 10 min of the session. These tasks were carried out under high- and low-stimulus environments. The low-stimulus condition involved white walls and a gray floor with only a 25-W lamp over the desk. The high-stimulus environment involved 25 large, brightly colored pictures, posters, and lettered signs. A cage of five mice was hung on the wall about 2 m in front of the child's desk, and popular rock music (Led Zeppelin's "House of the Holy") was played at about 75 dB. The investigators reported significantly less wrist ($F[1, 14] = 23.24$, $p < 0.001$) and ankle ($F[1, 14] = 9.88$, $p < 0.01$) activity under the high-stimulus condition as compared with the low-stimulus condition when the children were instructed to sit and wait for the experimenter to return. Significant reductions of wrist ($F[1, 14] = 8.96$, $p < 0.01$) but not ankle($F[1, 14] = 0.95$, NS) activity were reported under the high-stimulus environment in connection with the letter-circling task. These results contradict the hypothesis that "hyperactive" children, as identified by paper-

and-pencil tests and rating scales, are unable to inhibit motor activity in a highly stimulating environment. The evidence suggests that dull environments may lead to hyperactivity, which is consistent with more recent underarousal theories (Rosenthal, 1973; Satterfield & Dawson, 1971).

It is unfortunate that Zentall and Zentall (1976) did not publish their raw data or any descriptive statistics. They presented graphs where the ordinate is in arbitrary log units. Hence, this study does not allow comparisons with data from normal subjects to determine whether their subjects were significantly more active.

Millichap and Boldrey (1967) studied 9 boys and 5 girls aged 5 to 15 years referred for seizures, hyperactive behavior, and/or involuntary movements. This report concerns the control or pretest period for the four subjects, who later received either placebo or methylphenidate but not phenobarbital or prednisone. Actometers were placed on the dominant wrist for a 24-hr period. The AU/minute values for those who later received placebo, two boys (16.17 and 2.17 AU/min, respectively) and two girls (36.00 and 1.66 AU/min) averaged out to be 14.00 AU/min, with a standard deviation of 16.13 AU/min. The AU/minute values for the four boys (26.17, 16.17, 5.17, 15.00) who later received methylphenidate averaged 15.63 AU/min, with a standard deviation of 8.59 AU/min. All of these values were well below any level that could remotely be considered to indicate hyperactivity. The individual values below 10 AU/min probably indicate hypoactivity. However, it should be remembered that a 24-hr sample was taken, which means that perhaps eight or more hours of sleep was averaged in with data taken while the subject was awake. Extraordinarily long sleep intervals could thus suppress extremely high waking activity levels. It would have been better had the investigators reported data for sleeping and waking periods separately as they reflect functionally different situations.

Millichap and Johnson (1977) studied 24 boys and 4 girls aged 5 to 14 years who were diagnosed hyperactive and learning disabled. An actometer was placed on the nondominant wrist for 45 min. Unfortunately, they published their pretreatment data as a 28-bar graph. I measured the heights of these bars with a millimeter rule and converted the readings into AU/minute values for comparability. The mean equaled 26.74 AU/min, and the standard deviation was 17.15 AU/min. These values are about half the values reported for normal 5- to 12-year-old boys and very similar to 5- to 12-year-old girls reported by Schulman et al. (1965). It therefore appears that Millichap and Johnson's sample of "hyperactive" children was quite normal in their level of activity.

In sum, children who have been identified as hyperactive by teacher ratings and paper-and-pencil tests (1) are not more active than normal children and (2) are less active when exposed to more stimulating environments. Future investigators should collect day and night activity samples for at least 2 weeks to be confident that their sample is generally more active than normal before beginning any intervention.

Drug Studies

Another research strategy is to administer medication to children who have been identified as hyperactive by the medical and/or educational system. Table 8.5 summarizes the results of these studies in terms of the AU/minute associated with the various experimental conditions.

Cunningham and Barkley (1978) reported a dramatic wrist activity reduction from a no-medication baseline of 83.00 AU/min for Subject 1 to 19.17 AU/min while on medication. The wrist activity then increased to 70.00 AU/min during an ensuing placebo condition but returned to 29.00 AU/min during a subsequent drug condition. The effects of medication upon ankle activity were even more remarkable for Subject 1. His baseline value was 124.83 AU/min, which dropped to 6.17 AU/min during the first medication period (methylphenidate hydrochloride; i.e., Ritalin). Placebo was associated with 43.00 AU/min, but the second drug level remained at 39.50 AU/min. The effects for Subject 2 are equally dramatic.

Barkley and Cunningham (1979a) reported significantly ($t[19] = 3.44$, $p < 0.01$) lower wrist activity during the drug (Ritalin) condition (25.83 AU/min) than during the placebo condition (53.33 AU/min) for 20 boys referred by local physicians diagnosed as hyperkinetic. A similarly significantly ($t[19] = 4.08$, $p < 0.01$) lower wrist activity during the drug condition (33.33 AU/min) was reported relative to the placebo condition (56.67 AU/min). All children were tested in a playroom for 30 min.

Barkley and Cunningham (1979b) reported significantly ($t[13] = 2.05$, $p < 0.05$) lower wrist activity during a drug (Ritalin) condition (46.17 AU/min) than during a placebo condition (63.27 AU/min). The parallel ankle values (92.53 and 106.67 AU/min) were not significantly different ($t[19] = 0.83$, $p < 0.10$). The

Table 8.5. Means and Standard Deviations (in parentheses) of Wrist and
Ankle Actometer Data for Hyperkinetic Children During Off-
Drug Baseline, Drug, Placebo, and Drug Experimental Conditions

Study no. and investigator	n	Age[a]	Baseline	Drug	Placebo	Drug
			Wrist (AU/min)			
1. Cunningham &	1	5;6	83.00	19.17	70.00	29.00
Barkley (1978)	1	5;6	151.00	76.67	25.50	81.33
2. Barkley & Cunningham (1979a)	20	5-12		25.83	53.33	
3. Barkley & Cunningham (1979b)	14	5-12	72.00 (31.87)	46.17 (25.20)	63.27 (45.43)	
4. Millichap et al. (1968)	30	5-14	15.05	12.47	15.77	
Study no.			Ankle (AU/min)			
1.			124.83	6.17	43.00	39.50
			246.33	76.33	51.33	87.00
2.				33.33	56.67	
3.			123.73 (57.23)	92.53 (65.97)	106.67 (78.00)	

[a] 5;6 = 5 years and 6 months of chronological age; 5-12 = 5 to 12 years of chronological age.

reader should note that this study measured activity in a gymnasium setting rather than a playroom setting.

Millichap, Aymat, Sturgis, Larsen, and Egan (1968) studied the effects of medication on the activity of 26 boys and 4 girls aged 5 to 14 years (mean = 8 years). Actometers were attached to the nondominant wrist of each subject, and data were recorded over a 45-min period while the subject took psychological tests to evaluate responses to methylphenidate, placebo, and control conditions. The authors reported their results in terms of "actometer hours" per 45 min, which have been converted here to AU/min for purposes of comparability. The control condition produced an average of 15.05 AU/min, and the placebo condition produced an average of 15.77 AU/min. These two values were reported to be significantly greater than the average of 12.47 AU/min associated with methylphenidate therapy. It is important to note that these wrist results are substantially lower than would have been recorded in a free play situation.

Less encouraging results were reported by Millichap and Boldrey (1967), who administered a placebo to two girls and two boys aged 5 to 15 years as a control for judging the effectiveness of administering methylphenidate to four boys aged 5 to 11 years. Actometers were placed on the dominant wrist for a 24-hr period before treatment and another 24-hr period after treatment. No significant changes were found in either the placebo or the drug group. Placebo increased activity from a mean of 14.00 (SD = 16.13) AU/min to a mean of 16.50 (SD = 20.54) AU/min. Methylphenidate paradoxically increased activity from a mean level of 15.63 (SD = 8.59) AU/min to a mean of 42.28 (SD = 49.64) AU/min. This last difference was due primarily to one male subject increasing from 26.17 to 116.13 AU/min in response to chemotherapy. In sum, these results are contrary to what was hypothesized, and they are based on 24-hr behavior samples.

Millichap and Johnson (1977) measured the nondominant wrist activity of 24 boys and 4 girls aged 5 to 14 years for a pre and post 45-min period. Treatment involved dosages of Ritalin. The authors omitted reporting descriptive statistics, and consequently the present author had to measure the heights of 28 bars in a graph and then calculate the descriptive statistics. Nineteen of the 28 subjects showed some decrease in activity, while the other 9 subjects showed increased activity. The pretreatment mean of 26.74 (SD = 17.15) AU/min was reduced to 22.17 (SD = 11.27) AU/min. Hence, the drug effect was about 4.57 AU/min on average over the entire 1,440-min or 24-hr period, which totals to 6,580.8 AU ($t[27]$ = 2.14, $p < 0.05$). However, it is not possible to compare these results with other studies since the data were not reported separately for the sleep and waking periods. Rogers and Hughs (1981) placed actometers on the dominant wrist to measure the activity of nine boys aged 4 to 11 years and one 7-year-old girl before and after being placed for 6 weeks on Feingold's (1975) K-P diet or a diet that reduced sugar intake but did not restrict substances in the K-P diet. All children were being treated for hyperkinesis. The first condition required the child to point to cards having pictures of infants on them. The experimenter turned the 200 cards over at the rate of about 1/sec. The pretreatment mean (31.55 AU/min) was not significantly different from the posttreatment mean (9.98 AU/min) using a t test for matched pairs ($t[7]$ =

0.26, NS). However, there was a significant but unreported decrease in the pre ($SD = 20.44$) and post ($SD = 10.12$) variances ($F[8, 8] = 4.079$, $p < 0.05$). The second condition involved actometer readings from 4 to 6 P.M. at the child's house 5 days a week for 3 weeks, resulting in a total of 30 hr of recording per child. Subjects were divided into two groups on the basis of their pretreatment home actometer readings. Group I had a mean of 168.00 AU/min and a standard deviation of 35.22 AU/min; this was very similar to the subjects in Group II, who had a mean of 155.35 AU/min and a standard deviation of 30.15 AU/min. Only subjects in Group I received dietary restrictions. Their posttreatment mean dropped to 97.50 ($SD = 21.03$) AU/min, whereas subjects in Group II remained at 147.27 ($SD = 31.72$) AU/min. These posttreatment means are significantly different ($t[4] = 2.14$, $p < 0.05$, one tailed).

Behavior Disorder

Stevens, Kupst, Suran, and Schulman (1978) reported placing actometers on the dominant wrist and ipsilateral ankle of 13 boys aged 9 to 13 who were diagnosed as having a variety of behavior disorders and learning disabilities. A total of 40 1-hr measurements were obtained over a 2½-month interval in four situations representative of their day hospital program. The authors summated the wrist and ankle activity into a total activity score. They were unclear as to what units the actometer data were presented in, but Schulman characteristically uses AU/hour × 10 (-2). I therefore transformed their descriptive statistics into AU/minute for comparability with other studies. The means and standard deviations for the four situations are as follows: (1) classroom: $M = 156.07$, $SD = 77.98$ AU/min; (2) gym: $M = 823.20$, $SD = 231.39$ AU/min; (3) woodshop: $M = 274.45$, $SD = 125.63$ AU/min; (4) group therapy: $M = 243.22$, $SD = 154.42$ AU/min. Normal comparison values were obtained by summing over the wrist and ankle data reported by Schulman, Kaspar, and Throne (1965) for the two closest age groups of boys. The total activity was 114.16 AU/min for the 9- to 10-year-old boys and 75.17 AU/min for the 10- to 12-year-old boys. The average of these two age groups is 94.67 AU/min. The classroom activity of behavior-disordered boys was 1.65 times that of normal boys. The group therapy activity of behavior-disordered boys was 2.57 times that of normal boys. Pope (1970) reported values of 555.50 ($SD = 289.00$) AU/min for normal boys during a simple task, but a formal comparison cannot be made since the simple task was performed while seated and subjects moved about during the gym class.

Shaffer, McNamara, and Pincus (1974) conducted a 2×2 factorial study using 41 boys aged 5 to 8 years. Group 1 contained 8 boys who had neither brain damage nor a conduct disorder. Group 2 contained 13 boys who were considered to have a conduct disorder but no brain damage. Group 3 was comprised of 13 boys who had brain damage plus a conduct disorder. Group 4 contained 7 boys who had brain damage but no conduct disorder. All measurements were made during a 10-min free play period by attaching actometers to the dominant wrist and the ipsilateral ankle. The authors were very unclear about the units in which actometer scores were reported. They first said that "each [actometer] unit was taken to equal a one minute excursion by the large hand of the watch" (p. 8) but later said that "Each 'actometer unit' is equal to one complete revolution by the large hand of the actometer" (p. 10). These values differ by a factor of 60. Because their data contained high enough values that multiplying them by 60 gave impossibly large results, it was concluded that the actometer units were in minutes, not hours. It was also unclear whether the data reflected cumulative actometer units during a 10-min period or whether they had already divided by 10 to give AU/min. Dividing their data for the normal control group (Group 1) by 10 gave results that were about half the expected value. Not dividing by 10 yielded results about four times greater than expected. In short, it is not possible to interpret the descriptive statistics reported by these authors. Moreover, their data were not analyzed for main effects concerning conduct or brain damage, nor was the interaction term evaluated. Calculations by the present author suggest that collapsing across brain damage gave a mean of 219.47 ($SD = 111.20$) AU/min for boys without a conduct disorder and 323.46 ($SD = 149.86$) AU/min for boys with a conduct disorder. These means are significantly different ($t[39] = 2.34$, $p < 0.05$). Collapsing over conduct disorder gave a mean of 258.81 ($SD = 261.87$) AU/min for boys without brain damage and a mean of 313.35 ($SD = 150.01$) AU/min with brain damage. These means are not significantly different ($t[39] = 0.81$, $p > 0.10$).

In sum, it appears that boys with behavior disorders are more active than boys without behavior disorders. However, Stevens et al. (1978) took only 1-hr readings at a time, while Shaffer et al. (1974) took but 10-min measurements. Firm conclusions about hyperactivity and conduct disorders await longitudinal 24-hr studies.

Obesity

Much research and clinical treatment is devoted to the issue of obesity. It was therefore decided to review the single study using actometers with obese persons under a separate heading. This study by Rose and Mayer (1968) concerns the relationships between activity, weight gain, and calorie intake in infants.

Rose and Mayer (1968) obtained 24-hr wrist and contralateral ankle measurements from 13 male and 16 female infants aged 2 to 6 months over 2 successive days. The two wrist measures were added to the two ankle measures, and the resulting sum was divided by 4. The means and standard deviations were 44.23 (8.43) AU/min for males and 43.19 (11.90) AU/min for females. These means are very similar, indicating that no sex differences existed. Perhaps the most prominent finding was a significant negative correlation between activity and triceps skinfold density ($r[27] = -0.53$, $p < 0.01$), suggesting that the fatter children were less active.

Beale (1953) reported that the calories per day consumed by one sample of 46 normal 5-month-old infants ranged from 525 to 975 (median = 725). A similarly wide range was reported on a second sample of 67 normal 5-month-old infants, ranging from 530 to 1,025 calories per day (median = 806). Rose and Mayer (1968) hypothesized that differences in activity level might well account for this variation in calorie intake. Their study revealed a total calorie intake ranging from 630 to 930 calories per day ($M = 775$, $SD = 77$), which is comparable to the values reported by Beale (1953). Rose and Mayer reported a correlation of $r(27) = 0.47$, $p < 0.01$, between activity and total calorie intake, which supported their hypothesis that more active children ate more. This correlation increased to $r(27) = .53$, $p < 0.01$, when weight gain was held constant. This suggests a short-term activity–calorie relationship that is superimposed on a longer-term weight gain function. Taken together with the inverse relationship between activity and triceps skinfold density, one can conclude that although increased activity occasions increased food intake over the short run, those subjects who gain the most weight over time decrease their activity level. The relationship between activity and weight gain was not significant ($r[27] = -0.31$, $p > 0.10$) but was in the correct direction to be consistent with the preceding analysis. It appears that the relationship between activity and weight gain over several months is less linear than that between activity and short-term calorie intake. Future studies should record the subject's activity 24 hrs a day for an entire 6-month period to elucidate the functional relationships involved.

Counters

Normal People

Children

It is again refreshing to note that investigators have conducted at least two studies with normals, although they hardly constitute normative data. Foster, McPartland, and Kupfer (1977) randomly sampled 14 boys and 7 girls aged 8.7 (± 0.1 year) from the normal control group of another study. Counters sensitive to a 5° tilt were attached to both wrists and the right ankle during a 5-min adaptation period followed by a 28- to 32-min free play period in a playroom containing about 11 toys. The normal sample was then divided into a high-normal (10 subjects) group and a low-normal (11 subjects) group on the basis of the mean ankle counts per minute, which was 84.2 cpm. The activity data collected on these children are presented in Table 8.6. The mean split procedure conducted on the ankle activity data for identifying the high- and low-normal groups is responsible for the significant difference in ankle

Table 8.6. Means and Standard Errors of Motor Activity for High- and Low-Active Normal Children[a]

Site of attachment	High normal (n = 10)	Low normal (n = 11)
Dominant hand	131.6 ± 10.5	103.5 ± 9.7
Nondominant hand	124.6 ± 11.8	112.6 ± 10.8
Ankle	118.5 ± 7.27[b]	53.0 ± 5.9

[a] The two groups were dichotomized on the basis of the mean counts per minute for the right ankle of 84.2.

[b] $p < 0.01$ on the basis of a t test.

activity. Notice that no significant difference exists between either of the two hand measures. Hence, no reliable differences in activity were found between the dominant and nondominant hands in either "high active" or "low active" normal subjects. The more active children were reported to be shorter and have a significantly lower (more deviant) neurological rating, although they were still within normal limits. High-active normal children made significantly more errors on the Bender Gestalt Test and revealed significantly lower developmental level scores. Their school achievement was significantly lower, as was their self-concept relative to the less active children. It should be remembered that these persons were functioning normally in the school system even though the within-population variation was large enough for these differences between high-normal and low-normal groups to emerge.

Adults

Kast (1964) had 25 hospital employees (nurses and house staff) wear an activity counter on the forearm from 3 P.M. to 6 P.M. on three occasions 1 week apart. The 13 men had an average age of 35.85 years ($SD = 8.67$) and achieved the following average (and standard deviation) counts per 3 hr on three separate weekly occasions: 1,126.62 (118.15), 1,106.31 (138.07), 1,111.77 (100.23). The 12 women had an average age of 31.67 years ($SD = 11.20$) and achieved the following average (and standard deviation) counts per 3 hr on the same three weekly occasions: 1,186.58 (241.47), 1,112.50 (157.53), 1,089.33 (131.93).

LaPorte, Kuller, Kupfer, McPartland, Matthews, and Caspersen (1979) placed two Large-Scale Integrated Motor Activity Monitors (see McPartland, Kupfer, & Foster, 1976) on the nondominant ankle and on the subject's waist on the same side of 10 male physical education majors and 10 male non–physical education majors from 9:30 A.M. until 10:00 P.M. for 2 consecutive days. Table 8.7 gives the mean hourly trunk and ankle counts for the 20 subjects over the 2-day period. LaPorte et al. reported a correlation of $r(18) = .72$, $p < 0.01$, between the trunk and ankle measures. However, the average ankle reading of 156.7 counts/hr was almost twice the average trunk count of 80.5 counts/hr. This conforms with the casual observation that the legs move more than the waist during locomotion. The physical education majors were found to have significantly greater pooled mean counts/hr (199.41) than the non–physical education majors (99.02) ($F[1, 18] = 13.23$, $p < 0.01$).

Table 8.7. Mean Hourly Activity Rates for Trunk and Ankle Counts for 20 White Male Graduate Students of Similar Age[a]

	Hourly Trunk Counts		Hourly Ankle Counts	
Subject	Mean	SD	Mean	SD
1	20.43	2.84	54.29	14.58
2	21.14	6.60	59.22	30.58
3	21.58	26.14	133.72	72.29
4	34.57	29.04	78.21	44.54
5	44.72	43.76	154.36	34.31
6	44.93	41.99	92.93	36.76
7	52.22	20.44	177.36	72.53
8	58.07	48.02	115.71	175.64
9	76.00	17.71	130.65	47.35
10	77.07	11.52	137.86	17.49
11	80.14	59.62	142.93	89.91
12	83.79	37.77	186.14	11.27
13	95.00	66.29	157.78	63.92
14	97.64	45.30	191.72	20.92
15	102.36	33.46	181.43	59.56
16	106.57	61.05	301.43	295.19
17	131.57	123.19	222.79	125.52
18	132.64	57.28	280.50	194.70
19	135.14	86.42	93.50	57.50
20	194.14	113.81	233.50	130.70

[a] From LaPorte et al. (1979).

Notice that the mean values reported by LaPorte et al. (1979) are approximately one-third those reported by Kast (1964) when adjusted to read in terms of counts/hr rather than counts/3 hr. Some of this difference may be due to different operating characteristics of the two devices. Another proportion of the difference could be due to the fact that Kast sampled only 3 hr per day for a total of 9 hr, whereas LaPorte et al. sampled a larger portion of the day for a total of 25 hr. The longer measurement interval increases the probability that more types of activity, including resting, will be measured. It could be that Kast chose a 3-hr block during the busiest part of the subject's schedule. All else being equal, more confidence can be placed in data that are collected over longer time periods as they will tend to be more representative of the subject's modal activity level.

Behavior Disorder

Schulman, Stevens, and Kupst (1977) introduced a counter having biofeedback capabilities called the "biomotometer." The device produces a beeping signal through a crystal earphone every time the number of counts per interval exceeds some predetermined level. The device is typically attached to a belt above the hip on the dominant side. The subjects studied in the first investigation were 17 boys and 3 girls aged approximately 8 to 11 years who were enrolled in a day hospital program for emotionally disturbed children. The subjects were studied for 1 hr during two class periods (gym and woodshop) and during free play. Unfortunately, no descriptive statistics were presented. However, correlations were provided between the waist-attached biomotometer and the ankle- and wrist-attached actometers. The correlations between the waist and wrist were $r(18) = 0.38$, NS, for School 1; $r(12) = 0.65$, $p < 0.05$, for School 2; $r(9) = 0.39$, NS, for gym; $r(9) = 0.85$, $p < 0.01$, for woodshop; and $r(8) = 0.51$, NS, for free play. The correlations between the waist and the ankle were $r(18) = 0.55$, $p < 0.05$, for School 1; $r(12) = 0.75$, $p < 0.01$, for School 2; $r(9) = 0.64$, $p < 0.05$, for gym; $r(9) = 0.57$, NS, for woodshop; and $r(8) = 0.51$, NS, for free play. In summary, three of the five waist–wrist relationships and two of the five waist-ankle relationships failed to achieve statistical significance. Keep in mind that statistical significance simply means that the two groups are more related than two groups of random numbers. This criterion fails for half of the relationships, and the strength of the relationship for most of the remaining five is not great. Two conclusions follow. First, the caution against comparing actometer and counter data mentioned earlier is warranted. Second, the site of attachment is an important variable. The wrist experiences different forces than does the waist. Activity is not a unitary construct!

The biofeedback feature of the biomotometer was found to be useful in reducing the hyperkinetic behavior of an 11-year-old boy who also was reported to have a short attention span and in a 10-year-old boy who failed to complete his school work and repeatedly ran away from home (Schulman, Stevens, Suran, Kupst, & Naughton, 1978). A subsequent study of nine boys and two girls aged 9 to 13 also reported substantial activity decrements in 8 of 11 subjects using an instructions, feedback, and reinforcement package (Schulman, Suran, Stevens, & Kupst, 1979).

Anorexia Nervosa

Foster and Kupfer (1975) reported an intriguing case study concerning a 17-year-old female senior high school student having a monozygotic twin sister.she wore an activity counter on the wrist of her nondominant hand for the duration of her hospitalization. This patient was studied, but not medicated, for the first 97 days of her hospitalization. During this time her weight gradually increased from a low of about 78 lb to a high of about 113 lb. However, the more she weighed at 8:00 A.M., the more active she became that night (9:00 P.M. to 7:00 A.M.) ($r[83] = 0.77$, $p < 0.001$). During Days 98 to 132 she received chlorpromazine, with two results. First, her weight continued to gradually increase, up to about 124 lb. Second, the more she weighed at 8:00 A.M., the less active she became at night ($r[33] = -0.76$, $p < 0.001$). Daytime tube feeding increased her nocturnal activity more when she weighed more ($r[8] = 0.80$, $p < 0.01$). In short, the nearer she came to achieving her target weight, the more daytime tube feeding caused her to be active at night. The authors reported that it was their general clinical experience that improvement was associated with low nocturnal activity counts; the results of this study are consistent with this view.

The diagnostic applications of extended activity monitoring were also illustrated by this case study. The authors noted that the patient was particularly active on certain nights. It turned out that these nights typically followed one of the 34 family visits to the ward. The visitation effects were quantified as follows. The nocturnal activity of the target night was expressed as a percentage of the average nocturnal activity recorded from the previous and following nights. Five visits by the mother and father alone produced little augmentation in the patient's nocturnal activity ($M = +0.21\%$, $SE = 12.8\%$). However, the five visits where the twin sibling accompanied both parents resulted in a marked increase in nocturnal activity ($M = +41.41\%$, $SE = 30.4\%$). The patient's history revealed several traumatic separations from her dominant identical twin, and it was clear that this sister's presence on the ward greatly disturbed the patient's sleep. The four episodes of depersonalization and derealization were associated with lesser nocturnal activity ($M = -35.87\%$, $SE = 4.6\%$). A number of other findings of clinical relevance were also reported but cannot be described here for lack of space. In sum, this case study reveals the creative use of long-term continuous mechanical recording of activity to form stimulating clinical hypotheses in addition to documenting the effects of treatment.

Pedometers

Stunkard (1960) described the methodology of using pedometers to study physical activity in man. The pedometer is worn on the waist and is usually attached to a belt.

Normal Values

Children

Stunkard and Pestka (1962) reported data on 15 nonobese 12-year-old girls (range = 10 to 13) during 2 weeks at a summer Girl Scout camp and for the following week at home. The girls walked an average of 8.03 miles ($SE = 0.65$) per day at camp and an average of 5.75 miles ($SE = 0.89$) per day at home (see Table 8.8). This difference is not statistically significant ($t[14] = 2.07$, NS).

Adults

Dorris and Stunkard (1957) reported the mean and standard error of daily and weekly miles walked by 15 nonobese women averaging 40 years of age. They walked an average of 4.5 miles ($SE = 2.5$) each day and an average of 33.08 miles ($SE = 3.94$) each week (see Table 8.9).

Chirico and Stunkard (1960) reported pedometer data on 25 normal men aged 36.6 years on average. These people were chosen at random from hospital staff and medical and dental students. They wore pedometers every waking hour for 14 consecutive days. Their values ranged from 0.3 to 18.6 miles/day. The mean and standard error were 5.96 (0.88) miles/day (see Table 8.10).

The three control groups from these three studies provide consistent results. It appears that normal girls walk approximately 5.75 miles per day at home, normal adult women walk about 4.5 miles per day, and normal adult men walk about 5.96 miles per day. The weighted average (using sample sizes) of these three means equals 5.46, or nearly 5.5 miles per day.

Table 8.8. Distance Walked by 15 Pairs of Obese and Nonobese Girls While at Camp and Home[a]

Pair no.	Obese (miles/day)		Nonobese (miles/day)	
	Camp	Home	Camp	Home
1	12.0	10.6	11.8	6.3
2	9.7	–	9.4	–
3	8.5	11.6	11.5	12.6
4	8.4	2.9	12.0	8.2
5	8.0	–	7.3	–
6	7.6	3.0	9.5	3.2
7	7.5	–	6.3	–
8	6.9	7.0	5.7	5.0
9	6.3	3.3	4.2	1.7
10	5.9	–	5.3	–
11	5.8	1.7	10.0	7.6
12	5.6	3.1	7.6	5.2
13	5.5	3.4	6.1	4.3
14	5.2	5.8	7.2	5.3
15	5.0	2.9	6.5	–
M	7.19	5.03	8.03	5.75
SD	1.93	3.35	2.51	2.94
SE	0.50	1.01	0.65	0.89

[a] From Stunkard & Pestka (1962).

Gottfries, Gottfries, and Olsson (1966) reported data on 50 student nurses having a mean age of 23 years (range = 20 to 33). Unfortunately, the results were reported in thousands of steps taken rather than in miles walked. Moreover, no stride index was provided for each patient; therefore, no conversion to miles walked was possible. The mean number of steps, in thousands, taken over 7 consecutive 24-hr periods was 16.2, with a standard deviation of 4.19.

Obesity

Children

Stunkard and Pestka (1962) measured the physical activity of 15 normal and 15 obese Girl Scouts (average age = 12 years; range = 10–13 years) for 2 consecutive weeks while they attended

Table 8.9. Distance Walked by Obese and Nonobese Women[a]

	Weekly distances (miles)			Daily distances (miles)	
	Obese	Nonobese	Difference	Obese	Nonobese
	10.0	28.5	-18.5		4.1 ± 1.0
	23.0	17.5	5.5	3.3 ± 0.8	2.5 ± 1.7
	11.0	19.5	-8.5	1.6 ± 0.7	
	16.5	34.0	-17.5	2.4 ± 0.5	
	8.0	22.8	-14.8		3.3 ± 1.8
	7.8	16.5	-8.7	1.2 ± 0.4	2.4 ± 0.3
	12.0	39.5	-27.5		5.6 ± 2.4
	10.7	23.0	-12.3	1.5 ± 0.5	
	24.0	31.4	-7.4		
	8.3	30.5	-21.2	1.2 ± 0.4	4.4 ± 2.3
	5.5	64.5	-59.0		
	10.0	38.7	-28.7		
	10.2	61.7	-51.5		8.8 ± 1.2
	31.0	35.0	-4.0		5.0 ± 1.5
M	13.42	33.08	-19.61		
SD	7.45	14.74	17.77		
SE	1.99	3.94	4.75		

[a] From Dorris & Stunkard (1957).

summer camp plus the following week at home. The girls were matched for age, IQ, and camp group. Table 8.8 shows that the obese girls were equally as active as the normal weight girls both at camp and at home. The authors noted that energy expenditure is directly proportional to both activity and to body weight. They therefore defined a coefficient of activity (CA) to be the distance walked (D) times the quantity of the subject's percent overweight (W) plus 100, as per Eq. (1). The authors were unclear about which of two methods of calculating percent overweight were used, but they did report significantly greater energy expenditure for the obese girls when their CA values were compared. The mean percent overweight of the 15 girls was 36.9 $(SD = 14.3)$ using the Baldwin–Wood method (Baldwin & Wood, 1949) and 33.3 $(SD = 11.3)$ using the Stuart method (Stuart, 1949).

$$CA = D(W + 100) \tag{1}$$

Wilkinson, Parkin, Pearlson, Strong, and Sykes (1977) used pedometers to measure the activity of 10 obese boys and 10 obese girls, and an equivalent number of normal-weight control subjects during all waking hours for an unspecified number of days. Apparently they set the stride index to the same value on all pedometers and did not have subjects walk a measured distance. There-

Table 8.10. Distance Walked by Obese and Nonobese Men[a]

Pair	Occupation	Amount overweight (%)	Distance walked/ day (miles) Obese	Nonobese
1	Medical student	62	7.3	6.2
2	Clerk–typist	53	6.9	2.9
3	Traveling salesman	51	6.0	2.8
4	Stockroom clerk	54	5.8	18.6
5	Clerk–typist	44	5.2	4.7
6	Medical student	31	5.1	4.2
7	Dental student	41	5.0	4.1
8	Spray painter	29	4.7	2.0
9	Unemployed	54	4.7	10.3
10	Medical student	76	4.4	12.5
11	Watchman	35	4.2	7.8
12	Laboratory technician	58	4.0	3.1
13	Cook	92	3.9	4.1
14	Unemployed	63	3.5	4.3
15	Bartender	78	3.1	7.0
16	Medical student	30	3.0	6.2
17	Bartender	62	2.7	4.6
18	Teacher	40	2.4	4.4
19	Teacher	60	2.4	6.2
20	Bank teller	41	2.3	2.2
21	Laborer	56	2.0	17.0
22	Teacher	66	2.0	4.5
23	Medical student	76	1.8	2.7
24	Bank teller	64	0.7	6.4
25	Unemployed	40	0.3	0.3
	M	54.24	3.74	5.96
	SD	16.36	1.81	4.42
	SE	3.27	0.36	0.88

[a] From Chirico & Stunkard (1960).

fore, the unit of measure is not miles walked; it is arbitrary and of unknown size. Although these data cannot be directly compared with other studies, it is still possible to obtain a relative comparison of obese and normal-weight children within this study. The mean (and range) of activity units for the obese boys was 7.2 (3.6–12.6) compared to that of normal-weight boys, which was 9.0 (4.1–17.6). These data were not significantly different ($t[9] = 1.2$, NS). The mean (and range) of activity units for the obese girls was 8.7 (4.2–16.2) compared to that of normal-weight girls, which was 8.4 (5.3–13.6). These data were also not significantly different ($t[9] = 0.2$, NS). Hence, evidence exists that obese and normal-weight children are equally active even though we do not know how active that is.

Adults

Dorris and Stunkard (1957) studied the activity of 15 obese women averaging 42 years of age and 15 nonobese women as indicated earlier. The obese women were calculated to be 62% in excess of the weights considered desirable by the Metropolitan Life Insurance Company. Each subject wore a calibrated pedometer over her upper thigh for 1 week. The results are reproduced in Table 8.9, where it can be seen that the obese women walked but 13.42 miles per week (about 1.92 miles per day), whereas the normal women walked 33.08 miles a week (about 4.73 miles per day), or about 2.46 times as far as the obese women. Only one obese woman walked further than her normal control partner. This pattern was equally obvious in the daily data. Stunkard's (1958) article recapitulates these findings. It is interesting to note that the obese girls walked about 5.03 miles per day, whereas obese women walked about 1.92 miles per day, or only about 38% as far as their younger counterparts. This suggests that normally active obese teenagers become hypoactive as they grow older. Perhaps they cannot maintain the excessive energy expenditures necessary to move their overweight bodies around at normal speeds during their waking hours. This suggests a life-style change that accompanies chronic obesity.

Maxfield and Konishi (1966) used pedometers to measure the activity of 25 obese (15% overweight) women ($M = 76$, $SE = 9.5$ kg) and 25 normal-weight women ($M = 56$, $SE = 6.0$ kg) during one 48-hr period. The age of the obese women ($M = 42$, $SE = 13$ years) was matched to that of the control women ($M = 41$, $SE = 13$ years).

Thirteen of the obese and 14 of the control women had children at home. The pedometers were calibrated in an undescribed manner to enhance the similarity of their operating characteristics. Hence, it is unclear what the unit of measure is. The authors reported no statistically significant differences between the activity of obese and normal-weight women. Neither the type nor the magnitude of the statistical test used was reported.

The failure of Maxfield and Konishi (1966) to confirm the hypoactivity finding reported by Dorris and Stunkard (1957) may be due to either of two reasons. First, the Dorris and Stunkard subjects were 62% overweight, whereas the Maxfield and Konishi subjects were but 15% overweight. Perhaps the deficits in activity occur somewhere between these two levels of overweight. Second, Maxfield and Konishi studied their subjects for only 2 days. Perhaps a full week is necessary to detect the activity differences.

Chirico and Stunkard (1960) investigated the activity of 25 pairs of obese men ($M = 54\%$ overweight) matched for age ($M = 36$ years) and occupation (see Table 8.10). The obese men walked an average of 3.74 miles per day, whereas the nonobese men walked an average of 5.96 miles per day. These means are reliably different ($t[46] = 2.28$, $p < 0.05$). The variance of the nonobese men was also significantly greater than that of the obese men ($F[24, 24] = 5.96$, $p < 0.01$). Obese men appear to be uniformly underactive. It should be noted that the smaller variability associated with the nonobese men may be partly due to a floor effect given their low activity level. Obese women do not show a corresponding variability contraction relative to nonobese women.

Crisp and Stonehill (1970) reported having studied three obese patients from the time they got up in the morning until they went to bed at night. However, they did not calibrate their pedometers in miles, nor did they provide conversion indices for each patient to allow the reader to make such calculations. No numerical tables were provided. Even the ordinates of their figures were not labeled. Little more can be said about this study.

Anorexia Nervosa

Blinder, Freeman, and Stunkard (1970) reported the treatment of three cases of anorexia nervosa. Patient 1 was reported to have walked an average of 8.5 miles per day, including long walks and repetitive stair climbing. No further pedometer data were provided for any of the three patients. In conclusion, limited pedometer evidence exists showing that a 22-year-old anorexic female walks slightly less than twice as far as normal 40-year-old women.

Stabilimeters

Stabilimeters are devices that the individual sits or rests upon while changes in position are counted. This differs from the counting devices previously reviewed as the latter are attached to the subject, who is then free to move about his environment in a more or less natural manner. Stabilimeters require that the subject be brought to the recording instrument. However, stabilimetric cribs are naturalistic activity measures for infants, and stabilimetric cushions are naturalistic activity measures for invalids confined to a chair.

Stabilimetric Cushion

Normal Children

Juliano (1974) measured the activity of 80 normal public school children between the ages of 8¼ years and 11¼ years, using a stabilimetric cushion (cf. Sprague & Toppe, 1966) while taking the Matched Familiar Figures Test (Kagan, 1966). The total number of activity counts was divided by the time to take the test to obtain a counts per minute (cpm) unit of measure. The normal children obtained a mean of 5.02 cpm and a standard deviation of 3.66 cpm.

Hyperkinetic Children

Juliano (1974) reported stabilimetric data on normal and "hyperkinetic" children attending neighborhood schools. The "hyperactive" children all met the following five criteria: (1) They were in a special class due to learning and/or behavioral problems, (2) they were rated as "overactive" and "distractible" by their special class teachers, (3) the students' school records were consonant with the first two criteria, (4) a psychological diagnosis of hyperactivity was present if psychological testing had been administered, and (5) there was no evidence of brain injury, epilepsy, psychosis, or neurosis. Forty White male hyperactive children were selected in this way. Two normoactive children were randomly selected from each hyperactive child's class and served as a normal control group. All of the children were then given a concept-learning task while they sat on stabilimetric cushions for an unreported duration. The results indicated that the hyperactive group averaged 10.04 cpm ($SD = 4.98$), whereas the normal group averaged 5.02 cpm ($SD = 3.66$). This means that the hyperactive group accumulated significantly more counts per minute than did the normal group while taking the Matched Familiar Figures Test ($t[118] = 6.26$, $p < 0.001$).

Sprague, Barnes, and Werry (1970) measured the activity of 12 boys having a mean age of 7.85 years while they performed experimental tasks before and after drug administration. They reported the boys' activity measures in terms of mean numbers of movements per day without defining the length of a day. This prohibited comparison of their data with other studies. However, it did appear that lower activity was associated with methylphenidate than either placebo or thoridazine.

Ballistographic Chair

Werry and Aman (1975) reported data on 4 girls and 20 boys having an average age of 7 years, 9 months (range = 70–130 months) who were referred because either the school psychologist or the family physician diagnosed them as hyperkinetic. A within-group design was used such that each child received placebo, methylphenidate hydrochloride (0.3 mg/kg), a low dose of Haloperidol (0.025 mg/kg), and a high dose of Haloperidol (0.050 mg/kg) for 3 consecutive weeks each. A double-blind procedure was used that included a 2-day washout period between phases. Stabilimetric readings were taken during a Short Term Memory (STM) and a Continuous Performance Task (CPT) administered under each of the four drug conditions, along with certain other measures. The results from the STM task showed that an average of 147.0 cpm were obtained during the placebo condition. This figure dropped significantly to 78.9 cpm under the methylphenidate hydrochloride (Ritalin) condition. However, the counts per minute associated with the low (120.3) and high (148.8) Haloperidol conditions were not significantly different from the placebo condition. The Ritalin–Haloperidol differences were both significant. The results from the CPT task were not significantly different from one another. The authors argued that all subjects moved forward during this task while responding, thus triggering the recording device. The means for the placebo, Ritalin, and low- and high-Haloperidol conditions were 40.8, 36.8, 36.9, and 80.0 cpm, respectively.

Stabilimetric Cribs

Stabilimetric devices usually require that the subject be taken from his or her natural environment and placed in a laboratory setting where activity can be recorded. A major exception to this practice concerns stabilimetric cribs, which represent the infant's natural environment.

Irwin (1932) published perhaps the first study using a stabilimetric crib. He presented data on 73 full-term infants from birth to 16 days of age with one exception where recording continued until the child was 32 days old. The subjects were fed at 2:00 P.M. and 6:00 P.M., and their activity was recorded from 2:30 P.M. to 5:45 P.M. The data were presented in terms of counts (oscillations) per minute for each of the 13 consecutive 15-min observation periods. The mean counts per minute (and standard deviations) associated with the first, middle (7th), and last (13th) 15-min experimental period were: 17.2 (20.2), 26.6 (40.4), and 49.1 (59.7), respectively. Hence, a monotonic average increase in motility was reported over the entire experimental period. Since the first experimental period occurred after feeding and the third period occurred prior to feeding, it can be concluded that the infants' motility prior to nursing was more than double postnursing levels. These average results were mainly due to the 49 infants (67%) whose activity rose throughout the experimental period. Their first and third mean counts per minute and standard deviations were 16.2 (21.9) and 66.4 (42.6). The other 24 infants (33%) showed a substantial decrease in motility from the first to the third experimental period. Their mean counts per minute and standard deviations were 21.2 (22.3) and 6.9 (13.5). Hence, the less active infants increased (by 50.2 cpm) and the more active infants decreased (by 14.3 cpm) in motility over the experimental period from post- to prenursing time.

Campbell et al. (1971) studied 30 boys and 29 girls 24 hr a day in a stabilimetric crib and reported significant increases in mean activity level during the first 4 days of life. The counts per minute were 4.07 for the first day and increased to 6.10 on the second day, 6.87 on the third day, and up to 8.23 on the fourth day.

Sander and Julia (1966) also reported that neonatal activity steadily increased during the first 4 days of life while the subject remained in the nursery. Moreover, they also reported a very marked decline in activity when the infant was discharged and taken home. The rate of activity increase over the first 4 days at home was about 2 units versus a 26-unit increase during the first 4 days of life. Control subjects retained in the hospital beyond 4 days of life revealed no natural decrease in activity around 4 days of age. Hence, the dramatic decrease from 28 units to 2 units upon discharge and the 13 times slower increase in activity seem to be associated with discharge rather than any innate developmental sequence. These data are in general accord with those obtained using actometers.

Brackbill (1971) reported the effects of varying the number of modalities of stimulation upon the levels of activity in infants whose mean age was 26.58 days ($SD = 3.65$, range = 19–33 days). The auditory modality was stimulated by playing a tape-recorded heart beat sound at 85 dB against a background of ambient 65-dB noise level. Visual stimulation involved 400 w in the experimental and 50 w in the control condition. Proprioceptive-tactile stimulation was provided by tightly swaddling the child from the neck to the toes with long, narrow strips of flannel. Temperature stimulation was 31° C during the experimental and 25.5° C during the control condition. Motor activity during the control condition averaged 9.63 cpm. Any one stimulus increased motility to an average of 10.70 cpm. However, a combination of any two stimuli decreased motility to an average of 7.54 cpm. Any combination of three stimulations further reduced motility to an average of 5.98 cpm, and all four stimuli reduced motility further to an average of 2.96 cpm. These activity differences were statistically significant ($F[4, 95] = 34.37$, $p < 0.001$). The authors then described the average motility in response to sound (8.16 cpm), light (8.43 cpm), swaddling (3.44 cpm), and temperature (7.09 cpm).

Ultrasound

Peacock and Williams (1962) described an apparatus that generated ultrasonic (41 kHz) standing waves with sensors capable of recording alterations in these waves due to movement or to changes in position of objects within the room.

Daabs and Clower (1973) asked 10 male and 10 female undergraduates to sit quietly at a table for three 5-min periods during which time they were presumably to estimate how much time had elapsed. Activity counts were recorded at 15-sec intervals throughout these three periods. However, the data were presented in terms of the mean counts per minute over consecutive 5-min intervals. The average counts per minute for the three periods were 8, 6, and 20 cpm. This overall change in activity with time was statistically significant ($F[2, 36] = 8.40$, $p < 0.01$), indicating that even college students do not sit without increased movement for more than 10 min!

In a second experiment, the authors (Daabs & Clower, 1973) asked 10 other male and 10 other female undergraduates to sit sufficiently quiet in their seats so as to avoid activating a movement detection lamp. The mean counts per minute for the three 5-min experimental periods were 10, 3, and 18 cpm. These changes are also significant over time ($F[2, 36] = 16.65$, $p < 0.001$). Hence, "biofeedback" did not appreciably reduce the total activity, which equaled 34 units in Experiment I and 31 units in Experiment II. However, the movement in the middle biofeedback condition was half that reported in Experiment I.

Crawford and Nicora (1964) reported the use of ultrasonic procedures to assess the activity of a group of 30 men, women, and children aged 15 to 50 years who were confined to a simulated fallout shelter for 86 hr. The investigators used a 40-kHz tone generator and four ceramic transducers wired in parallel to cover the entire area of 240 sq ft. The results revealed a fairly regular circadian rhythm ranging from a low of near zero counts per hour to peaks near 2,500 counts per hour.

Electronic Accelerometers

Electronic accelerometers have the greatest potential for providing quantitative data regarding the physical forces associated with behavior, yet they are rarely used. The main reasons are probably the substantial cost of commercially available accelerometers plus the complexity or bulkiness of devices used to record the voltage outputs from the accelerometer. A welcome advance in this technology was presented by Wong, Webster, Montoye, and Washburn (1981). This device has two particularly useful features. First, the correlation with oxygen consumption suggests a similar correlation with caloric expenditure. Second, the device is attached to the waist, which allows one to use the person's body weight as the appropriate mass value when calculating force or energy quantities.

Ball, Sibbach, Jones, Steele, and Frazier (1975) used an accelerometer to activate a shock generator to control assaultive and self-destructive behavior in retarded persons. This application used the accelerometer as a trigger rather than as a measuring device. Such an application is mentioned only because it represents a partial awareness of the contributions that accelerometers can make to a study of behavior. The authors recognized that self-destructive and assaultive behaviors involve high levels of acceleration. Therefore, they used an accelerometer to detect and punish the behaviors that produced the high levels of acceleration.

Colburn, Smith, Guarini, and Simons (1976) used accelerometers in a similar way. They caused the output of an accelerometer to increment a counter. No quantitative behavioral data were presented as this article is a technical description of an apparatus.

Concluding Remarks

Some of the approaches to assessing activity have yielded regular patterns of results that have fairly straightforward theoretical implications. Other approaches appear to have generated only isolated bits of data. Most investigators using different devices fail to cite one another, and even investigators using the same devices do not cite each other as often as is warranted. This circumstance may be due largely to the fact that investigators of activity come from many disciplines across the fields of medicine and psychology, and they publish their results in widely scattered journals.

References

Alabiso, F. Inhibitory functions of attention in reducing hyperactive behavior. *American Journal of Mental Deficiency*, 1972, 77, 259–282.

Ball, T. S., Sibbach, L., Jones, R., Steele, B., & Frazier, L., An accelerometer activated device to control assaultive and self-destructive behaviors in retardes. *Journal of Behavior Therapy and Experimental Psychiatry*, 1975, 6, 223–228.

Barkley, R. A., & Cunningham, C. E. The effects of methylphenidate on the mother–child interactions of hyperactive children. *Archives of General Psychiatry*, 1979, 36, 201–208. (a)

Barkley, R. A., & Cunningham, C. E. Stimulant drugs and activity levels in hyperactive children. *American Journal of Orthopsychiatry*, 1979, 49, 491–499. (b)

Beale, V. A. Nutritional intake of children. I. Calories, carbohydrate, fat, and protein. *Journal of Nutrition*, 1953, 50, 223.

Blinder, B. J., Freeman, D. M. A., & Stunkard, A. J. Behavior therapy of anorexia nervosa: Effectiveness of activity as a reinforcer of weight gain. *American Journal of Psychiatry*, 1970, 126, 1093–1098.

Brackbill, R. Cumulative effects of continuous stimulation on arousal level in infants. *Child Development*, 1971, 42, 17–26.

Brumlik, J., & Yap, C. B. *Normal tremor: A comparative study*. Springfield, IL: C. C. Thomas, 1970.

Campbell, D., Kuyek, J., Lang, E., & Partington, M. W. Motor activity in early life. II. Daily motor activity output in the neonatal period. *Biology of the Neonate*, 1971, 18, 108–120.

Chapman, J. S. The relation between auditory stimulation of short gestation infants and their gross motor limb activity (Doctoral dissertation, New York University School of Education, 1975). *Dissertation Abstracts International*, 1975, 36, 1654B. (University Microfilms No. 75-21, 138)

Chirico, A. M., & Stunkard, A. J. Physical activity and human obesity. *New England Journal of Medicine*, 1960, 263, 935–940.

Colburn, T. R., Smith, B. M., Guarini, J. J., & Simons, N. N. *An ambulatory activity monitor with solid state memory*. Paper presented at the 13th annual Rocky Mountain Bioengineering Symposium and the 13th International ISA Biomedical Sciences Symposium, Laramie, Wyoming, 1976.

Connors, C. K. A Teacher Rating Scale for use in drug studies with children. *American Journal of Psychiatry*, 1969, 126, 884–888.

Crawford, M. L. J., & Nicora, B. D. Measurement of human group activity. *Psychological Reports*, 1964, 15, 227–231.

Crisp, A. H., & Stonehill, E. Sleep patterns, daytime activity, weight changes and psychiatric status: A study of three obese patients. *Journal of Psychosomatic Research*, 1970, 14, 353–358.

Cunningham, C. E., & Barkley, R. A. The effects of methylphenidate on the mother–child interaction of hyperactive identical twins. *Developmental Medicine and Child Neurology*, 1978, 20, 634–642.

Cunningham, C. E., & Barkley, R. A. The interaction of normal and hyperactive children with their mothers in free play and structured tasks. *Child Development*, 1979, 50, 217–224.

Daabs, J. M., Jr., & Clower, B. J. An ultrasonic motion detector with data on stare, restriction of movement, and startle. *Behavior Research Methods and Instrumentation*, 1973, 5, 475–476.

Davids, A. An objective instrument for assessing hyperkinesis in children. *Journal of Learning Disabilities*, 1971, 4, 191–197.

Dorris, R. J., & Stunkard, A. J. Physical activity: Performance and attitude of a group of obese women. *American Journal of Medical Science*, 1957, *233*, 622–628.

Feingold, B. F. *Why your child is hyperactive.* New York: Random House, 1975.

Foster, F. G., & Kupfer, D. J. Anorexia nervosa: Telemetric assessment of family interaction and hospital events. *Journal of Psychiatric Research*, 1975, *12*, 19–35.

Foster, F. G., McPartland, R. J., & Kupfer, D. J. Telemetric motor activity in children. *Biotelemetry*, 1977, *4*, 1–8.

Gottfries, C. G., Gottfries, I., & Olsson, E. Objective recording of arm and leg activity in normal and clinical samples. *British Journal of Psychiatry*, 1966, *112*, 1269–1278.

Haring, N. G. *Behavior of exceptional children.* Columbus, OH: Merrill, 1974.

Irwin, O. C. The distribution of the amount of motility in young infants between two nursing periods. *Journal of Comparative and Physiological Psychology*, 1932, *14*, 429–445.

Juliano, D. B. Conceptual tempo activity and concept learning in hyperactive and normal children. *Journal of Abnormal Psychology*, 1974, *83*, 629–634.

Kagan, J. Reflection–impulsivity: The generality and dynamics of conceptual tempo. *Journal of Abnormal Psychology*, 1966, *71*, 17–24.

Kaspar, J. C., Millichap, J. G., Backus, R., Child, D., & Schulman, J. L. A study of the relationship between neurological evidence of brain damage in children and activity and distractibility. *Journal of Consulting and Clinical Psychology*, 1971, *36*, 329–337.

Kast, E. C. Observations of psychomotor behavior as an index of psychopharmacologic action. *Journal of Neuropsychiatry*, 1964, 5, 577–584.

LaPorte, R. E., Kuller, L. H., Kupfer, D. J., McPartland, R. J., Matthews, G., & Caspersen, C. An objective measure of physical activity for epidemiological research. *American Journal of Epidemiology*, 1979, *109*, 158–168.

Mack, R. W., & Kleinhenz, M. E. Growth, caloric intake, and activity levels in early infancy: A preliminary report. *Human Biology*, 1974, *46*, 345.

Maxfield, E., & Konishi, F. Patterns of food intake and physical activity in obesity. *Journal of the American Dietetic Association*, 1966, *49*, 406–408.

McPartland, R. J., Kupfer, D. J., & Foster, F. G. The movement activated recording monitor: A third-generation motor activity monitoring system. *Behavior Research Methods and Instrumentation*, 1976, *8*, 357–360.

Millichap, J. G., Aymat, F., Sturgis, L. H., Larsen, K. W., & Egan, R. A. Hyperkinetic behavior and learning disorders. III. Battery of neuropsychological tests in controlled trial of methylphenidate. *American Journal of Diseases in Children*, 1968, *116*, 235–245.

Millichap, J. G., & Boldrey, E. F. Studies in hyperkinetic behavior. II. Laboratory and clinical evaluations of drug treatments. *Neurology*, 1967, *17*, 467–471.

Millichap, J., & Johnson, F. Methylphenidate in hyperkinetic behavior: Relationship of response to degree of activity and brain damage. In C. Conners (Ed.), *Clinical use of stimulant drugs in children*. Amsterdam: Excerpta Medica, 1977.

Peacock, L. J., & Williams, M. An ultrasonic device for recording activity. *American Journal of Psychology*, 1962, *75*, 648–652.

Pope, L. Motor activity in brain injured children (Doctoral dissertation, New York University, 1969). *Dissertation Abstracts International*, 1969, *30*, 2384A. (University Microfilms No. 69-21, 198)

Pope, L. Motor activity in brain injured children. *American Journal of Orthopsychiatry*, 1970, *40*, 783–794.

Rogers, G. S., & Hughes, H. H. Dietary treatment of children with problematic activity level. *Psychological Reports*, 1981, *48*, 487–494.

Rose, H. E., & Mayer, J. Activity calorie intake, fat storage, and the energy balance of infants. *Pediatrics*, 1968, *41*, 18–29.

Rosenthal, J. H. Neurophysiology of minimal cerebral dysfunctions. *Academic Therapy*, 1973, *8*, 291–294.

Sander, L. W., & Julia, H. L. Continuous interactional monitoring in the neonate. *Psychosomatic Medicine*, 1966, *28*, 822–835.

Saris, W. H. M., & Binkhorst, R. A. The use of pedometer and actometer in studying daily physical activity in man. Part I. Reliability of pedometer and actometer. *European Journal of Applied Physiology*, 1977, *37*, 219–228. (a)

Saris, W. H. M., & Binkhorst, R. A. The use of pedometer and actometer in studying daily physical activity in man. Part II. Validity of pedometer and actometer measuring the daily physical activity. *European Journal of Applied Physiology*, 1977, *37*, 229–235. (b)

Satterfield, J. H., & Dawson, M. E. Electrodermal correlates of hyperactivity in children. *Psychophysiology*, 1971, *8*, 191–197.

Schulman, J. L., Kaspar, J. C., & Throne, F. M. *Brain damage and behavior: A clinical experimental study*. Springfield, IL: C. C. Thomas, 1965.

Schulman, J. L., & Reisman, J. M. An objective measure of hyperactivity. *American Journal of Mental Deviance*, 1959, *64*, 455–456.

Schulman, J. L., Stevens, T. M., & Kupst, M. J. The biomotometer: A new device for the measurement and remediation of hyperactivity. *Child Development*, 1977, *48*, 1152–1154.

Schulman, J. L., Stevens, T. M., Suran, B. G., Kupst, M., & Naughton, M. J. Modification of activity level through biofeedback and operant conditioning. *Journal of Applied Behavior Analysis*, 1978, *11*, 145–152.

Schulman, J. L., Suran, B. G., Stevens, T. M., & Kupst, M. J. Instructions, feedback and reinforcement in reducing activity levels in the classroom. *Journal of Applied Behavior Analysis*, 1979, *12*, 441–447.

Shaffer, D., McNamara, N., & Pincus, J. H. Controlled observations on patterns of activity, attention, and impulsivity in brain damaged and psychiatrically disturbed boys. *Psychological Medicine*, 1974, *4*, 4–18.

Sprague, R. L., Barnes, K. R., & Werry, J. S. Methylphenidate and thioridazine: Learning, reaction time, activity, and classroom behavior in disturbed children. *American Journal of Orthopsychiatry*, 1970, *40*, 615–628.

Sprague, R. L., & Toppe, L. K. Relationship between activity level and delay of reinforcement in the retarded. *Journal of Experimental Child Psychology*, 1966, *3*, 390–397.

Stevens, E. A., Kupst, M., Suran, B., & Schulman, J. L. Activity level: A comparison between actometer scores and observer ratings. *Journal of Abnormal Child Psychology*, 1978, *6*, 166–173.

Strauss, A. A., & Lehtinen, L. *Psychopathology and education of the brain injured child*. New York: Grune & Stratton, 1947.

Stunkard, A. Physical activity, emotions, and human obesity. *Psychosomatic Medicine*, 1958, *20*, 366–372.

Stunkard, A. A method of studying physical activity in man. *American Journal of Clinical Nutrition*, 1960, *8*, 595–601.

Stunkard, A., & Pestka, J. The physical activity of obese girls. *American Journal of Diseases of Children*, 1962, *103*, 812–817.

Wasserman, E., Asch, H., & Snyder, E. A neglected aspect of learning disabilities. *Journal of Learning Disabilities*, 1972, *5*, 130–135.

Werry, J., & Aman, M. Methylphenidate and Haloperidol in children: Effects on attention, memory, and activity. *Archives of General Psychiatry*, 1975, *32*, 970–975.

Wilkinson, P. W., Parkin, J. M., Pearlson, G., Strong, H., & Sykes, P. Energy intake and physical activity in obese children. *British Medical Journal*, 1977, *1*, 756.

Wong, T. C., Webster, J. G., Montoye, H. J., & Washburn, R. Portable accelerometer device for measuring human energy expenditure. *IEEE Transactions on Biomedical Engineering*, 1981, *BME-28*, 467–471.

Zentall, S. S., & Zentall, T. R. Activity and task performance of hyperactive children as a function of environmental stimulation. *Journal of Consulting and Clinical Psychology*, 1976, *44*, 693–697.

Index